Springer Series on Behavior Therapy and Behavioral Medicine

Vol. 1 **Multimodal Behavior Therapy** *Arnold A. Lazarus*

Vol. 2 **Behavior Therapy Assessment** *Eric J. Mash and Leif G. Terdal, editors*

Vol. 3 **Behavioral Approaches to Weight Control** *Edward E. Abramson, editor*

Vol. 4 **A Practical Guide to Behavioral Assessment (O.P.)**

Vol. 5 **Asthma Therapy:** A Behavioral Health Care System for Respiratory Disorders *Thomas L. Creer*

Vol. 6 **Behavioral Medicine:** Practical Applications in Health Care · *Barbara G. Melamed and Lawrence J. Siegel*

Vol. 7 **Multimodal Handbook for a Mental Hospital:** Designing Specific Treatments for Specific Problems *Lillian F. Brunell and Wayne T. Young, editors*

Vol. 8 **Eating and Weight Disorders:** Advances in Treatment and Research *Richard K. Goldstein, editor*

Vol. 9 **Perspectives on Behavior Therapy in the Eighties** *Michael Rosenbaum, Cyril M. Franks, and Yoram Jaffe, editors*

Vol. 10 **Pediatric and Adolescent Behavioral Medicine:** Issues in Treatment *Patrick J. McGrath and Philip Firestone, editors*

Vol. 11 **Hypnosis and Behavior Therapy:** The Treatment of Anxiety and Phobias *J. Christopher Clarke and J. Arthur Jackson*

Vol. 12 **Child Obesity:** A New Frontier of Behavior Therapy *Michael D. LeBow*

Vol. 13 **Punishment and Its Alternatives:** A New Perspective for Behavior Modification *Johnny L. Matson and Thomas M. DiLorenzo*

Vol. 14 **The Binge-Purge Syndrome:** Diagnosis, Treatment and Research *Raymond C. Hawkins II, William J. Fremouw and Pamelia F. Clement, editors*

Vol. 15 **Behavioral Assessment in Behavioral Medicine** *Warren W. Tryon, editor*

Vol. 16 **Behavior Therapy Casebook** *Michel Hersen and Cynthia G. Last, editors*

Vol. 17 **The Covert Conditioning Handbook** *Joseph R. Cautela and Albert J. Kearney*

Vol. 18 **Problem-Solving Therapy:** A Social Competence Approach to Clinical Intervention *Thomas J. D'Zurilla*

Vol. 19 **The Psychological Management of Chronic Pain:** A Treatment Manual *H. Clare Philips*

Vol. 20 **Paradigms in Behavior Therapy:** Present and Promise *Daniel B. Fishman, Frederick Rotgers, and Cyril M. Franks, editors*

Vol. 21 **Innovations in Child Behavior Therapy** *Michel Hersen, Ph.D., editor*

Vol. 22 **Adolescent Behavior Therapy Handbook** *Eva R. Feindler and Grace L. Kalfus, editors*

Vol. 23 **Unifying Behavior Therapy:** Contributions of Paradigmatic Behaviorism *Georg H. Eifert and Ian M. Evans, editors*

GEORG H. EIFERT, Ph.D., is a Senior Lecturer in Clinical Psychology and Head of the Division of Psychology in the School of Behavioral Sciences at the James Cook University of North Queensland. Prior to moving to Australia, he had a faculty position in his native West Germany at the Goethe Universität in Frankfurt where he completed a doctorate on the acquisition and extinction of phobias. He also obtained a Graduate Diploma in Psychology at the Ruhr Universität in Bochum. Dr. Eifert is a Clinical Board Member of the *Australian Psychological Society*, has served several terms on the *National Council of the Australian Psychological Society*, and is a co-founder and past Chairman of the *Society's North Queensland Branch*. He is also on the Editorial Board of the *Journal of Cognitive Psychotherapy*.

IAN M. EVANS, Ph.D., is Professor of Psychology and Director of Clinical Training at the State University of New York at Binghamton. His interest in learning theory and its interface with clinical psychology was first stimulated by Alma E. Hannon's teaching at the University of the Witwatersrand in Johannesburg where he completed a B.A. Honours degree in Psychology. He then proceeded to the Institute of Psychiatry (Maudsley Hospital), University of London, where he obtained a Ph.D. on classical conditioning under Hans Eysenck. In 1970 he accepted a faculty position at the University of Hawaii where he was appointed full professor in 1982 shortly before leaving for Binghamton. Dr. Evans has also been interested in professional issues and was elected President of the Hawaii Psychological Association. He served for some years as Associate Editor of *Behavioral Assessment*, and on the Editorial Board of the *Journal of Behavior Therapy and Experimental Psychiatry*.

Unifying Behavior Therapy

Contributions of Paradigmatic Behaviorism

Georg H. Eifert
Ian M. Evans

Editors

SP

SPRINGER PUBLISHING COMPANY
New York

Springer Publishing Company, Inc.
536 Broadway
New York, NY 10012

90 91 92 93 94 / 5 4 3 2 1

Library of Congress Cataloging-in-Publication Data

Unifying behavior therapy : contributions of paradigmatic behaviorism
/ edited by Georg H. Eifert and Ian M. Evans.
    p. cm.—(Springer series on behavior therapy and behavioral
medicine : 23)
    "February 1989."
    Includes bibliographical references.
    ISBN 0-8261-4740-2
    1. Behavior therapy. 2. Behaviorism (Psychology) I. Eifert,
Georg H., 1952–   . II. Evans, Ian M. III. Series: Springer series
on behavior therapy and behavioral medicine : v. 23.
    [DNLM: 1. Behavior Therapy. 2. Behaviorism. W1 SP685NB v. 23 /
WM 425 U58]
    RC489.B4U55 1989
    616.89' 142—dc20
    DNLM/DLC
for Library of Congress   90-9408
                                                                         CIP

Printed in the United States of America

Contents

Contributors   *viii*

Foreword   *ix*
Hans J. Eysenck

Preface   *xv*

PART I: Overview

1. Paradigmatic Behaviorism's Contribution to Unifying
   Behavior Therapy: An Introduction   3
   Ian M. Evans and Georg H. Eifert

2. Paradigmatic Behavior Therapy: A Unified
   Framework for Theory, Research, and Practice   14
   Arthur W. Staats

PART II: Foundations for Applied Paradigmatic Behaviorism—Research, Language, and Personality

3. Research Foundations of a Developing Paradigm:
   Implications for Behavioral Engineering   57
   Karl A. Minke

4. Social Behaviorism, Interpersonal Determinants
   of Language Acquisition, and Implications for
   Language Intervention   81
   Jean A. Rondal

5. Affective-Cognitive-Behavioral Assessment: The
   Integration of Personality and Behavioral
   Assessment   98
   G. Leonard Burns

6. A Model for Research on Self-Regulation: Reducing
   the Schism Between Behaviorism and
   General Psychology   126
   Michael Rosenbaum

PART III: Areas of Application

7. Verbal, Emotional, and Imagery Repertoires in
   the Regulation of Dysfunctional Behavior: An
   Integrative Conceptual Framework for Cognitive-
   Behavioral Disorders and Interventions   153
   Jeffrey M. Lohr and L. Kevin Hamberger

8. The Acquisition and Treatment of Phobic Anxiety:
   A Paradigmatic Behavioral Perspective   173
   Georg H. Eifert

9. Semantic Behavior Therapy of Anxiety Disorders:
   An Integrative Approach   201
   Hamid Hekmat

10. Depression: Classification, Explanation, and
    Treatment   220
    Elaine M. Heiby and Arthur W. Staats

11. The Conceptual and Practical Evolution of
    Behavior Therapy with Children   247
    Frances E. Wilson and Paolo Meazzini

12. Social Behaviorism, Rehabilitation, and Ethics:
Applications for People with Severe Disabilities   268
Aimee Léduc, Alfred Dumais, and Ian M. Evans

PART IV: Conclusions

13. A Critical Appraisal of Paradigmatic
Behaviorism's Contribution to Behavior Therapy   293
Ian M. Evans, Georg H. Eifert, and Sheila A. Corrigan

References   *318*

Author Index   *359*

Subject Index   *365*

Contributors

G. Leonard Burns
Department of Psychology
Washington State University,
Pulman, Washington

Sheila A. Corrigan
School of Medicine
University of Mississippi
Medical Center
Jackson, Mississippi

Alfred Dumais
Department of Sociology
Faculty of Social Sciences
Laval University, Quebec, Canada

Georg H. Eifert
Division of Psychology
School of Behavioral Sciences
James Cook University of North
Queensland
Townsville, Australia

Ian M. Evans
Department of Psychology
State University of New York
at Binghamton
Binghamton, New York

Hans J. Eysenck
Institute of Psychiatry, University of
London,
London, England

L. Kevin Hamberger
Southeastern Family Practice Center,
University of Wisconsin—Parkside
Kenosha, Wisconsin

Elaine M. Heiby
Department of Psychology
University of Hawaii
Honolulu, Hawaii

Hamid Hekmat
Department of Psychology
University of Wisconson
at Stevens Point
Stevens Point, Wisconsin

Aimee Léduc
Department of Pedagogical Psychology
Faculty of Educational Sciences
Laval University,
Quebec, Canada

Jeffrey M. Lohr
Department of Psychology
University of Arkansas
Fayetteville, Arkansas

Paolo Meazzini
Department of Psychology,
University of Rome
Rome, Italy

Karl A. Minke
Department of Psychology
University of Hawaii
Honolulu, Hawaii

Jean A. Rondal
Institute of Psychology
University of Liege
Liege, Belgium

Michael Rosenbaum
Department of Psychology,
Tel-Aviv University
Tel-Aviv, Israel

Arthur W. Staats
Department of Psychology
University of Hawaii
Honolulu, Hawaii

Frances E. Wilson
Case Western Reserve Medical School
Cleveland, Ohio

Foreword

Behavior therapy, like *behaviorism*, is a term that has been used in so many different ways that it has lost meaning. I originally used it in the most restrictive sense as the application of the principles of learning and conditioning theory to the treatment of neurotic disorders, conceiving of these as being emotions of fear, anxiety, and depression acquired through a process of Pavlovian conditioning, in genetically predisposed persons, and curable by means of Pavlovian extinction. Note that the principles invoked might have a ready application to other areas and other types of behavior, but behavior therapy was restricted as a concept to the treatment of neurosis and neurosis only (Eysenck, 1959).

Skinner and his followers have used the term *behavior modification* to refer to a rather broader use of the principles of instrumental or operant conditioning. They seem to believe, in effect, that any human behavior can be changed by the appropriate action of reinforcement skillfully applied by the psychologist, and many of their applications relate to work in education, criminality, and psychosis. The use of the "token economy" in attempts to modify the behavior of criminals and psychotics is a notable example, but as far as neurosis in particular is concerned, there is an almost complete absence of use of this technique, which suggests that perhaps the management of emotional reactions and conditioned autonomic responses is more likely to fall within the purview of Pavlovian concepts (Kazdin, 1977b, 1982).

Staats's conception of *paradigmatic behavior therapy*, as explicated in his introductory chapter to this book, makes even wider claims. I think it would not be incorrect to say that paradigmatic behavior theory attempts to unify all the present-day theories of learning and conditioning, and apply them to all types of behavior. It is thus even more inclusive than Skinner's attempt, and certainly more inclusive than my own; its ambition appears to be nothing less than the unification of psychology. It remains within the stimulus–response (S–R) tradition by stating that (1) stimuli

can elicit emotional responses, (2) that stimuli can serve as reinforcers for instrumental behavior, and (3) that stimuli can serve
as incentives (directive or discriminative stimuli) to bring about
particular instrumental behaviors. In this way it attempts to unify Pavlov, Skinner, and Hull as well as contributions by other
theorists. It further seeks to unify animal and human research,
and it attempts to incorporate Pavlov's second signaling system
within the boundaries of its behavioristic framework. These are
all aims with which it is difficult to quarrel, and the rich harvest
of empirical results that Staats and his associates have gathered
has certainly made an important contribution to the psychological
literature.

When this theory is applied to efforts to improve human behavior,
the term *therapy* may perhaps be judged inappropriate, since linguistically it has more usually been used in connection with previously existing deficits or illnesses. On the whole, however, I feel
that it might be useful to retain the term *behavior therapy* for the
more limited area for which I originally coined it, and to use the
term *behavior modification* for the rather different and somewhat
wider area covered by Skinnerian explanations. What Staats is trying to give us is in fact a *behavior theory* that can be applied in
many different ways, and to many different problems; it might be
more accurate to refer to this as *applied behavior theory*, so as not
to mislead readers who associate the term *therapy* with psychiatric
problems of one kind or another.

There has, in recent years, been a theoretical quarrel between
traditional behaviorists of various kinds and so-called cognitive psychologists. This battle has always seemed to me a pseudo-quarrel
because a denial of cognitive processes is not a necessary part of
behaviorism, even though some influential individuals may have
taught that cognitive processes, and their recognition, must be regarded as a mentalistic error. In the same way a Russian commis-
sar, asked to adjudicate in a debate about whether behavior therapy,
as I had presented it, was in line with Marxist-Leninist philosophy,
declared after much furrowing of brows that "Eysenck is a left-wing
mechanist deviationist." Both the concepts and the conclusions are
essentially meaningless, and it is time psychology outgrew such
infantilisms (Rosenbaum, Franks, & Jaffe, 1983).

As is well known, Pavlov regarded words both as conditioned stimuli and conditioned responses, and Platonov was one of the first of
his followers to carry out empirical studies along these lines. It is
perhaps a major contribution of Staats to have pursued these concepts and issues for many years in considerable detail, and to have

made a number of fundamental experimental contributions to the integration of verbal behavior with the concepts of behaviorism in general. It is of course true that even the English associationists worked out laws of mental association that closely resemble Pavlov's laws of conditioning, indicating an essential similarity, but obviously this similarity had to be confirmed experimentally, and its laws much more clearly defined than was possible previously. This essential contribution of Staats to what I would prefer to call behavior theory comes out prominently in various chapters of this book, and constitutes one of its major strengths. No sensible behaviorist would deny that human beings have cognitions, that these can be expressed in language, and that they obey certain laws that are essentially similar to those discovered by Pavlov, Thorndike, and later behaviorists. To deny either the existence of cognitions or their lawful behavior seems to me nonsensical, and it is certainly not the sign of a good behaviorist to foreswear the use of such conceptions, however much he or she may be criticized for alleged "mentalism." It is the way concepts are used, not their nature, that defines a given psychologist as a behaviorist. There is a wide and a narrow sense in which the term *behaviorism* can be understood, and it is surely time now to slough off the narrow meaning of the term as having outlived its usefulness. In a very real sense "we are all behaviorists now," even though on smaller issues we may disagree with each other!

In spite of the much wider inclusiveness and sympathy for alternative points of view characteristic of the Staats approach, there is still in it insufficient recognition of the importance and centrality of the concept of the organism (0) within the S-O-R formula which is clearly an essential substitute for the old-fashioned S-R approach. Skinner, of course, made some obeisances to this concept of the essential organism by referring to a "history of reinforcement" as a crucial factor in behavior, but this clearly is little but a gesture. In actual fact we do not have histories of reinforcement for humans, and there is no obvious way in which these could be obtained. Repertoires of stress constitute one possible approach, but these have run into considerable conceptual and practical difficulties, and are of doubtful value; in any case, they cover only one particular kind of reinforcement, and cannot by any stretch of the imagination be regarded as an adequate operationalization of Skinner's construct.

Staats is rather more inclusive again in his acceptance of "personality" factors but seems to leave out entirely the absolutely central role of genetic factors. Fulker (1981) has summarized the evidence with respect to the three major dimensions of personality, and has shown conclusively that between one-half and two-thirds of the "true" variance for these personality factors is genetic in origin. More recent work, reviewed by Eaves, Eysenck, and Martin (1989), relies on very large numbers of monozygotic and dizygotic twins (with samples ranging from 12,000 to 15,000), and the results from numerous studies are remarkably unanimous, not only in emphasizing the contribution of genetic factors, but also in giving us information on the nature of the environmental factors involved.

Most personality theories, indeed practically all the best-known ones, involve between-family environmental variance, that is, events that differ from family to family, due to the nature of the relations between fathers and mothers on the one hand, and children on the other, to socioeconomic status, educational factors, and so on. Yet the evidence is pretty conclusive by now that it is within-family environmental variance that is responsible for the environmental part of individual differences in personality: that part of the variance which is produced by events accidentally differentiating between children in the same family, such as an accidental illness of one but not the other, or the accidental meeting of one but not the other child in a given family with a particularly inspiring or a particularly bad teacher. No theory of behavior can afford to disregard such well-established findings and paradigmatic behavior theory cannot claim to be truly paradigmatic if it leaves out of account fundamental facts of this kind.

Nor can it be said that these facts are too general to be of any specific interest. Seligman (1971), in his theory of "preparedness," has argued that certain types of behavior—in particular, phobic behaviors—are "prepared" in the sense that through evolution our nervous system has acquired the propensity of being much more easily conditioned to feelings of fear and anxiety for certain conditioned stimuli as compared with others. Going even further than that, Torgerson (1979) and Rose and Ditto (1983) have shown that quite specific phobias are inherited as such, as well as a general trait of neuroticism linking together all phobic disorders. Behavior therapists in the narrow (Eysenckian) sense can hardly avoid to pay attention to these facts in accounting for the origins of neurotic disorders in general, and phobias in particular. But of course the facts of genetics have much wider significance (Eaves, Eysenck, & Martin, 1989).

We can see that Staats is right in believing that the stage of psychology without a paradigm is slowly passing, and that a unification of several different approaches is taking place which will lead, or may already have led, to the development of a paradigm that can be usefully embraced by psychologists in general. This paradigm is fundamentally behavioristic, but without the disfiguring restrictions that single individuals like Watson and Skinner imposed on it. We are now much more ready to acknowledge the interaction of many different factors, including cognitive ones, in mediating observable behavior, including verbal behavior, and we are no longer afraid of postulating unobservable entities as part of the central organism intervening between stimuli and responses. Skinner's injunction to treat the organism as a black box and his hostility to physiological enquiry, which he shared with Watson, can now be seen to have been very much mistaken, impoverishing our search for causal elements in the mediation of behavior (Eysenck, 1967). Kelley (1987) critically examined the literature on the effects of hormones like adrenaline or peptides like ACTH on Pavlovian extinction and on the incubation of anxiety, and found that the experimental evidence strongly suggests that they play an important role in matters closely related to behavior therapy; such evidence cannot meaningfully be disregarded by anyone attempting to formulate an adequate theory of behavior. Injunctions like Skinner's, based essentially on a very unsophisticated type of materialist philosophy, should not be taken seriously by psychologists who have transcended the Cartesian dichotomy of body and mind and reject a priori prohibitions deriving from that ancient shibboleth.

We may, then, regard the present volume as an augury of better things to come: the abandonment of meaningless prohibitions based on primitive philosophical arguments, the coming together of many different areas of psychology in a mutually supportive manner, and the inclusion of cognitive and other events in a form of behaviorism less rigid and less rejecting than earlier versions. If paradigmatic behavior theory is still not quite wide enough in its inclusiveness, or sufficiently welcoming to genetic and biological concepts generally, then the answer must surely be that the logic of the approach exemplified in this book makes it essential to open the gate still further, and at least scrutinize the evidence that suggests that these factors have a very important and indeed vital role to play in mediating human behavior, and causing individual differences in such behavior. Paradigmatic behavior theory occupies what in politics is sometimes called the middle ground; it opposes primitive behaviorism as much as mentalistic cognitive theories, and attempts to combine all the best features of the many different approaches which have arisen in modern psychology. This surely is the way toward a future less driven by sectarian disputes, eponymous theorizing, and arbitrary rejection of alternative approaches. If we cannot unify psychology we will still be left with what William James called "the hope of a science," rather than a proper paradigmatic science of which we can be proud, and that we can with confidence apply to a great variety of human behaviors where improvement and healing are urgently needed. Staats is one of the central figures aiming at such a unification, and actively working toward it. This book is a monument to his efforts.

HANS J. EYSENCK
Professor Emeritus
Institute of Psychiatry
University of London

Preface

This book is a tribute to Arthur W. Staats's work in behavior therapy. It critically examines the major tenets of social behaviorism and samples the potential importance for the integration of behavior therapy offered by a paradigmatic framework. Partly to emphasize the concept of unification, partly because Art Staats has influenced scholars internationally, we selected contributors from all over the world. Patiently, they have allowed us to take considerable liberties with their chapters as we tried to reduce overlap and increase clarity, as well as contain the overall length of this book.

The history of our own collaboration also has a certain global quality, fortuitously directed by casual conversation. Having tea one afternoon in 1968 at the Institute of Psychiatry, University of London, Ian Evans heard Jack Rachman mention that Staats had moved to the University of Hawaii, where a behaviorally oriented clinical program was being established. Because of the great value for both behavior therapy and scientific clinical psychology placed on Staats's integrative work, this remark prompted an eager graduate student's letter of inquiry. Thus began Ian's 12 happy and enriching years as a faculty member in Honolulu and a colleague of Staats. One cold winter evening a few years later, wrestling with problems of animal conditioning at the Ruhr University in Bochum, West Germany, Georg Eifert asked visiting professor Jeff Bitterman to recommend an American clinical program with a strong scientific base. Naturally, Bitterman suggested the program in his own department and placed Georg in touch with Ian Evans. Georg arrived in Honolulu in 1977 on a Fulbright scholarship, and we worked closely together that year. This was obviously a perfect opportunity to explore social behaviorism at its source—and to appreciate the scope and fascination of Art's approach. This time was also the beginning of our collaboration and since then we have been able to meet and work together on an almost regular basis. The final editing of this volume was actually completed in upstate New York,

New Zealand, and Australia. Behavior therapy has always had this international character, just as it has always valued basic research, concern for theory, and self-criticism. It is to this spirit that we dedicate this examination of Staats's paradigmatic perspective.

We acknowledge with gratitude the advice and encouragement of Cyril Franks, Senior Editor of the Springer Series on Behavior Therapy and Behavioral Medicine, throughout the long gestation period of this project. His suggestions as well as comments by Dan Fishman and Fred Rotgers on the first draft of this book have been very helpful in the preparation of the final manuscript. We are also grateful to Ursula Springer and Barbara Watkins and other members of the Springer Publishing Company for their considerable patience and continued support of this project. Thanks are also due to James Cook University for providing a travel grant to assist with the completion of this book and to Anne Sharp, Department of Behavioral Sciences, James Cook University, for doing the artwork and typing of the final draft.

GEORG H. EIFERT
Townsville, Australia

IAN M. EVANS
Binghamton, New York

I

Overview

1

Paradigmatic Behaviorism's Contribution to Unifying Behavior Therapy: An Introduction

Ian M. Evans
Georg H. Eifert

Introduction

It is quite ironic, given its name, that behavior therapy has been so introspective a discipline over the years. Behavior therapists have repeatedly asked themselves who they were, what they should be called, whether they were really behaviorists, how the criterial attributes of their craft should be defined, and what they will look like when they get older. All the while behavior therapy has expanded rapidly; finding the answers to these questions, apparently, was not critical to progress—or at least to growth. The discipline has expanded in all directions, producing hybrids, like behavioral medicine, and specialties, like behavioral gerontology. It has undergone one cognitive revolution (roughly corresponding to the appearance of the journal *Cognitive Therapy and Research*) and is poised on the brink of a second (information processing, of which more later). It has tried disavowing its behavioristic origins in favor of a general empirical pragmatism, has become more professionalized along with clinical psychology, and has changed its sociological status from radical minority to prosperous, conservative majority. Although it has not fatally smitten its goliathan foe, psychoanalysis, it is certainly brazenly helping itself to the Freudian ancestral lands.

While all this has been going on, three aspects of behavior therapy seem to have survived unscathed. The first is that the original philosophical and historical structures of behavior therapy's evolution are still very clear. For instance, behavior analysts continue to maintain allegiance to a radical Skinnerian operant approach. So, too, one leading authority can still advocate the value of a stimulus–response (S-R) associationism model (e.g., Wolpe, 1982), and another completely exclude any facet of conditioning as a relevant phenomenon for psychological therapy (e.g., Bandura, 1978a). The second feature is that, despite apparently incompatible and contradictory perspectives, there is some kind of overriding value system or metatheory that ties the amazing diversity of "behavior therapy" together in some common sense of identity. And the third feature is that there is an ongoing concern in the field over the nature of its conceptual foundations. This suggests that there is considerable dissatisfaction with the discrepancies created by the opposing structural philosophies, and with the superficiality— probably mostly social in nature—of the common identity.

The goal of this book is to present a perspective on behavior therapy, the avowed purpose of which is to unify the conceptual foundations of the discipline. Our aim is to appraise the contribution that Arthur W. Staats's *social behaviorism* has already made to behavior therapy and to engender greater professional interest in its future potential. In the history of behavior therapy there have really been only two systematic or unifying positions developed: Bandura's social learning theory and Staats's social behaviorism. Bandura's perspective is well known and social learning theory is very widely cited as a general perspective. Staats's theoretical integration has received less formal attention but implicitly permeates much of the field. By attempting to redress this neglect, the book is quite personal and unashamedly partisan. We intended it to be essentially a festschrift, not of the purely laudatory type, but more of a critical examination of Staats's contribution to the goal of unity and its future for clinical applications.

Social Behaviorism

Both of us have been admirers of Staats's thinking since being exposed as undergraduates to the highly creative and original work *Complex Human Behavior* (Staats, 1963). It demonstrated that the intellectually satisfying rigor of neobehavioral learning theory could be extended to accommodate the obvious complexities of human thought and feeling. What particularly attracted us—as it did all the authors in this book—was the paradigmatic approach to the study of behavior. From Staats's early days as a graduate student, when he applied learning conceptions to such varied topics as schizophrenic speech, problem solving, and word meaning, to his most recent major attempt to establish a philosophy of science to unify all psychology (Staats, 1983b), he has been guided by the value of working within a consistent paradigm.

The scope of this paradigm was presented in 1975 in a comprehensive behavioral theory designed to integrate not only earlier behavioral models of learning, but concepts and research findings of nonbehavioral psychology as well. Arthur Staats used the term *social behaviorism* to describe this systematic position. The most fundamental characteristics of social behaviorism were the integration of classical and instrumental conditioning principles at the first explanatory level, and a logically consistent framework for incorporating language, images, thought, and other cognitive phenomena once rejected by behavioral theorists as mentalistic.

Although social behaviorism contained various specific and original propositions—some of which are of an explanatory nature—Staats's approach differed from the traditional behavioristic model of theory as exemplified by the theories of Hull and Skinner. For one thing, the approach was constructed as a blueprint whose general goal was to encompass and be heuristic in the traditional domains of psychology, such as social influence, development, abnormalities of behavior, and, of course, planful remediation and change—behavior therapy. The system blurred these traditional disciplinary boundaries in much the same way that a geological map, based on a more fundamental set of constructs, eliminates the national boundaries of a political map. With the development of his interest in a level of analysis that would unify existing scientific fields of study, Staats (1981) adopted the new name *paradigmatic behaviorism* to better capture the central theme of a framework theory. We have therefore used the term *paradigmatic behavior therapy* to label that subset of interests within the approach that is concerned with clinical applications.

Organization of the Book

Science is always conducted within a social network. The chapters that follow are composed by individuals who have employed, and in some cases embraced, paradigmatic behaviorism in their work as a result of personal, professional, and intellectual contact with Staats. Because of the great diversity offered by social behaviorism, he attracted numerous capable graduate students to the University of Hawaii, not only in psychology, but also in the College of Education, where he holds a joint professorship. Many of these students stayed in or returned to Hawaii where they have established successful careers and positions of leadership in the local community, but where their impact on the dissemination of social behaviorism has been of necessity diminished by the geographic isolation. Others have left Hawaii and taken up appointments all over the mainland United States and elsewhere, and some scholars have visited Hawaii from other countries. We have tried to capture the essence of this national and international circle in our choice of authors and will briefly identify their roles as well as introducing their topics.

Organizational Rationale

Progress within a discipline requires more than the spread of ideas among individuals. The fundamental goal of addressing the disunity in behavior therapy is to ensure the integration and use of new knowledge. This requires, first, a very broad theoretical framework—really a metatheory to guide both basic and applied research. This is provided by Arthur Staats in the next chapter. Second, a research base must be established for this framework and its major components (such as language and personality). Chapters 3 to 6 illustrate how this solid foundation for application can be developed. In our view many of the most heated theoretical debates in behavior therapy have been quite unproductive. A good example was the conflict between "cognitive" behavior therapists and those adhering to more traditional conditioning models. The conditioning models, because they did not make use of the social behaviorist paradigm, were quite simplistic, causing some behavior therapists (e.g., Meichenbaum & Cameron, 1982) to declare conditioning theory moribund—thus dismissing large areas of knowledge and turning to loosely formulated "cognitive" explanations.

The framework theory, therefore, must guide the translation of new knowledge into practice. The few attempts to analyze behavior therapy conceptually (e.g., Erwin, 1978) have not done so from the perspective of applied behavior therapy. An unfortunate separation has developed between the research literature and the day-to-day clinical practice of behavior therapy. Thus Chapters 7 to 12 sample the range of interventions for the treatment of various clinical disorders such as anxiety and depression, and applications in other socially relevant settings, like residential care. And finally, theoretical advances and clinical interventions based on the paradigm framework must be subjected to continuous critical appraisal, and this we do in the final chapter, Chapter 13. Let us consider the two major divisions of foundations and practice in a little more detail.

Foundations for Applied Paradigmatic Behaviorism (Part II)

The first chapter in Part II (Chapter 3) is by Karl Minke, who started his career as a graduate student with Staats and has continued as a close associate at the University of Hawaii ever since. What is significant about his contribution to this volume is that his chapter considers basic experimental research questions. It illustrates an epistemology for behavior therapy: a geological guide for those who want to map the infrastructure. Most books on behavior therapy nowadays are organized around different clinical disorders often following the current *Diagnostic and Statistical Manual of Mental Disorders* nosology the field used to deplore [third edition, revised (DSM-III-R)]. Few incorporate basic research to demonstrate the free flow back and forth between fundamental principles and their application. Behavior therapy's research questions are becoming self-generated and its contact with the basic science declining (see also Chapter 2). This is especially worrisome at a time when the scientist-practitioner model of clinical training is under fierce attack. The Boulder model is not uniquely identified with behavior therapy, but it was behavior therapy that gave it credibility by linking basic experimental research to practice.

To further emphasize that behavior therapy does ideally draw on diverse areas of research, the fourth chapter is on language development. Again, Jean Rondal would not be thought of as a behavior therapist nor would his work typically be cited in the clinical literature. He is a psycholinguist at the University of Liège in Belgium. In his chapter he discusses the interpersonal determinants of language acquisition and its implications for clinical interventions, acknowledging Staats's pioneering conceptual work and presenting data from his own research. We chose language to illustrate the multilevel theory approach because verbal phenomena have been so central to Staats's theory and such a stumbling block for the radical operant perspective. The blow Chomsky dealt to Skinner may be more dramatic than any the cognitivists have dealt to simplistic conditioning theory in behavior therapy, but there are parallels. The chief is that by *replacing* an overly simple model with an overly complex one, does little to enhance explanatory power (see also Chapter 13).

One of the seminal works in the history of behavior therapy was Eysenck's *Dynamics of Anxiety and Hysteria*, in which individual differences in emotional development were accounted for using conditioning mechanisms. But the importance of linking behavior therapy to personality theory that Eysenck advocated has never been taken very seriously, with the notable exception of Staats who shared the goal of formally incorporating personality constructs into his system. For this reason, we were especially pleased that Hans Eysenck agreed to write the foreword, and we have incorporated two chapters addressing the fundamental topic of personality.

In Chapter 5, Leonard Burns elaborates on the significance and functions of what Staats called the personality system, made up of basic behavioral repertoires. Burns does so by providing a metatheoretical framework for behavioral assessment that is very different from the traditional characterization of the behavioral perspective (e.g., Kanfer & Saslow, 1969) as interested only in observable samples of overt behavior. By detailing the personality level of theory in paradigmatic behaviorism, Burns promotes unification with the indirect methods of traditional testing. Tests represent verbal stimuli to which the individual's response indicates predictable beliefs and attitudes that will mediate future performance. If that stance triggers off memories of some of Rotter's work linking personality to learning in social behavior, it will come as no surprise that Burns completed his graduate clinical training at the University of Connecticut. Before that, however, he spent several very formative years as a student of Staats's in Hawaii.

Chapter 6, by Michael Rosenbaum, also emphasizes the importance of personality, but focuses more specifically on those functional repertoires that are involved in self-regulation. He articulates his theory of self-control and learned resourcefulness. The presentation is used as an opportunity to stress the need for behavior therapists to make use of the adaptive repertoires in a client's personality, rather than always concentrating on changing the negative aspects of a given problem. Rosenbaum provided an early impetus for our belief that there was a need for this book: during a conversation he asserted that Staats's contribution in outlining the role of specific behavioral repertoires in the regulation of dysfunctional behavior was being neglected by the present generation of behavior therapists. He was in an unusually good vantage point to survey the whole discipline of behavior therapy having served as principal organizer and chairperson of the First World Congress on behavior therapy in Jerusalem.

Areas of Application (Part III)

Arthur Staats is a Fellow in six divisions of the American Psychological Association and so it is rather difficult to categorize his professional allegiance within any of the traditional groupings! His role in clinical psychology has been as a researcher and theorist although he did complete the clinical degree requirements at the University of California at Los Angeles and a Veterans Administration hospital internship. He has participated in the clinical training program at Hawaii, although for a time he directed another graduate program in the psychology department that focused on the analysis of complex basic and applied human learning. Because this book is about behavior therapy, Chapters 7 to 12 provide examples of application that might usually fall within the domain of clinical psychology, but we hope the lack of rigid boundaries that characterizes unification efforts will be apparent.

Jeffrey Lohr and Kevin Hamberger (a former student of Lohr's at the University of Arkansas) analyze the multiple ways in which images, words, and other symbolic mediators regulate behavior. Their chapter serves as a conceptual introduction to the other applied chapters and could be a useful survey chapter for the reader who has had no prior familiarity with social behaviorism.

Lohr, and other doctoral students of Staats's at Hawaii, completed a number of laboratory studies modifying the emotional and connotative meanings of words. This represents one analogue for the complex pattern of interaction between therapist and client that actually takes place in behavior therapy. Wilson and Evans (1977) had suggested that social behaviorism allows for the interpretation of both the specific and "nonspecific" *social* influences of the therapist within a common conceptual rubric (see also Eifert, 1987). In addition, it seems a truism of therapy, and most other human interactions, that words—be they insults or praise, scary tales or erotic remarks—elicit emotional responses. Thus we have always recognized the importance of the early work of Hamid Hekmat and his colleagues. They took this truism, combined it with Staats's explication of how words can be construed as conditioned stimuli and higher—order unconditioned stimuli, and translated it directly into a "semantic" behavior therapy technique. In Chapter 9 Hekmat places these original clinical applications in their contemporary context. He describes a number of interesting changes to his earlier interventions that have resulted in an impressive variety of comprehensive and sophisticated treatment techniques.

Chapter 8, by Georg Eifert, focuses more specifically on the origins and treatment of phobic anxiety, one of the quintessential chal-

lenges for any theory in behavior therapy. This chapter shows how
inadequacies of the simple conditioning models of phobia can be
overcome by adopting a social behaviorist framework and by analyzing how the conditioning of self-statements is involved in both the
origin and treatment of anxiety. Eifert also provides a social behaviorist framework for "cognitive" interventions such as self-
instructional training and cognitive restructuring and their
treatment effects. The main impetus of his analysis is to help overcome the unfortunate and unnecessary schism between cognitive
and conditioning therapies.

It was in reference to the phenomenon of depression that the
recognition of the importance of verbal mediation gave the
strangely oxymoronic phrase "cognitive-behavior therapy" its im-
mense popularity. As a consequence, depression is one of the most
disunified and fragmented areas of study within clinical psychology.
Models and treatments as well as research into the biological,
operant, social, and cognitive determinants of depression are largely
unrelated and take little notice of each other. Chapter 10, by Elaine
Heiby (who came to the University of Hawaii as a young faculty
member) and Arthur Staats, is therefore an excellent example of
the unifying potential of paradigmatic behavior therapy. Their collaborative analysis of depression from a social behaviorist perspective is a particularly good challenge to the increasing tendency
within behavior therapy to neglect its early contribution to psychopathology in favor of acceptance of the validity and professional
dominance of medical model categories.

It is clearly implied in psychopathology that adult behavior disorders must have their origins in childhood, and yet abnormal child
psychology is a self-contained field of study. In addition to language
and personality, development was formally incorporated in social
behaviorism from the outset. A particularly important element of
Staats's approach was viewing behavioral development as both a
dependent and an independent variable in the study of causal influences. In Chapter 11, Frances Wilson and Paolo Meazzini map out
the conceptual commonalities between child and adult behavior
therapy by focusing on the metatheoretical issues involved—a long-
term interest of Meazzini's who is a professor at the University of
Rome. Wilson, a graduate of the Hawaii clinical program, has been
involved in behavioral pediatrics and neuropsychology. These relatively recent foci for behavior therapy emerge as a result of new
service settings and societal demands—which is perfectly
legitimate—but without a conceptual foundation they quickly become new professional oligarchies. While drawing upon a few practi-

cal examples from the vast material in behavioral applications to children, the major purpose of this chapter is to specify the framework.

Childhood represents not only processes of development but societal and environmental contexts—families, school, legal status, and so on—that significantly impact the contexts of intervention design. Similarly, paradigmatic behavior therapy must recognize elements of the context that are not inevitable components of the phenomena of interest but conventions of clinical practice. This is illustrated in Chapter 12 by Aime Léduc and Alfred Dumais. What they describe is the application of Staats's theory to a residential treatment program. But their message is much more fundamental. They demonstrate that a program, ostensibly using behavior therapy principles, can contain elements that are not intrinsic to these principles but a function of the social and intellectual circumstances of their implementation. Specifically, tactics such as depriving patients of basic rights or using punitive and aversive tactics are not fundamental parts of the behavioral approach, but superficial elements of practice. When a social behaviorist model was followed, the program looked very different; as Staats explains in his chapter, a framework theory must generate specific interventions that are compatible with the legal and ethical context of therapy. Léduc and Dumais present their analysis from the perspective of services in French Canada; Evans has added a related perspective from trends in special education and other services for people with disabilities in the United States.

An Invitation

Although not formally recognized, many of the authors of the following chapters contributed to the reviewing and editing of each other's contributions. However, we have not tried to impose absolute unity on the various authors. In other words, we have not suggested to them that there are a finite set of concepts and propositions that constitute social behaviorism and their task now is to present their given area of enquiry in these terms. To see a fully integrative attempt of that order, the reader should examine *Social Behaviorism* (Staats, 1975). We simply invited contributors with an interest in paradigmatic behaviorism to present their particular areas of expertise and interest.

The general framework theory that Staats articulates in the next chapter can be used in various proportions. Thus some of our contributors are paradigmatic behaviorists and project their own contributions within this theory. Other contributors employ large parts of paradigmatic behaviorism, but also combine their own different concepts and principles. And one or two have seen that a part of paradigmatic behaviorism can be a heuristic foundation in a particular area of psychology, but still use a conceptual framework and methodology from constituents other than those offered by paradigmatic behaviorism. Thus, Staats will argue, this compendium of chapters does not in every particular detail represent paradigmatic behaviorism, but it will do so in general. The book samples the different ways of employing the framework theory of paradigmatic behaviorism; it is not a complete or a fully consistent presentation of paradigmatic behavior therapy. It presents possibilities.

It might be helpful to suggest that there are levels at which Staats's contribution may be interpreted. (1) There are the specific theoretical positions that are a unique part of social behaviorism. A notable example is the affective—reinforcing—directive (A-R-D) theory, which suggests that the affective nature of stimuli—whether they be natural events or symbolic representation—endows individual stimulus events with three separate functions in the regulation of behavior. Another example would be the hierarchical ordering of basic behavioral repertoires. (2) Then there is the broader framework theory that is descriptive, somewhat post hoc in its explanatory capabilities, that seems to us to have enormous integrative potential. Its specific conceptual basis incorporates much of what is generally accepted in a behavioral position, and provides a rationale for judging the way phenomena and concepts not typically part of behaviorism might fit in. (3) And third, there is the general philosophical position that unification and integration would be good for the field and for science. This argument is thus in favor of reducing false antitheses in behavior therapy, but does not promote any particular theory for so doing. It indicates, however, possible directions to be taken in the huge task.

Paradoxically, the importance of unification within behavior therapy—far less psychology—became especially apparent as a result of the general neglect of social behaviorism in behavior therapy. One might have expected that any position that purported to integrate and unify different clinical domains would have captured the attention and appreciation of scholars in applied science, especially behavior therapy. Thus it is a continued source of surprise, and indeed frustration, to many of us who have intellectually valued social behaviorism, that Staats's position is not better known, appreciated, and cited. Hawaii's relative isolation and the density of the writing of the key works may have contributed. Also, social

behaviorism is built on, and incorporates, most of the earlier conceptual advances in behaviorism, so that its uniqueness is marked
by integration, not the rejection of past accomplishments. And the
generality and molecularity of some of paradigmatic behaviorism's
theoretical propositions do not lend themselves easily to the generation of the explicit experimental tests so sought after for doctoral
dissertation research. But very often the chief culprit has been,
quite simply, poor scholarship. If it had been the inadequacy of the
ideas that resulted in their neglect, social behaviorism would have
been subjected to damaging criticism, not simply ignored or been
unrecognized for the primacy of certain ideas very central to contemporary behavior therapy.

For some years Staats himself was preoccupied with these issues,
and some of his writings became occasionally strident. Not unnatu-
rally, he appeared self-laudatory as he attempted to focus attention
on the problem of inadequate citation practices in behavior therapy.
Eventually his frustration was subordinated to his insight that failure to credit social behaviorism for important principles was a manifestation of the general separatism that existed within behavior
therapy and psychology in general. This separatism was both a
cause and a consequence of the disunity within preparadigmatic
psychology which had so long concerned him. The fascinating and
important article he first wrote on this topic, with behavior therapy
as the illustrative area, was initially accepted for publication in the
American Psychologist, but, for political reasons, never published by
the journal. A major cause of the controversy was that Staats used
social behaviorism and social learning theory—the latter being specifically identified with Bandura, Mischel, and their associates—as
a case study of the failure to cross-reference closely related conceptual works.

This is not the place or time to rekindle the acrimonious controversy that arose. Bandura's contributions to the field of behavior
therapy, and the recognition of cognitive and social variables, are
secure and indisputable. Whether Staats's writings have been adequately cited in social learning and other major theoretical texts in
behavior therapy can be determined very simply by examining their
reference lists. In the next chapter Staats asks the reader to consider which broad approach—paradigmatic behaviorism, operant
(radical) behaviorism, or social learning theory—provides the best
unifying framework theory for allowing disparate sources of knowledge in behavior therapy to begin to fit together. If this book helps
the reader make such a judgment, and gives unification within a
paradigmatic approach a fair hearing, it will have served its purpose.

2

Paradigmatic Behavior Therapy: A Unified Framework for Theory, Research, and Practice

Arthur W. Staats

There is no question that the field of behavior therapy/behavior modification/behavioral assessment has grown into a large and successful professional-scientific field. Since initiation of the field in the 1950s and early 1960s it has expanded enormously in treatment techniques, findings, assessment instruments, analyses of problem behaviors, and specific approaches and orientations. A potpourri of valuable knowledge has been produced, with promise for continued impetus toward producing additional units of that knowledge.

Yet, like the whole of psychology, there is a great deal of disorganization of the knowledge that is currently available. There is not a systematically derived program that has been accepted as the basis for continued advancement of the field, a program that stipulates the directions to be taken at this junction of development. This is especially noticeable since there is not good understanding of just what the character of behavior therapy is or should be. For example, it has been said that behavior therapy should be a technology, which implies that the efforts of the field should be devoted to constructing new technological treatment methods. A similar expression has been that behavior therapy is a methodology (rather than a theoretical approach), that it is to be characterized by the way it goes about its tasks, that way being generally the use of the scientific method.

Such characterizations do not function well as guides to development of the field, for various reasons. First, these positions are vague, even in their methodological-technological realm, and convey no information regarding the phenomena to be concerned about, what conceptions to employ in analyzing the phenomena, how to employ what is already known concerning those phenomena, and so on. Such characterizations do not capture the broad significance for behavior therapy that behaviorism potentially entails, nor do they provide a context for our actions as scientists and professionals in the many activities in which we engage that are not guided by methods and technologies.

In fact, the early work in behavior therapy included much more than technological-methodological concerns. Most central was an interest in developing the potential of the field of learning for understanding and treating problems of human behavior. For example, I concluded my first published behavioral analysis of a problem behavior of a schizophrenic patient by saying "learning theory has reached a state where it has something to offer clinical theory *and practice*" (Staats, 1957a, p. 268). I needed to assert this because most of psychology—including the field of learning itself—was prejudiced against such possibilities. I emphasized the potentialities for practice, because at that time no one in United States psychology was analyzing actual clinical problems of behavior in straightforward principles of reinforcement. The point is that we nascent behavioral psychologists were interested not just in methods but in advancing a general approach whose principles directed us to new avenues of development.

Questions about the nature of behavior therapy arise because there is such a jumble of works and approaches, and because there is no accepted broad yet specific approach that provides the progressively advancing guidelines that a scientifically based endeavor requires. The most general purpose of the present book, as I see it, is to indicate that there is an approach that has been constructed to serve in the role of a framework theory providing such guidelines. The approach, with its roots in the period preceding the development of the behavior therapy movement, helped formulate the platform for and many of the substantive constituents of that movement. But it has continued to build throughout this period, adding important concepts, principles, and findings. This approach has reached the point where it is ready to be advanced as a framework theory with broad directions for further development of the field. Taking off from its name, Ian Evans has suggested that the subset of interests in the approach concerned with applications be further entitled *paradigmatic behavior therapy*.

This book thus has been organized to present works that have been composed by paradigmatic behaviorists and those who have employed parts of paradigmatic behaviorism. Each chapter analyzes how paradigmatic behaviorism can serve to unify a particular area of interest in behavior therapy. In writing this chapter I will take the opportunity provided by this organized context of works to characterize some of the general features of paradigmatic behaviorism's applied branch. Paradigmatic behavior therapy may be defined as the application of the framework theory of paradigmatic behaviorism (or parts of that theory). What is involved will be better understood after I have described the concept of the framework theory, which will be done throughout this chapter, beginning with some background analysis.

Philosophical Underpinnings of Behaviorism

Sometimes as behavior therapists we get caught up in the nitty-gritty of the specific—specific methods, techniques, analyses of particular problems, assessment instruments, and so on. The trees are dense, however, and preoccupation with them can interfere with stepping back and considering the general character of the forest. Behavior therapy has been task oriented and it is thus important to alert the field to the necessity of devoting attention to those general considerations. As will be seen, this is one of the guidelines that paradigmatic behaviorism provides for the field.

Although it is not a lively topic of consideration today, the development of behaviorism was intimately linked to a philosophy of science. Psychology began with an identification with natural science, a tradition that John Watson revivified in a manner that was congruent with the advancement of the philosophy of science called logical positivism. The second-generation behaviorists drew heavily from this philosophy and other related positivistic philosophies, and their works bear the characteristics of that philosophy (Staats, 1983b). For this reason it is important that we understand what that influence was.

It is critical to realize that logical positivism was a philosophy of science based upon observations of advanced theories in the natural sciences. Logical positivism took those theories to be the models of what science should be. Those theories, however, had certain charac-teristics that are not found in the broad sweep of psychology's con-cerns. The natural science theories were based upon precisely measured variables, whose interrelationships could be specified in impressive mathematical functions, and the totality could be ex-pressed in elegant axiomatic form like the classic forms of geome-try. Notwithstanding the differences in the sciences, many psychologists followed logical positivism and took the task of mak-ing psychology into a science to be the creation of theories that had those characteristics. Hull (1943, 1952) spent most of his career attempting to construct such a theory in the field of learning.

Logical positivism also laid great stress upon the empirical end of science and on the definition of scientific terms. Bridgman (1936) focused upon operational definition as the basis for science in a manner that was also reflected in psychology. Skinner's methodol-ogy was much closer to this, for which he has been criticized by philosophers of science. "It seems to be characteristic, but unfortu-nate, of science to continue holding philosophical positions long af-ter they are discredited. Thus, for example, Skinner's radical behaviorism, which insists on operational definition, came into prominence and dominated behavioral psychology well after most philosophers had abandoned the doctrine of operational or explicit definitions" (Suppe, 1977, p. 19). Skinner thus emphasized the em-pirical, technological aspects of science as these had been recognized in other sciences. His enunciated methodology for constructing the-ory aimed to advance from below, building observational generaliza-tions on top of other observational generalizations (Sidman, 1960), following classic empiricism of the type that Watson espoused (see 1930, pp. 18–19). This methodology never proved to be productive in psychology, or, contrary to popular conception, in the development of behavior therapy.

Psychology's Crisis: The Chaos of a Disunified Science

The method of taking the models for what psychology should be from the advanced parts of the natural sciences has unfortunate consequences, because psychology and the other behavioral sciences face different problems in theory construction (Staats, 1983b). Psy-chology faces conditions like those that prevailed at a much earlier time in the natural sciences, before those elegant, axiomatic, unified theories were created, a time when "there were almost as many views about . . . nature . . . as there were important . . . experimenters" (Kuhn, 1962, p. 13). In the early stages of the advanced sciences, there was unsystematic data collection and theorizing which produced a morass of unrelated, inconsistent, and, in a general sense, meaningless knowledge. It was also a time when there were relatively few scientists and few resources for manufacturing scientific products.

I have suggested that all sciences must go through that stage of disorganization before the methods of unification have been developed, in fact before the goal of unification has even arisen (Staats, 1983b). Psychology has not yet entered the stage of developing unification. It is a modern, disunified science. Its modernity makes the problems more difficult because, unlike the early natural sciences, psychology has many scientists, many sources of publication, many sophisticated apparatuses and methods, and many phenomena to study across a wide range of interests. These characteristics have resulted in the production of a bewildering profusion of unrelated knowledge elements. In psychology there are different theories, large and small, and different areas and methods of study in great abundance, and there are different general positions that separate psychologists and their works.

The theory that is needed in psychology is not of the type that has been described in logical positivism. The methodology for the needed theory has not been described by Hull or Skinner, or exemplified in their works. The huge theory problem that psychology faces—the problem of all the behavioral sciences—is to construct theoretical structures that provide frameworks for making some general sense out of the profligate, profuse chaos of knowledge elements produced in this divided and divisive science. The theory problem of psychology has been that of constructing and utilizing a framework theory that abstracts from the jumble a set of elements that can be ordered in close theoretical derivation, and that is relevant across the range of concerns of the science.

At first blush one may say that unification is not the recognized task of theory in psychology and that it is an impossible goal (Koch, 1981). There are many answers to such doubts (Staats, 1983b). A central answer is that the goal is not an option. The proliferative fecundity of the science has produced such a cornucopia of elements that without organization new findings already make the science less rather than more meaningful. Psychology's productivity combined with its disorganization sets the problem; the only question is how the problem is to be solved. It is also quite clear that even without making the problem explicit, the grand theories of psychology have attempted to solve that problem. At this point it is relevant that we consider the methods that have been employed in search of the solution.

Types Of Framework Theories

The field of behavior therapy has not yet taken as one of its tasks that of systematically selecting the general theory that it will employ to make meaningful and useful the range of knowledge elements that are relevant to the field's conduct. Behavior therapy has left the choice to the market place, that is, to unsystematic methods of selection such as organizational and theoretical partisanship. Historically, behavior therapy developed out of behaviorism in an eclectic manner that simply employed the basic conditioning principles common to all of the different and competing behaviorist theories (e.g., Hull's, Skinner's, Guthrie's, or Tolman's) The fact is that each of these second-generation theories failed, as has been attested to by opponents (e.g., Koch, 1981) and proponents (e.g., Follette, 1988). None of the traditional behaviorist theories established a continuing tradition of leading even the field of animal learning, or a continuing and mutually interactive relationship between basic and applied behaviorism, let alone establishing itself as a consensual approach in psychology generally. Despite the failure of second-generation theories, behaviorists still consider these theories to be models of what theory is and should be. In this sense the second-generation theorists and their theories have been reified. It is time the field begins to question and evaluate these models toward the goal of reaching a new understanding of what a general theory in psychology must be and how such theory can be constructed. At the same time, behavior therapy would be ill advised to throw out the baby with the bathwater and abandon behaviorism altogether—as some cognitive (behavior) therapists seem to favor. What we need is not a replacement of behaviorism with some type of cognitivism; we need a different type of behaviorist theory, one that is very different from second-generation behaviorist theories.

The Part-to-Whole Method

One of the most influential of the great theories of human behavior was Freud's psychoanalysis. This theory may thus be employed to illustrate an aspect of the methodology of constructing such general theories. Freud's theory was less than universal in that the sample of subjects that provided the data for the theory—middle-class Austrians with predominantly anxiety problems—was not very representative. A more general critique would recognize, in addition, that far less than the wide knowledge of psychology has served as the empirical-theoretical foundation for psychoanalysis. Yet psychoanalysis has been commonly considered to be a comprehensive theory that applies very generally to human behavior. The general methodology used in the construction of this theory was to study phenomena in a circumscribed part of psychology based on the assumption and speculation that the theory generally applied to human behavior.

This method is not restricted to psychoanalysis. Behaviorists, as another example, have employed the "part-to-whole method" also. Clearly, the main area of systematic study of second-generation behaviorists such as Hull and Skinner focused on animal learning. Their conviction was that the theories that they formed through this study of a part of psychology would be general to the whole of psychology, as we can see in Hull's preface to his book where he generalizes the theory he is about to introduce—a basic animal learning theory—to everything in the field of psychology:

> [This book] has been written on the assumption that all behavior, individual and social, moral and immoral, normal and psychopathic, is generated from the same primary laws; that the differences in the objective behavioral manifestations are due to the differing conditions under which habits are set up and function. (1943, p. v)

In different words Skinner (1953) sets forth the same methodology, and then proceeds to outline analyses that exemplify the methodology:

> Our conception of human behavior need not be *deduced* from the complex facts which it must eventually explain. We are not required, for example, to discover the characteristics of the political animal through a study of the facts of government. If the political animal is man himself, we may study him elsewhere and often under better conditions. A functional analysis of behavior provides us with a basic conception with which we may approach each of these fields [government, religion, psychotherapy, economics, and education] in turn. (p. 334)

It is important to realize what the characteristics of this methodology are, both explicit and implicit. The methodology consists of a two-level theoretical effort: (1) There is the work that establishes the basic principles of conditioning. This is the work that received the systematic application of the methods of empirical science. In this the previous findings of other researchers were integrally included, for example, the findings of the first generation of behaviorists. The work at this level is rigorous and systematic. (2) The second level of theory is devoted to explaining the phenomena of the most complex types of human behavior—including government and religion and so on—in terms of the basic principles. For this it is not necessary to make a systematic study of the "facts of government," following Skinner's statement, or any other area devoted to the study of human behavior. This is a monumentally important methodological position. The framework provides no basis for being concerned with the systematic study of human behavior made by those working in other frameworks. What is actually proposed is a reductionism that makes the empirical and theoretical findings of the nonbehaviorists superfluous. There is no basis here for a mutual, cooperative building of knowledge. That implicit methodology is made evident also by the fact that nowhere in any of Skinner's works will one see reference to the works of others including nonbehavioral works. Even in the study of a less global topic such as language, Skinner's analysis of verbal behavior (1957) includes no reference to the linguistic study of language or even to the work of other behaviorists (e.g., Cofer & Foley, 1942; Mowrer, 1954; Osgood, 1953; Razran, 1939; Russell & Storms, 1955).

In short, the behavioristic method of theory construction does not tell concerned behavioral scientists how to use the basic principles of animal learning, established by behaviorists, in conjunction with the knowledge of human behavior established by a variety of psychologists ranging from child developmentalists, through personologists, to social psychologists, psychological test constructors, and so on, let alone with the knowledge found in the fields of the social sciences. Not having a methodology for the unification of such knowledge, behaviorism's approach—beginning with Watson—has been generalization by exclusion. We can see this in Watson's rejection of not only introspection, but also of the phenomena that introspectionists—and currently cognitive psychologists—attempted to study. Radical behaviorists ruled large areas of study out of the realm of operant behaviorism—the works of personality theorists, psychological testing, and so on, in explicit statements (see Skinner, 1969, pp. 77–78, for an example) as well as in the implicit characteristics of the method employed. The same may be said for nonbehavioral attempts at general theory, of course, as was indicated in describing Freud's psychoanalytic theory. As other examples, personologists, child developmentalists, linguists, and other social scientists have been very explicit in their rejection of the relevance of

behaviorism and the study of animal learning for their areas of
interest. Psychological theories—regardless of their claims to
generality—have been local, specialized theories at heart.

Eclectic Combinations

Another theory methodology that is currently employed in psychology in the attempt to attain generality may be called the eclectic
combination. We can see social learning theory to be an example of
this in the field of behavior therapy. In its beginning (see Bandura
& Walters, 1959) Bandura's theoretical stance was traditional in
nature. When it began developing in the learning-behavioral direction it adopted the name provided by Miller and Dollard (1941) as
well as their emphasis on learning through imitation, and then
progressively included additional behavioral characteristics (Bandura, 1969), some from Skinner's basic operant and respondent distinction, and others like those of social (paradigmatic) behaviorism.
In more recent works, however, social learning theory has again
added concepts from traditional psychology. As Woll (1978) noted,
however, social learning theory's integration of cognitive psychology
concepts and behavioral principles has been eclectic, in a manner
that not only does not unify the concepts but instead involves "numerous inconsistencies" (p. 1). Woll has criticized this approach for
its eclecticism in a paper entitled *The Best of Both Worlds? A Critique of Cognitive Social Learning Theory:*

> I have argued that the movement made by social learning theorists to
> a cognitively-oriented, information processing approach represents
> more of a shift in terminology than a change in theoretical perspective
> or experimental strategy. The cognitive constructs proposed by social
> learning theorists bear little resemblance to and make minimal con-
> tact with their counterparts in cognitive psychology. (1978, p. 29)

In order for a general conceptual structure to serve as a heuristic
framework theory, the conceptual elements that are included in the
theory must be closely and explicitly linked. Without such a close
linkage the elements are simply thrown together, perhaps with terminological usages that suggest unification, but that provide no
avenues for using the principles of the one element with which to
consider the knowledge of the other, and vice versa. True unified
theory must provide the close linkage that allows derivational
movement from one part to the other. Only in this way can the
elements in the theory be joined to produce new, original combinations with which to understand phenomena formerly considered to

be different and unrelated. Thus, if social learning theory is going to employ concepts like information processing, coding, and cognitive transformations, along with learning principles, this should be done with the specific unification demanded for heuristic extensions. Woll says, however, "that the cognitive formulations offered by current social learning theory are misleading . . . and that they suffer from . . . ambiguities and imprecision" (1978, p. 21).

When one examines social learning theory it can be seen that it is not a precisely stated theory. The inconsistency and ambiguity that Woll has described with respect to its use of cognitive terminology also pervades its behavioral concepts. A primary example occurs in its basic principles of modeling which have been said to be as fundamental as classical and instrumental conditioning, but which have not been explicitly stated (Bandura, 1969, 1971). Moreover, in applying the theory to human behavior a wide variety of complex human activities—each involving different principles, and each different from the others—have been called modeling. Thus, activities such as communication, reading, learning through following instructions, emotion and image elicitation through symbols, and so on, are all considered to be examples of modeling. I would suggest that each area involves multiple principles and requires a particular analysis if the theory is to be heuristic. Modeling is used as a catchall concept, not a precisely defined theoretical term.

The part-to-whole theories of behaviorism have typically been systematically stated in their basic theory level, but have involved a less precise methodology in their theoretical extensions to areas of complex human behavior. Eclectic combinations may be imprecisely stated throughout. The methodology of paradigmatic behaviorism, to be described in the following section, calls for analysis, detail, and derivational explicitness throughout the range of its concerns.

Multilevel Theory: Paradigmatic Behaviorism's Method

Let us say that there are specialists in two fields of study, for example, animal learning and personality. Each specialist ordinarily will have only a hazy notion of the other field, while having detailed contact with his or her own. Typically, the animal learning theorist, if considering personality at all, will feel free in generally concluding that personality is at least in part learned. This may be done even without confronting and analyzing the knowledge of personality, and without considering what would make this field of knowledge suitable for such confrontation and analysis. The personologist, on the other hand, is no better able to put his or her field of knowledge into a form that would make it amenable to analysis in terms of learning principles. That is, the personologist does not specify what personality consists of in behaviorally relevant terms such that a learning analysis could be made of the knowledge in the field.

In such a case, although the two fields study events that in nature are very much related, this will not be evident in the knowledge produced by the fields. The relationship, to be revealed, demands the construction of *bridging theory* (or interlevel theory, see Staats, 1983b). That is, the knowledge of each field must be considered in a form that makes it susceptible to being related to the knowledge of the other. The bewildering knowledge elements of the field of animal learning, for example, must be examined for development of a smaller set of relevant principles and concepts. These must be stated in a form that allows them to be unified with suitably stated elements of knowledge from the field of personality. Furthermore, the principles taken from the two fields require further development of theory to be suitable for use in a unified theory. To illustrate, there are personality concepts that refer to complex cognitive characteristics that might be considered in terms of learning principles, if stated in appropriate behavioral terms. But this would also require that the learning principles first be elaborated appropriately. Even the the *basic* learning principles may not link well with the studies of cognition. A theory of language, derived on the basis of a learning analysis, may be necessary to bridge the gap between the simple learning principles and the concepts of the cognitive aspects of personality.

The various fields of psychology—learning, child development, personality, cognition, social psychology, abnormal psychology, clinical psychology, educational psychology, and so on—have all developed a bewildering complexity of idiosyncratic, specialized knowledge. To relate any two of these fields demands the type of bridging theory that has been briefly described, where the relevant elements of each field are stated in a manner such that they can be unified. Furthermore, these fields are typically related in a hierarchical manner such that bridging may first have to be accomplished between adjacent fields before the more distant relationships can be seen. The example involving the learning—language—cognitive relationship was one illustration. As another illustration, the field of psychopathology cannot be well understood in terms of basic learning principles until the learning and personality fields have been bridged, such that a learning theory of personality can be applied to the consideration of the phenomena of abnormal psychology (cf.,

Heiby & Staats, Chapter 10, this vol.; Staats, 1975, Chapter 8; Staats & Heiby, 1985). The fields of psychology in general can be considered to constitute a hierarchy of levels, requiring interlevel theory to form the bridges that enable the construction of a comprehensive, multilevel theory.

Finally, it should be realized that all general theories—Hull's, Skinner's, Freud's, and so on—only constitute framework theories; they can only address in systematic detail a small portion of the realm of psychology. In this sense they are all frameworks rather than completed, detailed structures throughout. Neither the part-to-whole method nor the eclectic combinations methods can succeed in providing a heuristic unified framework. Unified theory of comprehensive scope in psychology requires multilevel theory that confronts explicitly, and tightly relates in a bridging manner, the several fields of the science and the various problem areas within each field. This can first only be achieved in a framework fashion with the expectation that the framweork will be progressively filled. The next section will attempt to characterize more the multilevel theory structure of illustrate paradigmatic behaviorism, as summarized in Table 2.1.

TABLE 2.1 The Multilevel Theory of Social Behaviorism

Fields	Areas (examples)
Biological mechanisms of learning	Sensory psychology Brain and central nervous system Response systems Evolution of learning structures
Basic learning theory	Conditioning principles Generalizing principles: in stimuli, response systems, and species treated Motivation principles
Human learning principles	Complex stimulus-response learning Cumulative-hierarchical learning principles and others unique to humans Extending basic principles to human level
Child development principles	Language development, intelligence, and language-mediated modeling Sensory-motor development and imitation Emotional development through learning

(continued)

TABLE 2.1   The Multilevel Theory of Social Behaviorism (cont.)

Fields	Areas (examples)
Personality	Personality theory The personality systems: language-cognitive, emotional-motivational, and sensory-motor Personality and environmental interaction
Personality measurement	Theory relating behavior principles and personality measurement and assessment Integrating tests with theory (clinical, etc.) Constructing tests and behavior assessments
Social psychology	Attitudes and social cognition Interpersonal relations and group processes Personality processes, individual differences, and cross-cultural psychology
Abnormal personality	Deficits in the personality systems Inappropriate aspects of personality systems Diagnostic categories in terms of personality systems Interaction of personality and social systems
Clinical psychology	Behavior modification of simple problems Language-cognitive methods of treatment Personality change and measurement Children's problems and treatment
Educational psychology	Learning theories of school subjects Intelligence and readiness in school learning Problems of school learning Motivation and school learning
Organizational psychology	Personnel selection Motivation in organizational settings Behavioral analysis of jobs Organizational conditions and problems

Paradigmatic Behaviorism's Multilevels

Skinner (1950) indicated that in his view learning principles were not to be explained by reference to biological phenomena. Paradigmatic behaviorism, in contrast, sees a continuity of knowledge between the two, bridging the learning principles and the biological mechanisms that account for learning (Staats, 1975, Chapter 15). Thus, the physiology of learning might be considered the most basic level of the theory. Nevertheless, the basic level of theory for understanding the various fields concerned with human behavior for the present purposes will be considered to be the theory of learning, as the following will indicate.

The Basic Learning Theory Level

At the time paradigmatic behaviorism's basic learning theory was constructed, the field of animal learning was a buzzing confusion of different theories, experiments, findings, and methods, as it remains to this day. Pavlov had previously established classical conditioning, and Thorndike had established instrumental conditioning, as basic principles. Many studies had been conducted on both principles, and much was known about secondary principles such as generalization, discrimination, deprivation–satiation, and so on. The second–generation behaviorists accepted as their goal the construction of a general theory of learning. Each major theorist attempted to set forth his idiosyncratic theory aiming to best incorporate the principles and findings that had previously been produced. Although the materials they had at hand were the same to begin with, they came up with theories containing important differences. For example, Hull was a one-factor theorist—arguing that all learning occurred via reinforcement (1943). Skinner (1938) was nominally a two-factor theorist, but considered classical conditioning and emotional responding as totally separate from overt behavior which was learned through reinforcement. His focus on reinforcement made his approach in practice a one-factor theory. Later, two-factor learning theorists (N.E. Miller, 1948; Mowrer, 1947; Solomon & Wynne, 1954) posited that there were two types of learning processes that had a mode of interaction. Just exactly what that interaction constituted was never agreed upon (see Rescorla & Solomon, 1967), and these theories did not isolate and specify what the several functions were that stimuli could acquire—a central focus of paradigmatic behaviorism's learning theory—and extensions of two-factor theories to the human level, as in theories of word meaning (Mowrer, 1954; Osgood, 1953), lacked that specification.

In any event, the various theories stimulated a vast quantity of research. The rapid production of experimental findings amid the use of different methods, different languages of discourse, along with the competitions of the different theories, resulted in a confused, inconsistent, competitive mass of knowledge that was difficult to systematize for use in the study of human behavior. As Hilgard commented after reviewing just the major theories: "How can [learning] psychologists be helpful to other social scientists or to those who wish to apply their findings if they disagree among themselves on these fundamental matters?" (1948, p. 457).

The existence of the competing learning theories impacted upon those who attempted to apply learning to their interests in human behavior. There were those who used Hull's theory in applications (cf., Dollard & Miller, 1950; Rotter, 1954; Wolpe, 1950), Skinner's theory (Bijou, 1957; Lindsley, 1956), and so on. My own approach in the 1950s was to avoid commitment to any one learning theory. There was considerable overlap among them, when the terminologies were translated—indeed, they were all based upon much the same evidence and the principles provided by the first-generation behaviorists. Moreover, some of the new elements of each theory were productive. By the same token, each of the major theories contained useless elements, and elements that were in error and that would misguide applications. After all, those theories had been constructed explicitly to deal with the facts of animal learning, not those of human behavior. From the beginning, therefore, I felt that making one's focus of study the phenomena of human behavior changed the perspective. It called for the formulation of a different basic theory of learning that was constructed to have the characteristics important for its task. For example, Hull's (1943) axiomatic, mathematic, hypothetico-deductive emphasis had no value in studying human behavior. On the other hand, Skinnerian theory's emphasis upon schedules of reinforcement, disinterest in classical conditioning and ignorance of the emotion-behavior relationship, its restriction to the experimental analysis of behavior (operant chamber) methodology, its rejection of large areas of empirical, methodological, and conceptual knowledge, its restricted philosophy of science, and its inability to unify study in psychology made this theory inadequate in fundamental ways. Thus, from the beginning, paradigmatic behaviorism followed the notion of (1) selecting from the mass of animal learning literature the elements that could be used, when properly stated, (2) avoiding the disadvantageous elements, and (3) innovating the necessary new elements, to form a new basic learning theory in summary form with which to generally study human behavior. As an example of the innovation necessary, the various learning theories did not give a clear statement of the different functions that a stimulus could have (i.e., emotion eliciting, reinforcing, and directive), how those functions were acquired and could be changed, what the learning processes were that were involved, and how the processes interacted. Skinner's position that classical conditioning (of emotions) and operant conditioning (of behavior) are entirely separate was particularly disadvantageous for both animal and human behavioral research. Paradigmatic behaviorism's theory makes it clear, for example, that events important to classical conditioning take place during instrumental conditioning, and vice versa, and that instrumental behavior is ubiquitously changed via classical conditioning.

The second-generation theories employed the knowledge of the first-generation works of Pavlov, Thorndike, Watson, and others. However, the second-generation theories systematized the principles in different ways. Paradigmatic behaviorism's theory has likewise employed the works of the first two generations as background knowledge. But the process of the development of the basic learning theory of paradigmatic behaviorism has been described in part because it is different from that of the other two framework theories that have been mentioned herein. That is, operant behaviorism's basic learning theory (cf., Skinner, 1938) was composed as an animal learning theory, as was Hull's (1943) and the others of that genre. Paradigmatic behaviorism's basic theory has been composed with basic human as well as animal learning knowledge as fundamental. Most of its research has been conducted with humans, in clarifying, specifying, and extending the basic conditioning principles. Social learning theory (Bandura, 1969; Bandura & Walters, 1959, 1963), to continue the comparisons, may be seen to spring rather completely from the human level of study. Its focus has been on demonstrating the principles of modeling. This approach has not involved a systematic consideration of the animal learning principles or of constructing a new statement of basic learning principles based upon research of an animal or a human type to specify the basic principles involved. Social learning theory, actually, simply accepted Skinner's statement of the basic principles (see Bandura, 1969). In summary, operant behaviorism's basic learning theory (and the other theories of this generation) has the animal learning research perspective, and social learning theory's has the human research perspective. Paradigmatic behaviorism's theory, however, has both the animal and human learning research perspective. The result in each case is a fundamentally different basic theory structure.

At this point it is pertinent to summarize paradigmatic behaviorism's three-function learning theory. Its name was chosen to emphasize that it is the *functions* that stimuli can have for the behavior of the individual that is important. Using this perspective, when we cut through the various terminologies employed in order to describe the classic principles of conditioning, we can see that (1) stimuli can elicit an emotional response, (2) stimuli can serve as reinforcers for instrumental behavior, and (3) stimuli can serve as incentives (directive or discriminative stimuli) to bring on particular instrumental behaviors. If we look at the various theories we can see that the functions have been the focus of research but not in a clear manner that delineates and relates them, and that provides a basis for formulating a broad, unified theory. Different idiosyncratic characteristics have been given to the particular function, depending upon the nature of the experimental situation and apparatus used, and so on. For example, Hull used the term r_g (fractional anticipatory goal response) in animal-maze types of study, making it a different and less useful and general concept than that of an emotional response, although it has overlapping characteristics with the emotional concept. Skinner's concept of the discriminative stimulus (S^D) has characteristics that stem from the limited experimental situation in which it was studied, yet it overlaps in definition with what has been called more generally an incentive or, in the present approach, a directive stimulus. As another example, the concept of the reinforcing stimulus was also prominent in Hull's theory, considered as due to drive reduction, and in Skinner's theory, where it was defined only by its affect upon the strength of the behaviors it followed.

What is new in paradigmatic behaviorism's basic learning theory is the manner in which it defines the three functions of stimuli, describes the two basic processes and procedures of conditioning, and delineates the interaction of the two basic processes and consequently of the three stimulus functions. The theory states that different processes are involved in classical conditioning (emotional responses) and instrumental conditioning (motor responses), which agrees with operant learning theory. However, three-function learning theory indicates that instrumental and classical conditioning are inextricably linked. Unlike Skinner's theory, where emotional responding is considered as an epiphenomenon, not a determinant of behavior, three-function learning theory considers emotional responses and classical conditioning to be very fundamental Thus, *the ability to elicit an emotional response defines the reinforcing stimulus*—and this is a basic difference from both Hull's and Skinner's treatment of reinforcement. In three-function learning theory *a stimulus is a reinforcer because it elicits an emotional response,* either naturally or through previous conditioning. This is a central principle, with many implications both for the field of animal learning as well as for treating the phenomena of human behavior. In the mature organism, as a stimulus comes to elicit an emotional response—and in humans this can occur through a variety of procedures, many of which are vicarious—it will become a reinforcer in general, and a directive (incentive) stimulus that will control (tend to elicit) a large variety of instrumental behaviors. Positive emotional stimuli come to elicit a large class of "striving for" behaviors because those behaviors are many times reinforced by obtaining the stimulus—which is reinforcing. The converse is true with negative emotional stimuli. In the mature organism this learning has the effect that any stimulus that comes to elicit a positive or negative emotional response will *by this alone* gain the power to elicit a very large class of instrumental (including verbal) behaviors. Thus, in opposition to Skinner's position, classical conditioning causally affects instrumental behavior by affecting the reinforcing and directive powers of stimuli. Finally, deprivation is related to reinforcement value because deprivation increases the strength with which the stimulus involved elicits the emotional response (see Staats, 1988a, for a recent comparison of Skinner's theory with the three-function learning theory).

Because the concept of the emotional response is so central it needs more specification through further research. Let it be said here, however, that emotional responses may be indexed peripherally—by salivation, heart rate, or the galvanic skin response (GSR)—but they are essentially central nervous system phenomena (see Staats & Eifert, 1990, for a more detailed discussion). Although negative and positive emotional responses cannot be distinguished via such responses as the GSR and heart rate, they can be differentiated by the topology of peripheral responses in some cases (negative emotional stimuli lead to detumescence and decreased salivation, for example, in a manner quite the opposite of sexual stimuli and food, respectively). Moreover, physiological specification that distinguishes the anatomic brain centers for negative and positive emotional responses provides additional sources of definition.

The three-function learning theory (also called the A-R-D theory,

to name the *a*ffective, *r*einforcing, and *d*irective functions of emotional stimuli) incorporates all the findings concerning classical and
instrumental conditioning, and indicates new expectations as well.
It has been stated only in summary form as a framework theory
(Staats, 1970, 1975), but it is intended that this framework theory
of basic learning principles will be developed additionally through
theoretical elaboration and empirical specification. With respect to
animal learning, its potential can be seen in the fact that a less
general theory with some common features has arisen in recent
years in the context of explaining transfer of control studies (cf.,
Overmier & Lawry, 1979). I must add, however, that *various* areas
of study in the animal field could be better understood and researched in the context of the three-function learning theory.

The same is true for the human level of study. The various implications of the three-function learning theory also require systematic
verification, exploration, and elaboration with human subjects. Let
me illustrate how the basic principles can be used heuristically and
verified while at the same time that human motivational phenomena are studied. The principle is that deprivation of a positive
emotion-eliciting stimulus will increase the extent to which the
stimulus elicits the emotional response. This principle is derived
from Pavlov's early work and Finch's (1938) demonstration that food
deprivation increased salivary response to the conditioned as well as
the unconditioned stimulus. In terms of three-function learning theory, however, deprivation of the emotional stimulus should also increase the strength of the stimulus's reinforcing power (cf., Perin,
1942) and also its directive (incentive) value. These three-function
learning principles have been verified in laboratory research with
human subjects (Harms & Staats, 1978; Staats & Hammond, 1972;
Staats, Minke, Martin, & Higa, 1972; Staats & Warren, 1974). Food-
words were used as the conditioned stimuli to elicit an emotional
response that increased with food deprivation. It was shown that
deprivation also changed the other two functions of the food-word
stimuli. This set of studies illustrated one of the salient characteristics of three-function learning theory, that is, the manner in which
its basic principles have been experimentally extended with human
subjects and with stimuli important at the human level. One of the
most fundamental differences between Skinner's theory and paradigmatic behaviorism is that Skinner's theory has guided radical
behaviorists to neglect classical conditioning whereas paradigmatic
behaviorism provides the bases for many areas of research in classical conditioning, animal and human.

No one who seriously considers the knowledge of human behavior would reach the conclusion that the individual's emotional responding is not a determinant of her or his behavior. As such, understanding human behavior calls for understanding of emotional responding. Three-function learning theory provides the necessary principles whereas Skinnerian theory does not (see Staats, 1988b).

The Human Learning Theory Level

As has been indicated, the traditional strategy of behaviorism has been relying on learning theory based on animal research to provide the basic principles needed for the general task of explaining human behavior. When one stops and thinks about this strategy, its faults immediately become evident. Centrally, there are many things that must be added to the elementary conditioning principles to provide a basic theory suitable to the complex nature of the task. Although the animal conditioning principles are basic throughout the various levels of the theory of paradigmatic behaviorism, there are secondary principles that must be derived in the study of human learning and related to the basic principles. For instance, animal learning is studied in brief tasks requiring simple responses. Human behavior, however, involves extremely complex skills, acquired over very long periods of time. Let us take reading as an example. Learning to read involves thousands and thousands of learning trials and takes place over years of time. Furthermore, it takes place in a cumulative fashion that involves the child first learning certain repertoires of skills that then provide the foundation for the learning of other repertoires of skills that in turn enable other repertoires of skills to be learned (e.g., Staats, 1971a; Staats, Brewer, & Gross, 1970; Staats & Burns, 1981). Cumulative-hierarchical learning is typical in the achievement of complex human characteristics. Yet this process of learning is not studied in the animal learning laboratory, an absolutely central deficit. Paradigmatic behaviorism states that cumulative-hierarchical learning principles and the types of skills that can be produced thereby must be studied if we are to have a learning theory that can deal with the complexities of human behavior.

As another example, it has been recognized within paradigmatic behaviorism that most of the things that the human learns are not acquired solely on the basis of the elementary principles of conditioning. In its early form the approach used the term *vicarious learning* (Staats, 1963), a term that was also employed to describe modeling within social learning theory (Bandura & Walters, 1963). Social learning theory, however, considered humans' ability to learn vicariously as given, as basic, and proceeded to demonstrate how learning occurs through modeling. This puts modeling in competition with learning via the two other basic principles of conditioning, in a way that maintains the schism between behaviorist and traditional views. Paradigmatic behaviorism, in contrast, considered vicarious learning to take place on the basis of repertoires that themselves have been previously learned through basic conditioning. This is a fundamental difference. Some of these repertoires involve what in common sense would be called imitation or modeling. But many of these repertoires are not of that type. For example, much human learning takes place by means of language, which actually includes many different processes. For example, we can learn new instrumental skills through being told how to do something, or through reading instructions in a manual. To understand how that takes place, and why for some individuals such learning is difficult or impossible, and to be able to deal with such problems of learning, we need to analyze the repertoires that provide the foundation for the vicarious learning processes, and how those repertoires themselves are learned. The more detailed the theory we employ, the better will be our understanding and our ability to achieve positive results. Social learning theory has lumped a large number of such processes together, indiscriminately calling them modeling or vicarious learning, in a way that does not fully explicate what is involved and thus provides an incomplete guide for therapy. Each type of communication process, for example, calls for an explicit analysis of the repertoires involved. When we face a problem of communication, that is what we would need to know.

A prominent aspect of paradigmatic behaviorism has been the study of vicarious learning processes, much of it in the study of how language is learned (see Rondal's Chapter 4) and how language *functions* in providing the basis for additional learning. It is sufficient to give only one example, since there are later chapters in this volume that are based upon these developments. Early learning analyses began putting the consideration of the meaning of words within a learning framework (Cofer & Foley, 1942; Mowrer, 1954; Osgood, 1953: Razran, 1939). An early and continued part of my own research involved elaborating a systematic theory of the emotional aspects of language and the manner in which vicarious emotional learning can be produced through language (Finley & Staats, 1967; Harms & Staats, 1978; Staats, 1963, 1968a; Staats & Staats, 1958; Staats & Warren, 1974; C.K. Staats & Staats, 1957). This work involved the first behavioristic attempt to study experimentally the conditioning processes involved in language learning and function. One study showed how words come through primary classical conditioning to elicit an emotional response (Staats, Staats, & Crawford, 1962). It was said that the normal human learns a large repertoire of words that elicit a negative emotional response, and a large repertoire of word stimuli that elicit a positive emotional response.

But paradigmatic behaviorism was also concerned with the cognitive aspects of language, that is, with how language functions to affect behavior and to produce further (vicarious) learning. We know that language has important emotional functions. Can we understand these functions in the present context? An important function of emotional words is their role in the further development of the individual's emotional learning. The process is that an emotional word that is paired with another stimulus will transfer its emotional response to the other stimulus according to the principles of classical conditioning. An important type of communication involves pairing an emotional word stimulus with an event, object, or person, or with their verbal representation. This pairing will result in the object, person, or event coming to elicit the emotional response elicited by the emotional word. Most of what we call the individual's values, attitudes, goals, rewards, motivations, needs, and so on, involve the manner in which emotional responses have been learned to important life stimuli (or their verbal representations) through the process I call language conditioning. To understand the importance of language conditioning we must realize that individuals' values and attitudes are important determinants of their characteristic behaviors. The principles of animal learning by themselves do not provide the analyses by which to understand these aspects of human learning. We need to know also the human learning principles that derive from the basic principles.

It is important to make the methodology clear in this context, in view of the contemporary interest in cognitive theorizing. It should be noted that although paradigmatic behaviorism was involved in the initiation of the behavior modification movement (Staats, 1957a) and introduced a number of elements into that development (Staats, 1963), the theoretical position did not reject the importance of considering cognitive phenomena. On the contrary, paradigmatic behaviorism continued to build toward its goal of unifying empirically-based cognitive concepts and principles within its framework. Its works have empirically analyzed such cognitive-personality phenomena as purpose and goals, achievement standards, reasoning and problem solving, grammatical rules, communication, meaning, images, emotions, values, norms, and attitudes, to mention a few. This unifying goal is evidenced in many research articles that I authored and co-authored (see reference section of this book), in two books entitled *Complex Human Behavior* (1963) and *Learning, Language, and Cognition* (1968a), and of particular relevance for the present volume, in the article entitled *Language Behavior Therapy* (1972). The paradigmatic behaviorism treatment of cognitive phenomena differed, however, from the traditional cognitive approaches and the eclectic treatment that has been described with respect to social learning theory. Traditional cognitive approaches and the newer cognitive-behavioral eclectic approaches are essentially nonanalytic and do not employ multilevel theory construction methods as described herein.

Let us take the example of the negative thoughts of the depressed person. These have been considered in some theories as a cause of depression without the consideration of a more basic analysis of the cognitive phenomenon. Beck (1967, 1976), for example, considers depression to involve a negative view of the self, the world, and the future. The radical behaviorism position is to reject such theories. Paradigmatic behaviorism takes the view that reliably observed phenomena, such as the negative ruminations of the depressed patient must be analyzed. What do those ruminations consist of in behavioral terms? How are they learned? And how do these ruminations affect the individual and his or her behavior? While a complete analysis cannot be given here, paradigmatic behaviorism is interested in considering of what a negative view of the self, the world, and the future is constituted (see Chapter 10 by Heiby & Staats, this vol., for additional elaborations). For one thing, we might see that an important component consists of words that depressed persons emit out loud or to themselves. We then would be interested in how words can have emotion eliciting properties, as in creating dysphoria (see Rose & Staats, 1988, and Chapter 10, for a definition of dysphoria). We would be interested in the learning that went into the acquisition of such negative emotional words, in terms of individual differences in how particular words and word combinations elicit a negative emotional response as well as individual differences in the frequency in which such words are applied to the self, the world, and the future. We would also be interested in what actually constitutes the self and find that it is composed largely of language—cognitive repertoires with emotional properties. In making such an analysis, we would end up with a multilevel theoretical structure that advances from the basic principles of learning, through the human learning analysis of emotional word learning, to a consideration of more complex concepts such as the

self and, with these, into the consideration of depression. This is not
to say that practicing therapists will make that analysis for each of
their patients, but having a theory that includes the various levels
of the analysis will be of great benefit in understanding what depression is, and hence in the ability to deal with the problem.

The contemporary works that incorporate traditional (cognitive)
concepts, without explaining those concepts in terms of basic principles simply make themselves into traditional (nonbehavioral) theories. The advantages of behaviorism are thereby abandoned, for
such usages represent what Watson referred to as "mentalism."
There is a contemporary behavioral view that "what is now needed
is a comprehensive . . . perspective which includes environmental
determinants, biological foundations, systems theory, cognition and
society within some form of data-based social learning model rather
than the *status quo* applied behavior analysis approach which seems
to have dominated this field until now" (Franks, 1983, p. 70). Contemporary behavior therapy is now coming to accept the goals of
paradigmatic behaviorism that aim toward breadth through the inclusion of nonbehavioral knowledge. The trick, however, to incorporating traditional concepts and principles like biological and
cognitive processes or personality is doing so within the explanatory
power of behaviorism. This means linking the new concepts back to
the basic principles in the level-by-level manner of multilevel theory construction. Without that the attempts at unification are retro-
gressive.

The Child Development Level of the Theory

The purpose of the human learning level of the multilevel theory is
to describe in abstract form the advanced principles of human
learning, and to extend learning analyses to experimental analogues of complex human activities such as problem solving, communication, coding, imagery, purpose, information processing, and
so on. At the next level of theory the task is that of using the
preceding developments with which to consider the repertoires that
the individual learns in childhood. Child developmentalists have
described many of the important elements of child and adult behavior, including language-cognitive areas. But these must be analyzed
within the principles of the advancing, building theory. This has
been undertaken in such content areas as the development of motor
skills, including those involved in imitation, walking, toilet training, and so on, the development of intelligence and language, and
emotional learning (Staats, 1963, 1968a; Staats, Brewer, & Gross,

1970; Staats & Burns, 1981). One work devoted to the analysis of the development of grammatical language forms (Staats, 1971b) answered the Chomsky-inspired, psycholinguistic criticism of learning theories of language. This work included an analysis of how parents "train" their children in language—an analysis that later psycholinguistic studies verified, as Rondal has shown (see his Chapter 4, this vol.). Much additional theory and research is necessary in the analysis of child development. The start that has been made, however, provides a beginning basis for the practice of behavior therapy and is helpful in making sense of the widely divergent literature. It also serves as a basis for generating additional, new developments. Contrary to ahistorical approaches, such as the radical behaviorism approach to autism (see Staats, 1975, p. 62), the paradigmatic behavior therapy position is that we need to know—for prevention especially—what produces problems, and that makes the child development level of study very central. As with other levels, bridging theory construction is needed to resolve various problems such as the nature–nurture schism in child development study.

The Personality Level of the Theory

One of the sharpest schisms that has divided the knowledge of behavioral and nonbehavioral psychology has revolved around the concept of personality. Traditionally, psychology has considered personality as the central determinant of human behavior. In behavioral psychology the concept of personality has been rejected as mentalistic, that is, as the inference of an internal process that is supposed to determine behavior, when all one really has is the observation of the behavior itself. As a consequence of this schism, behavioral psychology has made little use of the knowledge accumulated in the fields of personality, personality measurement, or abnormal personality, and is diminished as a result.

Paradigmatic behaviorism, in contrast, has developed a bridging theory with which to unite the opposing fields. The approach was made explicit and labeled a *behavioral interaction* approach (Staats, 1971a), to indicate how the environment and personality interact to determine individual behavior. Other interactionist positions with somewhat similar goals have also been set forth, both within traditional personality theory (Magnusson & Endler, 1977) and within social learning theories (Bandura, 1977b; Mahoney, 1977; Mischel, 1973). Unlike these approaches which present little specification of what personality is, paradigmatic behaviorism has built its concept of personality in an objectively specified level-by-level way, beginning with the basic conditioning principles. The next more advanced level stipulates how humans learn complex repertoires of behavior via cumulative hierarchical learning processes, involving vicarious learning of various types. Study of such repertoires reveals that once acquired they affect the individual's experience, and later learning, and behavior. That is, they enter into the determination of behavior, along with environmental circumstances. As this theoretical structure gives personality a causal role, it then provides the basis for the analysis of traditional psychology's knowledge of personality.

The central aspect of this theory of personality is that of the *basic behavioral repertoire* (Staats, 1968a, 1971a, 1975). The individual, as an infant, begins to learn very broad basic behavioral repertoires in three areas, the sensory-motor, the language-cognitive, and the emotional-motivational. Let us take, as an example, the language-cognitive personality repertoire. It is composed of a number of sub-repertoires: the verbal-imitation repertoire, the verbal-emotional repertoire, the verbal-motor repertoire, and so on. Using the third as an example, the theoretical-empirical analysis reveals that the child learns to make specific types of motor responses to certain specific words. Words such as *push, pull, jump, walk, run, look, reach,* and so on, must through the child's learning come to elicit the appropriate motor responses. The verbal-motor repertoire forms the basis for the child's ability to follow instructions—the richer the repertoire, the better the child's ability. It is important to understand how this repertoire is learned, so that we can intervene successfully when the child has not developed it in the home situation. However, it is also important to understand how the repertoire enables the child to follow instructions and is thus basic to much later learning of the child—in further development of the child's personality repertoires. The weakness of Skinnerian theory in accounting for language-cognitive effects on behavior is not solved by the recent introduction of the concept of "rule-governed behavior" (Zettle & Hayes, 1982) since it is necessary to explain why "rules" affect people. Paradigmatic behaviorism's theory of the language repertoire, especially the verbal-motor repertoire, provides the general explanation needed.

The description of the basic behavioral repertoires, the analysis of how they are learned, and the way they help determine the characteristics of the individual's behavior and learning in new situations constitute a bridging theory framework within which to integrate the traditional study of personality with behavioral fields of knowledge, such as that of behavioral assessment (Staats, 1986; Staats &

Fernandez-Ballesteros, 1987). Thus, for example, we have a systematic fund of knowledge in traditional psychology concerning the concept of intelligence. This realm of knowledge has been completely divorced from behavioral psychology. In paradigmatic behaviorism intelligence is seen to consist of certain basic behavioral repertoires, primarily those of a language—cognitive sort. As one example of this general repertoire, we may refer again to the verbal-motor repertoire. We can consider the manner in which the repertoire is learned in straightforward terms (Staats, 1968a). However, we can consider the significance of that repertoire only by consulting the knowledge provided by traditional psychology. When we look at children's intelligence tests we can see, for example, that the ability to follow directions of increasing complexity with advancing age is a ubiquitous aspect of intelligence, part of many test items. A child who has learned a rich verbal-motor repertoire will as a consequence be more intelligent. Because the child can follow directions well, other things equal, the child will pass many items. Moreover, the child's ability will transfer into life's tasks, because the ability to follow directions of increasing complexity is basic to the learning tasks that the child will face in school. We cannot expect to understand fully and deal with problems involving intelligence, such as mental retardation or learning disabilities without an understanding of how such personality repertoires develop and how they function in the child's further development. Moreover, we cannot deal with problems of intelligence until we know how to produce development of child's basic behavioral repertoires that are relevant to intelligence, a problem whose basic solution has already been shown to be within the grasp of the approach (see Staats & Burns, 1981). This example has been given because it illustrates the multilevel theory development of paradigmatic behaviorism. At the upper end, having already specified the structures of the basic behavioral repertoires, the next level of advancement is the analysis of the traditional concepts of personality in terms of those repertoires. This analysis is intended to be very general, including interests, attitudes, the self-system, and traits such as sociability (see Staats, 1975, 1983a). Paradigmatic behaviorism calls for analysis of the many others that have not yet been treated. This is one of the new directions of research the framework theory provides.

Over the years, behaviorally oriented theorists have begun to accept the need for a concept of personality of the type that paradigmatic behaviorism has been proposing. We see, for example, Mischel (1973) changing his previous position and proposing cognitive and emotional constructs of personality, but these concepts have not been given clear behavioral definition in cognitive social learning theory. We need to ask what they are, how they are learned, and how and by what principles they work their effects upon the individual's behavior. Bandura (1977a), for example, has added the concept of self-efficacy to a position that formerly had no personality construct. There is, however, not much specification of just what constitutes self-efficacy, how the individual acquires self-efficacy beliefs, or the mechanisms and principles by which self-efficacy controls behavior (see also Eifert's critical comments, Chapter 8, this vol.). Furthermore, self-efficacy theory treats only a small part of personality. In this same area the paradigmatic behaviorism analysis (Staats, 1963, 1975) had seen the individual's self-concept as composed of parts of the language-cognitive and emotional-motivational repertoires in which the individual's own physical and behavioral characteristics, and the social reactions to them, are the operative stimuli. The self-concept forms part of the concept of the self-system introduced into paradigmatic behaviorism (see Staats, 1975, Chapter 5). Bandura (1978b) has also alluded to a self-system in his recent additions of personality concepts to social learning theory, but only in a rather general conception suggesting that the environment and person interact. Even radical behaviorists are beginning to add concepts that play the role of personality. Thus, for example, Baer (1976) describes the organism as the host of its own behavior. The concept of the behavioral repertoire is also creeping into radical behaviorism, without causal properties, however. But before these developments can become a theory of personality, like that of the basic behavioral repertoires, specification of their elements must occur. The several theories should be compared on how much specification each one provides.

It should be stressed that the development of a personality level of theory in paradigmatic behaviorism was a crucial step. It provides the basis for unifying large areas of important knowledge achieved within traditional psychology with the power, precision, and stipulation of a behavioristic methodology. By developing its bridging theory of personality, paradigmatic behaviorism provides new directions in the fields of personality measurement and behavioral assessment (see also Burns, Chapter 5), abnormal psychology (Staats & Heiby, 1985), and clinical psychology. I am not suggesting that paradigmatic behaviorism's work is complete, only that it has begun, and that the framework theory now has sufficient specification to serve as a foundation for new directions of theory and research development and applications.

Due to space limitations I cannot present the important personality measurement and behavioral assessment level of theory in this chapter, but Burns presents a detailed analysis of this area in Chapter 5 of this volume. He shows how the paradigmatic behaviorial conception of personality can serve to integrate traditional personality assessment and behavioral assessment. Overcoming this major schism will be an important step toward a unified science of psychology. I have also previously discussed these matters and outlined the importance of studying and understanding this level of theory for the design and evaluation of behavioral intervention programs (Staats, 1986, 1988a; Staats & Fernandez-Ballesteros, 1987).

The Abnormal Psychology Level of the Theory

The first attempt at composing a general behavioral taxonomy (and theory) of abnormal behavior was presented in my 1963 book. Later developments in behavior modification drew on this taxonomy and it was said to provide basic elements for development of the field of behavioral assessment (Goldfried & Sprafkin, 1974). With the elaboration of the theory of personality (Staats, 1968a, 1971a), however, the foundation was available for a more advanced theory of abnormal psychology (Staats, 1975). In brief, the paradigmatic behaviorism theory of psychopathology proposes that the three basic behavioral (personality) repertoires already described are learned in the individual's history, and are brought into play in any later situation that the individual encounters. The later situation and the personality repertoires, in interaction, determine the (normal or abnormal) behavior that the individual will display. This theory indicates five sites of study for an abnormal psychology (see also Figure 5.2, Chapter 5, this vol.). First there is the original learning period prior to the individual's present situation. That original learning period may contain deficit conditions or inappropriate conditions of learning. As a consequence the individual may acquire deficit personality repertoires in any of the three areas, or inappropriate personality repertoires. What the individual's behavior will be like in any life situation will also be a function of the particular situation as well as the individual's personality repertoires. The life situation itself may be deficit or inappropriate. Finally, the symptoms of abnormal behavior the individual displays may be deficit or inappropriate, as Eysenck (1960) originally indicated. The behavioral symptoms thus depend on the characteristics of the personality repertoires and on the life situation. Furthermore, the abnormal behavior ordinarily will result in environmental circumstances that will also affect the individual's personality repertoires, the later life situation, and hence later behavior, in a lifelong causal progression. The theory states that the traditional categories of psychopathology can be basically considered within these sites of concern. The autistic child, for example, has been considered in terms of the deficits and inappropriacies in the language-cognitive, sensory-motor, and emotional-motivational personality repertoires (Staats, 1971a, pp. 309–318). A systematic analysis is needed of the possible factors in the original learning conditions that resulted in those personality characteristics, as well as specification (through assessment and measurement) of those characteristics, on the deficits and inappropriacies of the present life circumstances that may interact with them. Paradigmatic behaviorism's theories of the emotional-motivational, language-cognitive, and sensory-motor repertoires should provide certain specifics by which to analyze the deficits and inappropriacies of the particular psychopathology. That is to say, by this type of analysis the framework provides a set of theoretical principles applying generally to the different categories of psychopathology. In general, the traditional categories of psychopathology can be considered to involve different deficits and inappropriacies in the several sites the theory indicates (Staats, 1975, Chapter 8). This enables a deeper and more unified analysis of abnormal behavior than an approach that considers each category to reflect a different type of mental disease or other causative condition. Moreover, the theory provides a specified explanation of abnormal behavior in a way that has been generally lacking in behavior therapy. The theory of abnormal behavior contains additional principles that cannot be elaborated here; however, other chapters in this volume demonstrate how the framework theory applies to anxiety (Eifert, Chapter 8; Hekmat, Chapter 9), depression (Heiby & Staats, Chapter 10), and rehabilitation (Léduc, Dumais, & Evans, Chapter 12).

Paradigmatic Behaviorism as a Framework Theory

The framework theories that exist in behavior therapy, or psychology generally, have not been systematically examined. Because these theories exert such a profound influence, this neglect is a deficit in our field that must be attended to systematically—as has already been mentioned in introducing the concept of the framework theory. With the summary of paradigmatic behaviorism in hand, however, the points involved can be elaborated to provide a basis for its use. We can also consider better what the functions are of a framework theory and why such theory is important. One thing to emphasize is that, in my opinion, all of the levels of paradigmatic behaviorism are relevant for the applied efforts of behavior therapists.

The Connective-Meaning Function

As I have said, psychology is an unguided confusion of a great multitude of works, cast in many different languages. The result is a potential knowledge pool of such vastness and diversity that it is virtually impossible for anyone to get a meaningful grasp even on particular specialty areas. I suggest that the modern disunified science of psychology produces a morass of inconsistent knowledge elements far beyond that known in the early disunified sciences. Consequently, psychology faces problems unknown in the natural sciences and requires its own philosophy of science (see Staats, 1983b). What is anomalous is that the various subfields of psychology cover areas important in understanding human behavior and the individual research and theoretical works are in good part well done and significant. Nonetheless, psychology has not generally discovered how to make meaningful sense out of the knowledge elements within and across its different areas. The typical clinician, for example, would grant that understanding child development, personality, social interactions (social psychology), educational problems, perception, communication, motivation, learning, and so on, would be very valuable in practice. But attempting to read and incorporate the works in the various specialty fields soon convinces one that this is an impossible task. What immediately becomes evident is that there are so many different, frequently antagonistic viewpoints, each couched in its own special language, that only confusion results.

Psychologists, including behavior therapists, need a guiding, framework theory at this stage of the science's development, to indicate to them what the important works are, and to interpret the variegated works into a unified theory framework. Such a theory can give them a basis for understanding in a meaningful way how the particular specialty area of study is related to the other specialty areas. The framework theory must be constructed to serve as the implement by which behavior therapists can draw knowledge from the various specialties, such as developmental psychology, personality, and social psychology. Without a good theory implement important, useful knowledge goes unknown and unused. This theory gap is one of the main reasons for the basic-applied schism. If behavior therapists employed a framework theory that helped them to translate each of these specialty areas of knowledge into the terminology of behavior therapy, their knowledge base would be greatly expanded. The greater the foundation the framework theory provides for the behavior therapist, the more useful it will be to her or him in the task of abstracting relevant information from the mass of materials each specialty area contains. In this sense the framework theory is essential to both clinicians and to academic-research psychologists. We must thus examine our framework theories—for example, operant behaviorism, paradigmatic behaviorism, social learning theory, cognitive behavior modification, and so on—for the extent to which they provide foundations for utilizing the knowledge of the different areas of psychology.

The Heuristic Function of Theory

The heuristic function of theory is a traditional consideration. Within logical positivism, theories were valued as axiomatic structures that permitted the derivation of empirical hypotheses according to the strict rules of mathematics or formal logic. These hypotheses then provided the basis for the conduct of experiments to test the theory. It should be realized that there are different considerations for theory in the disunified science, such as psychology, than for the advanced natural science theories. For one thing, we need models of theory other than those of axiomatic theory structures; we must understand the type of theory psychology needs to develop (Staats, 1983b) and the various functions psychological theory fulfils. One function has already been described—that is, the manner in which the framework makes materials mutually meaningful, increasing understanding of what otherwise is a confused complexity of knowledge elements. In addition, the heuristic value of theory involves the generation of hypotheses and experiemental and applied research. The framework theory should also lay out a general map for development of additional theory as well as suggest new areas of general empirical research and applications.

Let us take as an example a very general characteristic, the philosophy of science and methodology of theory construction within a framework theory. Skinner (1950) and his co-theorists (cf., Bayes, 1980; Sidman, 1960) have stated that psychology should be primarily empirically oriented, with theory deemphasized. This position gives no impetus to the continued study of the philosophy of the science of psychology, but gives impetus, rather, to the multiplication of technology and empirical findings. Although radical behaviorism has dominated general behaviorism for some two decades, it has not spawned any major philosophical works or advanced the philosophy of psychology past Skinner's original position—even in the face of strong criticism. In contrast, paradigmatic behaviorism places much importance on the analysis of the general character of the behavioral enterprise and has advanced in beginning form a new philosophy of the science of psychology. We cannot know what the needed development is for psychology until we have systematically considered what disunified science is like. We do not know what kinds of theory construction are relevant for our science until we systematically consider them. In addition to technological developments and empirical works, behavior therapists (and psychologists in general) should therefore be concerned with analyzing their science.

Unified positivism's analysis of the philosophy, history, and sociology of science (Staats, 1983b) calls for the multiplication of theoretical analyses that will perform the many unifications—large and small—that are needed. For example, unified theory is called for to integrate theory elements that superficially appear to be different but that are really the same. Unified theory is also called for to resolve schisms and important opposing knowledge fields such as the nature-nurture, personality-situation, and cognitive-behavior antagonisms. Unified theory is called for also to construct bridging theory between various separated areas of study in psychology. The methods for achieving these types of unification are described, at least in beginning form, but should be studied more systematically. Constructing unified theories of all degrees of size and importance should become a foremost task of behavior therapy and psychology generally.

In addition to the general philosophy and methodology, and the general guides that have been indicated thus far, framework theories differ in content, and these differences also serve as specific research guides. Radical behaviorism's rejection of the concept of personality and cognitive causation has led to the absence of conceptual development in these areas. Thus, radical behaviorism could not serve as a guide for integrating the work of traditional psychology, or for projecting behavioral work in these areas. For example, aspects of behavioral assessment were strongly influenced by radical behaviorism. As a consequence of using the framework theory of operant behaviorism, behavioral assessment has not systematically utilized valuable nonbehavioral knowledge of personality and personality tests (Burns, Chapter 5, this vol.; Staats, 1986).

In contrast, paradigmatic behaviorism, by constructing an empirically based behavioristic personality theory, introduces a great change in behaviorism that has not yet been recognized. Establishing a basis for linking closely and productively the knowledge of personality and personality measurement with behaviorism and behavioral assessment and research methodology provides new avenues for new areas of research and application. (Staats, 1988a). Behavior therapy must begin to study in detail the basic behavioral repertoires which constitute the differences in the emotional-motivational, language-cognitive, and sensory-motor aspects of personality. Theory development is necessary, as is an empirical specification of the personality concepts, and the development of instruments by which to measure those aspects of personality. Studies are necessary to specify how personality repertoires are learned and how they can be changed, and studies are necessary to specify how the personality repertoires determine specific behaviors across different situations, behaviors that may constitute clinical problems.

As another illustration, there is an important contemporary interest in integrating the many psychotherapies (e.g., Wachtel, 1977, 1987). Paradigmatic behavior therapy has contributed to this tradition with its behavioral analyses of *rapport, catharsis,* and *insight* (Staats, 1975, Chapter 9) and its treatment of *social behavioral humanism* (Staats, 1975, Chapter 13), as examples of unified theory with heuristic implications.

We can see in these areas a vast difference between operant behaviorism and paradigmatic behaviorism. Social learning theory falls somewhere in between. From 1963 on it became more and more like radical behaviorism with respect to personality, but in the middle 1970s began to include a concept of personality in its theory (Bandura, 1977a, 1977b, 1978b). Yet it has not defined what this concept is, with the exception of the part concerning self-efficacy (Bandura, 1977a), and it does not connect well the concept of personality to basic principles of behavior. As such, social learning theory does not provide the same heuristic guides as paradigmatic behaviorism.

There are many other differences among the framework theories that are important for the field of behavior therapy. It is essential that behavior therapists begin to systematically evaluate and compare their framework theories. It should be noted that paradigmatic behaviorism is a "theory of theories," that is, it has a framework theory or theories at each of its levels of interest, as shown in Table 2.1. For example, the personality level of theory takes the basic learning theory and the human learning level of the study of language acquisition and functions of language, and combines it with

traditional areas of research and knowledge such as intelligence and
the measurement of other aspects of personality. The abnormal psychology level of theory then enables this knowledge to be employed
in formulating a theory of mental retardation and learning disabilities (see Staats & Burns, 1981). At the clinical psychology level the
prior developments and others suggest many new lines of development. For example, the theory of language has provided a basis for
the analysis of verbal psychotherapy (Staats, 1972) in a manner
that gave boost to the cognitive-behavioral development and new
radical behaviorism and cognitive approaches (see Eifert, 1987;
Hamilton, 1988). As another example, at the educational psychology
level paradigmatic behaviorist theories of reading, writing, and
number concepts have provided the bases for research and many
applications; in fact, originally opening this and other fields to the
manipulation of token reinforcement (token economy) systems. At
the measurement level its analyses provide new foundations for
unifying behavioral assessment and traditional psychological measurement findings (see Burns, Chapter 5, this vol.; Staats, 1986).

There are many fields of psychology whose works are or could be
relevant to behavior therapy. It would be wonderful—a goal for
which to strive—if these fields had an orientation coincident with
behavior therapy's, such that the products of the fields would translate readily into behavior therapy. But this is not the case. In each
area, the scientists are occupied with their own agenda. They have
their own theory languages. They do not work to make their products useful to behavior therapy. If there are useful products in those
fields—and paradigmatic behaviorism argues that there are—these
products must be extracted and developed by behavior therapists to
serve their research or professional purposes. To do this, behavior
therapists need a framework theory that has the necessary heuristic
characteristics for the task, and the general framework theories in
psychology should be examined for the extent to which they have
such characteristics.

Before this topic is concluded, one other point must be emphasized: all of the various behavioristic (or learning) theories have
very large areas of similarity. There is heavy overlap, for instance,
in the principles employed in the second-generation theories of
Thorndike, Watson, Skinner, and Hull (Staats, 1983b, pp. 186–198).
It was the nature of disunified science, however, that these theories
were set forth as very different, to the point of mutual antagonism.
Each theorist considered his theory to be correct, and the others to
be all wrong, although each theory was constructed to account for
the same facts of learning. The fact is, most of the studies of condi-

tioning principles, including all the behavior therapy studies that have been conducted, *will fit any of the theories*, even though the studies have been generated from various theoretical perspectives.

For example, all of the studies in which reinforcement has been manipulated in a behavior modification procedure will support Thorndike's theory, Hull's theory, Miller and Dollard's theory, Skinner's theory, as well as paradigmatic behaviorism's theory which, actually, was among the first (Staats, 1957) to propose the extension of reinforcement principles to an actual case of a person with abnormal behavior. Frequently, those who adhere to one or another theory, have the feeling that behavioral research involving basic principles validates their particular theory, and not any other. But if the research involves the basic principles of classical or operant conditioning, its findings derive from and support all of the theories. What should be realized is that the distinctive contributions of the various framework theories of behaviorism come from the points where the theories *differ* and where they provide *different* heuristic guides for development. How heuristic the above mentioned theories have been for the development of behavior therapy and assessment will be judged only by historical analysis aimed at isolating the sources of the various principles, methods, and findings. How heuristic the theories can be for the future will require an analysis and comparison of the differences between the theories.

The World View Function

As already mentioned, various writers have suggested that behavior therapy should be a technology. However, problems for which there is a technology already developed, or one that can be developed, constitute a small portion of professional encounters. Frequently the problems met in general practice will require analysis and understanding in terms of some theoretical context of principles and the delineation of a treatment procedure. The more correct and profound the analysis and understanding, the better the therapist can deal with the problem. Complexities in human behavior problems are the rule rather than the exception, and solutions do not come about from knowing an ABAB behavior modification design, systematic desensitization, the token-reinforcer system procedure, or some such technology, as valuable as these have been to our work.

The practicing behavior therapist needs a conception of human behavior into which can be fitted the complex problems of human behavior that are encountered clinically. In addition to having knowledge of behavior principles and technologies, the behavior therapist should be someone who knows a great deal about human behavior, systematized, it is to be hoped, by the knowledge of the fields of psychology and the other behavioral sciences. Imperfect as they are, those fields constitute the systematic knowledge that is available. The principles of the animal learning laboratory do not tell us anything about economic systems, for example, and the manner in which industry in the Western countries is subject to fluctuations of activity that result in unemployment. Yet that knowledge may be important in the case of a patient whose depression involves loss of work as a precipitating cause. Important also may be the knowledge of how the unemployed individual's language-cognitive characteristics include strong negative evaluation of unemployment as a personal weakness, and how the patient's family, friends, and society support those ideas. Treatment of such a patient may involve verbal interactions aimed at changing the patient's own world view that gives foundation to his or her self-deprecating and depression-inducing ideas. In such a case the behavior therapist needs a theoretical framework that enables him or her to understand the various events that are relevant. Knowledge of these events occurs in various fields of study ranging from basic learning principles through the understanding of political and economic events. What the therapist needs in such a case is a large framework theory that serves as a world view. The more the various fields of knowledge within that world view can be fitted into a unified set of principles, the more useful that world view will be. Characteristics of the framework theory that should be evaluated concern its broadness, clarity, precision, profundity, and degree of unification involved. These will affect the utility of the world view the framework theory yields. These considerations have not been systematically considered by the field of behavior therapy. The behavior therapist should compare the framework theories of operant behaviorism (Skinner, 1969), paradigmatic behaviorism (Staats, 1975), and social learning theory (Bandura, 1977b) in this respect, too.

The Curriculum Planning Function

Recent years have seen the development of the doctor of psychology degree and the full development of the school of psychology, as a private institution and also as a separate school within the university. These developments are based upon the medical profession analogue. There is something that differentiates psychology from the medical profession, however, that should be considered. The medical profession is based in unified science fields. As a result, there is a large body of knowledge that is generally accepted in those sciences, and is considered to be a standard part of the medical student's training. The curriculum in any medical school is thus largely the same. This is not true, however, in clinical psychology where every clinical program is run in its own idiosyncratic way. Clinical psychologists trained in one university may thus differ greatly from those trained in another school.

The variation with respect to the training of behavior therapists is probably less than for clinical psychology as a whole, but nevertheless considerable in scope. Programs with an operant orientation present different training than programs with a social learning theory orientation or a general eclectic behavioral orientation. The definition of behavior therapy as a technology or a methodology provides a different guide for what would be learned than does, for example, the paradigmatic behaviorism framework. In other words, the framework theory also has implications for the training of behavior therapists. In programs in which the training of behavioral psychologists concentrates on operant conditioning, a great deal of emphasis is placed upon experience in the animal laboratory and in single-organism research methodology. Such study is thought to provide the basic principles that are sufficient, but in the paradigmatic behaviorism view this knowledge is inadequate and incomplete for understanding and treating human beings.

Paradigmatic behaviorism, in setting a different framework theory than operant behaviorism, also sets different goals for training behavior therapists. It says that knowledge in the various levels of theory that have been described provide important background for the behavior therapist. Since radical behaviorism and traditional psychology separate themselves so cleanly, training in one or the other is incomplete. Training for behavioral clinicians will only become standardized and inclusive when it becomes based upon a unified theory such as paradigmatic behaviorism that establishes a framework for unifying various works, concepts, and methods relevant to clinical psychology. It is time that behavior therapy (and psychology generally) come to understand the importance of the goal of unification within the common language of a framework theory so that an integrated view can result. Using paradigmatic behaviorism calls for progressive elaboration by faculty and students, since it is a framework theory as are the others. In any event the several exisitng framework theories should be compared in terms of how each provides a guide for curriculum design for behavior therapists.

This is an area that demands much development, with the goal of attaining unification and standardization. The framework theory of paradigmatic behaviorism is seen as an instrument with which to begin this effort. When such unification and standardization have occurred, behavior therapy will begin to exhibit the strength of professions based upon unified science foundations.

Conclusion

Psychology has had a philosophy-methodology for generating empirical knowledge and "local" theories, in abundance. Psychology, however, has not had a philosophy-methodology for constructing theoretical structures with which to bring the local elements into productive interrelation. There have been attempts to construct broad theories on the basis of the philosophy-methodology that is involved in the construction of the local theories. These attempts utilize the part-to-whole method already described. Such theories have occurred in behavioral as well as nonbehavioral psychology, in neither case in a way that has constituted much of a unification of the abundant, but antagonistic, knowledge elements of our field.

As I have tried to demonstrate in this chapter, paradigmatic behaviorism constitutes a comprehensive, unified theory as well as a philosophy-methodology for constructing such theories. During its more than three decades of development, paradigmatic behaviorism has, in addition to its specific areas of development, focused on the problems of such theory construction. My position has been that the positivistic methodology of behaviorism contained essential ingredients, that the principles of conditioning must be basic in any theory explaining human behavior, but that behaviorism did not understand the nature of constructing comprehensive, unified theory in psychology. In my opinion there is much knowledge in nonbehavioral psychology that is important and that must be included in an integral sense in the broad, framework theory. But utilizing that knowledge must occur in a certain way if the advantages of a behaviorism are to be retained. The methodology by which to accomplish this unification is that of the multilevel theory. The multilevel-theory-construction method says that there are bodies of important knowledge, at present considered to be antagonistic, that need bridging theory to remove inconsistencies and oppositions. Multilevel theory construction requires culling the irrelevant, but, more centrally, innovating the analyses that bring seemingly antagonistic elements within a common set of principles. When we begin constructing comprehensive theory across large areas we see that there is a level-by-level hierarchy involved. The illustration I gave in this chapter proposes that learning is basic to personality, personality is basic to abnormal behavior, and these are basic to the study of clinical treatment. While it might not be possible to consider an extensive range of the problems of clinical treatment solely within basic conditioning principles—one reason why traditional clinical psychology rejected behaviorism—a markedly better job may be done by a theory that includes the various intervening levels of theory. The antagonisms and seeming discrepancies between different parts of psychology occur, in my view, because the necessary bridging theory structures have not been presented. A multilevel theory structure like paradigmatic behaviorism is able to dissolve important, divisive discrepancies.

It should be emphasized that the method involved in multilevel theory construction is not eclecticism, that is, the combination of unrelated elements without unifying those elements. In paradigmatic behaviorism the rule is to keep everything tightly woven: the more advanced principles are linked in a derivational way with the more basic, even when there are intervening theory levels. The multilevel theory method involves a serious hierarchical theory-construction task. It is suggested that theorists, interested in developing behavior therapy (and psychology generally), as a unified scientific-professional area, should study these methods.

Most psychologists today are specialists, and as a consequence focus their interests somewhat narrowly. For example, the basic learning theorist may not be vitally interested in the advanced, human levels of theory, research, and application, while at the other end, the behavior therapist may no longer have a focal interest in the field of basic learning, except as it offers some principles of use in dealing with human behavior. This is a mistake for the basic learning researcher, for example, since that field is of interest in good part because its principles may be general to most organisms, including humans. This being the case, some of the resources of that basic field should be spent in constructing its knowledge for generalization to the study of human behavior (this is the theme elaborated upon by Minke in the next chapter). Showing generalization is central in advanced sciences. Moreover, the human perspective, it would be expected, would be heuristic in projecting lines of research and theory development that should be given concentrated attention. The reverse is also true, the behavior therapist would be better able to make his or her analyses of human behavior by utilizing the various relevant basic learning principles rather than a small sample of such principles. The present orientation does not deny that there are individuals with narrow interests in a special field who can be very productive. But specialization is not the only avenue for advancing our field.

Thus, while paradigmatic behavior therapy is a broad theory of various levels—that is, a theory of subtheories—and it has goals to be attained as such, it should be noted that each of its subtheories is intended to be heuristic in its particular area. The general framework theory of paradigmatic behaviorism, thus, can be used in various proportions. We will see this reflected in the present book. And, importantly, one of the resulting contributions of this book will be to demonstrate these different ways of employing the framework theory, ranging from specific uses to use of the whole framework.

Behavior therapy, at the time of its formation, drew much of its power from a part of the basic field of psychology: learning or behavior theory. This relationship must be revivified and strengthened. Moreover, the more that behavior therapy can utilize the various fields of psychology, in a unified manner, the more power it will acquire. A portion of the resources of the field should be devoted to exhausting the knowledge that it can draw from other levels (fields) of psychology. That is why behavior therapy must be interested in developing the best framework theory possible. For it is the framework theory that provides the mechanisms, the syphons, by which the wells of knowledge in psychology can be tapped. In my view, the most central implication of this book is the demonstration that a wide range of problems can be creatively treated within paradigmatic behaviorism's unified framework theory. As such, it is an adumbration of what behavior therapy (and psychology itself) could become as a unified science. Within that development lies enormous power that is as yet unrealized.

II

Foundations for Applied Paradigmatic Behaviorism— Research, Language, and Development

3
Research Foundations of a Developing Paradigm: Implications for Behavioral Engineering

Karl A. Minke

A defining characteristic of behavior therapy has always been its close links to the experimental science of psychology. However, the ideal or most productive form of this relationship has been hotly debated. In recent years there seems to have been less of an interactive relationship between applied behavior therapy and basic research, with behavior therapy becoming something more of a technology, empirically oriented, but drawing on its own autonomous research traditions. As Staats has argued in the preceding chapter, there are serious problems in attempting to derive a technology from a nonunified, preparadigmatic science. Thus, an ongoing endeavor in behavior therapy must be to define its relationship with the more basic fields of psychology. In this chapter I would like to consider the contributions a paradigmatic approach can make to the applied practitioner, or behavioral engineer, and to indicate how one of these contributions, the provision of a research base, can not only provide data, facts, and procedures for the applied psychologist, but can also add to the establishment and extension of the basic paradigm.

Contributions of a Paradigm
to the Behavioral Engineer

I have been defending the use of the term *behavioral engineer* over other labels for the applied behavioral psychologist for several years now—in spite of its mechanistic overtones (e.g., Minke, 1980). It is more general than terms such as *behavioral therapist* or *behavioral clinician* which imply concern with traditional clinical problems. While these more limiting terms are appropriate under certain circumstances, with the repudiation of the medical model and the acceptance of the view that "pathological" and "nonpathological" behaviors are learned and maintained according to the same principles, the distinction between classical clinical problems and other behavior problems becomes blurred and can be viewed in large measure as a historical anomaly. The use of a more general term fosters integration to the extent that it implies that the analyses and the findings of the behavioral therapist, the applied psychologist focusing on clinical behaviors, are relevant to those who are nonclinically oriented and vice versa.

Perhaps more important, the term *engineer*, as it is commonly employed today, refers to an individual who is responsible for using the concepts, procedures, and findings of a paradigmatic science to solve a variety of practical problems. Engineering disciplines that have built up around the physical and the biological sciences are much more closely tied to the basic science from which they derived than is the case in psychology. The engineer is well trained in fundamental science and follows the research and theoretical developments of the parent discipline carefully. Furthermore, the basic science is alert to the problems and observations of the engineer, applying its analytical, theoretical, and research methods to those phenomena considered important. The scientist-practitioner model predominates, and there is frequently no clear demarcation between the basic and the applied ends of the spectrum.

As Staats and others (e.g., Barlow, Hayes, & Nelson, 1984; Minke, 1986) have repeatedly emphasized, this situation is quite different from that existing today in general and clinical psychology, where there is a marked separatism between basic and applied science. An important aspect of the social behaviorism paradigm is its view of the hierarchical structure of a science. Whether one works at the basic end or the applied end of the continuum, one is employing the same fundamental principles, methods, and philosophy of science. Under this conception, modification of theory or principle at the basic level as well as findings at the applied level have effects all along the continuum. The term *behavioral engineer*, therefore, seems particularly appropriate as a label for the applied psychologist within social behaviorism, in that it denotes a number of characteristics identified with applied work in paradigmatic settings.

General paradigmatic development within psychology would have a number of specific advantages for any individual focusing on applications. First of all, it would offer a set of assumptions to guide one's work. Within social behaviorism, for example, when inappropriate behaviors occur or appropriate behaviors do not occur, it is assumed that the most important level of explanation lies in a learning history rather than in genetic factors or biological predisposition. This assumption is based on and in turn strengthens the recognition that the behavioral problem or deficit is modifiable through manipulation of the environment. To make the alternative assumption often implies that behavior problems cannot be altered at all or can be modified only through the manipulation of physiological variables. In social behaviorism, when a given procedure is ineffectual, it does not imply that the problem is uncorrectable—it simply means that one is not employing the proper procedure.

A paradigm also offers a set of theoretical explanations and constructs to account for the general observations concerning the nature of behavior constantly facing those working in applied settings. I suspect that the emergence of cognitive interpretations of behavior as the dominant approach in psychology in recent years is largely a function of the failure of behaviorism to attend to this variable. Classic behaviorism has come to be viewed as appropriate only to a subset of behaviors and limited in its application. This view is due in large part to traditional behavioral approaches ignoring or denying the existence of certain facts obvious to anyone working closely with behavior on a day-to-day basis. One of the crucial aspects of the integrative nature of social behaviorism lies in accepting the basic validity of these general observations and incorporating them into the paradigm by means of theoretical analyses and constructs. A sophisticated behaviorism can account for typically rejected concepts such as stagelike behavioral development or consistency of behavior across situations. A true paradigm within psychology would also allow the behavioral engineer to approach practical phenomena from a consistent framework rather than having to choose between a narrow, rejecting model and the overaccepting eclectic model which is so prevalent today.

Consistency is further fostered by the ability of a paradigm to provide a set of principles that can be applied throughout the behavioral domain. In social behaviorism these principles are the principles of learning. The higher-order (or more elementary) principles are those of classical and instrumental conditioning, while the lower-order ones are based upon combinations of the more elementary principles as well as principles unique to human behavior and not derivable from work conducted in the basic animal laboratory— as explained in the preceding chapter. Within a paradigmatic science research is constantly verifying, elaborating, and testing the limits of these principles, and the engineer associated with the science has these data constantly available for the development of his or her applied procedures.

One of the defining characteristics of a paradigm is the presence of a common view concerning methodology (Minke, 1987). On one level a paradigmatic science develops certain general procedures that can be employed across a wide range of situations, both basic and applied, to further its pursuits. For example, in biology there exist certain general techniques for gene recombination that serve as the basis for pure research in gene identification and function and that also serve as the foundation for the emerging applied field of genetic engineering. On a second level a paradigm provides a common methodological basis for carrying out research.

Social behaviorism continues to develop a methodological base along both these dimensions. For example, token reinforcement has been utilized as a laboratory procedure for the investigation of various basic research problems with children, such as determination of the course of development of basic behavioral repertoires like imitation, and it has served as the basis for a variety of applied programs (e.g., Kazdin, 1982). The applied psychologist also needs a systematic *research* methodology in order to evaluate the effectiveness of procedures and to accurately describe relevant behaviors and their milieu. The approach to research methodology taken by social behaviorism is based upon the assumption that the various methodological approaches that have been used in the past and are currently in use within psychology have important contributions to make to a unified science of behavior. The questions in a science, both basic and applied, must take precedence over the methods used in answering them. Too often it appears that questions are dismissed by the individual psychologist, not because the questions are unimportant, but because his or her particular methodology is not capable of dealing with them. It is important to recognize that different problems require different methods for their solution, and the view that only one specific methodological approach has scientific validity is stifling in terms of broadening our understanding of and control over relevant behaviors in the real world. If a question is meaningful in a scientific sense, it is incumbent upon the science to attempt to answer it, whether with existent methods or with new methods that might be developed within the basic precepts of the paradigm (Minke, 1987).

Implicit in most of what I have outlined to this point is a final contribution of a paradigmatic science to the behavioral engineer— the presence of a research base. It is the research base that provides validity to the other contributions. As the research literature accumulates, one gains confidence in the assumptions upon which the paradigm is based, in the theoretical analyses and constructs the paradigm produces, and in the principles the paradigm utilizes, as well as in the specific procedures and data defining the engineering discipline.

I would like to devote the rest of this chapter to providing examples of types of research important in establishing and extending a social-behavioristic paradigmatic approach to applied problems. Sidman (1960) began his methodological monograph by posing the classic question: "why perform experiments?" What follows is a personal answer to that question, an answer, coming from a paradigmatic perspective, that is quite different from that provided by Sidman, working in the radical behavioral tradition.

Types of Research Important in Developing a Social Behavioral Approach to Applied Problems

The following material essentially represents a personal analysis. Social behaviorism has guided my work and thinking across the years, and I view my area of specialization as the paradigm itself rather than any specific content area. As a function of this, my research and that of my students has covered a wide spectrum from basic to applied, and it is upon this work and the work of Staats and his associates that I will be drawing primarily for illustrations. This is not to imply that the work of others does not help to extend and elaborate the paradigm; one of the major dicta of social behaviorism is that the phenomena and observations of others represent data that must ultimately be incorporated into a complete theory of behavior, regardless of the theoretical orientation of the psychologist reporting them. In fact, it is further recognized that theoretical statements and constructs are often descriptive of realities of nature that must also be incorporated into the theory. However, until recently the work of Staats and those closely associated with him has been somewhat unique in its consideration of the paradigmatic as well as the more traditional implications of the research. This situation is rapidly changing, as attested to by the following chapters in this volume.

Research to Distinguish Among Competing Conceptions of Functional Repertoires

Although social behaviorism attempts to integrate the theoretical statements and constructs of other approaches into the general paradigm, there are times when such interpretations are contradictory to social behavioral assumptions. One way in which the paradigm is advanced is by directly testing these competing conceptions or their consequences against each other. Depending upon the results of such tests, either the paradigm is strengthened or an indication is provided that the paradigm needs to be changed in some fashion to accommodate the conflicting data. This type of research is particularly relevant to the behavioral engineer when the theoretical interpretations concern functional repertoires. Several of my graduate students have selected such a research strategy, choosing repertoires of great interest to behavioral engineering, but that at the time were usually analyzed in nonbehavioral terms.

The Basis of Aggression

In the late sixties one of my students, Lois Horton, became interested in the topic of aggression. Although drive-based theories of aggressive behavior were coming under attack, they were still prevalent in the psychological literature. Much of the negative evidence was coming from social learning theory and was directed at a specific consequence of Freud's catharsis theory, the notion that observing aggression in others should reduce one's own aggressive impulses and thereby decrease the probability of aggression in the immediately following time period, other things being equal. Bandura and his associates (e.g., Bandura & Walters, 1963) were demonstrating that observation of aggression in others led to an *increase* in later aggression rather than a decrease as predicted by catharsis theory.

However, there was a second implication of catharsis theory, shared by early learning interpretations such as the frustration-aggression hypothesis (Dollard, Doob, Miller, Mowrer, & Sears, 1939), that had received little experimental attention. This was the prediction that directly engaging in aggressive behavior should also result in less later aggression. Horton argued that from a social behavioral perspective aggressive behaviors could be regarded as instrumental responses operating according to the same principles affecting all other instrumental behavior. This interpretation would predict that to the extent the situation in the immediately following time period was similar to that present when the original aggression occurred (and was presumably reinforced), there should be an increase in aggression during the second period, due to the operation of generalization.

To test these competing predictions, Horton (1970) set up an experiment employing a group of intermediate-grade-level boys having a history of aggressive behavior. During each experimental session the boys played two different games in sequence, the first being a version of the card game "War" and the second being a version of the game "Steal the Bacon." Using a reversal design, aggressive responses (delivering hand slaps) or nonaggressive responses (taking poker chips from an opponent) were directly reinforced with a token reinforcement system within the context of the card game. The effects of these manipulations were assessed in the second game situation, where no reinforcement was given. It was found that direct reinforcement of aggression in the first time period resulted in an increase in later aggression, as measured by frequency of physical contact in the second game. Reinforcement of nonaggression in Game 1 led to a decrease in later aggression. Interestingly, whenever aggression was reinforced in Game 1 both the frequency and the intensity of the responses increased in Game 2. In fact, by the second reversal the physical contact responses in the second game had become so intense it was decided to terminate the experiment early rather than risk physical harm to the participants. No such increase in magnitude was discernible in Game 1 where the aggression was being directly reinforced. These results were contrary to those that would be expected on the basis of drive theories of aggression and were consistent with the generalization of reinforced responses interpretation suggested earlier.

Dyslexia as a Learning Phenomenon

A similar research strategy was adopted by another of my students, Martha Collette. Her master's thesis was conceived as a test of the generally accepted notion that dyslexia, a failure to learn to read despite persistent instruction and adequate intelligence, is due to neurological dysfunction stemming from genetic or maturational variables or from minimal brain damage. Such an etiology is inferred from the defining characteristics of the disorder: underachievement in reading, limited attention span, and poor visual and auditory perceptual ability. The implication of this assumption is that the disability is permanent; although some compensation is possible through specialized training, such individuals will remain dyslexic throughout their lives (e.g., Critchley, 1970).

Staats has emphasized the cumulative-hierarchical nature of much complex learning, including reading acquisition, pointing out that frequently the training procedures employed are dependent upon the prior establishment of general repertoires of learned behaviors. Unless these "basic behavioral repertoires" are well formed prior to the training situation, the complex learning cannot take place, at least with the procedures normally employed. Applying these conceptions to dyslexia, Collette argued that an inadequate learning history could explain not only the reading deficits found in dyslexic children, but the attentional and perceptual deficits as well. That is, attentional and perceptual behaviors can be viewed as basic behavioral repertoires that are normally acquired prior to formal schooling and that must be adequately formed before the child will profit from standard reading training. If learning deficiencies are present with respect to these repertoires, then one would expect to observe the syndrome defining dyslexia.

To distinguish between these two conceptions an experiment was conducted (Collette-Harris & Minke, 1978) in which six dyslexic and six nondyslexic children, matched with respect to age, IQ, and degree of reading remediation, were exposed either to standard, eclectic reading training in a private reading clinic or to Staats's token reinforcement remedial reading procedure. Staats's procedure relies minimally upon prior acquisition of the basic behavioral repertoires described above; instead it attempts to provide training in these repertoires simultaneously with training in reading. It was argued that if dyslexia was due to unalterable neurological factors then no procedure should be able to produce equal improvement in reading ability in dyslexic and comparable nondyslexic children no matter how effective these procedures were, since they could not alter the neurological impairment. At most, they would provide the dyslexic child with a certain degree of compensatory skill.

After 40 hours of training it was found that children given Staats's procedure had improved an average of 16.45 months in reading as measured by a standardized reading achievement test, compared to an average improvement of only 1.28 months for the children exposed to the traditional procedures. More important to the present discussion, however, was the finding that the dyslexic children exposed to the Staats procedure showed slightly more improvement than the nondyslexic children, although the difference was nonsignificant. Even more revealing was the finding that the Staats procedure produced such great improvement in the perceptual and attentional measures used to diagnose the dyslexic children in the first place that these children would no longer be diagnosed as dyslexic or even learning disabled on standard examination.

For her doctoral dissertation Collette (1979) focused on another aspect of the dyslexia problem, the so-called pathognomic signs of dyslexia. There seems to be general agreement that dyslexic children tend to make certain types of errors in reading, spelling, and handwriting. Such errors include reversals, rotations, insertions, substitutions, omissions, and so on. It is generally assumed that these errors, while not unique to dyslexic children, occur more frequently and for longer periods in dyslexic than in nondyslexic children and reflect underlying neurological deficits. However, upon surveying the literature, Collette found that no norms existed reporting the incidence of these pathognomic signs.

To generate such norms she devised 49 dependent measures to assess the frequency of the various pathognomic signs discussed in the literature. Data were collected from 26 dyslexic children with ages ranging from 12 to 14 years, 19 nondyslexic remedial readers, matched with the dyslexic children for age, IQ, and degree of reading retardation, and 96 children reading within 6 months of grade level. On 44 of the 49 measures the children reading at grade level made significantly fewer errors than the dyslexic and nondyslexic remedial readers taken together. When the dyslexic and nondyslexic remedial readers were compared to each other, however, neither analyses of variance, discriminant analyses, nor a factor analysis yielded any meaningful differences between these two groups, although all types of analysis indicated differences between nonremedial and remedial readers. Her data suggested that the "pathognomic signs of dyslexia" were characteristic of remedial readers in general rather than simply children diagnosed as dyslexic.

Research to Indirectly Observe Implicit Events

Social behaviorism differs from other contemporary approaches to applied problems in how it treats inferred constructs. It recognizes that not all important explanations in a science are based directly upon causal relationships among immediately observable events. Although there are those in psychology who argue that the only meaningful explanations are of this nature (e.g., Skinner, 1966), most other sciences do not restrict themselves in this fashion. For example, the gene was used in an explanatory fashion in biology, the molecule in chemistry, and the atom in physics long before technology was advanced enough to make such entities directly observable.

Psychology also has a history of employing inferred events as explanations for behavioral phenomena. Psychologists employing this technique frequently feel they are conceptualizing actual events and entities and usually have a degree of faith concerning their actual existence. Unlike the situation in the physical and biological sciences, however, this faith may well be unjustified. Before such inferred constructs were used in an explanatory fashion within the other sciences, their validity was established by means of a complex logical and experimental technique that may be called *indirect observation* (see Staats, 1975). The logic of indirect observation protects the science against errors of inference by arguing that before an inferred implicit event can be used in an explanatory fashion, the existence of two sets of independent causal relationships must be demonstrated, one relating the implicit event to observable antecedent events and a second relating observable consequent events to the implicit event. In other words, it must be demonstrated that the inferred implicit event has both dependent and independent variable properties within the context of the observable variables in the situation. This is done experimentally, usually across a series of studies in which each of the hypothesized sets of causal relationships are held constant in turn and manipulations are performed to demonstrate the operation of the other. Only after the two sets of causal relationships have been demonstrated to operate independently can the inferred event be given explanatory properties. Continued experimentation of the sort described can then be conducted in order to specify the particular characteristics of the implicit event.

The scientist utilizing indirectly observed constructs believes in the actual existence of the inferred entities, and each experiment that verifies a prediction made on the basis of such constructs increases this belief. The scientist in such a case assumes that the indirectly observed constructs are potentially directly observable. The history of science suggests that when indirect observation has been carried out carefully this is a good assumption. Numerous instances can be found where indirectly observed constructs later became directly observable as a function of improved techniques and instrumentation.

An important and continuing research task within social behaviorism involves carrying out indirect observation of theoretically derived constructs and events. For example, basic to many analyses within the paradigm has been the concept of emotion, which is conceptualized in terms of classically conditioned implicit responses. Emotional responding is seen as the basis for the principle of reinforcement itself, as exemplified by Staats's affective-reinforcing-directive (A-R-D) formulation, as well as the primary event involved in such topic areas as attitudes and connotative word meaning. The literature bearing upon the indirect observation of these implicit emotional responses is too vast to review in detail here, but some indication of the breadth of this endeavor can be outlined.

Studies that have treated the emotional response as a *dependent* variable have frequently involved establishing it as a conditioned response to some stimulus using classical conditioning procedures. The prototype experiment in this regard was performed by C.K. Staats and Staats (1957), who paired nonsense syllables a number of times with positive and negative words. It was found that after such pairings the nonsense syllables were rated on Semantic Differential scales in a fashion similar to that of the meaningful words with which they had been paired.

Support for the contention that this represents a classical conditioning phenomenon has come from studies that have manipulated variables known to affect classical conditioning in systematic ways. Such variables included number of conditioning trials (Staats & Staats, 1959), extinction (Carlson, 1971), partial reinforcement and deprivation-satiation conditions (Staats, Minke, Martin, & Higa, 1972), and their predictable effects illustrate the existence of one of the two sets of causal relationships necessary for the indirect observation of the inferred emotional response.

Several studies have looked at the set of causal relationships present when the inferred emotional response is treated as an *independent* variable. For example, in an early study (Staats, Staats, & Crawford, 1962) first-order conditioning procedures were used to establish a conditioned negative emotional response to a previously neutral meaningful word by pairing the word repeatedly with either a loud noise or electric shock. After these pairings it was found that the meaningful word was rated negatively on a Semantic Differential scale. More important for the point being developed here, the

intensity of the rating was correlated with the intensity of a galvanic skin response (GSR) that was being measured concurrently. In
another experiment Solarz (1960) had subjects either pull a lever
toward themselves or push the lever away from themselves in response to both positive and negative meaningful words. He found
that the latencies were shorter for the pulling response when the
stimulus words were positive than when they were negative and
that the pushing response latencies were shorter for negative words
than for positive ones. Using a similar procedure and employing
food words with deprived and satiated subjects, Staats and Warren
(1974) demonstrated that deprived subjects learned to pull the lever
toward themselves in the presence of food words significantly faster
than they learned to push the lever away in the presence of the
same type of word.

Studies such as these go far in establishing the validity of the
emotional response (it should be noted that Martin & Levey, 1978,
1985, also have successfully employed indirect observation procedures in studying the classical conditioning of affective responses).
However, the studies described have been subjected to alternative
interpretation in terms of demand awareness. It is argued that subjects become aware of the experimenter's hypothesis, and this
awareness is what mediates the measured performance. Although it
is standard procedure in these studies to attempt to identify aware
subjects and delete them from the analysis, it has been suggested
that the methods used to assess awareness are not sensitive enough
to detect any but a few of these individuals. When more elaborate
postexperimental awareness questionnaires are employed, many
more subjects are classified as aware, and, more important, those
remaining do not show the predicted conditioning effect (Page,
1969). Staats (1969) has argued that such elaborate questionnaires
in fact induce awareness in all but those subjects who are inattentive to the experimental situation and who therefore are not
expected to condition under any circumstances. Following 10 years
of inconclusive research on this issue, Warren (1978) may have
resolved the controversy when he found that unaware subjects did
indeed show the conditioning effect when an awareness questionnaire that was empirically demonstrated to be free of both types
of bias was employed. Related to this conclusion is the finding of
Martin and Levey (1978) that evaluative conditioning occurred
both when subjects were unaware of the direction of changes in
evaluation and when they attributed these changes to irrelevant
causes.

Research to Demonstrate the Validity of Principles

Staats has characterized social behaviorism as a third-generation behavior theory. This characterization refers to the fact that the approach builds upon the principles, concepts, and analyses that have preceded it as well as introduces novel developments of its own. This does not indicate that older conceptions are accepted without modification. Rather, earlier work is incorporated in a selective, integrated fashion; those concepts and principles that have not proved productive are discarded while those that have continued relevance are maintained. All too frequently in psychology, however, when a general approach has proven faulty, all concepts associated with that approach tend to be ignored as well, even if some of these have continued validity when viewed in a new context. It is important that such principles receive continued validation so that they may be maintained and integrated within the current framework.

An example of a principle that has received little attention in the literature in recent years and yet has continued relevance for understanding a variety of phenomena in human learning is the acquired-distinctiveness-of-cues (ADC) hypothesis of Miller and Dollard (1941). This hypothesis contends that attaching distinctive cue-producing responses (e.g., words) to similar stimuli provides them with learned distinctiveness, decreasing the extent to which instrumental responses will generalize from one stimulus to another.

Several years ago, Paul Ban, another student of mine, became interested in investigating the continued viability of the ADC hypothesis in the context of a phenomenon in the area of stimulus generalization, the central tendency effect. It seems that if an instrumental response is established to a stimulus (S+) and then generalization testing takes place employing an asymmetric test series (a test series in which all test stimuli fall on one side of the stimulus continuum from the S+), maximum responding does not occur to the original training stimulus. Instead, peak responding tends to occur to a test stimulus halfway down the test series (Thomas, 1974). Using a line-angle dimension, Thomas and Thomas (1974) found that this central tendency effect could be inhibited with human subjects if prior to the generalization testing they were required to label the S+ line angle as if it were the time on a clock face. They interpreted these findings within the framework of adaptation-level theory, concluding that the clock-time label categorized the domain within which the adaptation level effects could be manifested and arguing that the inhibition was to be expected whenever the concept identified by the label was isomorphic with the stimulus dimension employed in the generalization test (e.g., every line-angle test stimulus could be labeled with a distinctive time on a clock face).

Ban argued that the inhibition of the central tendency effect could also be understood in terms of the ADC hypothesis; attaching the label to the S+ merely made it more distinctive. If this interpretation is correct then any label, whether it defined a conceptual category that could be related to the test stimuli or not, should produce the inhibition. Ban tested this prediction by replicating the Thomas and Thomas experiment employing two words selected at random as labels, one word selected from a list of high-imagery words and one selected from a list of low-imagery words. He hypothesized that high-imagery words may be more distinctive than low-imagery ones and therefore might produce greater inhibition. As predicted, the labeling conditions did produce inhibition of the central tendency effect. However, Ban's study and a later replication (Ban & Minke, 1984) failed to support an imagery effect; all words, regardless of their imagery value, resulted in complete inhibition. Taken together, these two studies lend support to the ADC interpretation of the inhibition phenomenon and suggest that the ADC hypothesis has continued validity as a general principle of behavior and as the basis for applied procedures for increasing the discriminability of physically similar stimuli through verbal means.

Of course, as paradigmatic development continues, it is almost inevitable that new principles will emerge as well. Staats's affective-reinforcing-directive (A-R-D) formulation can be viewed in this light. The validity of this notion is being repeatedly demonstrated in experiments specifically designed for this purpose as well as through reinterpretation of experiments performed under different theoretical orientations. For example, the research on emotional responses discussed in the section on indirect observation can be understood in this context, the studies utilizing classical conditioning procedures to establish the emotional response demonstrating the A function and the studies employing the lever pushing and pulling task the D function.

Several studies have focused on the R properties of such stimuli as well. For example, Finley and Staats (1967) demonstrated that positive words, as measured on Semantic Differential scales, would strengthen a motor response in 12-year-old children when applied contingent upon that response, while negative words would suppress the response. In another experiment (Harms & Staats, 1978) deprivation conditions were manipulated in a task where subjects had the option of making a left-hand response or a right-hand response. Food words were delivered contingent upon making the left-hand response. It was found that more left-hand responses were made by the food-deprived subjects than by the satiated subjects.

In addition to the experiments already described several other experiments, although not discussed in these terms, seem to demonstrate rather directly the D function of A-R-D stimuli. For example, Nunnally, Duchrowski, and Parker (1965) found that the length of time a child would attend to a nonsense syllable depended upon whether that syllable had previously been paired with positive, neutral, or negative events. In a similar fashion, Silverstein (1973), employing adult subjects, found that individuals would spend more time looking at pictures rated positively than pictures given a neutral rating and would be more likely to select the positive picture as a keepsake. The transfer of control phenomenon (e.g., Trapold & Winokur, 1967), where repeated prepairing of a stimulus with reinforcement increases the rate at which that stimulus can later be established as a discriminative stimulus for an instrumental response, is understandable in these terms as well.

Although more research of the sort described is necessary to raise the A-R-D formulation from a theory to a firmly demonstrated principle, it has proved extremely useful to social behaviorists interested in developing experimental-theoretical analyses of functional repertoires and procedures for modifying these repertoires. This can be seen by its repeated recurrence throughout the remainder of this volume. This research base is rapidly developing, as will be attested to in other chapters, and it is to be expected that soon the term *A-R-D theory* will be supplanted by the term *A-R-D principle* in the social behavioral literature.

Research to Establish the Multilevel Nature of the Paradigm

As has been previously indicated, one of the areas in which separatism has traditionally been the norm in psychology is with respect to basic as opposed to applied science. Social behaviorism takes the position that applied science should be firmly based upon the elementary principles identified and studied in the basic laboratory. When this is done, there is a mutual contribution of each type of science to the other. New principles and findings from the basic laboratory are available for potential use in functional settings; as these elementary principles are extended to deal with significant human behavior problems they must frequently be modified and elaborated in ways that suggest elaborations at the basic level as well. In addition, successful application of basic principles in applied settings serves to validate those principles as well as to provide evidence concerning their generality. It is this continual interplay among the levels of the domain of our science that Staats is referring to when he calls social behaviorism a multilevel theory (see Chapter 2, this vol.).

A good example of research designed to demonstrate the applicability of principles studied in the basic laboratory to applied settings is to be found in Staats's work on the acquisition of cognitive repertoires in young children. Across the years this research has focused primarily upon three repertoires representative of complex cognitive behavior having clear functional value in the real world: number concepts, writing, and reading. Following a theoretical analysis of these repertoires based on learning principles, a set of procedures was developed and applied in a research fashion with a single subject, Staats's daughter Jennifer, beginning when she was 1½ years old. Procedures and analyses were revised on the basis of this experience and two further lines of research were established.

The first of these involved moving from the more naturalistic setting employed with Jennifer to a more controlled laboratory setting. The first study resulting from this line of research (Staats, Minke, Finley, Wolf, & Brooks, 1964) was designed to test the ability of the apparatus and procedures to maintain a young child's behavior over the long periods of time required if one is to study the acquisition of complex cognitive repertoires. Two 4-year-old children participated for 40 sessions, each session 20 minutes in length. It was found that across sessions the children worked at high, steady rates, with the work behaviors at the end of each session being just as strong as at the beginning. A second study (Staats, Finley, Minke, & Wolf, 1964) demonstrated that the children's work behaviors were indeed under the control of the reinforcer system employed rather than some other aspect of the procedures or apparatus. In general, the results obtained with these children paralleled the results that are typically obtained with lower animals engaging in simple learning tasks.

While additional studies were being conducted in the controlled laboratory situation, involving different reinforcement schedules, different populations of subjects, and so on, a second line of research was begun in which the procedures developed with Jennifer, modified on the basis of findings from the laboratory studies, were employed with additional children in a more naturalistic setting. The initial purpose of this research was to assess the generality of the procedures across children and experimenters.

As it became clear that the results being obtained with different children were paralleling those obtained with Jennifer (and as my skills as an experimenter improved), the focus of the research shifted from the general procedures and the basic behavioral repertoires underlying complex cognitive learning to the specific learning tasks being employed. Children were taught not only how to read the alphabet but how to write it as well; several microexperiments were conducted in the context of the overall training to evaluate theoretical analyses in such as areas as concept formation with respect to consonants, whole word versus phonics training, and so on.

Research such as this is not only of direct interest and usefulness to the behavioral engineer, but in addition it adds to his or her confidence in the basic principles upon which the procedures are based. In addition, it strengthens the basic science by suggesting that the principles are heavyweight, in that they have powerful effects in situations less tightly controlled than those in which they are traditionally studied and with behaviors of greater functional significance. In a multilevel paradigm such as social behaviorism, however, it is to be expected that not only will laboratory-derived principles have relevance for the applied psychologist, but that principles conceived and studied in applied settings will have relevance for certain basic laboratory phenomena as well. A study currently underway in my laboratory can be used as illustration.

A phenomenon studied extensively in the basic animal laboratory has been peak shift. If responding is established to a stimulus using extradimensional discrimination training and then a generalization gradient is obtained, it will be found (at least with a symmetrical test series) that peak responding occurs to the original discriminative stimulus. If, however, responding is established using intradimensional discrimination training, then maximum responding during generalization testing will not occur to the discriminative stimulus; the peak of the resulting generalization gradient will be shifted to a value on the generalization continuum away from the S-delta. As far as I can determine, peak shift has never been demonstrated to occur other than following intradimensional operant discrimination training, and the phenomenon has usually been explained in terms of the interaction of excitatory and inhibitory gradients established through reinforcement and extinction respectively. According to A-R-D theory, however, the basis for excitatory and inhibitory tendencies are positive and negative emotional responses, respectively; reinforcement and extinction procedures can be viewed as classical conditioning situations, in which the stimuli present act as conditioned stimuli (CS) and the occurrence or nonoccurrence of reinforcement acts as an unconditioned stimuli (UCS) for the appropriate emotional response. In other words, any procedure, not just discrimination training, that would condition positive and negative emotional responses to two stimuli along a common continuum should produce peak shift. We have been able to provide support for this conclusion in several recent studies by inducing peak shift through verbal means, attaching the labels "same" and "different" to two different stimuli along a line tilt dimension in one case, and pairing line angles with randomly selected evaluative words in another.

Research to Provide Analysis of Functional Behavioral Repertoires

Since a true paradigm strives to be all encompassing of the phenomena within its domain, an important activity within paradigmatic science is the extension of principles, theoretical constructs, and assumptions to phenomena heretofore not considered by the paradigm. Before the theoretical constructs of social behaviorism can be applied to new behavioral repertoires, however, those repertoires must be observed and described, frequently with greater specificity than has occurred previously in the psychological literature. Until such description has taken place, detailed theoretical analyses may well be fruitless. Studies designed to provide this sort of description are a legitimate form of research within the paradigm, and can frequently add to the development of the paradigm by providing previously unreported observations to which the paradigm's principles and theoretical constructs can be applied. Such descriptive studies are particularly relevant to the behavioral engineer when the repertoires involved are functional (or dysfunctional) in real world settings.

Speech Fluency in Stuttering

One such repertoire, of major practical concern, is fluency of overt speech. Although a number of theoretical models have been developed to account for speech dysfluencies, in particular stuttering, there is a lack of precise descriptive data available against which to evaluate these models or to provide the basis for new theoretical extensions. This is largely due to methodological constraints. For example, it is generally accepted that stuttering is accompanied by hypertensive muscle responses in the throat, mouth, and laryngeal areas, and several major theories of stuttering are based upon the assumption that these hypertensive muscle responses occur in a specified temporal relationship to the stuttering episode. However, until recently no data have been reported describing the orderly changes in speech muscle activity occurring prior to, during, and after specific speech responses within the same individual. This was probably due to the inherent variability found when continuous physiological response measures such as those produced by use of an electromyograph (EMG) are employed.

Ban (1979) found a way around this problem by integrating continuous EMG data into 1-second units, allowing for the production of orderly descriptive profiles of speech muscle activity for individual subjects that were uncontaminated by the high variability normally encountered. These semicontinuous measurements were taken at several sites from people who stuttered, and yoked-control individuals who did not, as they spoke a list of single words. Ban found that the increase in muscle tension accompanying episodes of stuttering occurs primarily during the overt speech act itself and is accompanied by a much longer recovery period than observed when a word is spoken fluently. Furthermore, the profiles obtained on nonstuttered words from those who stuttered parallel those obtained on all words from the nonstuttering controls. Ban had no particular theoretical preconceptions concerning the learning mechanisms involved in stuttering prior to the collection of his data; the descriptive data generated can serve as the basis for the beginnings of such an analysis.

There are times, however, when a phenomenon suggests a general theoretical approach but in the absence of specific descriptive data one cannot determine just how the theoretical analysis should be applied. This was the problem faced by another of my students, Cindy Ikenaga, as she started her work on syllogistic problem solving, an area almost totally ignored in the behavioral literature although one that has generated a great deal of cognitive research (e.g., Huttenlocher & Higgins, 1971).

A Social Behavioral Analysis of Problem Solving

Advances in our understanding of problem solving are of considerable importance for unifying behavioral and cognitive therapy. Eifert (Chapter 8, this vol.) has outlined how problem solving can be conceptualized in social behavioral terms and employed in cognitive-behavioral therapy. Despite the renewed interest in clinical problem solving (Goldfried & Davison, 1976), however, there have been few attempts to draw upon basic research investigating the processes involved in problem solving to design and improve clinical interventions. Ikenaga has added to this basic research base by utilizing Staats's (1963) suggestion that many problem solving situations could be conceptualized in terms of three sequential stages: (1) a labeling response stage; (2) a reasoning sequence stage; and (3) a motor response stage. In other words, an individual facing a problem would first label relevant features of the environment. The stimulus properties of this labeling response would elicit appropriate reasoning sequences (i.e., implicit verbal response sequences), the stimulus properties of which in turn would elicit appropriate motor behavior (the problem solution).

Although Ikenaga (1982) was sure this type of analysis could be applied to the syllogistic situation, involving as it does complex implicit reasoning, she could conceptualize a number of different specific ways this could be done. Therefore, she decided to examine performance in such a situation in a more molecular manner than had been employed previously, to see if a particular mode of application suggested itself. She presented subjects with a set of syllogism problems of the form "John is taller than Sam; Sam is taller than Fred; who is the tallest? a) John b) Sam c) Fred" by means of a microcomputer. Each problem was presented one premise at a time, and each sentence was erased by a subject-initiated key press before the next was displayed. This allowed her to obtain separate latency measures for each of the three statements in the problem. Prior research employing these types of problems at most took overall latency measures based upon simultaneous display of all three statements.

When these data were summarized across problems, an interesting function was obtained and is depicted in Figure 3.1A. Very little time was spent with the first premise; this is to be expected, since at this point nothing more than reading and perhaps some implicit rehearsal can occur. A much longer latency was obtained with respect to the second statement. Since the second statement was of the same length as the first, this additional latency was almost assuredly reflecting time spent in implicit reasoning. When the third statement (the actual question) was presented, average latency was actually shorter than to the first statement when the problem was ultimately solved correctly. Under these circumstances the latency seemed to reflect reading and the selection of the an-

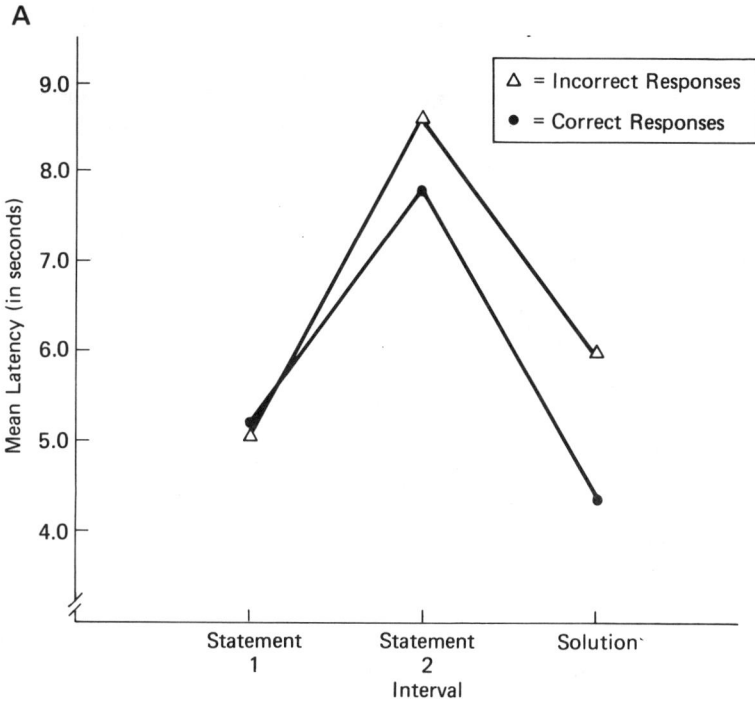

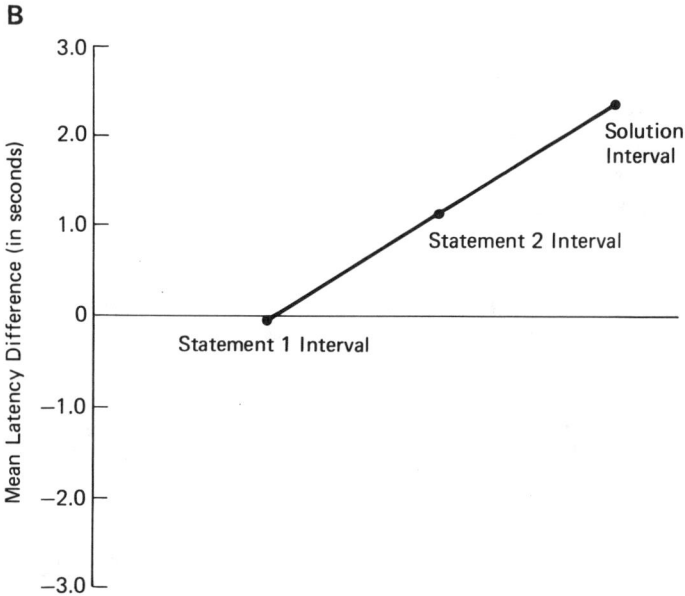

FIGURE 3.1A: Mean response latencies to each problem statement as a function of whether the problem was ultimately solved correctly or incorrectly. **B:** Mean latency differences (incorrectly solved problems minus correctly solved problems) for each statement.

swer, but little or no reasoning. The three-stage model seems to fit these data quite well, with the reading of the first premise corresponding to the labeling stage, the performance with respect to the second statement reflecting the reasoning stage, and the performance in the third step representing the motor response stage.

The shape of the function changed, however, when we examined problems that were ultimately answered incorrectly. Although the latency to the first statement paralleled that obtained with problems solved correctly, a longer latency occurred to both the second and the third statement (question). In fact, the differences in latencies for correct and incorrect problems increased steadily across the intervals (see Figure 3.1B). Ikenaga speculated that on those problems they ultimately solved incorrectly, subjects produced faulty reasoning sequences in the presence of the second statement; logical inconsistencies might have occurred and the subjects may even have attempted to run through the reasoning sequences again, thus adding to the response latency. The fact that the latency to the third statement was higher than to the first under these circumstances suggests that subjects, when faced with the actual question, could label that they did not have the answer readily available, engaged in further reasoning, and ultimately missed the question anyway. We have been able to replicate these basic findings with respect to linear syllogistic reasoning (Sato, 1987), but an investigation currently underway suggests that additional mechanisms may be operating with respect to categorical syllogisms.

Conclusions

These studies and research programs, as well as many others, some of which will be elaborated in later chapters, represent the ever expanding research base of social behaviorism. Such research activity is a never-ending enterprise in a paradigmatic science, and much still needs to be done in each of the categories discussed. Nevertheless, this research base goes far in establishing the validity of the precepts of the paradigm. The nature and scope of this research, along with the usefulness of the paradigm's constructs, have led a number of psychologists, particularly at the applied end of the continuum, to have sufficient faith in the efficacy and power of the paradigm to begin calling themselves social behaviorists. Even more make use of social behavioral concepts and analyses in their professional activities.

None of the studies described in the preceding pages would be considered classic applied research. Some have obvious utility to behavioral engineering in that they deal with functional repertoires of immediate concern to the discipline. Horton's experiment in aggression, Collette's work in dyslexia, Ban's research in stuttering, and Ikenaga's study in syllogistic problem solving fall into this category. Others, while typically conducted in settings far removed from those of interest to applied psychologists, are of ultimate concern as well, in that they establish the validity of the principles and inferred constructs used in their daily activity. I believe the studies dealing with indirect observation are particularly important in this regard. I suspect that the ability to incorporate cognitive events that are nondirectly observable into a systematic behavioral approach has been one of the most appealing features of social behaviorism to the applied psychologists who have aligned themselves with the paradigm. Perhaps more than any other factor, it is this characteristic that has allowed social behaviorism to provide explanations for complex behaviors and to integrate the findings and conceptions of other approaches.

Traditional applied research is conducted for a variety of reasons as well. Some studies are designed to demonstrate the effectiveness of a particular procedure. For example, one of my early research projects was concerned with the development of a procedure to produce limb movement and hand-eye coordination in a child with cerebral palsy (Minke & Heard, 1964). Others are designed to extend the generality of a procedure already demonstrated. Staats's research in remedial reading can be viewed in this light. After demonstrating the effectiveness of the procedure with a single child (Staats & Butterfield, 1965), several studies were conducted that demonstrated the utility of the procedure with different types of children and instructional technicians in different settings (Staats, Minke, & Butts, 1970; Staats, Minke, Goodwin, & Landeen, 1967).

Still other applied studies are conducted for the purpose of evaluating specific parameters of a procedure. For about the past 12 years most of my applied work has centered around an instructional method for use in the university classroom, developed by John Carlson and myself, that we call unit mastery instruction. This instructional system can be viewed as a version of the personalized system of instruction (PSI) that evolved within radical behaviorism (Johnston & Pennypacker, 1971; Keller, 1974). Because of the broader social behavioral perspective concerning academic behavior that underlies our specific procedures, however, we felt that our instructional system was sufficiently different to justify a new name. Within the context of our introductory psychology course taught with this method, we have manipulated such variables as the availability of lectures, the method of assigning students to tutors, the quiz question format, and the mastery criterion to determine the most effective values of these parameters.

Finally, applied research frequently centers around the evaluation of specific objectives. In our unit mastery course we have formally compared our instructional system to the traditional lecture method, have demonstrated improvement in study behaviors as a function of experiencing the course, and are currently evaluating the effectiveness of specific remedial procedures employed with some students. Summaries of most of these studies can be found in Minke (1988).

It is important to recognize that to the extent the applied procedures and techniques derive from the paradigm, research of this sort is critical for the validation and elaboration of the paradigm itself. Successful employment of procedures that are developed using the assumptions, constructs, and methodological principles of the paradigm provides, in the end, the strongest evidence of all concerning the paradigm's viability. For this reason, it is particularly exciting to see evidence of the successful application of social behavioral principles in clinical and remedial settings as described in Chapters 7 through 12 of this book.

Acknowledgments

In addition to the colleagues and students referred to in the preceding pages I would like to thank Earl Hishinuma, Keith Sato, and Sandy Tadaki for their assistance in the more recent research described. Research projects in my laboratory are always collaborative efforts, and these students have all contributed in various important ways.

4

Social Behaviorism, Interpersonal Determinants of Language Acquisition, and Implications for Language Intervention

Jean A. Rondal

Anyone familiar with the early development of behavior therapy would agree that teaching speech to nonverbal children was one of the first major clinical contributions to behavioral intervention (e.g., Hewett, 1965; Lovaas, Berberich, Perloff, & Schaeffer, 1966; Wolf, Risley, & Mees, 1964). All these classic studies were carried out within a relatively simple operant conditioning paradigm (cf., Sloane & MacAulay, 1968), although a few attempted to integrate learning principles with more traditional speech therapy techniques (e.g., Nelson & Evans, 1968) and to move from speech to grammatical target behaviors (Guess, Sailor, Rutherford, & Baer, 1968). Another important early therapeutic contribution was Staats's (1957a) demonstration that schizophrenic speech could be manipulated by social reinforcement contingencies, which initiated an intensive research effort into understanding the social influences on language and other behavior in very seriously disturbed individuals. Not only the nature of the audience, but other facets of the individual's own behavioral repertoire influence expressive language, so that some evidence began to accrue that anxiety affected conversational ability and speech fluency (Gray & England, 1969; see also Minke, Chapter 3, this vol.).

Generally, these and other behavioral analyses of language phenomena were carried out quite separately, so that researchers interested in teaching children to use a covert verbal mediator to enhance self-control would typically not connect these efforts to studies of teaching children overt verbal repertoires to enhance communication and social interaction. In social behaviorism, however, the study of language as both an independent and a dependent variable has been a central concern from its very beginning (Staats, 1963, 1968a). Unlike some of the other behavioral formulations, social behaviorism did not rely on only one or two mechanisms for explaining all language development and its subsequent regulation and use. Nevertheless, learning processes were certainly considered critical, and in this sense Staats's position shares important assumptions with other behavioral perspectives, in stark contrast to the nativist assumptions of some psycholinguistic theories. It is of interest to note that behavioral clinical approaches to language intervention continued their development with little or no attention to the theoretical and empirical controversies that have raged over the mysteries of language acquisition and development. This is unfortunate, since the controversies result in refinement of some positions and increasing support for others, so that social behaviorism's elaborated position has obtained some credence, whereas Skinner's (1957) radical behavioral position has fared less well. The purpose of this chapter is to consider current trends in theory and research on language acquisition and suggest the more sophisticated clinical applications that can logically follow.

General Paradigms
of Language Acquisition

According to Reber (1973), three broad and conflicting perspectives could be distinguished within developmental psycholinguistics: associationistic, process, and content approaches. This is similar to the commonly adopted distinction that theories of language acquisition fall into the categories of behavioral, cognitive, and linguistic theories. Central to the content (linguistic) approach is the belief in the existence of a specific nativist content of the human mind, a faculty of language that is directly responsible for linguistic functioning. This faculty is assumed to contain a special system, the "language acquisition device" (LAD), the content of which is a set of substantive and formal universals. Substantive universals are those concerned with the description of the natural language. Formal universals are concerned with the nature of the generative rules found pertinent in linguistic theory for describing natural languages, such as the transformations that map deep structures onto surface structures (Chomsky, 1965). Briefly said, on the basis of the linguistic input that he or she receives, a child develops sets of hypotheses allowing him or her to organize and account for the input data by using the formal and substantive universals stored in the LAD.

The role assigned to learning in this orientation is modest. Innate dispositions and maturational processes are held to be mainly responsible for transforming a nonlinguistic infant into a fluent speaker-receiver. Rather than learning a language, children are viewed as actually selecting, through the linguistic input they are confronted with, the appropriate evidence for building an internal representation of the grammar of the language. Any content approach must begin with a theoretical model of language assumed to reflect the internal grammar of the mature speakers. The linguistic theory generally used for this purpose is the "standard" generative and transformational grammar written by Chomsky (1965) and its further refinements and modifications (see Chomsky, 1980; McNeil, 1970; Wexler & Culicover, 1980). The acquisition process is assumed to take place in stages. It is guided by a universal hierarchy of categories. At the early stages, there are only few classes and the rules used to generate utterances are simpler and pretransformational. At later stages, the classes become highly differentiated and the generative rules are more complex and transformational.

There are a number of variations of the process (cognitive) orientation (e.g., Bever, 1970; Sinclair, 1982; Slobin, 1973). They all, however, assume that the regularities observed in the acquisition of the natural languages do not derive in any direct manner from innate process mechanisms, but rather that children acquire their language as a result of general cognitive abilities. These abilities differ for different theorists but they make it possible for the children to abstract the regularities in the language heard. These theories differ from linguistic theories in that learning as well as biological development are central issues, although learning is viewed as an information-processing operation. For instance, Bever (1970) and Slobin (1973) have proposed a series of interpretive strategies that could be used by the children to understand the sentences addressed to them and to extract grammatical information. General informative principles like "pay attention to the ends of words" (because this is reflected in the acquisition of inflectional systems) or "avoid exceptions" are thought to play a role in the acquisition process, while being based at the same time on the emerging cognitive capabilities of the young child.

The associationist position as a potential psycholinguistic paradigm has developed directly out of the behaviorist school of thought, in which language performance is regarded as a set of learned behaviors. The full complexity of language behavior is assumed to develop through the chaining and combining of stimulus-responses connections. The possible role of biological components of language behavior are usually acknowledged but clearly environmental factors are given predominance. The associationist theorists like to indicate that any conceptualization of a possible biological predisposition for language acquisition and language use in humans will remain "lettre morte" without a sound theory of behavior and behavior development to which it can be related.

Prior to Staats's attempts at integration, there were essentially three traditions within behavioral psychology regarding language: (1) the neo-Hullian tradition as exemplified in particular by Osgood (1971) and Mowrer (1960); (2) the verbal learning tradition, exemplified by such individuals as G.A. Miller (1962), Ervin-Tripp (1964), and Jenkins and Palermo (1964); and (3) the radical behavioral tradition of Skinner's (1957) *Verbal Behavior*. Staats, in accordance with his concept of a third-generation learning theory, selectively integrated these traditions, especially the first two. Skinner's analysis, interestingly enough, has had minimal impact on the language literature except to have served as a convenient "whipping boy" for critics of behavioral approaches. It can also be said that Staats has recognized from the beginning the significance of linguistic observations as providing data that must be considered in a behavioral account. The process of combining linguistic and learning theory analyses calls for recognition: (1) that linguistic observations are valuable as such; (2) that language, including grammatical "rules," may be learned; (3) that theoretical analysis may be made of grammatical rules in terms of the stimulus-response mechanisms involved; (4) that experimental learning procedures can be used to test the theoretical analysis; and (5) that teaching procedures can be based on these findings (Staats, 1974).

Social behaviorism does not rely on only one or two mechanisms for explaining all of language development. On the contrary, the theory argues that language development is an extremely complex phenomenon, involving all the mechanisms suggested by the second-generation theorists at various times—in particular, direct, verbally-based, training experiences provided by parents. Staats (1963) is replete with examples based upon this assumption, and

Moerk's analyses of the "Harvard children" data—to be discussed presently—provided strong empirical support for the occurrence of such experiences and has described in some detail what the specific nature of these types of experiences are. The criticisms of the second-generation theories were really predicated on the fact that those earlier learning theories were arguing that all language could be explained on the basis of one or two principles (e.g., shaping through deliberate parental reinforcement, or the establishment of word associates). So pointing out that parents often do not provide direct social reinforcement for a correct grammatical construction or that word association norms do not reflect the complexity necessary to account for the sophistication of adult speech does not necessarily discount the theory; the theory simply argues that *sometimes* these mechanisms are operating, along with others. Therefore, the theory is supported by the demonstration that these events *do* take place; furthermore, it specifies other types of events that should occur if language is learned in the way described, and many (if not all) of these events are "interactional" in nature.

The Interactive Viewpoint in Language Acquisition

The scientific study of language acquisition demands at least two types of detailed information: (1) information on the children's linguistic forms, meaning and uses and their evolution in time; (2) information on the language the child is exposed to and its evaluation in time. As surprising as it may sound, this second series of information has not been available in sufficient amount before the seventies, making any attempt to understand and explain language acquisition virtually impossible. Typical contributions to the once-called "pedolinguistics" (e.g., Taine, 1876) in the last quarter of the 19th century and in the first half of the 20th century involved detailed descriptions of the children's vocabularies, formal classes, articulatory errors, morphosyntactical forms, and so forth, and their evolution in time. This evolution was analyzed for itself in a sort of environmental vacuum, as little or no information was gathered on the conversational antecedents and consequents as well as on the situational and interpersonal contexts of children's speech.

This criticism of one-sidedness can be extended to contemporary contributions. For example, the work of Slobin (1982) on universals and particulars of grammatical development in languages such as English, Turkish, and Serbo-Croat only documents aspects of children's productions and receptive abilities, with little information on the speech to which the children are exposed from both. Chomsky (1965) asserted: "It seems clear that many children acquire first or second languages quite successfully even though no special care is taken to teach them and no special attention is given to their progress" (p. 200). This alleged lack of care and attention in parents and the ill-nature of the speech usually heard by the child, together with the relatively short period of time identified for basic language acquisition, make it logically necessary for Chomsky and followers to postulate a very strong innate predisposition for grammatical construction in human beings. Fortunately, one is not obliged to make such drastic assumptions regarding human nature.

First, it is clear that language acquisition is not completed by 5 years. Actually, language mastery including metalinguistic awareness is not completed before adolescence. Second, Chomsky's claim that no special care is taken to teach language to children and that no special attention is given to their progress is simply wrong. A large number of systematic studies of parent–child verbal interactions in the process of language acquisition clearly attest to the contrary. Reviews of this literature (Rondal, 1981, 1983; Rondal, Harrod, & Charlier, 1985) clearly indicate that mothers' speech to language-learning children is simplified in every respect: phonological, lexical, semantic structural, morphological-syntactical, and pragmatical. Mothers' speech is well articulated, slower, lower in rate of dysfluencies, and well marked by pauses at sentences boundaries. The lexicon used is simpler. The speech produced is lexically less diverse. The number, the diversity and the complexity of the semantical relations expressed are reduced. Mothers' speech is well formed in terms of morphology and syntax. It is shorter and formally simpler than the speech exchanged between adults. Also, maternal speech addressed to children tends to be repetitive. The available data on fathers' speech to children (see Rondal, 1980, for a review) indicate that fathers' speech is also simplified and adapted to the children's level of language development. Data have also been gathered (e.g., Shatz & Gelman, 1973) indicating that children, starting around 6 years of age, are able to modify the prosodic, lexical and syntactical properties of their speech when addressing younger children. Whether they have younger siblings or not does seem to matter in this development (Shatz & Gelman, 1973). It can be said, therefore, that the whole familial linguistic environment of the language-learning child is sensitive and adapted to his or her changing linguistic level.

Parents' speech changes as the children's linguistic capabilities develop. Mothers and fathers not only adjust their speech to the children's linguistic capabilities, they also react to what the children say and how they say it (Moerk, 1972, 1975, 1980a, 1980b; Rondal, 1978a, 1978b, 1978c, 1980). Two categories pertaining to the feedback dimension of parental speech to their children can be distinguished: (1) the evaluative reactions and (2) the corrective reactions. Both types of reactions aim at the formal as well as the content aspect of the children's utterances. The often quoted claim by R. Brown (1973) that parental reactions rest only on the content of the children's speech to the exclusion of the structural properties of speech is groundless (Newport, Gleitman, & Gleitman, 1977; Rondal, 1978a). The tendency observed in parents to modify and to adapt their speech to the language level of the children is found across social classes and has been documented for various languages and cultures (see Rondal et al., 1985, for a review). Generally, all these findings support the theoretical analysis originally made by Staats (1971a, 1971b) who described in detail the interactive social and linguistic stimulus events likely to influence children's language development.

The Effect Question

An important question remains, however, as to whether fathers' and mothers' linguistic adaptations to their children's language do have an effect on language acquisition. K. Nelson (1977) has supplied the first clear demonstration that parental recasting of children's utterances does indeed facilitate syntax acquisition.

A related issue is whether variations in parental frequency of use of certain linguistic structures significantly affects the acquisition of these structures. A negative opinion in this respect was that of R. Brown (1973). On the basis of his analysis of data pertaining to the "Harvard children" (Adam, Eve, and Sarah) and their parents, he asserted that frequency of input is not a significant variable in language acquisition. Brown's opinion was reproduced many times and long considered to be the final word on the subject. Moerk (1980b), however, challenged this view, after having obtained the original transcripts from Brown and undertaking a systematic reanalysis of the data. Moerk's results flatly contradict Brown's conclusion for seven grammatical morphemes (plural, *in, on,* present progressive, possessive, past regular, and past irregular). For the other seven morphemes studied by Brown and reanalyzed by Moerk (i.e., uncontractible copula, articles, third-person regular, third-person irregular, uncontractible auxiliary, contractible copula, and contractible auxiliary) the interval between the point in time when the parental input frequencies were established and the time when the rank orders for acquisition were made is 6 months and more (up to 14 months). With long intervals between the establishment of the input frequencies and the children's uses, serious methodological problems are likely to arise. For the morphemes reanalyzed, the items more frequently used by the parents of the children are the first to reach the productivity criterion set by Brown (i.e., correct use in at least 90% of the obligatory contexts) for each of the three children. For all morphemes included, the product-moment correlation coefficient between input frequency and age of acquisition is $-.56$ in the case of Adam. For Sarah this correlation is $-.66$, and for Eve it is $-.67$. Thus, when properly analyzed, Brown's data clearly show that input frequencies are important. Analyses of mother-child interactions centering around the correct use of particular linguistic constructions suggest that densely spaced repetitions within relatively short periods of time are highly conducive to the productive mastery of these constructions (e.g., prepositional phrases).

The clinical implications of this reanalysis would be enhanced if the precise natural parental teaching strategies could be described. Fortunately, Moerk (1980a) has identified 40 teaching techniques in the mothers of the "Harvard children." The total range of transcripts extends over a time span of 9 months for Eve and her mother when Eve was between 18 and 27 months, and a time span of 8 months for Adam and his mother when Adam was between 27 and 35 months old. Among the teaching techniques differentiated were conditioned reward, conditioned punishment, expansion of child's utterances, exact self-repetition, obvious correction of child's utterance, imitation of child's utterances with substitution of items, building up sequences of own utterances, breaking down sequences of own utterances, conveying that the preceding utterance was linguistically incorrect, and many others. The following five categories together account for approximately 53% of all maternal interventions (which accrued at a rate of 5.8 per hour): expansions, perseverance of a specific morpheme or morpheme category, replacement of a major word or constituent within an unchanged frame, frame variation without meaning change, and perseverance of a vocabulary item.

The arguments in favor of a parental language-teaching hypothesis are quite convincing, in my view. It explains why parents maintain a level of speech complexity only slightly higher than that of the child, although it is quite possible to communicate satisfactorily at fairly similar speech levels of complexity. It also explains the numerous instances of evaluative and corrective feedback found in parental speech to language-learning children. The exact relationships do need further investigation. Furrow, Nelson, and Benedict (1979), for example, showed that mothers' simplification of constructions were associated with later language growth; the greater the number of nouns, verbs, pronouns, and copulas used by the mothers when their children were 18 months old, the less advancement shown by the children over time (up to 27 months). My own position (see also Rondal, 1983) is that a *dynamic* concept is required, by which is meant that there must be moment-to-moment changes in the adult's verbal adaptations to the child's speech, allowing change over time and therefore linguistic progress in the children.

There are three implications of this perspective that should be mentioned. The first relates to the conditions under which certain classes of grammars are learnable, which Wexler and Culicover (1980) have tried to establish. In its simplest form, these authors have been concerned with demonstrating that a certain class of grammars is learnable, given assumptions about three sets of entities: (1) the nature of the input data, (2) the mechanism that selects the appropriate grammars from a set of possible ones, and (3) the notion of correctness. They have sought to disprove the thesis that the input of the child is especially tailored to the child's linguistic needs, emphasizing in particular the lack of evidence that children were provided with negative information about the grammatical status of strings in their language (Atkinson, 1982; Wexler & Culicover, 1980). However, as I have reported elsewhere (Rondal, 1978b), maternal speech addressed to toddlers contains between 7 and 23% of evaluative instances according to the situation (fewer such reactions are recorded during mealtime than during free play or story telling). Between 2 and 4% of these evaluative instances are negative ones. If one adds to this the explicit corrections and expansions, it seems that the significant part of parental reactions to children's productions is informative to the child, either regarding the truth value of his or her productions and whether a given string of morphemes belong to the grammatical system of the language, or can at least be considered close enough to what this system demands to be accepted momentarily.

A second issue emerging from the dynamic interaction perspective is that the child obviously does not have a passive role, but is an active participant and learner. These essential behavioral processes are too complex to be given adequate treatment here, but it should be noted that the social behavioral conception of personality consisting of basic behavioral repertoires—both an effect and a cause of behavior—is very relevant in this context. If the child is an active learner, then response mechanisms such as attention as well as a variety of perceptual processes must underlie language learning in the cumulative-hierarchical fashion suggested by Staats (1968a, 1975). Thus, for instance, the nonvocal reciprocal sensitivity established between mother and infant as early as 2 or 3 months might be an important precursor to conversational interaction. Certainly up to 6 months of age only the mother's vocal behavior exhibits constant evidence of dependent control in the dyadic interaction, but by the end of the first year, normal infants show many social interactional skills necessary for further learning—for instance, waiting a reasonable time between vocal productions for the partner to contribute to the protodialogue.

This leads to a third important issue. If language learning is related to the interactions between children and parents, and if language learning is related to more fundamental perceptual and learning skills in the way described above, it suggests interesting implications for beginning to link the literatures on the acquisition of intelligence (see Burns, Chapter 5, this vol.) as well as the clinical work on disturbed or disrupted interactional patterns between parent and child. Typically, the consequences of maternal neglect or physical abuse, as well as subtle disturbances in child–parent relationships, are viewed in terms of emotional development and the appearance of specific behavior problems such as hyperactivity or aggression. In paradigmatic behavior therapy, however, language is given a very important role in mediating aberrant behavior, such as failing to provide a directive function to impulsive motor behavior; another example is mislabeling which may evoke affective responses such as anxiety or hostility in situations that are not in reality threatening (see Chapters 7 through 9, this vol.).

My discussion has thus far been about language acquisition. Yet a critical aspect in a social behaviorism perspective is to understand not just the acquisition of subsequent grammar but the acquisition of linguistic functions, such as in social interaction, self-regulation, and so on. Parents provide linguistic input not just in terms of grammatical structure but in terms of context: parents who use inductive (reasoning) strategies in discipline are further encouraging verbal problem-solving skills that can be used by the child. Similarly, the accurate or inaccurate labeling of situations and events provides the child with attitudes, beliefs, and values that direct later responding according to A-R-D principles. Of the many areas where these concepts could be illustrated I will focus the remainder of this chapter on clinical applications to language disorders, where the function of the language repertoire acquired by the child has recently become better recognized.

Language Disorders and Intervention

In this section I will consider certain research data pertinent to language development in children whose language acquisition has not, for various reasons, followed the expected course of development. I hope it will become clear, that a learning-based, interactional view of language has much relevance for clinical remediation, representing a significant conceptual advance over the more simplistic behavioral perspective that has guided much behavioral clinical work. For example, in keeping with the suggestion made earlier that all aspects of language need to be considered in a unifying theory, speech fluency is related to verbal exchanges between parent and child: Egolf, Shames, Johnson, and Kaspisin-Burelli (1972) identified several negative patterns of behavior in the parents of children who stuttered. These patterns were verbal aggression, silence, and interruptions. Therapy targeted toward encouraging parents to reduce these negative responses and increase positive reactions to the child's verbal accomplishment did lead to an increase in fluency both inside and outside the therapeutic sessions. It should be realized, of course, that, as in the case of linguistic and social responses developed toward autistic children, it is possible, indeed likely, that parental reactions are consequences, not causes of stuttering, and many serve to exacerbate an already existing problem. Another illustration of social responses influencing language has been supplied by Wulbert, Inglis, Kriegsmann, and Mills (1975). They found that the mothers of language-delayed children were more critical, less responsive, and generally less involved than mothers of age-matched and mentally retarded children. Although these maternal behaviors might have played a causal role, I would argue that mothers of language-delayed but otherwise normal children experience frustration and fail to adapt to their children's language peculiarities, unlike the mothers of Down's syndrome children. Let us consider the literature on this latter topic in greater detail.

Children with Mental Retardation

The systematic study of the linguistic environment of children with mental retardation can be traced back to the studies of Siegel at the University of Minnesota in the sixties (e.g., Siegel, 1967). At that time, however, only the speech of the adults surrounding the children was studied, but not the speech of the children themselves. The first truly interactive studies were conducted by Marshall and collaborators (Marshall, Hegrenes, & Goldstein, 1973) who compared speech interactions between parents and handicapped and nonhandicapped children in a free-play setting. They analyzed their data according to Skinner's verbal operant categories and reported more mands and echoics and fewer tacts and intraverbals in the speech of the mentally retarded children and their mothers. Another early study (Buium, Rynders, & Turnure, 1974) involving both a free-play and structured interaction compared the speech of mothers of Down's syndrome 2-year-olds and of nonhandicapped children. The latter used longer utterances and more advanced types of sentences and linguistic structures. On this basis, Rynders and his associates concluded that the linguistic environment of Down's syndrome children is different from that of nonhandicapped children, an interpretation that was overgeneralized, with some authorities arguing that adult speech to mentally retarded children was deficient and involved restricted linguistic codes.

These conclusions, of course, fail to take into consideration the possible effects of the children's level of linguistic development on the speech of the adults. In order to prove that adult speech to mentally retarded children is deficient, one has to show that there are deficits when the handicapped and nonhandicapped children are at comparable levels of language development. My own large-scale study of 42 children (half of whom had Down's syndrome) and their mothers was designed to investigate this issue. The children were matched at three levels of mean length of utterance (MLU), using R. Brown's (1973) criteria. Other language production measures were computed on the children in order to check the validity of the MLU matching: type-token ratio (an index of lexical diversity), upper bound or longest utterance in the corpus, proportion of utterances without verb, and number of modifiers per utterance. A semantic structure analysis adapted from Chafe (1970) was made. These analyses yielded no significant differences but one between the two groups of children at each MLU level. The only difference was with type-token ratio and favored Down's syndrome children over the nonhandicapped controls. The nonhandicapped and the Down's syndrome children therefore were at comparable linguistic levels but, of course, they differed widely in chronological ages. For instance, at MLU Level 1, the average age was about 4 years for the Down's syndrome children versus 23 months for the nonhandicapped children and at MLU Level 3, the average age was about 10 years for the Down's syndrome children versus 30 months for the nonhandicapped children.

The speech of the mothers was thoroughly analyzed in its numerical, lexical, syntactical, semantical, pragmatical output, and language-teaching aspects (see Rondal, 1978a, for more details). No significant difference was found in maternal speech to the Down's syndrome and the nonhandicapped children at each MLU level, but there were numerous significant differences in maternal speech across MLU levels for the comparison children as well as for those children with mental retardation. This indicates that mothers of Down's syndrome children do indeed make appropriate linguistic adjustments when mentally retarded and nonhandicapped children are matched in terms of productive linguistic level.

Even when matched for MLU, there remain deep-seated syntactic differences between nonhandicapped and mentally retarded children. Down's syndrome children tend to produce sentences that are syntactically less sophisticated. Operations of reversing the order of the first nominal and verbal elements in asking questions (e.g., "Is he coming?") and sequentially combining main and secondary verbs in sentences (e.g., present or past participle "I found a toy broken") are less advanced in Down's syndrome children even when they are producing sentences of comparable length to those of nonhandicapped children. Another interesting difference relates to behaviors that are possibly more basic in the cumulative-hierarchy of language development. We found (Gutmann & Rondal, 1979) that nonhandicapped children produced more imitative verbal responses than Down's syndrome children, so that the latter group may not be making full use of a valuable language-learning strategy.

The studies I have mentioned, as well as others, indicate that mothers' speech to mentally retarded children is formally and functionally appropriate for language growth in their children. This means that the ground is sound and solid if one wants to use and rely on the families in language intervention with mentally retarded children. There is no apparent need to drastically change the linguistic environment of children with mental retardation as some have hastily suggested. However, this does not mean that parental speech to mentally retarded language-learning children cannot be improved in terms of maximizing the efficiency of the parents in teaching language to their children through verbal interaction, which will contribute to speeding up the language development process in the handicapped children as much as possible. Social skills must be developed in conjunction with conversational skills (Leifer & Lewis, 1984), and parents encouraged to be less directive and more teaching oriented (Cardoso-Martins & Mervis, 1985). This is a different issue from the one regarding the deficit question in parental speech to mentally retarded children, and it can be raised for the parents of nonhandicapped children as well (e.g., Metzl, 1978).

Hearing-Impaired Children

Before concluding with some clinical implications of this position, it is worth mentioning briefly a few interesting findings from interactional studies of children who are hearing impaired. Very few data seem to have been published on the oral and gestural exchanges between deaf or nondeaf parents and their deaf (or nondeaf) children. Regarding the use of sign language, there are some reasons for explaining this lack of data. Until a few years ago, the manual communication systems have been virtually ignored by linguists, educators, and psychologists. Manual communication was dismissed as concrete, iconic, and tied to the here and now. Its use was discouraged with young deaf children for fear that it would inhibit the development of speech and the oral language. Perceptions of the nature and value of the manual communication systems, for example, sign language, have drastically changed in recent years with the progressive realization that hearing-impaired children exposed to manual communication from an early age are superior in academic achievement, social adjustment, and oral language skills to those not exposed to manual communication (Moores, 1978; Moores & Maestas y Moores, 1982).

As a result, several researchers have started to study the acquisition of sign language by hearing-impaired children using psycholinguistic techniques (see Rondal & Henrot, 1984, for a review). As a representative example, consider the study by Maestas y Moores (1980), who videotaped mother–child interactions in families with deaf parents. A variety of interaction patterns were analyzed, including signing on the child's body, modeling signing style, fingerspelling, signing and rhyming, and cross-modal communication, that is, from signing to speaking and vice versa. The study gives valuable information on the early communicative patterns of deaf and nondeaf infants and their deaf parents. It indicates that much of what has been described in the early interactions of hearing mothers with their infants also applied to deaf mothers and their infants: by approximately 16 months, the infants born to deaf mothers make use of all available means of communication. They take the initiative in dialogues, respond to the partner, and combine the sign language units in acceptable utterances. The acquisition of a first communicative competence (in the sense of Hymes, 1974) therefore appears to be largely independent of the communicative channel used preferentially.

A second representative study was conducted in Australia by Cross, Morris, and Nienhuys (1980), who observed three groups of hearing mothers in dyadic interaction with their children. The children in one group were 26 months old and had normal hearing, in another group they were about the same age but had a severe or profound hearing loss, and in the third group were equally hearing impaired but were 15 months old, on average. The third group's MLU in speech samples was not dissimilar to the first group. Maternal speech to the children was analyzed for MLU, syntactic complexity, propositional contents, types of sentences, verbal fluency, number of utterances per conversational turn, and so forth. On each of these indices, maternal speech addressed to the hearing 2-year-olds was significantly more complex than to the deaf children, even to the oldest ones. Cross et al. (1980) add that the formal complexity of the speech of the mothers to the deaf children in both groups can be equated to that of the speech usually addressed to hearing infants around 6 months of age according to the current literature. Therefore it would appear that the speech addressed by hearing mothers to their young deaf children may be exaggeratedly simplified. It may be difficult for hearing parents to evaluate correctly the receptive language competence of their hearing-impaired children and thus properly calibrate the level of complexity of their speech.

Implications and Conclusions

One of the strongest implications of the work reviewed is that as a general rule, families can, and typically do, provide a suitable linguistic environment for language development in children with handicaps. This supports the general trend toward "normalization," the maintenance of children with handicaps in their home environments, and the provision of educational services in integrated settings. If children at an early age are placed outside the home and, specifically, into environments consisting primarily of relatively uninvolved paid caretakers and other children with severe language delays, the quality of the language learning context has declined drastically. At the same time, the parents of children with handicaps can probably be helped to be even more effective as "teachers" of language, and there are a large number of early intervention programs that attest to the value of this approach. MacDonald (1982), for example, has developed a curriculum for professionals to guide parents, based on the need for conversational interactions between child and parent that are progressively matched. What the linguistic analyses of early language development seem to clarify is that behavioral interventions designed according to simple principles of reinforcement, shaping, and other strategies of direct instruction can be greatly enhanced by considering the social interaction patterns whereby effective parents adjust and regulate their own verbal behavior in complexity and style according to the needs of the child. Natural environments do not, of course, include only adults in the acquisition process. Peers are also quite capable of fine-tuning their speech and adjusting it to the development level of children with handicaps with whom they are interacting (Guralnick, 1978).

We do not yet know the relative contribution of different sources of influence on children's language, but these may be issues for clinical assessment. Social behaviorism's theory of language emphasizes its multiple functions. Obviously the major purpose of language is to communicate with others, so for children whose repertoire of effective communication skills may be limited, the development of such skills—by whatever means—should, perhaps, take educational precedence. This seems to have been recognized in the education of deaf children (cf., Baker & Battison, 1980) and of children with autism (Fay & Schuler, 1980), and children with severe disabilities in general (Reichle & Karlan, 1985). In contemporary special education, great stress is placed on the teaching of verbal/linguistic skills that will be functional, which often means individual tailoring of educational goals. For instance, if a child is exhibiting a seriously disruptive negative behavior that seems to serve a communicative function, then a specific verbal response such as asking for help, expressing a dislike, and so on, would be particularly valuable (Donnellan, Mirenda, Mesaros, & Fassbender, 1984).

In the absence of an integrative theory, the educational focus on one important feature of language learning sometimes results in neglect of others. Thus the stress on instruction focused on functional objectives sometimes seems to detract from teaching responses that may be necessary prerequisites. The value of a cumulative-hierarchical learning perspective (Staats, 1975) is that such principles are not incompatible. Although not fully reviewed in this chapter, there seems to be good empirical support for promoting language in children with handicaps by enhancing protoconversations and joint attention and joint action leading to lexical reference in the infant. It is arguable from developmental psycholinguistics that a nonverbal repertoire of consistent responses to objects is a precursor to the development of a receptive and expressive vocabulary. Essential features of the process (cognitive) orientation to language acquisition can be incorporated within paradigmatic behaviorism without the contradictions evident when certain cognitive stages are presumed necessary for language learning. Reichle and Karlan (1985) point out the logical inconsistencies in decision rules for implementing augmentative communication systems when some of these rules refer to cognitive development (such as object permanence) and some to practical but important social considerations such as the family's and the professional speech therapists willingness to use a nonspeech communication system. They argue that the use of a nonspeech system along with efforts to establish speech would allow the child to communicate early on and thus facilitate not only language development but also positive social interactions with the environment—the positive cumulative learning hierarchy that Staats has described and which will be illustrated in the next chapter. Decision rules that relegate the introduction of a nonvocal system to a later age only after a child has experienced significant failure to communicate with speech do not appear to be supported by the empirical literature or a theoretical consideration of the crucial role of *communication* (and not merely speech) to social development (Reichle & Karlan, 1985).

It is also not too far fetched to consider important features of the motivational system, including a history of "success" experiences in which the child has been able to learn that words function as stimuli for social events and are thus tools for changing and regulating one's environment. I have emphasized an interactional approach and tried to show its importance for linking linguistic analyses of language acquisition with the assumptions of paradigmatic behaviorism's "third-generation" learning theory. Undoubtedly, many of the details need to be filled in, however, the heuristic implications for clinical and educational interventions with language have, I hope, been highlighted.

5

Affective-Cognitive-Behavioral Assessment: The Integration of Personality and Behavioral Assessment

G. Leonard Burns

Several of the chapters in this book suggest that a causative concept of personality is important for the integration and advancement of behavior therapy. This chapter will elaborate on this theme by an explicit focus on paradigmatic behaviorism's personality conception. It is indeed one of the most valuable assets of paradigmatic behaviorism that it is a "behaviorism with a personality" (Staats, 1986). My purpose will be to attempt to show how this particular conception of personality can unify the schism between traditional personality and behavioral assessment. I will introduce this topic by discussing some of the characteristics of a preparadigmatic science as well as presenting a brief overview of Staats's multilevel, hierarchical approach to theory construction.

Just as psychology is divided and fragmented by many schisms (Staats, 1983b), so is the field of personality, where a schism exists between the view that internal personality processes determine behavior and a view that behavior is determined by external events. A second schism is found in the area of measurement. One side takes the view that the goal of measurement is the assessment of internal, causal personality processes for prediction and classification (diagnosis), while the other side takes the view that the goal of measurement is the quantification of behavior. Another such schism is found in the area of psychotherapy between the view that the goal of therapy is to change internal personality processes and the view that the goal is to modify behavior directly through the manipulation of environmental events.

Behaviorism has traditionally attempted to reduce such schisms by the rejection of the methods, concepts, and findings of the nonbehavioral sides (Burns, 1988). Staats describes this and other types of theory construction methodology in greater detail in his chapter, referring to this particular one as "generalization by exclusion." As traditional behaviorism's unification methodologies are inadequate, it is necessary to formulate a set of principles that are able to integrate productively the positive findings from both sides of the schism, the outcome being the unification of the two separate, antagonistic areas of knowledge—such as the integration of personality and behavioral assessment, which is the theme of this chapter. First, however, I will outline the issues that divide personality and behavioral assessment.

The Schism Between Behavioral and Personality Assessment

As is characteristic of any emerging area of study, there has been an exponential growth in behavioral assessment. This expansion is represented by texts (e.g., Bellack & Hersen, 1988; Nelson & Hayes, 1986) and journals (*Behavioral Assessment and Journal of Psychopathology and Behavioral Assessment*) as well as by texts that redefine the concept and apply behavioral assessment to new areas (Kendall & Hollon, 1981; Merluzzi, Glass, & Genest, 1981). A major emphasis in the early development of behavioral assessment has been to indicate how the approach differs from (and is better than) traditional personality assessment (e.g., Hartmann, Roper, & Bradford, 1979; Mischel, 1968). While recent years have witnessed an increased concern within behavioral assessment for such traditional psychometric concepts as reliability and validity, the general focus continues to be on behavioral assessment as something distinctly different from personality assessment.

Hartmann and his associates (1979) have compiled the various ways that behavioral assessment has been contrasted to personality assessment. These authors suggest that the two approaches differ in their conception of personality, the hypothesized causes of behavior, the role of behavior (sign vs. sample), the importance of history, the consistency of behavior, the uses of data, and the methods, time, and scope of assessment. Within the personality assessment approach, personality is usually defined as enduring, internal processes that are assumed to be the causes of behavior. Behavior is conceptualized as a sign or index of these internal processes—that is, behavior is important because it provides the means to assess the more critical processes. There is also a focus on the historical antecedents of the adulthood personality dynamics (e.g., early childhood experiences). Behavior is expected to be consistent across time and situations given the assumption of causation by enduring, internal processes. In turn, data, as an index of the personality processes, are used to make decisions about etiology, diagnosis, and prognosis, with treatment attempting to change internal processes if such is considered theoretically possible. Finally, in terms of the methods, time, and scope of assessment, the approach favors indirect and more global measures.

Behavioral assessment, in defining itself as something in opposition to the personality approach to assessment, has taken a contrasting view on each of the above points (Hartmann et al., 1979). First, behavioral assessment has traditionally rejected a causative conception of personality. *Personality* is defined as a dependent variable (behavior) determined by the environment. In the liberal behavioral view personality is defined as covariations among behaviors making up a response class, such as compliance (Voeltz & Evans, 1982). In contrast, radical behaviorism seeks covariation between environmental events or manipulations and a specific behavior or operant (e.g., the covariation between the manipulation of the rate of reinforcement and the rate of responding).

The assumed causes of behavior within behavioral assessment, as indicated above, are environmental events rather than internal processes. Behavior is considered a sample of some larger universe of behavior as opposed to a sign of underlying personality processes. In regard to the role of developmental factors, behavioral assessment takes an ahistorical approach, with the primary focus being on the current environmental conditions that maintain behavior. Behavior is also assumed to be situationally specific since the hypothesized causes of behavior are situations rather than enduring, internal processes. Data, the behavioral sample, are the problematic behaviors, and treatment strategies are evaluated in terms of their ability to bring about changes (increase or decrease) in certain dimensions (frequency, latency, duration, amplitude) of the behavioral sample. Finally, the assessment is more complete the more direct, frequent, and situationally specific the behavioral sample.

The key issue—basic to the other differences—is whether behavior is viewed as a sign or a sample. Kirkland (1978, p. 14) pointed out that the pivotal idea in the shift from trait to behavioral assessment revolves around the dictum that the behavioral sample measures nothing beyond itself so that there is no theoretical basis for inferences beyond the behavioral sample. As Mischel (1972) correctly noted, the no-inference assumption means that sample predictor behavior should be as similar as possible to the behavior used on the criterion measure. In contrast to the no-inference viewpoint, the sign approach assumes that an inference can be made from the behavioral sample to internal personality processes as well as an inference from the internal processes to some future behavior.

This issue, the nature of the inference from the behavioral sample, is a crucial difference between personality and behavioral assessment that must be resolved for a productive integration of the respective knowledge bases of these two areas. For example, I have noted earlier (Burns, 1980) that the strict adherence to the no inference assumption would rule out the use of any form of measurement (e.g., self-report inventories, interview, standardized tests) that did not directly sample criterion behaviors in the environmental situation of interest; if the sample of behavior from one population is used to make a decision about a different population of behavior that has not been sampled, then there is a clear violation of the above assumption—the "other population" in this case is not some underlying trait (internal process) but, rather, a different nonsampled population of behaviors.

Consider the following example: I ask an individual the number of cigarettes he or she smokes per day by means of a questionnaire and I also directly observe the number of cigarettes the person smokes on a given day. These two behavioral samples represent different populations of behavior and, as such, the no-inference assumption of behavioral assessment does not provide a theoretical framework for making an inference from the behavioral sample of the questionnaire to the behavioral sample of direct observation, or vice versa. A researcher could argue that criterion validity is a sufficient rationale to justify the inference from the first behavioral sample to the second (e.g., does self-report on the questionnaire predict smoking behavior?). However, such "dust bowl empiricism" may make the development of behavioral assessment more disorganized than if there was an explicit theoretical framework to indicate how an inference can be made from one behavioral sample to another. I must stress that the issue of making an inference from one behavioral sample to another behavioral sample is different from the traditional inference of personality assessment—an inference from a behavioral sample (questionnaire or direct observation of smoking) to internal personality processes (self-destructive id impulses).

Paradigmatic behaviorism assumes that the behavioral sample can measure something beyond itself and provides a theoretical rationale for this assumption within a behavioral framework. This assumption is the key to the integration of personality and behavioral assessment. I will now describe how the theory attempts this integration. This will first involve a discussion of the personality level of the theory, since this provides the foundation for a discussion of the measurement level.

Paradigmatic Behaviorism's Personality Level of Theory

As indicated already, one of the continual schisms between behavioral and nonbehavioral approaches has been in the area of personality. The rejection by behaviorism of the assumptions of traditional personality theory (i.e., internal causation, continuity, and generality assumptions) in favor of environmental causation and situationism resulted in a considerable amount of controversy between the two positions (e.g., Bem, 1972; Kenrick & Braver, 1982; Mischel, 1968, 1969; Rushton, Jackson, & Paunonen, 1981; Wachtel, 1973). As an outgrowth of the futility of an extreme either/or position, the focus shifted to an interactional emphasis (Bandura, 1977b; Bem & Funder, 1978; Magnusson & Endler, 1977; Mischel, 1973, 1977, 1979). This shift was largely the result of a set of empirical studies that demonstrated that personality-by-situation interactions account for more behavioral variance than their separate effects (see Magnusson & Endler, 1977). In other words, rather than the situation or the individual's personality determining behavior, behavior came to be treated as the result of a continuous interaction between individuals and the situations they encounter.

It is important to indicate that this shift to an interactional viewpoint has been labeled as a rediscovery of the past by some (e.g., Jackson & Paunonen, 1980) referring to earlier interactional theory of personality such as Julian Rotter's social learning theory. In his original formulation of the theory, Rotter (1954) put forth a concept of personality and personality–environment interaction within a cognitive learning framework. He also indicated how various measurement procedures (e.g., structured interviews, questionnaires, and behavioral tests) could be used to assess three dimensions: behavior, a person's expectancy for the obtainment of certain goals, and the reinforcement value of these goals. Rotter also very early described the importance of the psychological situation for the prediction of goal-directed behavior (Rotter, 1960). His social learning theory thus clearly antedated some of the more recent developments in Bandura's and Mischel's social learning theories.

In the transition to an interactional approach, Bandura's and Mischel's social learning theories introduced a personality level into their theories (e.g., Bandura's internal cognitive events, Mischel's person variables) as well as interactional principles (Bandura, 1977b, 1977b; Mischel, 1973). However, several questions arise as to the exact nature of personality within these formulations—for instance, whether traits are causal entities, summary labels for behavior, mediators or intervening variables—and in regard to the nature of and data base for interactional principles (Buss, 1977; Krauskopf, 1978; Staats, 1980). The trend seems to have been for former situational positions to have adopted a personality level and interactional principles without deriving these developments in a systematic way. This lack of specificity in regard to what is meant by person variables (personality), the environment, and how the two interact, is a weakness and poses theoretical and practical problems. That is, if the person and environmental variables remain as global, poorly specified conceptions, then the possibility of actually obtaining specific, analytic accounts of how the two jointly produce behavior and additional learning is reduced (cf., Staats, Chapter 2, this vol.). Though somewhat overlooked by the developments toward an interactional position, paradigmatic behaviorism's goal has been to conduct this type of specific analysis of personality and the environment, as well as to enumerate the various forms of interaction between the two.

Basic Behavioral Repertoires and Their Interaction

Within paradigmatic behaviorism, personality is defined as consisting of basic behavioral repertoires of skills (Staats, 1975). It is hypothesized that while these basic behavioral repertoires (BBRs) are learned through prior experiences, the repertoires also function in a causative and interactive manner with other BBRs and the stimulus situation in affecting the subsequent behavior, experience, and learning of the individual. Paradigmatic behaviorism thus considers personality to be both a dependent and an independent variable (see also Figure 5.1).

This conception of personality has several features important to

E ⟶ BBRs ⇄ B ⇄ E

| Past Environmental Situations | Personality Repertoires | 1. Behavior 2. Experience 3. Learning | Environment |

E

Current Environmental Situation

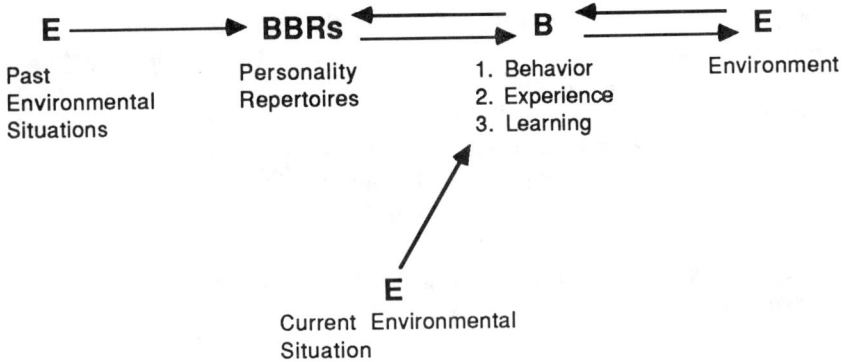

FIGURE 5.1 Paradigmatic behaviorism's personality conception.

the unification of behavioral and nonbehavioral approaches to personality. The specification of these features of the BBR concept will indicate how personality and the environment are treated in paradigmatic behaviorism as well as the nature of the behavioral interactional principles. The specification of a BBR will provide information on (1) the constellation or population of the behaviors making up the BBR; (2) the specific learning conditions necessary to establish the BBR; (3) the importance of the elements in BBR as prerequisites for the acquisition of additional skills within and across BBRs; (4) how the BBR and the situation exert a joint influence in producing behavior; and (5) how the BBR will reciprocally interact with the environment to determine subsequent learning (i.e., the elaboration of the BBR and the establishment of new BBRs) as well as the behavior of the individual in later situations (Burns, 1980).

Personality is thus considered to consist of BBRs. While these BBRs are learned (i.e., a dependent variable), the repertoires, once learned, also have a causative influence in determining the individual's behavior, experience and subsequent learning. The BBRs have this causative influence in several ways. First, the behavioral elements within the BBR or the BBR itself are often prerequisites for the acquisition of additional elements within the BBR or other BBRs. For example, the child's verbal-imitational BBR (i.e., the child's ability to repeat sounds, words, and phrases) is a prerequisite repertoire for the acquisition of the object-labeling BBR. That is, the child must be able to imitate the words of the adult prior to being able to produce labels for objects (Rondal, Chapter 4, this vol.).

The above example represents the situation where one BBR is a prerequisite for another BBR. The other variation is where the elements within the BBR facilitate the acquisition of additional elements within the same BBR. For example, the child's sensory-motor—imitational BBR (e.g., the child's ability to copy various geometric shapes with a pencil) is acquired in a process that requires many learning trials to add the first behavioral elements to the repertoire. However, these skills make the addition of the subsequent skills more and more rapid so that after sufficient training the child is able to copy novel geometric shapes with a high degree of accuracy on his or her first attempt (Staats & Burns, 1981).

The principle that Staats has used to describe these two situations (i.e., where one BBR is a prerequisite for another and where the elements within the BBR facilitate the acquisition of additional elements within the same BBR) is the principle of *cumulative-hierarchical learning* (Staats, 1968a). These two examples also represent an indirect *personality–behavior interaction*. The interaction is considered indirect because here the personality repertoire does not directly cause the behavior but rather determines subsequent behavior by producing circumstances that will determine whether or not other behaviors are acquired or maintained.

The second way that the BBR can have a causative influence on behavior is through the BBR and the current situation impacting the individual's behavior. This represents a *personality–environment interaction* in that both the BBR and the situation determine behavior. The strength of paradigmatic behaviorism's personality—environment interaction position is the analytic manner in which personality (BBR concept) and the environment (specific stimulus events) are defined, as well as the more precise specification of the interaction. An experiment (Staats & Burns, 1982) that exemplifies this analytic approach will be described later.

A third way that the BBR can have a causative influence is in the form of a *personality–environment–personality interaction* (Staats, 1971a). Here the BBR affects the individual's social and physical environment in ways that result in the further elaboration of the BBR; or the BBR and situation produce behavior, experience, or learning that then results in additional personality development. Once the BBR has been changed in this reciprocal process, the individual's behavior in later situations will also be affected (i.e., the personality repertoire affects the environment, the environment then affects the personality repertoire, and then the modified personality repertoire and some future situation produce behavior, etc.). What constitutes the independent or dependent variable in this process is arbitrary since it depends upon the particular focus (i.e., where the behavioral stream is demarcated).

An example may help to clarify this particular type of interaction. Consider the individual whose learning experiences have produced inappropriate or deficit BBRs for certain situations in the area of social competence. These inappropriate or deficit BBRs result in behavior (e.g., inappropriate verbal behavior such as sexist remarks) that changes the person's social environment (e.g., avoidance of the person by others) which then results in the addition of more inappropriate behaviors to the BBRs or the missed opportunity to learn more appropriate behaviors. These modified BBRs then produce additional behavior that further affects the environment, which further affects the personality repertoires. Clients with interpersonal difficulties often seem to be caught in such cumulative downward spirals.

Paradigmatic behaviorism also assumes that a person's physical attributes can determine the response of the social environment and, in this manner, influence the further development of the repertoires. For example, the more attractive child is expected to experience more positive responses from other people than the less attractive child. As a consequence the more atractive child will have greater opportunity for positive social interactions that will further facilitate the development of social skills and a more positive self-concept. Physical attributes may thus be treated in a way similar to personality repertoires in their role in the determination of behavior, experience, and future learning. Such an analysis has received additional support from recent clinical research reporting an inverse relationship between physical attractiveness and self-perception of mental disorder (Burns & Farina, 1987) and actual severity of mental disorder (Farina, Burns, Austad, Bugglin, & Fischer, 1986; Farina et al., 1977).

This section has described the BBR concept and some of the behavioral interactional principles. I will now describe some specific BBRs in greater detail and indicate how these repertoires are organized into three general personality systems.

Tripartite Personality Conception

Many classification schemes have been proposed for the understanding of personality (e.g., the classification schemes by Freud, Rogers, Eysenck, Cattell) or to guide assessment (e.g., triple response mode assessment, multimethod-multibehavior matrix). Paradigmatic behaviorism suggests that in a descriptive sense it is useful to consider personality as consisting of three broad personality systems: the *emotional-motivational personality system, the language-cognitive personality system,* and the *sensory-motor personality system.*

Several of the other chapters describe the acquisition and function of these repertoires in the context of clinical problems. Here I will attempt to provide a general overview of paradigmatic behaviorism's conception of personality to show how it provides the theoretical structure for the integration of personality and behavioral assessment. Thus, rather than focusing on any specific clinical content area as some of the following chapters do, I will focus more on the overall theoretical framework. First, however, it is important to emphasize that this tripartite personality conception is meant to be descriptive and not meant to indicate that these structures actually exist within the individual (Staats, 1975). Also, it should be understood that it is the complex interaction between the BBRs in the three personality systems that provides the theoretical rationale for the integration of personality and behavioral assessment. Later in the chapter I will also describe how paradigmatic behaviorism's tripartite personality conception differs from triple-response mode assessment.

Emotional-Motivational Personality System

The emotional-motivational system consists of environmental and behavioral stimuli that elicit positive and negative emotional responses in the individual (e.g., work stimuli, political stimuli, sexual stimuli, food stimuli). The individual's personal, familial, social, and cultural experiences determine which stimuli become part of the emotional-motivational system, as well as which particular stimuli elicit positive or negative emotional responses. The three functions of emotional stimuli are deduced from combining classical and instrumental conditioning principles. That is, emotional stimuli have attitudinal, reinforcer, and directive functions, as discussed more fully by Lohr and Hamberger (Chapter 7, this vol.).

A central aspect of the approach is that empirical specification is necessary to validate the theory's conception of personality and its implications for traditional personality measures. In a series of these early studies (Staats, Gross, Guay, & Carlson, 1973), the Strong Vocational Interest Blank was employed to select individuals with different emotional-motivational systems. It was demonstrated that test items on the Strong have attitudinal and reinforcer stimulus functions and that individuals approached and avoided stimuli consistent with their vocational interests as defined by a summary score on the Strong.

A more recent study along similar lines (Staats & Burns, 1982) was designed to test for a personality–environment interaction in terms of the directive stimulus function (i.e., to show how the individual's emotional-motivational system and the stimulus situation jointly determine behavior). The results showed that individuals who had opposite emotional-motivational systems in terms of religious stimuli—as assessed through their scores on the Allport–Vernon–Lindsey Study of Values—responded differently when presented with the same stimulus situation: high-religious individuals approached religious words more rapidly than low-religious individuals; low religious individuals avoided religious words more rapidly than high-religious individuals; high-religious individuals approached religious words more rapidly than they avoided such words; and low-religious individuals avoided the religious words more rapidly than they approached them. Thus, on the basis of a summary score traditionally used to index the overall strength of an individual's religious values within a trait framework, it was possible to predict how individual differences would be determined by a different set of religious stimuli. When individuals were presented with the same stimulus situation, the differences in the emotional-motivational system were shown to produce differences in behavior—thereby demonstrating one way that this particular personality system can have a causative role in the determination of behavior.

These studies suggest how the concept of the emotional-motivational system is relevant for understanding the development and function of such traditional personality traits as values and vocational interests. The theory also proposes that individual differences in the emotional-motivational personality system are relevant for understanding part of what is meant by such traits or constructs as masculinity-femininity, extraversion-introversion, the self-concept, and so on. Finally, the theory shows how it is possible to consider the test items of some personality inventories to have affective-reinforcing-directive (A-R-D) value, and thus to indirectly measure the A-R-D value of environmental events or behaviors represented by the items.

Language-Cognitive Personality System

As Rondal described in the preceding chapter, another major schism in psychology is between the cognitive (nativistic) and behavioral approaches to language (e.g., Piaget and Chomsky vs. Watson and

Skinner). In a general sense the cognitive approaches have been concerned with the development of language from somewhat innate cognitive structures and with the functions of language, while the behavioral approaches have focused on language as a learned verbal behavior, thus ignoring the causative role of language. A goal of paradigmatic behaviorism over the years has been to integrate the acquisition and function of language within a behavioral framework. This has involved an attempt to describe the learning principles involved in the acquisition of language repertoires, as well as describing the causative, personality functions of these language-cognitive repertoires, which I will now briefly describe.

The *verbal-motor BBR* consists of the population of words, phrases, and sentences that control motor behavior (e.g., run, come, see, examine, "Pass the salt," "Please complete a mental status examination on the patient."). This repertoire is crucial to many aspects of our daily functioning, and it is also crucial to therapy since it is involved, along with other repertoires, in the client's ability to carry out explicit therapeutic instructions. Such might occur with an overly self-critical client who has difficulty accepting appropriate compliments from others. Here the therapist might say to the client something as follows: "When someone gives you a compliment, rather than negating it, make eye contact with the person and say thank-you." In a subsequent session when the therapist praised the client for the completion of a particular homework assignment and the client negated this compliment, then the therapist could prompt the client to label what had just occurred in the therapeutic interaction. This provides a behavioral interpretation of the concept of "insight" in therapy. Moreover, the theory has used other language repertoires (e.g., the verbal-emotional) to deal with "nonspecific" aspects of therapy such as rapport, empathy, and so on (Staats, 1972; Wilson & Evans, 1977).

The *verbal-emotional BBR* consists of the population of words and phrases that elicit positive and negative emotional responses and thus also have reinforcer and directive stimulus functions (A-R-D value). The two studies described earlier indicated how test items can serve these functions. Since the words are hypothesized to have similar A-R-D value to the objects and events represented by the words, how the individual responds to the words provides information on how the individual will respond to the objects and events. Directly measuring the verbal-emotional BBR in the language-cognitive system indirectly assesses the role of the emotional-motivational system in determining behavior. As Rosenbaum proposes in the next chapter, this repertoire may play a role in the development of the individual's self-concept since people employ the words in their verbal-emotional repertoire to label their own behavior (e.g., good, bad, wonderful, awful, depressing, attractive, intelligent). Later chapters (e.g., Eifert, Hekmat, Heiby & Staats) describe the importance of this particular repertoire for behavior therapy.

The *word-image, image-word,* and *image-motor BBRs* reflect individual differences in the ability of language stimuli to elicit images, the ability of individuals to describe their images, and the ability of images to guide motor behavior, respectively (Staats & Lohr, 1979). For example, a client's ability to describe his or her dreams and wishes is partly determined by the image-word repertoire. In turn, the word-image BBR is involved in many behavior therapy procedures where words are used to elicit images (Hekmat, Chapter 9, this vol.; Lohr & Hamberger, Chapter 7, this vol.).

The various *labeling BBRs* (e.g., picture, multiword, object, self, and social labeling repertoires) are relevant to many facets of a person's adjustment. At a very early age the child begins to learn labels for various objects and pictures of objects (e.g., car, shoe, tree, knife, stove, etc.). This repertoire is very important for the child's adjustment and all the major intelligence tests for children include test items to sample the picture and object labeling repertoires (Staats, 1963). Later the child learns to label classes of objects (e.g., fruits) which become increasing complex (e.g., living things) as well as various attributes of objects (e.g., color, size, shape, texture). Finally, as the child's labeling skills continue to develop, he or she learns to label the actions of others or natural events (jumping, crying, relating, judging, competing) and to label his or her own behavior and physical characteristics. By the time the child becomes an adult, the social and self-labeling BBRs are very complex and can be the source of much happiness or unhappiness. For example, much of my own therapy time with clients involves an attempt to move their social and self-labeling repertoires in a direction more isomorphic with consensual reality (e.g., "How is it that you believe you are a bad student when your GPA is 3.8?" "What might be some other reasons your boss had a frown rather than her being mad at you?" "Your friends seem to view you as an attractive and socially skilled person yet you do not consider yourself such."). Given that BBRs are assumed to have causative properties, a change in the self-labeling repertoire in a more positive direction is expected to result in better adjustment. Deficits in appropriate labeling are also implicated in a variety of psychological disorders (e.g., anxiety and depression, see also Chapters 8 through 10, this vol.).

Although I have described some of the BBRs in the language-cognitive personality system separately, it is their simultaneous functioning that is relevant to the understanding of the role of language in such areas as the individual's reasoning, self-concept, and world view. A simple example is when someone labels his or her boss as being upset and then proceeds to reason that "the boss must be mad at me—did I do something wrong—oh, I do everything wrong" with the negative emotional response produced by these reasoning sequences leading to avoidance of the boss or anxiety in the presence of the boss. More complex examples of the simultaneous functioning of the BBRs in the language-cognitive system are presented in the next chapter.

Sensory-Motor Personality System

While instrumental behavior was discussed earlier in the context of the emotional-motivational system (e.g., approach or avoidance instrumental behavior) and in the discussion of the language-cognitive system (e.g., motor behavior under the control of language), the sensory-motor personality system deals with the vast individual differences that are found in instrumental or sensory-motor skills. Many areas of human functioning such as athletic skills, sexual skills, musical skills, social skills, and vocational skills may be viewed as partly involving individual differences in the sensory-motor personality system. Another area relevant to the sensory-motor personality system is in regard to the young child learning the many motor skills important for development: toileting, eating, crawling, standing alone, walking, reaching for objects, imitating the motor actions of others, holding a pencil, tracing and copying shapes, and so on. For example, a series of experiments has studied in detail how young children acquire a sensory-motor-imitational BBR in the process of learning to copy and write the letters of the alphabet, as well as the function of this repertoire for subsequent learning (Staats & Burns, 1981). It has traditionally been thought that the child's ability to copy geometric shapes is related to maturation (e.g., the idea that a child who can copy a square at age 5 will not be able to copy a diamond until age 7). However, the experimental-longitudinal research conducted within the framework of paradigmatic behaviorism—where a very detailed record of every stimulus, every response (letter-writing trial), and every reinforcer is kept over an extended period—shows in a specific manner the lengthy learning process involved with this particular repertoire, a process requiring thousands of learning trials. Variations in sensory-motor skills are thus considered to constitute an important aspect of personality.

The BBR concept and the behavioral interactional principles provide a basis for a causative concept of personality, continuity, and generality assumptions within a behavioral sample approach. The BBR concept and interactional principles also provide the basis for paradigmatic behaviorism's tripartite view of personality, consisting of the emotional-motivational, language-cognitive, and sensory-motor personality systems. In turn, the tripartite personality conception provides a framework for a tripartite approach to assessment (affective-cognitive-behavioral assessment), and thus the possibility of the integration of personality and behavioral assessment—the focus of the next section.

Paradigmatic Behaviorism's Measurement Level of Theory

The measurement methods of personality assessment have mainly involved paper-and-pencil assessment devices (intelligence tests, objective and projective personality tests) and interviews. The data that are obtained by these methods are viewed as tapping internal personality processes, with such data traditionally being used to make decisions about diagnosis, etiology, and prognosis. In contrast, as indicated earlier, the goal of behavioral assessment is the quantification of behavior (amplitude, frequency, duration, latency) in a situation that is as close to the criterion situation as possible.

Paradigmatic behaviorism's personality conception provides a means to integrate these two approaches to measurement (Staats, 1986; Staats & Fernandez-Ballesteros, 1987). This integration involves two main aspects. The first is the specification of five sites for assessment. These sites are (1) the original learning of the personality repertoires, (2) the personality repertoires, (3) the current environmental situation, (4) the current behavior in a particular situation, and (5) the impact of behavior upon the environment which then further affects behavior and the personality repertoires.

The second aspect is the specification of how one sample of behavior can provide information about another nonsampled population of behavior (e.g., under what circumstances self-report can predict nontest behavior). An implication of the second point is that the directness/indirectness of a behavioral sample is a function of whether the behavioral sample is being used to make inferences to the population of behavior from which the sample is drawn (a direct inference), or to make inferences to a nonsampled population of behavior (an indirect inference). Thus, in the present approach, the

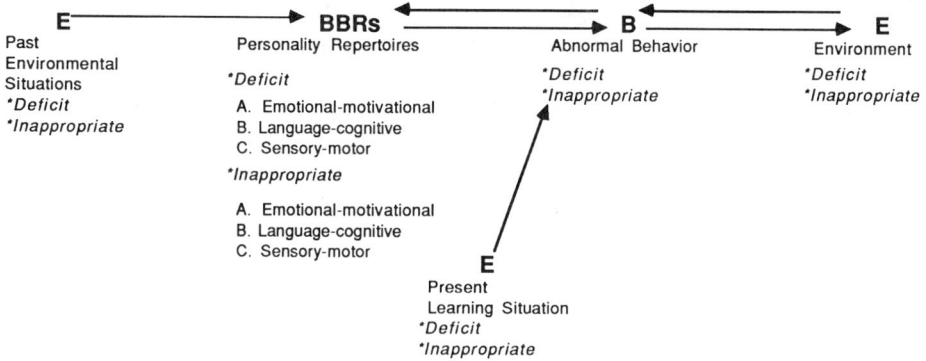

FIGURE 5.2 Paradigmatic behaviorism's conception of abnormal behavior and abnormal personality. (Based on Stats, 1975.)

directness or indirectness of a measurement method is determined by the nature of the inference and not by measurement method. Figure 5.2. based on Staats (1975), shows the five assessment sites that are involved in paradigmatic behaviorism's conception of abnormal behavior. I will now attempt to show how paradigmatic behaviorism can unify personality and behavioral assessment by discussing each of these sites.

Assessment of the Original Learning of the BBRs

Obviously, the processes involved in humans learning to be humans are complex and occur over long periods of time. As described above, Staats has argued in favor of an experimental-longitudinal methodology that permits the detailed study of the acquisition of the repertoires. This research has focused on how young children learn language, reading, arithmetic, writing, and verbal concepts (Staats & Burns, 1981; Staats, Minke, & Butts, 1970). While there is much research left to do in the study of the acquisition of the BBRs that facilitate adjustment, this research has, nonetheless, shown that it is possible to specify some of the BBRs important to the child's adjustment, to indicate the learning principles involved in the acquisition of the repertoires, and to study in a detailed and analytic manner the child's learning of these repertoires.

This knowledge has implications for the treatment of problems as well as the prevention of problems. For example, in Chapter 3 Minke describes a study (Collette-Harris & Minke, 1978) where

Foundations for Applied Paradigmatic Behaviorism

prior research on the acquisition of the reading repertoires allowed the design of a successful treatment program for dyslexia. Another study by Ryback and Staats (1970) showed that the parents of children with dyslexia could successfully employ the treatment procedures to improve their children's reading skills. Other studies (Staats, Minke, & Butts, 1970; Staats, Minke, Goodwin, & Landeen, 1967) have demonstrated that various nonprofessionals are able to use the treatment program in the amelioration of reading problems. Though it is not possible to assess in a direct manner the past learning of a person who has just entered the clinic for treatment, the point here is that knowledge of the acquisition of the repertoires will help in attempting to establish the deficit BBRs or change inappropriate BBRs. It should also be pointed out that knowledge of the normal acquisition process is also relevant for parents, teachers, and other educators in order to use such knowledge for the prevention of problems.

Assessment of the Personality Repertoires

A major aim of measurement procedures that focus on the personality repertoires, the second of the five sites in the assessment model, is to look for deficits in or inappropriate aspects of BBRs in regard to a particular assessment question. By discussing how each of the personality systems can be assessed, I will suggest possibilities for using the tripartite personality conception to make an inference from one behavioral sample to a nonsampled population of behavior.

Assessment of the Emotional-Motivational System

The *direct measurement of the individual's emotional-motivational system* involves the observation of which stimulus events elicit approach (striving toward) and avoidance (striving against) behavior, which stimulus events function as reinforcers, and which stimulus events elicit emotional responses. It is the covariation between these three functions of stimuli in the emotional-motivational system that means that the measurement of one function will provide information on the other stimulus functions. For example, if young children elicit sexual arousal in a person, then such children would also elicit a class of approach behavior as well as positively reinforce the behaviors that brought the person in contact with them. The following measurement methods are commonly involved in the direct assessment of the emotional-motivational system: (1) the direct observation of behavior in the relevant environment by trained observers; (2) physiological recording of emotional responses to stimuli in the relevant environment; (3) participant monitoring (e.g., a parent monitoring a child's dog phobia by keeping a record of the child's approach and avoidance behavior in regard to dogs, the length of time the child remained in the presence of various dogs, indices of nervousness in the presence of dogs, etc.); and (4) self-monitoring (e.g., the individual recording what stimulus events are approached and avoided in the relevant environment—parties he or she attended, length of time there). Each of these measurement methods allows the direct assessment of one or more of the three functions of stimuli in the individual's emotional-motivational system.

Analogue stimulus situations can also be employed in the direct assessment of the emotional-motivational system (e.g., clinic playrooms, behavioral avoidance tests). For example, Eyberg and Robinson (1982) developed a structured playroom interaction that allows the assessment of bonding between parent and child along with other aspects of the parent–child interaction. This procedure was developed to provide a clinic measure of conduct disorder in young children as well as to measure the effect of parent–child interaction therapy on this childhood problem (Eyberg & Matarazzo, 1980). In terms of the current discussion regarding the direct measurement of the emotional-motivational system in analogue situations, this procedure measures the degree to which the child's behavior has positive or negative A-R-D value for the parent as well as the parent's A-R-D value for the child. For example, if a parent has negative A-R-D value for the child, then the child will avoid, strive against, hit, argue with, and/or run away from the parent since the parent (or the parent's verbal command) elicits a negative emotional response in the child. The parent in this example would also be ineffective as a positive reinforcer for the child.

The point of this example is that it is possible to create analogue environments that allow the direct assessment of the emotional-motivational system. The indirectness of this procedure (i.e., the inference) is in terms of the stimulus (clinic to home) and time dimensions. Analogue situations can thus provide a direct measurement of the emotional-motivational system, with the external validity or inference being partly dependent upon the degree of perceived similarity across the stimulus dimension.

The *indirect measurement of the emotional-motivational personality system* is accomplished through the measurement of the verbal-emotional BBR in the language-cognitive system. It is possible to assess the verbal-emotional BBR directly by measuring the directive stimulus function of words (e.g., rating of the words on a pleasant-unpleasant semantic differential scale), the emotional or physiological responses elicited by the words, or the reinforcing value of words. Since many of the self-report inventories (e.g., Strong Vocational Interest Blank, Study of Values, Minnesota Multiphasic Personality Inventory (MMPI), Reinforcement Survey Schedule) contain items that require individuals to indicate what they like or dislike, find pleasant or unpleasant, prefer to do or not to do, and so on, this type of test item measures the verbal-emotional BBR by assessing the directive stimulus function of the words making up the test items. The theory thus suggests that an inference can be made from the direct measurement of the verbal-emotional BBR to a nonsampled population of behavior determined by a certain aspect of the emotional-motivational system, because the emotional responses elicited by the words will be similar to those elicited by the environmental and behavioral events that the words represent.

The emotional-motivational personality system can be indirectly assessed in other ways as well. For example, retrospective ratings by others can be used to measure indirectly the rated person's emotional-motivational system. This indirect measurement of the rated person's emotional-motivation system is accomplished by directly sampling various labeling BBRs in the language-cognitive system of the individual providing the ratings. Thus, if I was asked to rate my friend's political values, the assessment would focus on my social labeling BBR or my ability to label his or her political behavior accurately.

The individual's emotional-motivational system can also be indirectly assessed by the measurement of the A-R-D value of pictures, video and audio recordings (e.g., the person's penile tumescence response to pictures). In this example one would be directly measuring BBRs in the language-cognitive system (e.g., picture labeling, verbal-emotional, word-image and image-word BBRs) in order to assess indirectly certain aspects of the person's emotional-motivational system (i.e., how the person would response to the actual events represented by the video tapes). It is the relationship between the BBRs in the language-cognitive and emotional-motivational systems that provides a theoretical basis for how one sample of behavior can provide information on a nonsampled population of behavior.

Assessment of the Sensory-Motor System

The sensory-motor personality system can be directly measured through the direct observation by trained observers of the individual's sensory-motor skills in the relevant environmental situation. Self-monitoring can also be used to measure this personality system directly. Each of these measures can provide a direct measure of the individual's sensory-motor skills in particular areas such as recreation, vocational, or social skills. This is not meant to imply that the sensory-motor system is the sole determinant of behaviors representative of the above constructs. Repertoires in the other two systems are relevant as well. This issue will be addressed shortly.

The sensory-motor system can be indirectly measured through the measurement of complex self-labeling BBRs in the language-cognitive system. Such self-report inventories as the Guilford-Zimmerman Temperament Survey, Rathus Assertiveness Inventory, and various behavioral checklists contain items that require individuals to judge the quality of their sensory-motor skills. Thus, just as the individual learns to label the skills of others or to self-monitor his or her own skills in the relevant situation, so can the person respond to test items that inquire about his or her sensory-motor skills (e.g., "You usually make eye contact when listening to people").

Retrospective ratings by others, as when a parent completes a rating scale on a child (e.g., Eyberg Child Behavior Inventory, see Eyberg, 1980; Robinson, Eyberg, & Ross, 1980), is another method that can indirectly measure an individual's sensory-motor system by directly measuring the labeling BBRs in the language-cognitive system of the parent. Items on this questionnaire include: (1) "Has poor table manners," (19) "Destroys toys and other objects," (27) "Physically fights with sisters and brothers," and (36) "Wets the bed." In this example it is the labeling BBRs of the parent that are being directly assessed to provide information on the sensory-motor skills of the child (e.g., aggressive sensory-motor skills). This point again indicates how the behavioral sample can measure something beyond itself—that is, how a sample of behavior that measures certain BBRs in the language-cognitive system of the parent can provide information about a nonsampled population of behaviors in the sensory-motor system of the child. Of course, there may be a lack of isomorphism between the sensory-motor skills of the child and the labeling repertoires of the parent. This issue, rather than leading to the absolute rejection of indirect measurement, is treated as an additional source of information to incorporate into the assessment model.

Assessment of the Language-Cognitive System

As mentioned earlier, the causal properties of the BBRs in the language-cognitive system are relevant to understanding such traditional constructs as self-concept, intelligence, problem solving, beliefs, and values. The direct measurement of the repertoires in the language-cognitive system involves the assessment of the BBRs that make up the above constructs and others. For instance,· many of the test items on the Stanford-Binet and Wechsler intelligence tests directly sample some of the BBRs in the language-cognitive system and the predictive value of intelligence tests stems from the relevance of the BBRs sampled by test items to individual functioning and adjustment in various situations. For instance, since the labeling repertoire is relevant to the child's functioning and further learning, a sampling of the repertoire will allow predictions to be made regarding how the repertoire will determine future behavior. This is the manner in which paradigmatic behaviorism accounts for the predictive value of intelligence tests. It should also be noted that R.O. Nelson (1980) extended this analysis with her discussion of how behavior therapists might use intelligence tests.

Since a major focus of paradigmatic behaviorism has been on the development and function of language (Rondal, Chapter 4, this vol.), it also provides a theoretical framework for the current interest in cognitive assessment within behavioral assessment and therapy (e.g., Kendall & Hollon, 1981). For example, the interest in cognitive assessment on the role of self-statements in psychopathology is treated by paradigmatic behaviorism as one aspect of language function (see Eifert, 1987; Chapter 8, this vol.). The idea of self-statements or inner speech consisting of multiple BBRs is an important contribution that makes the distinction between cognitive assessment and behavioral assessment unnecessary.

I have attempted to show in this section how the BBRs in the three personality systems can be directly or indirectly assessed by various measurement methods. A key issue was to indicate how paradigmatic behaviorism provides a theoretical rationale for how one sample of behavior can provide information about another, nonsampled population of behavior. I will now describe the other sites for assessment.

Assessment of the Present Stimulus Situation

Figure 5.2 shows why it would be important to assess the current stimulus situation in addition to the BBRs. One reason for this is that it is the current situation and the BBR that determine behavior, experience, and learning. A second reason is that the BBRs in the language-cognitive system and the emotional-motivational system help to determine how the current situation is perceived, labeled, and emotionally experienced by the individual. A third reason is that the situation can be deficit or inappropriate for adjustment (Staats & Burns, 1982). Just as inappropriate or deficit past learning conditions can give rise to inappropriate or deficit personality repertoires, so can a deficit or inappropriate current stimulus situation help to maintain maladjusted behavior. A good example of this is the failure of treatment generalization to occur because the client has returned to a deficit or inappropriate situation which maintains the problematic behavior.

Assessment of Behavior

Figure 5.2 indicates that a fourth site for measurement is the actual deficit or inappropriate behavior that the individual displays in a given situation. In a traditional clinical context—for example, the *Diagnostic Statistical Manual of Mental Disorders*, third edition revised (DSM-III-R)—this assessment site deals with what has been labeled as the symptoms of abnormal behavior. Is there any real difference between the assessment of "symptoms" or abnormal behaviors and the assessment of BBRs in the three personality systems? I see this issue as a subtle, but crucial point in the unification of personality and behavioral assessment. That is, the abnormal behavior (symptom) can be viewed as a single behavioral element from a population of behavioral elements from one or more BBRs. The abnormal behavior is a symptom in that it is the product of a BBR and a situation, with the BBR being populated by many behavioral elements or possible "symptoms." This matter is relevant to paradigmatic behaviorism's treatment of symptom substitution and other traditional clinical topics (Heiby & Staats, Chapter 10, this vol.; Voeltz & Evans, 1982).

Assessment of the Environment and Behavior–Environment Interactions

The fifth assessment site deals with the response of the social environment to the person's behavior or, stated slightly differently, the impact of the person's behavior or attributes on the environment (Figure 5.2). For example, a particular assessment question could require information on the environmental response to the person's behavior. This is important because a person's deficit or inappropriate behavior can create a deficit or inappropriate environment for the person, with this deficit or inappropriate environment then leading to further deficit or inappropriate behavior as well as deficit or inappropriate personality development. An example of a deficit behavior creating a deficit environment would be when the child's language deficits lead to the placement of the child in the deficit environment of an institution. In turn, the child's deficit behavior can also create an inappropriate environment. An example of this would be when the child's failure to acquire toilet skills results in punishment for accidents. In this situation the deficit in the child's skills has created an inappropriate and aversive environment that then further compounds the child's problems. This is discussed further in Chapter 12 by Léduc, Dumais, and Evans. This reciprocal interaction between behavior and the environment can thus result in the additional development of inappropriate personality repertoires and/or the missed opportunity to learn more adjustive repertoires.

There are two additional points relevant to this discussion. The first is that Figure 5.2 involves a time dimension, of significance for the three assessment sites that deal with the environment (i.e., past learning conditions, the present stimulus situation, and the environmental response to the behavior). What is the environmental response to the behavior at one point in time becomes the present stimulus situation at a later point in time and at a still later point in time the past learning conditions.

The final point here is that personality and behavioral assessment have differentially focused on the five sites in Figure 5.2. For example, behavioral assessment has stressed the present stimulus situation, the behavior and the environmental response to the behavior. In turn, traditional personality assessment, as noted earlier, has stressed the assessment of internal personality processes and antecedent events. Paradigmatic behaviorism's model of abnormal behavior and assessment brings the different focuses together into an integrated and comprehensive framework. The interests of neither approach are rejected by fiat, but the integration is not eclectic. The integration is instead accomplished within a consistent set of principles as well as being part of a larger theoretical system. In the next section I will suggest how the five assessment dimensions are relevant to some current issues in behavioral assessment.

Current Trends in Behavioral Assessment

Within behavioral assessment there are at least two developments that suggest the emergence of a concept of personality. One trend is the increased interest in the study of covariations between various samples of behavior. The second is the triple-response-mode assessment concept. While these two topics are related, I will first discuss the relevance of paradigmatic behaviorism to the study of behavioral covariation, followed by a discussion of the triple-response mode assessment concept.

Behavioral Covariation

A current interest in behavioral assessment is the covariation between behaviors (Evans, 1986; Evans & Scheuer, 1987; Voeltz & Evans, 1982). As I indicated earlier, paradigmatic behaviorism argues that a behavioral sample can measure something beyond itself (i.e., provide information on a nonsampled population of behavior). This point is the key to the integration of personality and behavioral assessment and to guiding the study of covariation. For example, the theory indicates how the assessment of the verbal-emotional BBR in the language-cognitive system by means of a questionnaire in a clinician's office can provide information on how an aspect of the emotional-motivational system and a different stimulus situation (work) will determine a different class of behavior (e.g., approach or avoidance) at a later time. This example involves a generalization across the personality dimension (language-cognitive to emotional-motivational), the measurement dimension (questionnaire to direct observation), the setting dimension (clinician's office to work situation), the behavioral dimension (check marks on a questionnaire to approach or avoidance behavior), and the time dimension.

Evans (1986) criticized the triple-response-mode concept of fear and pointed out that "mode"-by-measurement method confounds have often clouded the question of covariations across behavioral samples (i.e., measuring the physiological domain by physiological recordings, the cognitive domain by self-report, and the motor domain by direct observation, thus confounding domain and method in the study of covariations across domains). However, in the above example I have intentionally "confounded" each dimension to stress how paradigmatic behaviorism's theoretical framework can guide the investigation of causal and correlational covariations across behavioral samples.

This framework for assessment allows for a greater degree of complexity than I will be able to develop at this time since various degrees of consistency or confound can occur across the measurement dimensions of paradigmatic behaviorism depending upon the measurement question. For example, the research question might require one to hold constant the personality system (verbal-emotional repertoire in the language-cognitive system), the stimulus setting (word stimuli), and the time (same day) and to vary the behavior (an emotional response and instrumental response such as a button press, marking a questionnaire, approach-and-avoidance behavior) and measurement method (quantification of a physiological response such as amount of salivation, quantification of the speed of approach-and-avoidance behavior, direct observation of whether the person made a right or left button press, questionnaire). This example is from a series of studies by Staats and associates on the emotional properties of language (Harms & Staats, 1978; Staats & Hammond, 1972; Staats, Minke, Martin, & Higa, 1972; Staats et al., 1973; Staats & Warren, 1974).

There is thus a good deal of complexity involved in paradigmatic behaviorism's theoretical framework for the study of covariation. This is an area where the framework needs to be spelled out in greater detail, and while I have only outlined the relevance of the approach for the study of behavioral covariations, I hope it reveals the potential of the approach for the integration of the research on covariation. I will now discuss how the approach can be applied to understanding traditional psychological constructs by considering paradigmatic behaviorism's tripartite personality system.

Triple Response Mode: The Example of Social Competence

Stimuli with A-R-D functions, such as stimuli in the verbal-emotional BBR, can be measured by physiological techniques, by questionnaire, and by the direct observation of motor behavior. This one repertoire, the verbal-emotional, can thus be measured in each of the domains of the triple-response-mode assessment model. The triple-response-mode approach is atheoretical compared to paradigmatic behaviorism. In paradigmatic behaviorism the three personality systems are considered to consist of specific BBRs, with the goal of measurement being to sample the population of behavioral elements in the BBR or the BBRs relevant to the construct. Since the theory describes how the BBRs are related, it provides a specific framework to guide the study of covariation. I will attempt to clarify these points by a brief discussion of the construct of social skills or social competence.

An inspection of the social competence literature reveals that there is a lack of consensus over definition. Bellack (1983) noted that there is no agreement as to the definition of social skill. Whereas some authors argue that the definition should exclude cognitive and perceptual factors, others advocate the inclusion of such aspects. In his own work, Bellack emphasized the central role of molecular elements in combination with a limited set of cognitive and social perceptual factors. In spite of this definitional problem, researchers have been willing to posit how the construct is relevant to adjustment (see Bellack & Morrison, 1982, for a list of the areas the construct has been applied to). It is also common to have the "social competence" model contrasted with other models of interpersonal adjustment such as the "conditioned anxiety" model, the "cognitive or social perception" model and the "physical attractiveness" model (Nelson, Hayes, Felton, & Jarrett, 1985). In the social competence or skill deficit model the individual's interpersonal problem is considered due to an inadequate or deficit repertoire of skills. The conditioned anxiety model assumes that the skills are present but that anxiety interferes with performance, while the cognitive model assumes that the problem is caused by the person's negative evaluation of his or her behavior and/or the inappropriate labeling of interpersonal situations. Finally, the physical attractiveness model assumes that the interpersonal difficulties result from the negative reaction of others to the person's physical appearance.

Rather than viewing the models in competition with each other, I see the models as corresponding to different aspects of paradigmatic behaviorism's conception of abnormal psychology, with the five sites shown in Figure 5.2 providing the basis to formulate a comprehensive treatment of social competence construct. For example, a judgment of social competence (i.e., an environmental response regarding the adequacy of a person's behavior given the requirements of a particular situation) would be viewed as partly a function of the BBRs in three personality systems. Social incompetence might be a result of deficit or inappropriate repertoires in the sensory-motor system (e.g., too little or too much eye contact, too few or too many gestures, too little or too much touching, standing too close or too distant).

Social incompetence might also be a result of deficit and/or inappropriate repertoires in the language-cognitive system. An example here would be when the individual's social labeling repertoire has deficits (i.e., the individual has not developed the necessary skills to label social interactions) or when this repertoire has inappropriate aspects (e.g., the person labels interpersonal situations in an inappropriate manner). In either case the faulty cognitive repertoires could result in interpersonal difficulties.

Given the complexity of a construct like social competence, assessment will probably indicate difficulties in all three personality systems as well as reciprocal interactions between the repertoires in the three systems. The interactions could result in a "downward spiral" such as where the avoidance of social situations restricts opportunities to learn language-cognitive or sensory-motor skills relevant to this situation, with this resulting in further anxiety and avoidance. It is important to stress that many possible reciprocal interactions could occur here (e.g., inappropriate repertoires in the language-cognitive system result in faulty social appraisal which results in inappropriate behavior which then results in social rejection followed by increased anxiety and avoidance). It is also possible that the primary problem might be more specific to a particular personality system (e.g., conditioned anxiety as specific to the emotional-motivational system, faulty cognitive appraisal as specific to the language-cognitive system, or deficit motor skills as specific to the sensory-motor system). Paradigmatic behaviorism's comprehensive approach to assessment would, however, provide a framework to isolate the major area of difficulty as well as to guide the search for possible reciprocal interactions between repertoires.

The above discussion has primarily focused on the relevance of the personality repertoires for an understanding of social competence. However, the other four sites in the assessment model are relevant as well. For example, a thorough explanation of social competence would also require knowledge of the demands of a particular situation and the criteria by which the environment (judgments by other) evaluates a person's behavior as socially competent or socially incompetent in that particular situation. Thus the present situation, the behavior in that situation, and the environmental response to the behavior are important assessment sites. In addition, it is important to understand the acquisition process of the repertoires relevant to social skills. This knowledge can help prevent problems associated with social incompetence or help to design treatment programs to ameliorate problems. This knowledge of the acquisition process is also relevant to the manner in which paradigmatic behaviorism attempts to establish a close relationship between etiology, assessment, diagnosis, and treatment. In the ideal sense, assessment would determine which of the various sites was deficit or inappropriate in regard to a particular question, with the knowledge of the normal acquisition process then providing a framework for intervention. In regard to treatment, paradigmatic behaviorism introduces the idea that personality can be changed (i.e., the modification or the establishment of personality repertoires) in addition to changing specific problematic behaviors.

Conclusion

I have attempted to indicate how paradigmatic behaviorism's personality and measurement levels of theory can integrate the schism between personality and behavioral assessment. At the personality level of theory, the BBR concept, the behavioral interaction principles, and the tripartite personality conception were suggested to provide a theoretical framework to integrate behavioral and nonbehavioral approaches to personality. I then suggested that the personality level provides the foundation for the measurement level, thus indicating how paradigmatic behaviorism's multilevel theory attempts to bridge the various fields of psychology. The measurement level of the theory involves a time dimension (past, present, and future environments), a setting dimension (analogue and relevant environments), a personality dimension (tripartite personality conception and behavioral interactional principles), a behavioral dimension and a methods-of-measurement dimension (e.g., self-report, direct observation). These various dimensions provide an explicit rationale for direct and indirect inferences within assessment (i.e., how a sample of behavior can provide information about the sampled population of behavior and how a sample of behavior can provide information about a nonsampled population of behavior, respectively). Finally, I discussed how paradigmatic behaviorism's measurement model provides a framework for the study of behavioral covariations and psychological constructs. I believe that the careful application of the theory to these two areas in particular will provide useful information for behavior therapy as well as further specification of the theory.

6

A Model for Research on Self-Regulation: Reducing the Schism Between Behaviorism and General Psychology

Michael Rosenbaum

Since the introduction of Watsonian behaviorism into psychology three major concepts have clearly divided various theories in psychology. These include the concepts of personality, information processing, and unconsciousness. I think there is no area in psychology where the behavioristic rejection of these concepts created more serious conceptual difficulties than in the area of self-regulation and self-control. The early signs of these difficulties can already be detected in Watson's book on behaviorism.

Although Watson (1924, p. 222) stated strongly that "situations always dominate us" and that personality is only "the sum of activities that can be discovered by actual observations of behavior over enough time," he preached to his students the following: "I am just trying to show you that our way of acting in certain situations is almost automatic. Some of us know these kinds of weaknesses in ourselves and we are constantly on the watch for them. . . . Every man can watch his own way of acting and he will often be surprised when he comes to face the real stimuli that touch off his actions. . . The individual when he really faces himself is often almost (if not quite) overcome by what is revealed—infantile behavior, unethical standards, smothered over by the thinnest veneer of rationalization. Nakedness of 'soul' can be faced only by the truly brave" (p. 238). Who is the "person" who watches his own activities? By what process does this individual "know" his own behavior? Furthermore, it is clear from this quotation that Watson believed that certain knowledge is unconscious and that only the "truly brave" are willing to face such knowledge; are these individuals less "defensive" that other individuals, as psychoanalysis would have hypothesized? Obviously, Watson believed that individuals are partially responsible for their own behavior and hence they could be expected to self-regulate their own actions and thinking.

Watson (1924) devoted a whole chapter to the concept of "personality," but did so reluctantly: "The behaviorist usually likes to discard psychological words that have no precise meaning and that are so laden down by bad history, but through some perversity of his nature he is trying to keep the term personality because it does fit so beautifully into his general psychological system" (p. 216). Admittedly, 60 years later we as behaviorists are still "perverse" and I think we cannot deal effectively with issues such as self-regulation without resorting to concepts such as personality, information processing, and unconsciousness. Only by accepting the legitimacy of these concepts can we reduce the theoretical schisms in psychology and contribute to the construction of a unified psychological theory that Staats has been advocating for many years.

I begin with a brief discussion of the place of these concepts in contemporary behavioral approaches, with particular reference to the study of self-regulation. These concepts deserve a more extensive discussion and are presented in order to provide the reader with background information relevant to a more unified model of self-control behavior. The term *process-regulating* cognitions is introduced to describe a specific kind of behavioral repertoire whose function is to regulate the processes by which individuals control their own behavior. I then turn more explicitly to the domain of self-regulation and consider the function of process-regulating cognitions. The next sections are mainly devoted to the role of personality (basic behavioral repertoires) in the process of self-regulation. I will focus in particular on the role of learned resourcefulness, a hypothetical personality repertoire of self-control skills, presenting both findings from my own laboratory as well as from other investigators.

Personality, Information Processing, and Consciousness in Self-Regulation

Personality

The traditional concept of personality is based on the following assumptions: (1) there are internal processes that determine an individual's behavior in a specific situation; (2) individuals have enduring characteristics that are consistent across time and situations; (3) individuals differ from each other in their enduring characteristics (hence, central to any personality theory is the measurement of individual differences); and (4) there is a need to look at the "whole" person, not just at specific behaviors or cognitions, because personality is characterized both by parts and by relationships among these parts.

In the early stages of the development of behavior therapy, none of these assumptions were admissible. Behavior therapists focused on environmental determinants of behavior, neglected individual differences, and targeted treatment toward specific behaviors. Staats's attempt to develop a personality theory within the general framework of behaviorism represented a notable exception. However, recent developments within behavior therapy indicate that the underlying assumptions of the personality concept are gaining respect, although the concept itself is still somewhat of a taboo, particularly in radical behaviorism (the term *personality* is not listed in the cumulative subject index for *Behavior Therapy* for 1970 to 1982). The growth of behavioral assessment and the number of publications centered on the need to match clients' characteristics to specific treatments seem to indicate greater acceptance that there are individual differences and that individuals possess certain enduring characteristics (Voeltz & Evans, 1982). With the advancement of cognitive approaches to treatment, internal processes are increasingly well accepted. Further, complex models that describe self-regulatory processes (e.g., Kanfer & Gaelick, 1986) and multiple determinants of complex behaviors (e.g., Bandura, 1977b, 1978b), all attest to the fact that behavior therapists look now at the "whole" person and not just at specific behaviors that are unrelated to each other.

By presenting an integrated model of self-regulation I will attempt to make a persuasive case that personality is a useful concept in understanding human behavior when personality is viewed as consisting of systems of skills that an individual has learned since birth. In social behaviorism these systems are called basic behavioral repertoires or personality repertoires. A major characteristic of the social behaviorism conception is that personality is both a cause and an effect of behavior. Since Staats has written extensively on this theory and its major elements are described throughout this volume (e.g., Burns, Chapter 5), I will not elaborate on Staats's personality concept except to demonstrate its usefulness in the study of self-regulation.

Information Processing

Staats (1981), Bandura (1978a), and others have pointed out a major schism in the conceptualization of human behavior. On the one hand, human beings are perceived as "active, striving, self-directing, cognitively aware, and purposive organisms who help determine their destinies and in so doing have a measure of freedom" (Staats, 1981, p. 240), while on the other hand there is a passive, mechanistic concept of humankind.

Let us examine this distinction more carefully. If we assume that psychological research abides by the rules of science that strive to predict human behavior, then we cannot assume that human beings are free to choose their own behaviors. Thus, those who perceive humans as free agents who determine their own behavior cannot at the same time look for rules and laws that govern human behavior. Similarly, the distinction between an "active" and a "passive" model of human behavior is more artificial than real. Usually what is meant by this distinction is whether the cause of human behavior is presumed to be originating from "within" the individual or from forces "outside" of the individual. Today, however, most psychologists would agree that human behavior has multiple causes and that this is no longer an issue that divides psychology.

The dividing line, however, runs between those who explain all of human behavior, even the most complex kind, in terms of a conditioning model and those who explain human behavior in terms of information-processing models or cybernetic models. For instance, proponents of the information-processing position argue that the explanation of human cognitions in terms of basic conditioning principles—or as being the antecedents and consequences of overt verbalizations—fails to recognize the relevance of human structural characteristics in the processing of information, the widely different processes associated with different types of cognitive events (e.g., visual imagery, decision making, or attribution), and the different methodological problems in studying these diverse events (see Kanfer & Gaelick, 1986; Kanfer & Hagerman, 1985).

Staats has proposed a "multilevel" learning theory (see Chapter 2, this vol.) which has at the basic level the elementary conditioning principles that were established in animal studies. However, "in formulating a human learning theory these principles require selection, elaboration, abstraction and formulating elements that may not emerge from animal studies" (Staats, 1981, p. 242). Social behaviorist theory allows the integration of basic conditioning principles with the more complex forms of human learning and information processing that Kanfer and his colleagues refer to thus overcoming a major source of disunity in contemporary psychology. In other words, various levels of phenomena must be confronted in the study of human behavior, and these levels require additional theoretical development.

This chapter is concerned with such a development, and assumes that processes involved in the encoding and decoding of information, in decision making, in establishing expectancies for future events, in social judgments, and in making causal attributions could not be effectively described and explained solely at the basic level of conditioning principles. A unified theory of human behavior must find a way of integrating the two models of human behavior without damaging either model's conceptual utility. Kanfer and Hagerman (1985) made the important observation that the research on information processing models lends itself most readily to integration with learning-based behavioral views because it (1) meets stringent methodological requirements for data collection; (2) deals with well-controlled variables affecting clearly defined behavioral measures; and (3) deals with universal characteristics of the human organism in the encoding, storage, and retrieval of information that act as modifiers, facilitating or constraining both learning and reproduction of various behaviors.

Carver and Scheier (1982) noted that some proponents of behavioral theory have been moving steadily in the direction of cybernetic models of self-regulation. Kanfer's research and conceptualization of the self-regulation process is one of the best examples of this trend. I believe that such a trend leads to a greater integration of various conceptions of human behavior, and contributes significantly to our understanding of self-regulatory processes.

Consciousness Versus Unconsciousness

Goldfried and Merbaum (1973) are the only authors who have attempted to introduce the concept of consciousness into a behavioral definition of self-control: "Self-control represents a personal decision arrived at through *conscious deliberation* for the purpose of instigating action which is designed to achieve certain desired outcomes or goals as determined by the individual himself" (p. 12, italics added). By *conscious deliberation* these authors mean that for individuals to self-regulate their behavior they must be able to verbalize their goal and to specify each of several steps they will take to alter their problematic behavior. Consciousness is thus equated with the ability to label one's actions and cognitively plan for the future. Similarly, Staats (1975, p. 466) has attributed awareness and self-direction to the individual's language-cognitive personality repertoire. Active cognitive processes often associated with self-regulation such as problem solving are explained in terms of "a sequence of conditioned sensory responses" (Staats, 1975, p. 182).

In recent years certain prominent behavior therapists (e.g., Mahoney, 1982; Meichenbaum & Gilmore, 1984) have introduced the concept of "unconsciousness" into cognitive-behavior therapy. According to Meichenbaum and Gilmore (1984) unconscious determinants of behavior are thoughts and actions that are not "noticed or appreciated" by the person. These words do not define the term *unconsciousness*, they are just substitute labels. However, certain processes that were subsumed by Meichenbaum and Gilmore under the label of "unconsciousness"—such as thinking styles and automatic behaviors and thoughts—seem important for the understanding of self-regulation. Furthermore, it is common sense to think of self-regulation as a "conscious" process and automatic nonself-controlled behaviors as occurring "unconsciously."

Thus any theoretical statement of self-regulation would seem to require some reference to behaviors that are subsumed under the labels "consciousness" and "unconsciousness." However, since these terms have had such a long history in psychology they carry with them surplus meanings. Instead I propose that a distinction be made between "automatic mindless behaviors" and "thoughtful behaviors." Well-established habits and cognitions are considered to be automatic ("unconscious"), not always because persons are unaware of them at certain times, but because they affect current behavior in a uniform and automatic way. Most personality repertoires can be considered to function on an "unconscious," automatic level, whereas cognitions that are involved in the regulation of behavior (such as judgments, evaluations, and expectations) function on a "conscious" level. The role of these two kinds of behaviors in the self-regulatory process will be discussed in the following sections.

Toward a Unified Model of Behavioral Self-Control

The model to be presented here attempts to solve the three major schisms identified in the previous sections. It is based on a number of assumptions that are widely shared in psychology today. First of all it is assumed that there is no single cause of behavior and that behaviors are in reciprocal interaction with situational, personality, and biological variables. Changes in one of these domains affects all other domains in various degrees. Models of human self-regulation behaviors developed by Bandura (1977b), Kanfer and Gaelick (1986), and Staats (1975, 1981) are in basic agreement with this assumption.

These models also share the assumption that human behavior is goal directed. Behavioral goals are the symbolic representation of future consequences. Goals can be evaluated on three major dimensions: proximity, globality, and relative value. Individuals strive to achieve long-range goals as well as proximal goals. Bandura and Schunk (1981) found that distal goals have less effect on human motivation than proximal goals. Hence individuals often adopt proximal subgoals in order to achieve a distal goal that is highly valued. Goals may be defined in global terms such as "to be a good person," or in more specific terms such as "producing good grades in school". The more the goal is defined in specific terms, the greater the impact of the goal on current behavior. On the other hand, the more global the goal is, the more threatened the individual feels when obstacles arise on his or her way to achieving the goal. Furthermore, the same goals may be valued differently by different individuals. The motivating impact of goals on behavior is determined by each of the above dimensions.

The behavioral models of self-regulation developed within the framework of social learning theory (Bandura, 1977b; Mischel, 1984) and social behaviorism (Staats, 1975) emphasize the role of learned competencies and skills in the self-regulatory process. Mischel (1984), for instance, viewed the ability to delay gratification both as a psychological process and as a basic human competence. In an impressive series of studies, Mischel and his colleagues have demonstrated the reciprocal interaction between personality and situational variables in the process of delay of gratification (e.g., Mischel, 1983). Both situational factors (such as the salience of the reward) and the cognitive-attentional skills (such as the ability to divert and control attention and cognitive control of frustration) influence children's ability to delay immediate gratifications. Rosenbaum and Ben-Ari Smira (1986) have extended Mischel's findings to an adult population. Similarly, Staats (1975) described the role of basic behavioral or personality repertoires in self-directed behavior. Basic behavioral repertoires are "constellations of complex skills which are evoked by many situations but also have the quality of providing the basis for additional learning" (Staats, 1975, p. 63). In social behaviorism these personality repertoires are thought to be learned from an early age according to the principles of conditioning and cumulative-hierarchical learning. Social learning theory, on the other hand, hypothesizes that basic human competencies may be learned not only by conditioning principles but also by principles derived from cognitive and information-processing models.

I have identified a specific subset of basic behavioral repertoires that I have labeled *process-regulating cognitive (PRC) repertoires*. The PRC repertoires are basic behavioral repertoires whose specific function is to regulate the processes by which the individual determines his or her own behavior. The PRC repertoires are equivalent to the cognitive functions of the "self-system" in Bandura's (1978b) social learning theory. According to Bandura the "self-system" refers to cognitive structures that provide reference mechanisms and to a set of subfunctions for the perception, evaluation, and regulation of behavior. From an early age the individual learns to monitor events, to assign meanings to events, to attribute causality to what has happened, and to develop expectancies for the future. The PRC repertoires are activated when the smooth flow of habitual behavior is disrupted. They in turn activate other behavioral repertoires or competencies while being in constant interaction with environmental and physiological determinants of behavior as will be described in the following sections and schematically in Figure 6.1.

Problem-solving skills and behaviors are part of the individual's PRC repertoires. They include the following kinds of cognitive behaviors: identification of the problem, definition of the problem, attribution of causality, evaluation of one's ability to solve the problem, generation of alternatives, decision making, application of previously learned skills to solve the problem, evaluating the solution by comparing it to a standard, and self-reinforcement. When PRC repertoires are not activated the individual's behavior is considered to be "automatic" and "unconscious." The PRC repertoires describe the person's "conscious," "nonautomatic" behavior. Hence by introducing the concept of PRC repertoires into a general model of behavioral self-control, the schism between unconscious-conscious

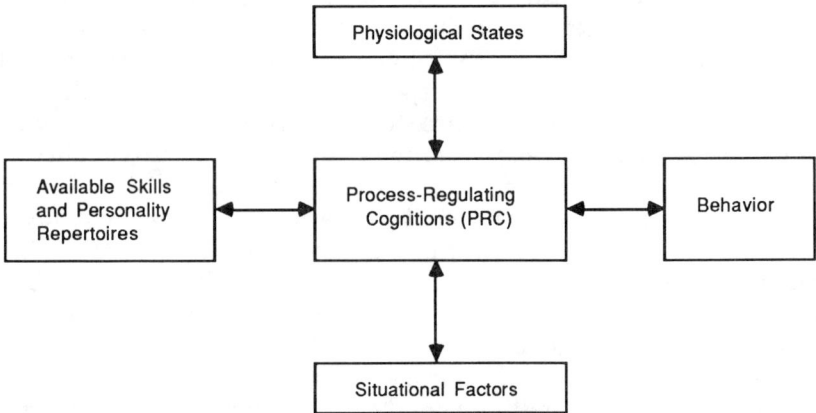

FIGURE 6.1 Schematic representation of the interactions among factors that reciprocally determine "nonautomatic," "conscious" behavior.

behavior is resolved. Figure 6.2 offers a description of the behavior on an unconscious level, namely, without the mediating effects of PRC repertoires.

Process-Regulating Cognitions and Self-Regulation

Well-learned behaviors and well-established habits characterize automatic behavior. Speaking one's mother tongue, driving a car, or brushing teeth are often performed without employing any self-regulating cognitions. Langer and her associates (e.g., Langer, Blank, & Chanowitz, 1978) have amply demonstrated that familiar activities may be performed in a "mindless" fashion. When behaviors are performed without thinking, or without what I have labeled here as process-regulating cognitions, they are often labeled by the person as behaviors that occur "automatically" or "unconsciously."

Since behaviors are involved in a continuous reciprocal interaction with personality, environmental, and physiological variables, any change in one of these variables may lead to an interference with the smooth performance of these behaviors. Physiological factors might be a source of disruption. Pain, high level of arousal, fatigue, hunger, and so forth might interfere with the smooth execution of well-established behaviors. Similarly, situational factors, ei-

Physiological States

Available Skills
and Persoanlity
Repertoires

Behavior

Situational Factors

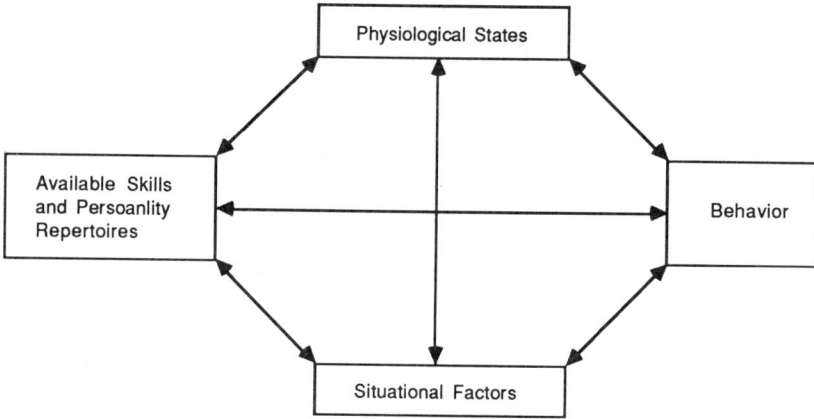

FIGURE 6.2 Schematic representation of the interactions among factors that reciprocally determine "automatic," "unconscious" behavior.

ther in the form of actual physical obstacles or in the form of social pressures and unfavorable responses from other individuals, may interfere with behavior. Other persons may provide the individual with new information that is inconsistent with well-held beliefs. Changes in one's belief systems, or schemata, may interfere with habitual behaviors that are associated with these beliefs—for example, if a heavy smoker is induced to believe that smoking may lead to cancer. Most cognitive therapies focus on disrupting the maladaptive belief system of the individual as a way of introducing behavioral changes through self-regulation (Beck, 1976; Ellis, 1962, 1983).

Kruglanski and his colleagues (Kruglanski, 1980; Kruglanski & Klar, 1985) developed a cognitive-motivational theory that postulates the conditions in which individuals would generate cognitions when faced with new sources of information. In other words, the theory attempts to predict in motivational terms when human actions will be thoughtful and rational and when they will be mindless and automatic. Within the present conceptual model, the question may be phrased: When do individuals employ PRC repertoires to regulate their behavior and when not?

Three major "epistemic motivations" have been identified: the need for cognitive structure, the fear of invalidity, and the need for specific conclusions (Kruglanski & Klar, 1985). The needs for an immediate and firm knowledge (need for structure) and for information that would be consistent with a given specific point of view (a conclusional need) reduce the potential interference of new and inconsistent information on behavior. Consequently, less "thinking" is required. On the other hand, those who fear being mistaken (fear of invalidity) are likely to generate numerous alternative hypotheses on a given topic and to attend prudently to all available information on the problem. Under these circumstances the individual would "think" a lot before he or she decides to act or to form new attitudes. In a similar vein, Kruglanski and Klar (1985) predicted that "mindless" behavior would be more likely to occur when the subjects are under a high need for structure, and less likely to occur when they are under a high fear of invalidity or when information inconsistent with schema is made available and salient.

Thus situational, motivational, and physiological factors may determine the extent to which goal-directed behaviors are disrupted. The disruption serves as a signal to engage in the self-regulatory cycle (Kanfer & Gaelick, 1986) which is guided by the PRC repertoires and is potentially influenced by the person's personality repertoires. The role of other personality repertoires in the self-regulatory process will be described in greater detail in the next section.

In Figure 6.3, I present a schematic overview of a self-regulation model. The model is based on information processing or cybernetic ideas, as are other self-regulation models (Carver, 1979; Kanfer & Gaelick, 1986) that provided the stimulus for the present model. Kanfer and Gaelick's (1986) model, however, assumes that self-regulatory processes are mainly directed at attainment of an expected reinforcement, whereas the present model postulates that self-regulatory processes are mainly directed at eliminating actual or potential factors that interfere with current ongoing goal-directed behaviors.

One of the most important PRC repertoires is the ability to detect changes within oneself and in the external environment. This was often referred to as "self-awareness" or "self-consciousness" (Carver & Scheier, 1982). Without this ability the whole self-regulatory process cannot be initiated. However, individuals quite often adhere to well-established behavioral patterns without being aware that circumstances have changed and that they have to modify their behavior if they wish to attain their desired goal. This kind of behavior has been labeled "denial" and interpreted as a psychodynamic defense mechanism. For example, a person following myocardial infarction may insist on returning to his or her pre-illness normal activities as though nothing has happened. Research has shown that patients' use of denial may make for better coping

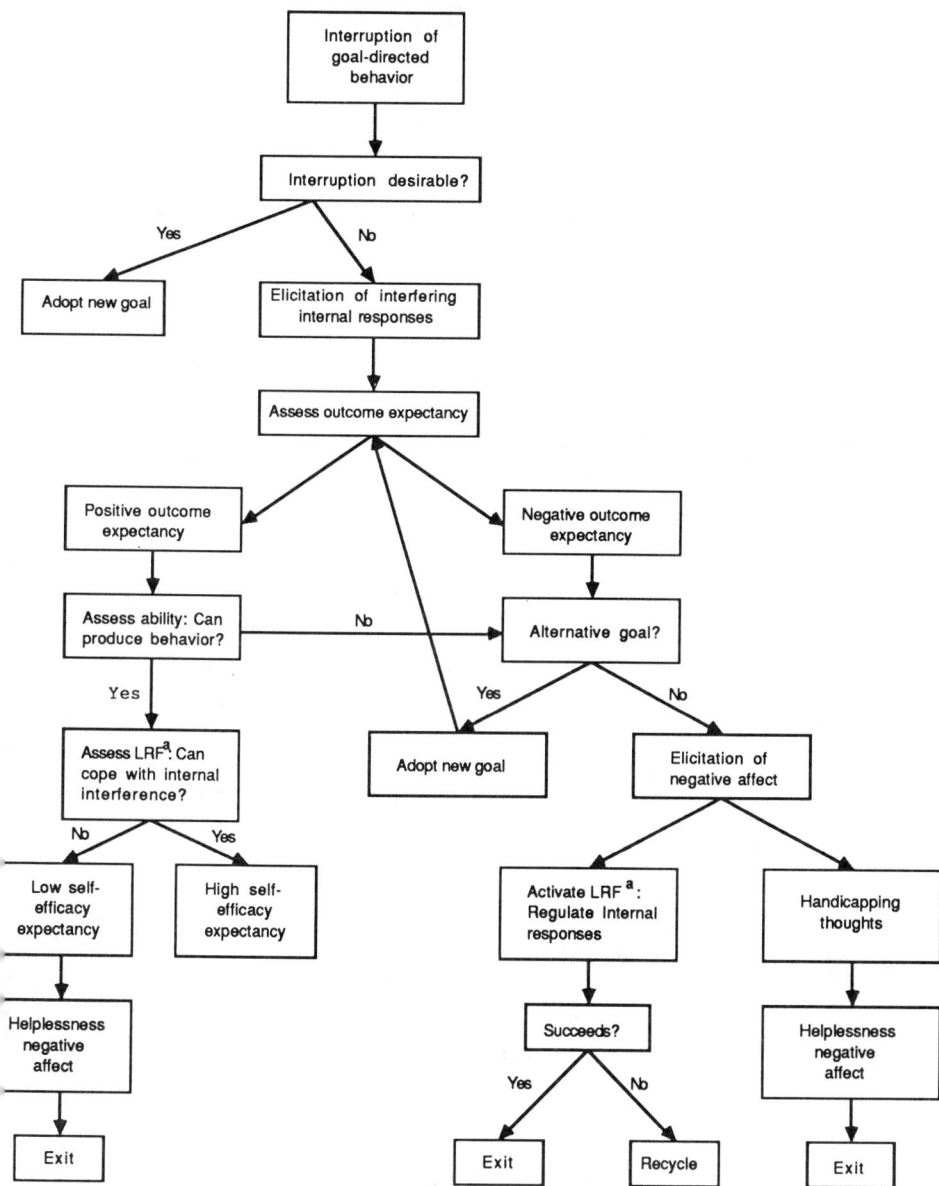

FIGURE 6.3 Flowchart description of the self-regulatory model.

[a] LRF = Learned Resourcefulness.

with the early stress of illness in the coronary care unit. In the long term, however, patients may limit their chances of recovery by ignoring important medical recommendations (Krantz & Deckel, 1983). Obviously then, without the perception that circumstances have changed, the process of self-regulation cannot begin.

The next stage involves a cognitive appraisal of the disruption. The disruption may be perceived by the person as either desirable or as threatening. Sudden illness, for instance, may be appraised in positive terms if it interrupts a boring and a nonstimulating daily routine and carries with it potential financial and social rewards. Individuals in such circumstances may easily adopt a new behavioral goal that is compatible with illness behavior. For example, they may adopt the "sick role" and enjoy all the benefits that are entailed: removal of responsibilities and increased support from other family members. In such cases, the process of self-regulation ends once the individual can easily adopt the new goal of being a "patient."

However, when the disruption is perceived to be negative and it evokes negative emotions and ruminations that interfere with current behavior, then the self-regulatory process continues its operation. This process is guided by expectancies for the attainments of goals in the future. These expectancies are based on evaluations of current behavioral resources (i.e., personality repertoires), situational factors, and the physical state of the organism. The more salient and the more immediately available information is to the individuals on any of these factors, the greater the impact on their future expectancies.

Bandura (1978a, 1984) has proposed two basic expectancies that are important in guiding human behavior: outcome and self-efficacy. Outcome expectancies refer to the belief that the desired goal will be obtained if the person follows a well-specified course of action. Self-efficacy beliefs, on the other hand, refer to the person's expectation that he or she is fully capable of performing the acts needed to attain the desired goal. According to Bandura, judgments of self-efficacy also determine how much effort people will expend and how long they will persist in the face of obstacles or aversive experiences. When faced with difficulties people who entertain doubts about their capabilities tend to slacken their efforts or give up altogether, whereas those who have a strong sense of efficacy exert greater effort to master challenges. Efficacy judgments are based on past success in mastering similar situations, perceived personal capabilities, vicarious experience (observing models), verbal persuasion, and the physiological state of the organism. The expectation that behavior will produce a specific outcome is based on the perceived responsiveness of the environment (Bandura, 1984). This is essentially similar to the original theory of learned helplessness (Seligman, 1975), which postulated that people become inactive and depressed if they are led to believe that their performances will go unrewarded (response-outcome independence).

Bandura (1977a) hypothesized that self-efficacy judgments are in part a function of the individual experiencing successful performance. Similarly, Seligman (1975) assumed that outcome expectancies are in part a function of the person's history of contingent reinforcement. The present view, however, is that individuals learn a set of cognitive skills by which they interpret their experiences and modify the impact of situations on their behavior. People learn how to self-regulate their behavior by acquiring the abilities to adopt behavioral goals and to evaluate their attainability. In order to judge whether certain behavioral goals can be reached, individuals have to apply a set of skills that help them evaluate their own competencies and environmental contingencies. This kind of skill is part of the PRC repertoires. There is some research on how children learn to set behavioral goals, but there is almost no research on how children learn to judge their specific abilities (i.e., their self-efficacy) or how they learn to evaluate the responsiveness of the environment to their own behavior (i.e., response-outcome relationship).

Within the conceptual framework of the present model, outcome and efficacy expectancies develop through the activation of PRC repertoires, and they play a major role in the self-regulation process. When an undesirable interruption occurs, individuals must first judge whether the original goal is still attainable under the new circumstances (outcome expectancies), and following that, whether they are capable of coping effectively with various disruptions and interferences (self-efficacy expectancies). To put it in a nutshell, the continuous evaluations of possible behavioral outcomes and of one's behavioral capacities against these outcomes is the major motivating force behind a person's self-regulation.

Figure 6.3 depicts how these two expectancies guide the self-regulatory process. At each point in the sequence the individual judges whether or not the original goal is attainable. If it is judged to be attainable, then the individual decides whether he or she is capable of removing the obstacles encountered. If individuals conclude that they have the inner resources to cope with the goal-interfering factors, then they will continue to stick to the original goal. However, if they conclude that they lack these resources, they either may despair and feel helpless or they may search for alternative goals. If the search for alternatives is also fruitless, the individuals may feel trapped and helpless. Yet if an alternate goal is judged to be attainable, self-efficacy judgments are once again activated and the self-regulatory sequence continues.

According to the present model the self-regulatory process terminates at the point when individuals follow their behavior without "thinking"; behavior is performed in an automatic manner. This may occur when a desired goal is obtainable without any interference or when the individual concludes that the goal is not obtainable and he or she cannot do anything to reach it. In the latter case the individual feels apathetic and helpless. Rehm's (1977, 1984) work strongly suggests that some cases of depression are produced by deficits in self-regulation.

One final point should be stressed. Since self-regulation involves active attention, there are natural limits to one's ability to handle many behavioral disruptions simultaneously. If there are too many such disruptions, individuals will fail to adequately self-regulate their behavior. Consequently, behavioral disorders such as anxiety reactions and depression may ensue. McGrath (1976) has applied the label "stress" to such situations that a person perceives as presenting a demand which threatens to exceed the person's capabilities and resources for meeting it.

The Role of Situations and Personality in Self-Regulation

In the previous section I have described how situations, personality repertoires, and physiological factors can be instrumental in initiating the self-regulatory process by causing an interference in the smooth flow of an ongoing behavior. In this section I will briefly describe how these factors affect the process of self-regulation once it has started. I will devote, however, more space to the potential role of personality repertoires in the process of self-regulation because of my own work in this area. Although I recognize the importance of physiological factors, it is beyond this chapter to provide any extensive discussion of their role in this process.

Situations have three major functions in the process of self-regulation. First, they may elicit personality or behavioral repertoires. Second, they determine how much pressure will be put on the self-system. If there are too many changes in the environment that call for attention and self-regulation, the individual cannot adequately self-regulate his or her behavior. Third, the environment, especially the social environment, provides individuals with feedback on their performance that influences their expectations for the future. When feedback is negative or noncontingent, individuals either may abandon any attempt to obtain the original goal or may search for new and more rewarding goals. Individuals may often observe other persons in similar situations and may develop outcome expectations on the basis of the feedback others receive and disregard the feedback they themselves receive. Furthermore, observing similar others perform certain behaviors under adverse conditions may increase people's self-efficacy expectancies. The effects of situational variables on the self-regulatory process were extensively researched and reported by Bandura and his colleagues (e.g., Bandura, 1984).

However, relatively little research was carried out on the role of personality repertoires or individual differences in the process of self-regulation. At various points of the self-regulation process personality variables play an important role. They determine the direction in which the process of self-regulation may proceed, if at all. The process of self-regulation begins with what Lazarus and Folkman (1984) call "primary appraisal" and Nerenz and Leventhal (1983) call "representation." At this stage, individuals perceive a disruption or an interference in their regular ways of behaving. As I have already alluded to in the previous section, individuals could simply deny that there is any problem and ignore any disruptions or interferences. For instance, Lazarus and Folkman (1984, pp. 132–135) and Taylor (1983) have emphasized the advantages of self-deception and illusions to terminally ill patients, and the illusion that "life goes on as usual" could indeed be adaptive as long as the patient cannot do anything toward recovery. However, when patients are required to alter their behaviors in order to enhance their recovery, such an illusion can be disastrous.

We do not yet have much empirical information on individual differences and the use of denial. There is some evidence in the literature that depressed patients are more realistic in their self-perceptions than nondepressed persons (Lewinsohn, Mischel, Chaplin, & Barton, 1980). Furthermore, nondepressed in comparison to depressed individuals overestimate the predictability of and control they have over positive outcomes and underestimate the predictability of negative outcomes (Alloy & Abramson, 1979). This issue is an important one and calls for extensive research.

Behavior in general and self-regulation in particular is guided by the kind of goals individuals are striving to achieve. Across the years Staats has dealt at length with how goals and behavioral standards are acquired and how they direct behavior. According to Staats (1975), behavioral goals and standards are part of the emotional-motivational system which by definition is a personality repertoire. Goals can be represented by verbal means or by sensory images. Social behaviorism was among the first behavioral theories to consider images in self-standards and achievement motivation. Already in 1968, Staats wrote the following:

> The child does not set standards for himself spontaneously; although he may carry them "within," they are learned and it is important for a human learning theory to indicate the mechanisms involved. Thus, as one example, we may observe a boy alone practice a certain "move" in football until he is "satisfied," that is, *until he has attained some internal standard.* The standard stimulus within, as one example, may be a conditioned sensory response (image) which the boy acquired from observing a more skilled player. The novice actor may practice a walk or gesture in the mirror until he attains the standard of an internal image. The painter or musician acquires similar sensory standards through a long history of conditioning and continues working on a piece until the standards are matched and reinforcement is produced. (pp. 454–455)

Since this was written almost every model of self-regulation developed thereafter included the principle that individuals reinforce themselves by matching their responses to an internal standard (Bandura, 1969; Carver, 1979; Kanfer & Gaelick, 1986). Staats maintains that these standards constitute a personality characteristic. Yet there is little research on how different personality repertoires affect the kinds of standards individuals adopt. In the behavior therapy literature there is indication that depressed individuals set overly stringent personal standards for performance (Beck, 1976; Rehm, 1984). However, there is some evidence that those who are depressed do not differ from normal controls in this respect (R. Kanfer & Zeiss, 1983; Nelson & Craighead, 1977). The ability to search for alternative goals is probably a function of people's problem-solving abilities, intelligence, and resourcefulness. Thus, one's goals are part of one's personality repertoires.

There is, on the other hand, considerable evidence on the relationship between personality characteristics or repertoires and subjects' outcome expectancies. "Locus of control" is a personality construct and defined as a generalized expectancy pertaining to the connection between personal characteristics and/or actions and experienced outcomes (cf., Lefcourt, 1982). Individuals who hold the generalized belief that outcomes are not determinable by one's personal efforts (external locus of control) also construe events to be beyond their control and hence they act in a helpless manner. There is considerable evidence (summarized by Lefcourt, 1982) linking internal locus of control with good adjustment to stress. In the present model of self-regulation internal locus of control orientation effects people's continued efforts at self-regulation, by influencing them to expect outcomes to be related to their own efforts.

Seligman and his co-workers (e.g., Seligman, Abramson, Semmel, & von Bayer, 1979) identified another personality repertoire that affects outcome expectancies and may produce depressive mood. They have labeled this repertoire as "attributional style." Individuals who generally attribute failure to internal, stable and global factors may give up attempts at self-regulation when confronted with actual failure. These individuals are likely to become depressed and helpless. On the other hand, individuals who habitually attribute failure to external, unstable, and specific factors are less likely to become depressed.

To date there is fairly strong evidence that individuals who are depressed habitually make internal, stable, and global attributions for failure and external, unstable, and specific attributions for success. There is weaker evidence, however, that attributional styles can lead to depression. Seligman (1981) reported that students who, 8 weeks before they failed an examination, had made global attributions for failure on a questionnaire (Seligman et al., 1979) tended to become depressed following their failure. On the other hand, Manly, McMahon, Bradely, and Davidson (1982), who used the same attributional styles questionnaire, found that women's prenatal attributional style failed to predict depression following childbirth. Lewinsohn, Steinmetz, Larson, and Franklin (1981) also found that depressive attributions and other depressogenic cognitions accompany depression but may not precede it.

I think that the failure of an attributional style questionnaire to predict depression is mainly the failure of models that assign a single cause to complex behaviors (see also Heiby & Staats, Chapter 10, this vol.). The picture is considerably more complicated, as the present self-regulatory model suggests. If anything, attributional style can probably best predict outcome expectations and the findings reported by Seligman and his associates also suggest that certain attributional styles are part of a depressive personality repertoire. Depression is, according to the present model, reciprocally determined by situational, physiological and personality factors that guide the self-regulatory process.

Outcome expectations undoubtedly play an important role in the self-regulatory process, as do expectancies about one's personal efficacy. Whereas locus of control and attributional style, as components of personality repertoires, probably affect outcome expectancies, learned resourcefulness (Rosenbaum, 1983) can be viewed as a personality repertoire that mainly affects certain kinds of self-efficacy expectations. This will be discussed in the next section.

Learned Resourcefulness and Self-Regulation

In recent years my colleagues and I have been studying the role of personality repertoires in the process of self-regulation. We have identified one personality repertoire that appears to be of great importance for self-regulation. It is a repertoire of self-control skills that previous research in the area of cognitive-behavior therapy has revealed as being effective in self-management and coping (Goldfried, 1980; Kanfer & Gaelick, 1986; Meichenbaum, 1977). Following Meichenbaum (1977) this personality repertoire was labeled "learned resourcefulness" and was operationally defined as a repertoire of behaviors and skills by which a person self-regulates internal responses that interfere with the smooth execution of an ongoing behavior.

A person's learned resourcefulness is activated during the self-regulatory process at the point in the sequence (Figure 6.3) at which he or she decides to pursue the initial goal in spite of disturbing internal stimuli such as anxiety, depressed mood, anger, and so forth. For example, two individuals may be equally anxious when asked to speak before an audience. Nonetheless they may differ in their resourcefulness. The resourceful individual may employ various skills to minimize the effects of anxiety on performance in public whereas the less resourceful person may succumb to his or her anxiety.

Individuals who succeeded in the past to self-regulate their internal responses and resourceful individuals who have acquired the skills needed for it may expect to do so also in the future. One's learned resourcefulness is an important information source for self-efficacy judgments in addition to those sources originally identified by Bandura (1977a). According to the present view, highly resourceful individuals judge themselves more efficacious in coping with the emotional strains involved in completing difficult tasks, whereas those rated lower in resourcefulness judge themselves inefficacious in coping with demands and consequently are likely to dwell more on their personal deficiencies and their self-worth than on the task at hand (Rosenbaum & Ben-Ari, 1985). The extent to which one judges oneself to be resourceful will determine whether one will continue efforts at self-regulation.

We have found the Self-Control Schedule (SCS) (Rosenbaum, 1980b) to be a useful instrument for assessing learned resourcefulness. The behaviors assessed by the SCS cover the following content areas: (1) use of cognitions and self-instructions to cope with emotional and physiological responses; (2) application of problem-solving strategies (e.g., planning, problem definition, evaluating alternatives, and anticipation of consequences); (3) ability to delay immediate gratification; and (4) a general belief in one's ability to self-regulate internal events. Redden, Tucker, and Young (1983) as well as Richards (1985) provided further evidence as to the psychometric adequacy of the SCS. A factor analysis of the scale done by Redden et al. (1983) failed to indicate a clear, strong factor structure. It should be noted here that the four content areas mentioned above were used only for the construction of the scale and should not be viewed as subscales. Persons who scored above the median score of the SCS are referred to as high resourceful (HR) persons and those who scored below the median score as low resourceful (LR) individuals. In all our studies we obtained a wide range of scores on the SCS which indicates that there are large individual differences in learned resourcefulness. Although resourcefulness could probably be assessed by additional tests, all the studies referred to in this chapter measured resourcefulness by the use of the SCS.

In a number of studies (Rosenbaum, 1980a; Rosenbaum & Palmon, 1984; Rosenbaum & Rolnick, 1983) we found that HR subjects did not differ from LR subjects in their perceptions of the aversiveness of an event, but they differed in how they coped with aversiveness. HR subjects are challenged by stressful and difficult situations and they persist in their efforts at self-regulation, whereas LR subjects tend to feel helpless and easily give up their efforts to master their own behavior in face of obstacles. Hence one's resourcefulness does not determine whether or not one would initiate self-regulation when confronted with disruptions, but it keeps the self-regulatory process going once it has started.

Furthermore, the model proposed here specifies that learned resourcefulness as a personality repertoire influences self-efficacy judgments and not outcome expectations. However, in reality there are many occasions where outcome expectations cannot be separated from self-efficacy judgments. Bandura (1984) suggests a number of such conditions: when outcomes are strongly inherent in actions, or when extrinsic outcomes are fixed at a minimal level of performance. Rosenbaum and Hadari (1985) found that among normal controls, but not among depressed and paranoid patients, outcome expectancies were strongly associated with general judgments of personal efficacy. From a purely logical point of view, beliefs in personal efficacy and behavior/outcome expectancies should be independent of each other. The fact that we are capable of producing a certain behavior does not guarantee in any way that this behavior will produce the outcome we desire. Yet persons with no psychiatric history tend to think so more than psychiatric patients. Rosenbaum and Hadari (1985) attributed this phenomenon to the illusion of control phenomenon (referred to already in this chapter) which was found among normal control subjects, but not among psychiatric patients (Alloy & Abramson, 1979; Golin, Terrell, Weitz, & Drost, 1979). There is some evidence to indicate that HR subjects are more prone to develop illusions of control than LR subjects. Rosenbaum and Palmon (1984) found that regardless of the severity level of their disorder, HR individuals with epilepsy believed more strongly that they could control their seizures than LR individuals with a seizure disorder. Yet in laboratory studies we did not find the illusion of control phenomenon among HR subjects.

In two laboratory studies (Rosenbaum & Ben-Ari, 1985; Rosenbaum & Jaffe, 1983) that focused on the role of individual differences in learned resourcefulness on the development of helplessness, w were able to separately manipulate outcome expectancies and judgments of personal efficacy. In the Rosenbaum and Jaffe (1983) study, outcome expectations were experimentally manipulated by external reinforcers and resourcefulness by SCS selection criteria (Rosenbaum, 1980b). As in a typical learned helplessness study, subjects were first administered a treatment with inescapable, escapable, or passively received noise. The degree of debilitation produced by these conditions was subsequently measured on a solvable anagram test. The major finding was that HR subjects who had reported the characteristic use of an extensive repertoire of self-controlling behaviors were more immune to the induction of helplessness than LR subjects who had endorsed a more limited repertoire of this nature. In fact, it was only among the LR subjects that performance deficits reported to be associated with the learned helplessness phenomenon (e.g., Hiroto & Seligman, 1975) were reliably reproduced. However, the important findings for the present discussion were in subjects' responses to the postexperimental questionnaire. HR subjects did not differ from LR subjects in their outcome judgments when the noise was uncontrollable; both groups equally believed that the noise was uncontrollable, but HR subjects believed more strongly that they could cope with the disturbing effects of this noise.

In many situations in our lives we are well aware that we cannot control certain outcomes, but that we can control our reactions to these outcomes. In such cases learned resourcefulness and self-efficacy expectancies play a crucial role. In the Rosenbaum and Ben-Ari (1985) experiments we demonstrated that HR subjects cope differently with uncontrollable situations than LR subjects. As predicted from the self-regulation model, HR subjects used more statements indicating positive self-evaluations and task-oriented thoughts and less negative self-evaluations than LR subjects during exposure to uncontrollable failure.

We (Rosenbaum & Palmon, 1984) extended these findings to a "real-life" situation and investigated how persons with epilepsy who are continuously exposed to uncontrollable seizures cope with their disability. We found that subjects' psychological adjustment to epilepsy is a joint function of their resourcefulness and of the extent to which they are exposed to uncontrollable epileptic seizures. HR individuals who were exposed to low and medium frequencies of epileptic seizures were less depressed and less anxious, and coped better with their disability than LR individuals exposed to the same amount of seizures. In the high-frequency range of epileptic seizures there were no significant differences in adjustment level between HR and LR individuals; both groups were abnormally anxious and depressed. Probably only in the milder forms of epilepsy would a personality factor such as learned resourcefulness play a role in psychological adjustment. However, in the more severe forms of epilepsy, the neurological disorder may be more detrimental to one's adjustment than one's learned resourcefulness. Obviously, there are biological limits to the self-regulatory process.

A behavioral repertoire such as learned resourcefulness was also found to play a significant role in therapies that are based on self-management techniques. Smith (1979) found that a weight reduction program based on self-management techniques was more effective with HR women than with LR women both in terms of weight and habit changes. Furthermore, fewer HR women dropped out of the program than LR women. A study by Simons, Lustman, Wetzel, and Murphy (1985) suggests that subjects' resourcefulness could be used for matching patients with treatments. In their study, HR subjects who were clinically depressed benefited more from cognitive-behavior therapy (based on self-control techniques) than LR depressed patients, whereas the reverse was true for pharmacotherapy. It should be noted here that initial levels of depression were unrelated to subjects' assessed resourcefulness. These investigators speculated that cognitive therapy utilized the skills and abilities of HR patients and hence it was more effective with them. Furthermore, HR patients might have been more positively oriented toward a cognitive treatment that emphasized self-help than LR patients. On the other hand, the pharmacotherapy approach was more congruent with the LR patients' expectations of the therapy.

Bandura (1977a) has argued that a whole range of therapeutic procedures are effective because they strengthen the patients' perceived personal-efficacy, which influences the initiation and persistence of coping behavior. The above studies suggest that this would be especially true for HR clients. Many psychotherapeutic procedures either train subjects in various self-control, resourceful behaviors (Meichenbaum, 1977) or harness the clients' already existing repertoire of resourcefulness toward the solution of their current problems. These treatments might be especially effective with HR clients.

Conclusions

In this chapter I tried to demonstrate the need for multilevel theory, using the study of self-regulation as an example. It was suggested that without adequately incorporating the concepts of personality, information processing, and consciousness, the process by which individuals self-regulate their own behavior cannot be fully understood. Although these concepts were rejected by traditional behaviorism, prominent behavior therapists, such as Bandura, Goldfried, Kanfer, Lewinsohn, and Meichenbaum, have adopted some of these concepts in their exploration of self-management for want of other explanatory mechanisms. In recent years, as I have documented here, these concepts have been slowly gaining legitimacy within behavioral approaches, although they are often presented as alternatives to, rather than extensions of, behavior theory. The current Zeitgeist, however, favors a rapprochement among various points of view in psychology, and in this spirit the chapter was written.

I presented a theoretical model for research on self-regulation. This model, on the one hand, is heavily based on previous theoretical and applied work done in the area of self-regulation, and on the other hand, it is based on the principles developed by social behaviorism and social learning theories. To some extent the model described here represents a theoretical extension of social behaviorism into areas and concepts that were not previously discussed by Staats such as information processing and process-regulating cognitions. My viewpoint is that social behaviorism provides excellent guidelines and principles for the study of human behavior rather than a set of strict rules that cannot be violated. Furthermore, in order for a theory to stay alive and useful it has to be subject to continuous changes and modifications, as is the model of self-regulation that was presented here.

III

Areas of Application

7

Verbal, Emotional, and Imagery Repertoires in the Regulation of Dysfunctional Behavior: An Integrative Conceptual Framework for Cognitive-Behavioral Disorders and Interventions

Jeffrey M. Lohr
L. Kevin Hamberger

The conceptualization and treatment of psychopathology is experiencing renewed interest in intrapsychic or cognitive and even "unconscious" determinants of behavior (Meichenbaum & Gilmore, 1984). However, these cognitive processes are not restatements of Freudian or Ego-Analytic theorists. Quite surprisingly, many of the proponents of cognitive concepts are closely identified with behavior therapy. As a consequence, the conceptual orientation is one that has been widely described as "cognitive-behavioral." It is one that has garnered a great deal of intellectual interest and one that has shown some promise in the assessment and modification of disordered behavior. While the merits of "the cognitive-behavioral revolution" have been widely debated (Eysenck, 1987; Latimer & Sweet, 1984; Mahoney, 1977; Miller & Berman, 1983), it is a conceptual orientation that will have a distinctive impact for some time to come. Our purpose is not to further the polemic but to consider how important psychological constructs subsumed under social behaviorism may aid in making the "cognitive-behavioral" model less of a contradiction in terms.

Cognitive-behavioral approaches, as presently conceptualized, lack a comprehensive and integrative model of functional mechanisms. If such a model is not forthcoming, the cognitive-behavioral model will dissipate into a morass of techniques and isolated mechanisms. We hope to show how Staats's concept of the basic behavioral repertoire provides such a comprehensive framework. We will first briefly review how behavioristic models have attempted to conceptualize hypothetical constructs that serve as molar explanatory mechanisms of disordered behavior. The bulk of this chapter, however, will be devoted to the involvement of verbal and emotional repertoires in cognitive-behavioral interventions and a reformulation of mechanisms of change using the concept of the basic behavioral repertoire outlined in Chapters 2 and 5 of this volume (see also Staats, 1972, 1975).

Behaviorism and Explanatory Constructs

Radical behaviorism focuses upon overt (motor) behavior and the manner in which it is acquired and maintained. Behavior is treated strictly as a dependent variable under the control of environmental variables functioning as independent variables. Early behavioral models also suffered limitations in proposing the explanatory power of language-mediated processes. Radical behavioral accounts of language (Skinner, 1957) emphasized language as a dependent variable and rarely discussed the adaptive functions that language serves. Such a position eliminated the functional role of both verbal and cognitive mechanisms by fiat. It is at this point, we believe, where social behaviorism has made a distinct contribution. It is Staats's (1975) contention that well-learned and hierarchically organized behavior can function in the determination of other organized behavior. A common thread that runs through the description of these repertoires concerns the nature and function of language processes.

Social behaviorism, therefore, is concerned with language in a way that is not possible in traditional behaviorism. In Chapter 4 by Rondal, language was conceptualized as the consequence of social and cognitive influences, but language also plays a functional role in the acquisition of new behavior and in the regulation of previously acquired behavior. Social behaviorism's view of human behavior is based upon hierarchically organized language-mediated repertoires. These repertoires serve mediational functions for verbal and nonverbal behavior because the elements that compose them provide response-produced cues. Repertoires are hierarchically organized in that elemental units (responses) are related in a fashion by which they constitute a higher-order response class. Repertoires are learned in a cumulative fashion by means of which elemental stimulus-response (S-R) relationships are combined in higher-order organizations of skilled behavior.

Traditional behavioral views consider only the linear structure of behavior through the process of shaping and chaining. In addition, the functional control of any previously acquired behavior is limited to the elicitation of the next response in a chain of behaviors. The functional relationship of classes of behavior or of a class of behavior to its constituent elements is not included. Social behaviorism's approach provides for the analysis of organized repertoires in cross-situational and long-term behavioral consistencies. In addition, Staats (1972) shows how these repertoires function in the regulation of disordered behavior. A complete description of the three major basic behavioral repertoires, their subrepertoires, and the affective-reinforcing-directive (A-R-D) functions of salient stimuli is provided in Chapters 2 and 5 of this volume (see also Staats, 1975).

Language Repertoires in the Regulation of Dysfunctional Behavior

Cognitive-learning therapies differ from traditional psychotherapeutic approaches in that language is not only the medium of intervention, but language further serves as the focus of therapy. Language processes are here considered both target (dependent variable) and mediator (independent variable) for wider and more generalized effects of intervention. The rationale for this position arises from the premise that if language exercises control of behavior, then alterations in the functions that language serves can effect changes in the behavior represented by the content and structure of language. Social behaviorism thus provides cognitive-learning therapies with a therapeutic rationale and a mediational S-R paradigm founded on basic behavioral repertoires. We would like to turn our attention to some clinical applications of verbal-cognitive mechanisms subsumed by this approach.

Language Control of Overt Behavior

The idea that self-generated internal speech is crucial in the development of the self-direction of behavior is not a recent one. Luria (1961) and Vygotsky (1962), investigating the nature of language and cognitive development, provide early and extensive research into the manner in which self-generated language operates in the control of simple motor responses. These studies suggested that self-directed behavior in the older, language-proficient child functions in the same way that the child's behavior is guided by the speech of others.

Research investigating child behavior in complex social contexts also supports the hypothesis that self-verbalizations can direct overt action. In a correlational study, Ross and Karoly (1977) found different mother–child interaction patterns for children selected on the basic of self-control as measured by delay of gratification, a problem-solving task, and teacher ratings. In problem-solving situations, children showing high self-control tended to make more statements of internal control processes and frequent response-contingent outcome statements in comparison to children showing low self-control. Mothers of high self-control children prompted the use of self-control statements and used more overt cues in assisting self-control whereas mothers of low self-control children were more critical, intrusive and directly controlling of the child's behavior. Low self-control children appeared to rely more on the mother to control and direct, were more rule-oriented, and complained more about the task. While the data are correlational, it appears as if the mother–child interaction pattern in low self-control children is not conducive to the development of task-relevant, self-directed verbalizations in problem-solving tasks. Camp (1977) has also described what appears to be a production or control deficiency in the use of verbal mediators in aggressive boys. Aggressive and nonaggressive boys were reliably discriminated by immature and irrelevant private speech, response latency during covert self-commands for slow activity, and inhibition errors.

In addition to correlational data, experimental evidence suggests that verbal stimuli can acquire directive control over clinically relevant nonverbal behavior. For example, Kanfer, Karoly, and Newman (1975) employed self-statements designed to reduce fear and avoidance of the dark. Training involved the teaching of self-statements (e.g., "I am a brave girl") to increase tolerance of the dark and showed increases in length of time spent in the dark at posttest. Karoly and Dirks (1977) report a study where two groups of children were assessed for their ability to tolerate an effortful physical task. Training sought to establish correspondence between verbalizations about the ability to perform the task and the overt behavior required. Reinforcement of correspondence between saying and doing led to increased performance of the task.

Correspondence and Self-Instructional Training

The earliest attempts at therapeutic training procedures that were specifically designed to increase the directive control of verbal behavior over nonverbal behavior involved either "correspondence" training (Risley & Hart, 1968) or "self-command" training (Palkes, Stewart, & Kahana, 1968). In the former, training was aimed at the positive contingent reinforcement of agreement between doing and saying for purposes of verbal generalization on subsequent tasks. In the latter, the purpose was to verbally model and "encourage" the use of self-statements to increase reflective and deliberative behavior. Israel's (1978) summary of the correspondence training literature indicates that correspondence between verbal and nonverbal behavior is greatest under conditions of say-do contingent reinforcement and may show maximal generalization (see also Eifert, 1987). These findings are interpreted as support for the development of verbal control over nonverbal behavior and may be a mechanism that is separate from any correspondence shown under nonverbal-verbal training. We suggest that verbal self-instructional training represents a general and sometimes unspecified means of developing generalized verbal-motor repertoires. Correspondence training represents a specific technique (say-do reinforcement) for increasing such verbal-nonverbal control.

Self-Regulatory Systems and Plans

In addition to environmental consequences, there are internal consequences (i.e., self-criticism or self-praise) that, according to Mischel (1973), may be dispensed contingent upon an individual's approximation to self-imposed standards and goals. Through a set of contingency rules, an individual guides or regulates his or her behavior in the absence of, or despite, external contingencies. Such rules may be represented as verbal-motor or verbal-emotional repertoires that are hierarchically organized into more generalized plans or strategies. For example, in order to attend a baseball game, a child must plan and execute a number of subplans with the necessary subgoals, such as asking for and receiving parental permission, seeking and obtaining the money for an admission ticket, and finally arranging and procuring transportation. Each of the subgoals may, in turn, require a number of subordinate plans requiring more simple verbal-motor, verbal-emotional repertoire units.

Using this framework, the analysis may be extended to clinically relevant behavior such as attentional deficits and impulsivity. These clinical syndromes may result from an absence of self-goals or self-regulation, although it is more probable that they are a function of self-goals set too low and/or inadequate self-regulation (see also Kendall & Braswell, 1985). This latter idea is supported by self-regulation studies examining goal-setting and self-reinforcement behavior. Even young children will impose rules and regulations upon themselves for self-reinforcement despite immediately available gratification (Bandura & Perloff, 1967).

Another possible explanation of attentional deficits and impulsivity is that such children do not mediate their behavior with self-praise or self-instructions that help obtain subgoals and eventually major goals. In either case, the absence of adaptive self-regulation plans or the operation of maladaptive plans can be construed as elements of the verbal-motor repertoire. The modification of the repertoire involves two major features: (1) the strengthening of the discriminative control of verbal stimuli over motor behavior, and (2) the elaboration of the verbal and emotional components. Correspondence training focuses upon the former and self-instructional training focuses upon the latter. Initial training requires the acquisition and strengthening of elemental S-R units and generalization training requires the training to higher-order components. Such repertoires are more "generative" in nature because they are composed of not only elements of what to do, but also rules of how to do it. Meichenbaum (1977) suggests that rule-governed behavior serves as the self-control mechanism for more elemental units of behavior. The acquisition of rule-governed behavior facilitates the generalization of self-instructional training. From a social behavioral perspective, such learning involves S-R elements to propositions by which the elements are organized and functionally related.

Language Control and Emotional Behavior

The development of the verbal-motor repertoire involves not only the acquisition of self-guiding plans and the establishment of self-imposed plans but also the establishment of self-imposed goals. To the extent that plans and goals are compatible, they can serve as effective incentives for verbally mediated motor behavior. A person having specified an organized plan to reach an attainable goal has good reason to provide verbal and material self-reinforcement when the goal is obtained. However, if self-produced goals or standards are unrealistically high, self-reinforcement will be nonexistent. Reinforcement, therefore, would be inadequate to maintain either a plan or its constituent behavioral elements. In addition, the inability to obtain the goal may meet with consistent self-condemnation in the form of punishment. Such a pattern of contingencies would lead to further suppression of the verbal-motor repertoire. Just as important, continual self-condemnation may lead to the elicitation of negative conditioned emotional responses to the verbal representation of self-concepts ("I am just no good") and to self-deprecatory expectations of outcome ("I will never be any good"). Unrealistically high self-goals could be self-produced from faulty personal constructs or attributions (e.g., "I should be perfect, but I am not, and therefore I am awful"). With this example, we can begin to see the manner in which verbal and emotional repertoires can interact. The affective nature of the verbal stimuli can serve to elicit strong, negative emotional arousal. The self-referential nature of the labeling and the syllogistic structure of the reasoning process serves to direct and project the negative affect upon the individual producing the verbal response. The dynamics of these processes are particularly pertinent to an understanding and explanation of depression (see Heiby & Staats, Chapter 10, this vol.).

The so-called cognitive-behavioral paradigm has experienced great popularity based upon the proposition that verbal labels, expectations, and causal attributions have functional implications for an individual's emotional and instrumental reactions. Labels, in addition to being verbal descriptors of objects, can have emotional or attitudinal value depending upon past association with pleasant or harmful events or with other emotional words and concepts. Expectations are higher-order verbal constructions that are predictions of future events that may be negative, neutral, or positive in affective valence. Attributions are yet more abstract verbal constructions relating the causal effect of some prior event upon some consequent event. Both the prior events and the subsequent event may have affective valence. The logical (or paralogical) connection between one affectively valenced verbal response ("I am not perfect") and another ("therefore I am terrible") may have a devastating emotional effect upon the person engaging in the verbal behavior.

In the clinical realm, the ability to anticipate and change self-produced elements of the verbal-emotional repertoire is an important component of the self-control process, including the control of emotional reactions. The specification and modification of self-produced verbal responses can be employed in the elicitation of emotional behavior. The following discussion will emphasize the nature and function of verbal-emotional repertoires as employed in cognitive or rational restructuring in adult behavior disorders in emotional arousal.

Two early proponents associated with cognitive-behavioral treatments, Beck (1967, 1976) and Ellis (1962, 1983), developed their theories and procedures in reaction to dissatisfaction with their psychoanalytic backgrounds. Upon closer inspection, Beck's theory possesses some striking similarities to psychoanalytic theory. It is intrapsychic and emphasizes a structural model of cognitive organization. Beck proposes that human behaviors are controlled by cognitive structures and that affective dysfunction follows therefrom. Such structures are relatively enduring components of the total cognitive organization. Cognitive structures are further composed of schemata. Schemas appear to be self-statements that often consist of rules that, in turn, function to screen, code, and evaluate incoming information. Hence, incoming information is organized into psychologically meaningful facets. Such screening and organizing allows the person to orient in time and space with respect to the interpreted stimuli. Such orientation involves either affective or instrumental responses, or both. The affective and/or behavioral responses, in turn, provide further stimulus information to be processed.

In psychopathology, the orderly matching of stimuli with appropriate schemata is upset by the intrusion of "primitive" idiosyncratic schemata. These idiosyncratic cognitive schemata ordinarily exert minimal influence on integrated thinking but when the cognitive organization becomes "dislocated," the idiosyncratic cognitions produce a powerful stream of irrational self-statements. The result is incongruity between the stimulus situation and resultant schemata. Such incongruity gives rise to the misapplication of labels and rules to various situations resulting in paralogical processes including arbitrary inference, selective abstraction, and overgeneralization. These cognitive processes then mediate maladaptive emotional and instrumental behaviors.

Ellis (1962) also formulated a theory concerning the interaction of verbal and emotional processes, although his is perhaps not as molecular as Beck's. In short, Ellis posits that individuals acquire faulty cognitions, that is, syllogistic reasoning processes, beliefs and interpretive rules of events. To the degree that the person's cognitions are irrational and illogical, emotional dysfunction (anxiety in particular) will be manifested. The person's emotional response, then, is not to some external situation, but to related value-oriented and interpretive cognitions about the external situations. In order to treat emotional disorders, the faulty cognitive and belief systems, as well as overt behavior, must be changed.

As clinically innovative as these models might be, they both suffer from the lack of a coherent and comprehensive theory that can incorporate both functional and dysfunctional processes. Viewed paradigmatically, however, both of these theories can be interpreted in a social behavioral model by analyzing the basic behavioral repertoires involved. Ellis's model emphasizes the operation of verbal-emotional repertoire components. These include words, phrases, and verbal concepts that elicit physiological and affective responses. The syllogistic reasoning process that proceeds from verbal description to arbitrary inference and to catastrophic conclusion clearly represents hierarchically organized elements of the verbal-emotional repertoire. Beck's paralogical reasoning processes relate more directly to elements of the language-cognitive repertoire which indirectly articulate with elements of the verbal-emotional repertoire.

In order to draw social behaviorism's contribution to cognitive-behavioral treatments more clearly, we now turn to a more detailed analysis of basic repertoires and then apply the analysis to relevant forms of psychopathology.

The Regulatory Functions of Labeling and Reasoning Repertoires

The operation of the language-cognitive repertoire has important implications for problematic human behavior. The importance of language is that it enables a person to communicate, solve problems, reason, plan, interpret information, and so on. Language repertoires constitute the knowledge of a person allowing him or her to predict events and to respond to stimuli in the form of reasoning and solving problems. Three factors are generally involved in reasoning and problem-solving processes. The first is the manner in which the relevant stimuli are labeled. The second factor concerns the verbal sequence made to the labels. Finally, some overt act is often elicited and represented by the specific verbal responses.

Language-cognitive responses that are elicited by nonlanguage stimuli (physical objects) give rise to labeling repertoires. Labeling repertoires are learned, beginning with concrete or classes of objects, proceeding to more complex labeling processes, giving rise to grammatical classes. One example of complex labeling repertoires is social and self-labeling. Complex combinations of stimuli are labeled as anger, boredom, acting suspiciously, or feeling depressed. Not only do we learn external situations, events, and people, but we also learn to label our own behaviors as stimuli. Labeling processes also have important implications for effective reasoning and problem solving. The emotional valence of the labels may affect reasoning. To the degree that the label is inaccurate and elicits a highly negative or positive emotional response, the reasoning process is also likely to be adversely affected, directly interfering with adaptive behavior, or indirectly leading to maladaptive behavior.

The initial labeling of a stimulus situation often elicits a sequence of additional verbal responses. The particular word association sequence elicited by a label is idiosyncratic to the person, based on his or her unique learning history. To the degree that the word association sequence is consistent with the observed events, the associated reasoning and problem solving will be facilitated. Further, if some overt behavior is the end point of the reasoning, then the behavior may be appropriate or inappropriate depending on the consistency of the reasoning sequence in relation to the actual events.

As noted above, labeling repertoires also include the labeling of our own behaviors. As human behaviors become more complex, more elaborated constellations of behavior are organized. One result of this increased complexity is development of a self-concept. The self-concept consists of complex repertoires of attitudes, interests, values, and beliefs that pertain to the perceived self. Such labels acquire emotional value and, consistent with the above discussion, influence subsequent reasoning and problem-solving processes. The emotional characteristics of the self-labels and subsequent self-statements are important, not only in influencing the person's own reasoning and behavior, but also in determining the responses of others to the person. For example, self-statements concerning personal worth give rise to reasoning processes leading to overt behaviors that, in turn, constitute stimuli eliciting the response of others. Hierarchies of verbal-cognitive behaviors are constructed that interact and form cumulative hierarchies. Such cumulative hierarchies form the basis for facilitating the rapid learning of new response patterns in terms of reasoning, planning, vicarious learning, imagining things never concretely experienced before, and so forth. These are all "cognitive" activities. As such, they are learned language repertoires. Hence, we would argue, language repertoires form the basis of both intrapersonal (cognitive) and interpersonal activity.

Applications of Verbal-Cognitive Repertoires to Abnormal Behavior

Abnormal behavior may be conceptualized in two possible ways within the present model. The first application has to do with deficits in the language-cognitive repertoire. The second application has to do with the verbal-emotional repertoire. Deficits in the language-cognitive repertoire affect social and personal adjustment because many important reasoning and labeling repertoires are absent. More likely, however, is the operation of maladaptive verbal-cognitive processes. When labeling repertoires are faulty, the subsequent reasoning processes and overt behaviors will also be inappropriate. For example, in the case of speech anxiety, some objective event (giving a speech) is inappropriately labeled as dangerous. As a result of higher-order classical conditioning, the word "dangerous" will elicit a negative emotional response along with an associated verbal reasoning sequence that suggests that "it is horrible to have to put one's personality on the line by giving a speech." Hence, subsequent overt behavior, such as avoidance of public speaking situations, may be maladaptive in that the person fails a speech course or does poorly in a profession that requires verbal presentations.

Language-cognitive repertoires also provide an explanation for "defense mechanisms." The function of verbal-cognitive defenses is to reduce anxiety, punishment, or other negative consequences. In relation to the speech-anxious person, he or she may explain failure in the course by saying "I don't like the structure of the course" or some other such statement. Generally, such defensive measures are acceptable to others in the person's social world, and are not regarded as abnormal. However, if the defensive statement is not veridical, the person will receive socially aversive consequences for exhibiting defensive behavior. Such inappropriate defensive verbal-cognitive behavior is dysfunctional because as the language becomes more idiosyncratic, it becomes less effective to the person in mediating adaptive overt behaviors. If the individual mislabels reality via such defensive statements, he or she effectively prevents appropriate social disapproval and personal aversive consequences that would possibly function to modify the problematic behavior.

So far, we have analyzed the maintenance and modification of maladaptive cognitive and emotional processes in the "metalanguage" of the basic behavioral repertoire. It is incumbent upon a paradigmatic approach to identify the manner in which it provides a more coherent or a more explanatory model of cognitive processes than those provided by "cognitive" theorists (Beck, 1976; Ellis, 1983;

Landau & Goldfried, 1981). We argue that the concept of the basic behavioral repertoire is more specific than concepts such as schemata, irrationality, distortion, and the like. More important, the learning mechanisms that are subsumed by basic behavioral repertoires have been subjected to extensive experimental analysis (Staats, 1975). Unlike single-function theories, Staats's three-function theory allows for a more detailed understanding of how the two primary mechanisms of learning interact in the modification of attitudinal, reinforcing, and directive functions that language serves.

The process of "language behavior therapy" (Staats, 1972) involves the analysis of how cognitive structures are acquired, maintained, and modified. A molecular analysis of these cognitive processes is necessary to understand their function. Staats (1975) notes that by teaching clients to discriminate situations and events that give rise to maladaptive self-statements and overt behaviors, they can learn to change their own behaviors. The client is taught to make new labeling responses to certain problematic classes of stimuli that ordinarily set the occasion for maladaptive behavior. Changes in labeling frequently (but not always) result in different emotional responses to the new label, thus also providing a new directive stimulus for different, more adaptive reasoning and behavioral responses. New reasoning (self-statements) sequences are also taught that, again, provide new emotional and directive conditions for other self-statements or overt behaviors. Such a conceptualization is entirely consistent with the cognitive therapy process and procedures discussed previously (Meichenbaum, 1986). Staats's (1975) conceptualization, however, provides for a rapprochement between elemental, peripheralistic behavioral emphases and more centralistic cognitive approaches. It should also help to overcome the extensive, unnecessary and unproductive controversy in behavior therapy between "pure behaviorists" and "cognitivists". The following chapters will further elaborate on how social behavioral theory can provide a unifying framework for the various cognitive-behavioral treatments of common psychological dysfunctions such as anxiety (Chapters 8 and 9) and depression (Chapter 10).

Basic Behavioral Repertoires and Imagery Representation

Behavior therapy procedures have often relied upon the use of imagery when direct presentation of fear-producing stimuli has been difficult or impossible. Some of the most extensively used procedures have been systematic desensitization, covert extinction, covert sensitization, imaginal flooding, guided imagery, and rational imagery. This is somewhat paradoxical, from a behavioristic point of view, because of the inherently "cognitive" nature of the imagery process. It is not surprising, therefore, to find no comprehensive model of imagery structure and function in the behavior therapy literature. Lang's (1977, 1984) model emphasizes the verbal-propositional nature of imagery function and analyzes fear reduction as information processing. However, a more comprehensive model requires that the developmental and structural components of imagery also be explicated.

Behavioristic analyses of imagery began with the application of mediational mechanisms. N.E. Miller's (1959) conception of cue- and drive- producing responses provided a vehicle by which imagery could be considered as a mediational variable. Imagery could then be understood in terms of learning mechanisms that governed other mediational variables, such as conditioned fear and covert instrumental responses. However, N.E. Miller's (1959) treatment of imagery was tangential, and he discussed it only in an attempt to demonstrate the explanatory utility of mediational constructs in general. At the same time, however, other researchers using mediational constructs were more directly interested in explicating the nature and acquisition of imagery processes. In its most elemental form, imagery was analyzed in terms of classically conditioned sensory responses (Mowrer, 1960; Staats, 1961; Staats, Staats, & Heard, 1961).

In addition to a mediational analysis of the development of imagery processes, Staats's view has also emphasized the structure and function of imagery. Imagery function involves not only passive mediational mechanisms with cue properties, but also constructive and integrative properties that exercise directive functions in gathering additional information from the physical environment. Staats has attempted to extend the analysis of imagery function from simple verbal learning/conditioning phenomena to a complex analysis of the interaction of basic behavioral repertoires involving verbal, emotional, and motor components.

The Imagery Basic Behavioral Repertoire

It has been argued (Staats & Lohr, 1979) that language gives imagery much of its scope or applicability. The use of language to denote characteristics of objects not present to the sensory system provides for the utilization of cognitive representations of physical objects or events. Language is thus employed in the elicitation or construction of imagery, and imagery is utilized in the elicitation of verbal representations of other symbolic events. From a social behavioral point of view, imagery processes are subsumed under the verbal-image and image-verbal repertoires. The most basic function unit of the verbal-image repertoire is the unit-image word. Unit-image words elicit elements of a larger composite image. The elements many be components of may different images and physical stimuli. These imagery characteristics represent concepts such as roundness, loudness, heaviness, whiteness, sweetness, and so on.

The characteristics of imagery that are elicited by unit-image words are typically referred to as features of denotative meaning. Unit-image words come to acquire denotative meaning through first-order and higher-order classical conditioning. When verbal stimuli are consistently paired with objects eliciting a common sensory response, a portion of that response is transferred to the neutral verbal stimulus. Staats and his associates (1961) showed that pairing nonsense syllables with words having a higher-order denotative characteristic (roundness or squareness) resulted in the transfer to a nonsense syllable. Sensory preconditioning effects (Bitterman, Reed, & Kubala, 1953; Brogden, 1947) and some aspects of mediated generalization (Phillips, 1958) have also been interpreted as a function of conditioned sensory responses. Concept words for roundness, colorfulness, and loudness are those that have come to elicit one or more conditioned sensory responses. The sensory responses may represent either single (i.e., redness) or synthesized (i.e., sharpness) sense modalities depending upon the nature of associations developed in acquisition or upon the immediate environmental context in which they are employed. In addition, the multiple production of several unit-image words may be used to reconstruct or even synthesize complex imaginal representations. That is, words can be combined in a manner that will assemble or elicit a new compound image (Staats, 1975). While isolated unit-image words may elicit individual conditioned sensory responses (dark, stomach, against, triangle, hair, white) a more familiar order of presentation may elicit a qualitatively different picture (dark, triangle, hair, against, white, stomach). The language-cognitive analysis helps to explain the sensory experience of a complex imaginal stimulus in the absence of the primary experience. It occurs through the sequential elicitation and structural organization of unit-image responses. Because the unit-image responses have stimulus properties, the stimulus properties can be assembled in a manner analogous to that of constructing a puzzle.

In addition to an explication of the way in which words function in determining the imagery experience, imagery can function in the determination of verbal or other motor behavior. This process involves another behavioral repertoire, the image-verbal repertoire. In this case, however, simple or compound images, with their sensory stimuli, may serve as cues for a detailed verbal description of some past or future experience. Individuals learn to label their internal conditioned (and constructed) sensory responses in the process of learning a verbal labeling repertoire. Thus, one is able to report daydreams, nocturnal dreams, and other similar private events through the vehicle of language. These internal mediators may serve as more than cues for the description of mental content, however. Paivio (1971) has suggested that the operation of imagery is an extremely powerful mediator in the learning of verbal stimuli and in important memory functions. The primary function of verbal-image and image-verbal repertoires is to provide a basis for the vast multiplication of human experience. Individuals with different verbal-image and image-verbal repertoires will experience the same language stimuli in different ways. Limitations or deficits in these repertoires will result in deficits in experience.

The imagery component of the language-cognitive repertoire subsumes functions for other repertoires, such as the emotional-motivational repertoire. The image compound referred to above (dark, triangle, hair) may elicit a strong emotional response after sufficient experience with stimulus represented by the image compound. At the most elemental level of acquisition, Lohr (1976) has found that connotative (emotional) and denotative meaning can be acquired in a simultaneous fashion based on the mechanisms of classical conditioning. Subjects were presented with some nonsense syllables printed in red letters and some printed in white letters. The nonsense syllables were paired with words having either strong positive or strong negative meaning. The results showed that subjects rated the red syllables as more colorful than the white syllables, and rated their evaluative meaning (pleasant-unpleasant) based on the type of words with which they were associated.

Kirchner (1970) has shown that paired associate learning is enhanced when evaluative stimulus words also elicit a sensory response. In addition, the interaction of conditioned sensory responses and conditioned emotional responses may be seen in sensory preconditioning, a form of mediated generalization. If a blue light is consistently paired with a verbal stimulus such as the word *azure*, the sensory response will be conditioned to the word. If the word *azure* is then paired with faradic shock, a conditioned response such as heart rate will be conditioned not only to the word *azure* but also to the conditioned sensory response which the word has previously acquired. When the blue light is presented alone, the blue sensory response will also elicit the conditioned heart rate response which was previously conditioned to the mediating image elicited by the word *azure*.

In a more concrete manner, the interaction between connotative and denotative meaning has been applied to the analysis of the development and modification of racial attitudes. The pairing of positive and negative stimuli, such as food or the loss of money, with color concepts (black-white) leads to transfer of evaluative meaning to racial concepts and attitudes toward persons denoted by the color concept (Trayman & Witte, 1976; Williams & Edwards, 1969). Other research has shown that preexisting racial color concepts in children can be modified by pairing the color concept with words having positive connotation (Parish, 1974; Parish, Shirazi, & Lambert, 1976). In the context of the repertoire analysis, verbal-image and verbal-emotional repertoires are modified or developed through language learning and such repertoires then exercise functional control over objects represented by the image.

Applications of Imagery Repertoires

The mediation of emotional responses is not limited to concept-image words. This analysis also suggests that an image compound may serve to elicit strong emotional reactions even when the unit-image components may not. A clinical example of this phenomenon is phobic imagery which will be discussed in the following chapter by Eifert. Image-produced emotional reactions may be of an appetitive or aversive sort depending upon one's direct or language conditioning history. The nature of the emotional mediatory is also capable of eliciting instrumental behavior which may be directed toward or away from the object denoted by the image. Staats (1968a) proposes that stimuli that acquire an attitudinal (emotional) function also exercise directive stimulus control independent of direct reinforcement contingencies. Images that are capable of eliciting emotional responses may mediate instrumental behavior directed toward the denoted object more effectively than just the emotional mediatory alone. For example, Berkowitz and Knurek (1969) showed that aggression generalized to persons denoted by a proper name follows the classical conditioning of a negative attitude toward the name. Subsequently, Turner and Layton (1976) demonstrated that aggression was facilitated when memory-induced mediators had both imagery and negative connotative components. These findings imply that the imagery sensory responses serve to cue and direct the affective and behavioral components of strong emotional reactions.

The induction of affective states using verbal imagery instructions is standard behavior therapy procedure. Methods of constructing imagery with aversive characteristics have long been employed in procedures (e.g., flooding) designed to modify conditioned fear responses and the escape/avoidance behaviors that fear mediates. Therapeutic imagery has often been considered iconic representation of three dimensional space (Danaher & Thoresen, 1972; Stampfl & Levis, 1967; Waters & McDonald, 1973). Following Pylyshyn's (1973) criticism of iconic imagery, several researchers have demonstrated that therapeutic imagery also consists of verbal stimulus and response propositions (Grayson & Borkovec, 1978; Lang, 1984). Both iconic and propositional representations have been shown to mediate physiological correlates of fear (Weerts & Lang, 1978). Similarly, fear has been modified through extinction of fear conditioned to iconic representations (Wilson & Davison, 1971) or by direct modification of response propositions through imagery instructions (Grayson & Borkovec, 1978). In both cases, imagery has been modified through verbal instructional means. New unit-image responses are elicited, reorganized and practiced in a manner similar to skill acquisition. Physiological arousal then changes as imagery content is modified.

A reciprocal process has also been demonstrated. It has long been presumed that the reduction of fear arousal through relaxation training leads to modification of fear imagery (Evans, 1976). The empirical research on the effect of relaxation upon imagery vividness, however, has not been supportive of the presumption (Rehm, Mattei, Potts, & Skolnick, 1974). Our own research (Hamberger & Lohr, 1980; Lohr & Rookey, 1982) indicates that it is imagery controllability that improves as a function of relaxation training. A social behavioral analysis suggests that the verbal-image repertoire is modified through interaction with the verbal-emotional repertoire. The verbal induction of a relaxed emotional state leads to more efficient elicitation and organization of unit-images.

The image-compound concept has also been utilized as a mediational mechanism in the operation of self-direction and self-reinforcement. Anticipated rewards in the form of image-compounds can serve as directive stimuli for organized, goal-directed behavior. In this fashion, the attitudinal value of self-presented incentives and the informational value (concreteness) of the imaginal representation both serve to regulate goal-directed behavior. The manner in which image-compound incentives are represented has important implications for self-direction, as in the case of resistance to temptation. Initial research demonstrated that young children could resist temptation to proscribed edibles by distraction (Mischel, 1974) or by presenting a symbolic representation (picture) of the reward during the delay period (Mischel & Moore, 1973). The role of imagery in the representation of reward was also shown to have systematic effects upon ability to delay gratification (Moore, Mischel, & Zeiss, 1976). When children transformed pictures into "real" rewards, resistance to temptation was decreased. When real rewards were imaginally transformed into pictures, resistance to temptation was increased. This pattern of results was explained in terms of the connotative and denotative characteristics of the anticipated reinforcing stimulus. When directly presented, the motivational (emotional) characteristics of the blocked stimulus increase the likelihood of the proscribed response. In imaginal representation, however, the denotative (informative) characteristics of the blocked stimulus served to guide and maintain reward orientation without the motivational stimulus for consummatory behavior. In order to test this hypothesis, Moore (1977) asked children to imagine either "real" rewards or "pictures" of rewards. Children were then instructed to focus on either the arousal or informational properties of the imaginal representations. The results showed that arousal instructions led to less delay in the "picture" group but did not influence delay in the "real" group. Conversely, informational instructions increased delay in the "real" group but had no effect upon delay in the "picture" group. These findings support the theoretical analyses of the interaction between the sensory and motivational components of the image-compound and their regulation of instrumental behavior.

The social behavioral conceptualization of imagery has been extended to the establishment of self-standards (performance criteria). The ability to present anticipated rewards in both their directive and informative characteristics represents the terminal link in a chain of symbolically rehearsed or planned responses. For example, if one is to give a particularly important speech (in terms of its imagined consequences), a series of responses and intermediate consequences must be organized to influence the probability of favorable outcome. Just prior to receiving the reward (applause), a series of verbal responses must be emitted in an organized fashion. In order to find one's self behind the podium, one must effectively wend one's way through a tangle of chairs and people. In order to begin wending, one must find oneself at the appropriate building, the appropriate gathering, and at the appropriate time.

One can thus elaborate sets of sequentially organized subrepertoires that must be established as necessary preconditions for the delivery of the primary reinforcer. The complexity and motivational value of the image-compound of the reinforcing stimuli may serve a self-presented conditioned discriminative (incentive) stimulus that may strengthen flagging or inadequate behavior earlier in the response chain. The vigor, strength, alacrity or precision of the behavior may thus be construed as a molecular element of more complex self-standards of behavior. The imaginal representation of these behavior propositions will serve as criteria for the self-reinforcement of self-directed behavior.

The social behavioral theory of imagery is a useful heuristic in explaining the compound and constructive nature of imagery, that is, the manner in which verbal stimuli are compounded to elicit a constructive representation having characteristics (or functions) that are not subsumed by any one (or several) of its elements. An earlier anecdotal example implied that grammatical order to the verbal constituents may be a necessary requirement for the elicitation of an image-compound and that prior experience (familiarity) with constituent elements would facilitate the construction of imagery. At present, little research on this aspect of imagery and imagery function has been conducted. The social behavioral conceptualization promises to be a useful heuristic device by which such research could be generated.

Conclusions

Cognitions as language-based mediational processes have been detailed with reference to their development, integration, function and modification. In discussing the development and integration, we have treated language-based cognitions primarily as dependent variables. The interactive learning processes responsible for the development and organization of these language mediators were identified as a means of demonstrating their explanatory value. It was suggested that complex human learning processes could be applied to the development of those cognitive mediators. Our discussion of the modification and function of language-based cognitions has emphasized their role as both dependent and independent variables. At a higher level of analysis, we have attempted to show how basic behavioral repertoires function in the regulation of general patterns of behavior. Cognitive-behavioral interventions employ not only language as a tool, but also make it the focus of change. Modifications of language and associated cognitions have been implemented with the intent of providing rapid and generalized effects of intervention upon complex cognitive skills and social behavior. The social behavioral model thus provides a heuristic by which the nature and function of language may be directly applied in the amelioration of disorders. The value of this heuristic can be judged in the next five chapters, in which language repertoires (and other response systems) are analyzed in the context of specific topics of clinical concern.

8

The Acquisition and Treatment of Phobic Anxiety: A Paradigmatic Behavioral Perspective

Georg H. Eifert

Of all behavioral and emotional problems, theories and treatments of phobic anxiety have attracted the greatest interest during the development of behavior therapy over the last 30 years. This is not surprising given the prevalence of phobias in the general population which is as high as 11% in the United States and 13% in West Germany (cf., Öst, 1989). According to Öst, the majority of phobic complaints in the general population consists of specific phobias and behavioral interventions usually achieve a clinically significant improvement in 75 to 85% of treated cases—and a slightly lower success rate of 65 to 75% for persons suffering from agoraphobia and social phobia.

In this chapter I will undertake a conceptual analysis of the acquisition and cognitive-behavioral treatment of phobic anxiety from the perspective of social (paradigmatic) behaviorism. This approach to adult psychotherapy was originally outlined by Staats (1972) and described in detail in this volume in Chapter 2 by Staats and Chapter 7 by Lohr and Hamberger who touched on many facets of complex behavior and its dysfunction. I will concentrate on theories and treatments of phobic anxiety and show how social behaviorism accounts for both the direct and indirect verbal-symbolic acquisition and treatment of phobic anxiety. I thereby hope to provide a unifying framework to guide the research of both "traditional" and "cognitive" behavior therapists and help to overcome this artificial and separatistic distinction (see also Eifert, 1985). Furthermore, the chapter is intended to make a contribution toward closing the gap between theory and application in behavior therapy.

The Inadequacies of Simple Conditioning Models of Phobic Anxiety

In behavior therapy it has become customary to operationalize phobic anxiety as fairly dramatic changes in three "response systems": the physiological (e.g., perspiring, heart palpitations), the verbal-cognitive (e.g., negative evaluations and statements), and the motor-behavior system (escape and avoidance behavior). Although this "triple-response-mode" concept of anxiety has been widely accepted, it is not without its critics. For example, Hugdahl (1981) argued that if each component is a measure of the underlying phenomenon (fear) but each of the three components is also capable of representing the phenomenon itself, are we not identifying different phenomena rather than the subcomponents of a unitary entity such as fear? Evans (1986) points out that some "modes" are easily misinterpreted and constantly confounded with the different methods of measurement. For instance, neither can the cognitive mode be equated with the subjective experience of fear, nor is the cognitive mode or response system the same as self-report measures. Evans therefore suggests abandoning the notion of measuring traitlike unitary constructs such as fear through different "modes" of behavior. We should focus instead on examining the structural interactions and relationships between different response repertoires.

The original behaviorist position (e.g., Eysenck & Rachman, 1965) views anxiety as the product of a classical conditioning process, in which a neutral stimulus is paired with an unpleasant event or aversive unconditioned stimulus (UCS) that elicits a strong negative emotional unconditioned response (UCR). The formerly neutral stimulus becomes a conditioned stimulus (CS) that is capable of eliciting a negative conditioned response (CR)—"anxiety"—more or less similar to the original UCR. Conditions conducive to the development of phobias are: (1) the intensity of the fear or pain elicited by the UCS, (2) the number of pairings between fear/pain and the neutral or conditioned stimulus, and (3) contextual factors such as confinement and darkness (see Rachman, 1977). In order to reduce the unpleasant consequences of anxiety, the individual learns to escape and subsequently avoid the anxiety-provoking stimulus or situation. This operant learning of avoidance behavior was considered to be responsible for the maintenance of anxiety: as the individual never confronts the CS, the CR cannot extinguish.

The simple conditioning theory of the acquisition and maintenance of fear has been extensively criticized on theoretical, empirical, and clinical grounds (e.g., Marks, 1977, 1987; Rachman, 1977; Rachman, Craske, Tallman, & Solyom, 1986) with conclusions varying from improving and refining conditioning models to declaring them dead. I will attempt to demonstrate that a social behavioral framework can overcome the major limitations and shortcomings of the simple conditioning model.

Certain phobias are more common than others. For example, snake fear is much more common than dental fear or fear of injections (Agras, Sylvester, & Oliveau, 1969). This selectivity of phobias was not sufficiently considered in the early conditioning model. Not every "neutral" stimulus that is paired with an aversive UCS is likely to become a powerful CS. According to Seligman's (1971) "preparedness theory," only biologically significant stimuli are likely to become phobic stimuli when associated with trauma. The predictions that such phobias are acquired rapidly and are highly resistant to extinction have received empirical support in a number of well-controlled experiments by Öhman and his associates (reviewed by Öhman, Dimberg, & Öst, 1985). On the other hand, the notion that these conditioned responses are unaffected by verbal-cognitive manipulation once they are acquired has been qualified in two experiments by Eifert (1984b) and Eifert and Schermelleh (1985), which will be discussed in a later section.

Not all phobias begin with one or several clearly determinable traumatic experiences. It has been repeatedly argued (e.g., Marks, 1977) that only a few phobias are the result of direct traumatic experiences. For instance, Kleinknecht (1982) studied the origins and remission of fear in a group of members of the American Tarantula Society. He found that vicarious learning and information were not only responsible for the original acquisition of fear, but the vast majority of subjects also attributed remission of fear to acquired knowledge and observation of spiders. Similarly, Murray and Foote (1979) reported that most of their snake-phobic subjects had very little personal experience with snakes; in fact, the more experience subjects had with snakes, the less they feared them. Extreme anxiety was largely the result of a variety of observational and instructional experiences that communicated negative information about snakes. As one subject reported, "Basically my fear was ingrained by my parents and reinforced by TV and movies. Snakes are always evil there" (p. 493). However, I do not agree with assertions (e.g., Marks, 1977) that the finding that some phobias are the result of vicarious and instructional learning is damaging to a conditioning model of fear acquisition. On the contrary, provided we have extended the conditioning model to take account of the specific forms of *human* learning rather than simply transferring the basic animal conditioning principles to account for human behavior, we would expect humans to acquire phobias by verbal-symbolic means *as well as* direct traumatic experiences. Social behavioral theory explains, and in fact predicts, this phenomenon by stating that verbal and symbolic stimuli (e.g., images, observations) can elicit similar negative emotions to external aversive stimuli that are involved in actual traumatic experiences. In other words, phobias need not be the results of one or two traumatic incidences; they can develop gradually through a number of verbal-symbolic learning experiences.

The high resistance to extinction and the increased intensity of conditioned fear and avoidance behavior cannot be explained by a simple conditioning model without resort to additional assumptions. Each successful reduction of the CR by means of escape or avoidance of the CS constitutes an extinction trial since the CS-CR connection is not reinforced by the UCS. The conditioned anxiety response should subsequently diminish as well as the instrumental behavior supposedly motivated by it. Eysenck (1982) explains the maintenance and increase of UCS-unreinforced conditioned anxiety by the process of *incubation*. Assuming that the conditioned anxiety response (CR) has drive properties, it will serve UCS functions and act as a reinforcer to the extent that the anxiety response resembles the unconditioned fear response. In view of critical comments (e.g., Bersh, 1980) that incubation has been only rarely and mostly retrospectively observed in humans, the more recent supportive findings for incubation theory coming from carefully controlled experiments with humans (e.g., Sandin & Chorot, 1989) are worth noting. Incubation, therefore, is a valuable concept because it complements the social behavioral explanation of the process by which self-generated emotional stimuli, such as negative labels and images, can maintain and exacerbate an existing fear. Referring to adaptation level theory, Lauterbach (1979) argued that the increased intensity of phobic reactions may be due to changes in the perception of phobic stimuli. These perceptual changes could be a result of phobic individuals' tendency to avoid progressively weaker and greater numbers of anxiety-related stimuli.

In her review of animal studies, Mineka (1979) found the relationship between fear and avoidance behavior to be much more complex than originally assumed. Studies revealed a disassociation between avoidance behavior and fear (measured by physiological arousal): neither does extinction of fear automatically and always lead to a decrease in avoidance nor is fear extinction a prerequisite for a decrease in avoidance; conversely, extinction of avoidance behavior is not always accompanied by a parallel reduction in fear (see also Mineka, 1987). Some of the most critical findings for the two-stage theory of fear and avoidance come from a recent study by Rachman and his associates (1986): when agoraphobic clients were encouraged to escape from situations if they felt too anxious, neither were escapes followed by increases in fear nor did they strengthen subsequent agoraphobic avoidance. Rachman and his colleagues suggest that the option of escaping—the knowledge that one can escape— served to increase the clients' sense of control and thereby reduced their fear. The heightened sense of control and the reduced fear even generalized to novel tasks and situations.

It is obvious that the simple conditioning theory of fear is neither comprehensive nor adequate, but its weaknesses are not fatal either. However, all of the above findings strongly suggest that the two-stage theory must be revised and expanded. The following sections will show that cognitive-behavioral theorists have abandoned conditioning theory without replacing it with a new readily testable theory. At the same time, the theoretical and empirical framework of social behaviorism is comprehensive and has gone beyond the limitations of early conditioning models by adding new theory levels to account for complex human behavior; therefore it has the potential to serve as a unifying framework for cognitive-behavioral approaches to phobic anxiety.

Social Learning Perspectives of Anxiety Acquisition and Reduction

Cognitive and social learning approaches emphasize the adaptive abilities of individuals and their active role in controlling their behavior through self-generated stimuli. Stimuli are selectively attended to, perceived, transformed, labeled, and categorized before a person responds to them. Bandura (1977a) postulated a "reciprocal determinism" or interaction of individuals and their environment stressing that situational and personal variables constantly influence one another. Expectations are believed to be of particular importance in mediating human learning and behavior, and aversive experiences, either of a personal or vicarious sort, create expectations of injurious effects that can activate both fear and defensive behavior. When formerly neutral stimuli are associated with painful experiences, it is not that the stimuli have become aversive but that individuals have learned to anticipate aversive consequencies (Bandura, 1977a, 1978a).

The crucial questions to be asked are: what are the advantages of such social learning perspectives, and what more do they offer than social behavioral theory? Although it was initially hoped (e.g., Wilson, 1978) that social learning approaches would lead to the development of more effective treatment methods for anxiety, more recent reviews have not been able to substantiate such hopes (cf., Eifert & Craill, 1989; Latimer & Sweet, 1984). On the contrary, even staunch proponents of cognitive behavior therapy have consistently emphasized that performance-based treatment methods are significantly more effective in producing behavior change than methods that rely on verbal, imaginal, or vicarious interventions (Meichenbaum & Cameron, 1982). Similarly, Ellis (1979) conceded that pure cognitive restructuring works relatively poorly for almost any kind of phobia. Phobic individuals must act against their "irrational beliefs" if they really want to overcome them.

Wilson (1978) also referred to the heuristic functions of social learning theories because they could integrate three regulatory systems in a comprehensive yet testable framework: (1) the antecedent system which is controlled by classical conditioning, (2) the consequent system which refers to the effects of operant conditioning and reinforcement on behavior, and (3) a mediational system operating with a variety of symbolic processes. Yet assumptions on the interrelatedness of regulatory systems generally leading to statements like "cognitions influence behaviors, which influence environments, which influence cognitions . . ." are examples of incomplete causal analyses and tautologous explanations (Mahoney, 1977). Cognitive behavior therapists are still faced with the task of stating the psychological principles and rules underlying the reciprocal determinism of person and situation variables: "Without specifying what these are, how they are learned, and how they have their effects, a theory that says it includes cognitions as a central element does so only on a general philosophical level" (Staats, 1980, p. 214). One of the most important tenets of cognitive-behavioral approaches is that it is not the situation per se, but the way a person perceives it that determines whether or not anxiety will be experienced. In their cognitive theory of anxiety, Beck and Emery (1985) emphasize the role of idiosyncratic perceptions and "faulty cognitive styles" (e.g., selective attention, misperceptions, catastrophizing) without, however, explaining the origin of these misperceptions. Similarly, Ellis views anxiety as the result of irrational interpretations and appraisals of persons and events blaming a self-defeating negativistic human nature for these distortions. Zettle and Hayes (1980) rightfully criticized this pseudobiological account for failing to explain the origin of irrational beliefs.

It is unfortunate and unnecessary for cognitive behavior therapists to operate in such a "conceptual vacuum" (Eysenck, 1982, 1987), and I find it difficult to understand why almost all cognitive-behavioral proponents have ignored social behaviorism. Paradigmatic behaviorism specifies the psychological principles by which language and symbolic stimuli (e.g., images) interact with affect and overt behavior in the acquisition, maintenance, and treatment of anxiety. In other words, a cognitive-behavioral structure including a personality level of theory has always been central in social behaviorism accounting for individual differences in responses to situations and indicating how these personality differences determine differences in behavior. For example, a series of studies (Burns, Chapter 5, this vol.) provided evidence that differences in emotional-motivational repertoires affected which emotional stimuli were perceived, evaluated, experienced, and responded to. These personality differences also determined which new emotional responses were learned.

Applying these principles to the analysis of phobic problems, it follows that whether potentially frightening stimuli (e.g., a formal social situation) will be perceived and experienced as fearful depends in part on the unique characteristics of the individual's basic personality repertoires. These in turn are determined by prior learning experiences with the actual stimuli and/or their sensory-verbal representations in words, images, photographs, movies, and so on. Evaluative statements people make about potentially phobic stimuli or about themselves would be expected to have stimulus function in eliciting affective responses and motor behavior. Eysenck (e.g., 1982) has repeatedly stressed that the omission of personality variables from the traditional behaviorist position has been one of its greatest weaknesses. Paradigmatic behaviorism with its personality level of theory and interactional principles is a major step toward overcoming this problem in the analysis of anxiety.

Self-Efficacy: A Unifying Theory of Behavior Change?

Rather than adopting a paradigmatic behavioral approach, the general field of behavior therapy has paid much more attention to the concept of *self-efficacy*, which is supposed to fulfil a unifying purpose. Bandura (1978b) claims that anxiety and avoidance behavior are not causally related but that both are a function of an individual's perceived lack of coping skills to deal with an anxiety-provoking event. This lack of perceived self-efficacy produces high arousal in individuals when they are confronted with feared situations. Thus, what makes people afraid is mainly their perceived inability to cope with potentially aversive events. Interestingly, Bandura has repeatedly stated that anxiety should be eliminated most effectively through performance-based techniques rather than by cognitive manipulations. In several experiments (summarized in Bandura, 1978a, 1984) Bandura and his associates found significant increases in self-efficacy following a successful treatment of phobias; these increases in perceived self-efficacy are considered to be the causal factor responsible for the success of therapy.

Bandura's contention that the concept of perceived self-efficacy may provide a unifying framework to explain and predict therapeutic changes was already widely criticized in a 1978 issue of *Advances in Behaviour Research and Therapy,* and the criticisms are as valid today as they were more than a decade ago. Many authors were particularly critical of Bandura's assumption that self-efficacy expectations should play a causal role in producing behavior change. While acknowledging the important role of language and imagery, Eysenck regarded mastery and failure expectations as epiphenomena or by-products of behavioral changes rather than their cause. Similarly, Borkovec considered self-efficacy as a potentially important reflection rather than a mediator of behavioral change. In a reply to these criticisms, Bandura (1978b) pointed out that anxiety is, in large part, self-generated and the product of self-referent thoughts and verbalizations rather than automatically evoked by conditioned stimuli. He also criticized (rightly, in my opinion) the narrow and restrictive view of treating thoughts as mere epiphenomena. "Does conceptualizing cognitive activity simply as a by-product of physiological change encourage experimentation that will deepen our understanding of human thought and action?" (p. 254). As will be discussed later, there is indeed empirical evidence that at least some of the arousal and anxiety experienced by individuals when confronted with a phobic stimulus is self-generated and affected by the individual's appraisal of the situation. On the other hand, Bandura's (1984) distinction between self-referent thoughts and conditioned stimuli is untenable and reflects an anachronistic view of contemporary conditioning theories. For example, Martin and Levey (1985) have repeatedly stressed the importance of "evaluative cognitions" and how these can be modified through conditioning interventions. There is considerable evidence that through higher-order conditioning certain words and images can come to function as unconditioned stimuli capable of generating anxiety and direct avoidance behavior.

Referring to the three-systems model of anxiety, Bandura (1978b) argued that thought, physiological arousal, and overt behavior operate as reciprocally interacting factors rather than as loosely linked components or as conjoint events. However, as Staats (Chapter 2, this vol.) criticized, social learning theorists have not specified and concretized the dynamics and organization of these interactions. For instance, how do thoughts, verbal stimuli, emotional arousal, and behavior influence one another? How exactly do behavioral techniques influence a phobic person's perceived self-efficacy? Instead of providing clear answers to these crucial questions, Bandura (1978b) expressed a feeling of growing discontent with the view that human behavior can be adequately explained in terms of autonomic and instrumental conditioning and claimed that reciprocal determinism cannot be explained by conditioned anxiety theory.

Self-efficacy theory has also been criticized on a number of methodological grounds. Kazdin (1978) noted that the primary data used to draw conclusions about self-efficacy are correlations of answers to questionnaire items and approach scores in behavior tests. As the items used to assess self-efficacy (e.g., holding a snake) are identical in the questionnaires and behavior tests, and as both are administered closely in time and presented in the same hierarchical order, some correlation would be expected. Similarly, Eastman and Marzillier (1984) pointed out that Bandura's experiments merely show that people can make reliable predictions about their future behavior where tasks are discrete and outcomes limited. None of Bandura's experiments demonstrate the main tenet of self-efficacy theory: namely, that changes in perceived self-efficacy are the central mediating mechanism underlying all therapeutic change. In other words, neither high correlations between self-efficacy and overt behavior nor the finding that self-efficacy is higher after rather than prior to treatment proves that these changes in self-efficacy actually mediated or caused the behavioral change. A change in perceived self-efficacy could indeed itself be a function of another variable, or as Borkovec (1978) put it, a reflection rather than the cause of behavioral change.

Self-efficacy theory has been discussed in some detail because it is a very prominent example of a social learning or cognitive approach to the acquisition and treatment of anxiety. It reflects the necessity and advantages of going beyond a simple conditioning model by emphasizing the important role of symbolic processes in human learning and behavior. However, it also exemplifies the flaws and potential dangers still inherent in these approaches. I fully concur with the following critical evaluation of self-efficacy theory by Eastman and Marzillier (1984):

> We are in sympathy with the view that fearful and other behavior is at least partially determined by cognitive or personal factors. One of these factors may well be a sense of one's own efficacy. But we are skeptical that this is the all-pervasive and potent source of behavior change that Bandura claims it to be. (p. 226)

Verbal and symbolic stimuli are only one source of behavioral regulation and even if their modification leads to anxiety reduction, it cannot be concluded that they actually caused the phobic problem in the first place or that they are causally related to the occurrence of anxiety. Coyne (1982) criticized the persistence of the mechanistic assumption that cognitions are causal entities and warned against the pitfalls of considering cognitions as linearly causal antecedents of other psychological phenomena. And yet even with conceptions like "reciprocal determinism," cognitive-behavioral proponents have tended to concentrate more on what is happening within the person than between the person and the environment. There is a certain one-sidedness and imbalance in the explanation and treatment of anxiety and depression favoring cognitive variables. What Mahoney (1977) described as "the lack of ideological balance of today's cognitive revolutionaries" is indeed still one of the most serious challenges to and conceptual problems of cognitive-behavioral approaches.

To summarize, while cognitive-behavioral approaches have enlarged the number of techniques to alleviate phobic anxiety, the argument that the social learning perspective has generated more effective treatment methods still remains to be substantiated by clinical outcome studies (cf., Eifert & Craill, 1989; Latimer & Sweet, 1984; Miller & Berman, 1983). Furthermore, the supposedly heuristic function of social learning theories in their present inadequate conceptual form (Eysenck, 1987) must be questioned because the psychological principles underlying interactions between the environment, cognition, and behavior have not yet been specified.

A Paradigmatic Behavioral Formulation of Anxiety Acquisition and Treatment

The major implication of social behavioral theory for understanding anxiety disorders is that—while sufficient—it is not necessary for an individual to have an actual traumatic experience to develop a phobia. The association of inappropriate or negative emotion-eliciting verbal-symbolic stimuli with certain objects or situations is sufficient for those objects and situations to acquire aversive properties. Considering the potential conditioning trials that are available in a person's lifetime, intense anxiety reactions can easily be accounted for on the basis of language or other forms of symbolic conditioning. Acknowledging and explaining this important role of language and symbolic stimuli in a paradigmatic framework is one of the most valuable contributions of social behaviorism to unifying the field of behavior therapy.

The Role of Language Conditioning in the Acquisition of Phobic Anxiety

Humans acquire a verbal-emotional repertoire consisting of a very large number of words that come to be emotional stimuli. Hence phobias with no history of overt aversive conditioning could have been acquired vicariously and/or by means of semantic classical conditioning. It is not necessary for an individual to have a traumatic experience with an object to develop a phobic response. "Instead the association of the verbal stimulus with other negatively evaluated stimuli would be sufficient for that object to acquire aversive properties" (Burgess, Jones, Robertson, Radcliffe, & Emerson, 1981, p. 234). Phobias based on misinformation are a result of verbal classical conditioning in which inappropriate negative emotive labels are associated with particular stimuli and situations. Information transmission is therefore not an additional factor to conditioning—as Rachman (1977) maintained—but a subset of verbal classical conditioning. Words serve an important symbolic function in providing individuals with emotional experiences without exposure to the actual physical stimulus or event. As the emotion-eliciting, reinforcing, and directive functions of emotive verbal stimuli are interrelated, it means that following conditioning a phobic stimulus will not only elicit a negative affective response but also lead to avoidance behavior. Accordingly, the phobic person is reinforced for every behavior that reduces the aversive impact of fear.

The above model may be summarized and clarified using the example of a simple animal phobia. Such a phobia may be the result of direct classical conditioning (e.g., if a person is attacked by a snake), or vicarious conditioning (by observing another person being attacked), or if negative verbal stimuli (e.g., dangerous, vicious, slimy) are frequently paired with the sight of a snake. In fact, it is often the combination of these processes that leads to the development of a phobia. For example, persons who were attacked by a snake are more likely to make negative statements about snakes and may be further conditioned through their own language responses. The more often this happens, the more likely is the development of a phobia. Frequent semantic self-conditioning could also explain the gradual fear increase in persons with a long history of their phobia (Lauterbach, 1979). In other words, despite the lack of any overt UCS-UCR reinforcements, phobic individuals may increase their anxiety level through their own language responses. In Eysenck's (1982) terminology one could describe this as "self-produced incubation of fear."

There are a number of measurement problems that make it difficult to assess whether self-verbalizations actually control overt behavior or whether they are merely a verbal commentary to individual emotional experience and behavior (Eifert & Lauterbach, 1987). In fact, it is quite conceivable that they can be both! Beck and Emery (1985) propose that panic attacks are precipitated by inappropriate statements, thoughts, and images that signal danger: "The crucial element in anxiety states...is a cognitive process that may take the form of an automatic thought or image that appears rapidly, *as if by reflex,* after the initial stimulus (e.g., shortness of breath), that seems plausible, and that is followed by a wave of anxiety" (p. 5, italics added). The reference to the reflex-type character of these thoughts and images is very interesting because it indicates the involvement of classical conditioning in the formation of such "cognitive reflexes". These views are quite congruent with the social behavioral model: verbal or symbolic stimuli, which may be elicited by some physiological change or environmental event, can actually precipitate and intensify anxiety.

The Role of Imagery in Phobias

In addition to being "simple" language stimuli with affective, reinforcing, and directive (A-R-D) functions, phobic word stimuli are able to elicit sensory responses (images) in the indiviudal on a conditioned basis. These conditioned sensory responses are often reduced in vividness and completeness (Staats, 1975) and occur along with rapidly occurring chains of thoughts that cognitive behavior therapists seek to detect and "deautomatize" (Meichenbaum, 1977).

Images are sensory responses with stimulus characteristics that can also elicit verbal responses and other instrumental behaviors. Staats (1975) pointed out that individuals learn to label their sensory responses. So when a composite image is elicited, these images often also elicit labeling responses such as self-statements. If images or sensory responses are idiosyncratic, distorted and of negative value, the resulting verbalizations are also likely to be negative and may lead to feelings of anxiety and avoidance behavior (see also Lohr and Hamberger, Chapter 7, this vol.).

The relationship between imagery and self-verbalizations is particularly striking in persons with social fears or agoraphobic problems who constantly pair negative thoughts and verbal stimuli with images of panic and disaster in potentially frightening situations. This means that such persons do not need to have direct reconditioning experiences to remain phobic and continue to avoid these situations. They may condition themselves by providing their own verbal-symbolic stimuli that elicit negative emotional responses. For instance, one of my agoraphobic clients used to imagine having a panic attack or fainting in a supermarket with a group of people rushing toward her and staring at her. This (highly unlikely) imagined event led on to self-statements such as, "This is dreadful; it must never happen to me and I should not go into supermarkets". Thus, "irrational" images and thoughts were sufficient to induce anticipatory fear and the avoidance of a particular situation, even though she had never actually experienced a panic attack in a supermarket. Similarly, persons with social phobias often have images of people staring at them while they are performing everyday activities such as eating, drinking, and writing; such images lead them to engage in highly negative self-statements and avoid situations where they think they might be stared at.

A social behavioral model of phobias may also help to build a bridge to information-processing models of fear and studies investigating schemata of feared objects and situations. A *schema* is a prototypical abstraction of a complex object (Landau & Goldfried, 1981). It helps to structure, organize, and interpret new information and also facilitate the storage and retrieval of old information. Schemata of phobic and nonphobic individuals differ in important aspects. For instance, Landau and Goldfried found that dog-phobic persons attended exclusively to cues associated with the animal's propensity to harm humans, whereas nonphobic persons were more likely to categorize dogs according to their color and relative size. I believe the explanatory power of the schema concept could be enhanced if schemata were regarded as specific sensory responses or complex combinations of images that are elicited on a conditioned basis. A phobic individual who has learned the appropriate imaginal word repertoire may be told about a dog that is big, furry, and has a big mouth and experience a composite image that elicits an emotional response. Staats (1975) noted that such word concepts can be infinitely combined, so that there are ample possibilities for sensory experience to occur solely on the basis of language, without requiring primary direct experience. Moreover, it is not necessary to provide a person with a complete description of the phobic stimulus to elicit a sensory response and anxiety. Because of prior experiences and associative learning, the complete sensory response or "phobia prototype" (Lang, 1984) may be elicited by activating only some elements of the composite image. Lang also found in his studies on phobic imagery that the likelihood and intensity of a phobic response is influenced by the completeness of the stimulus information that elicits the image.

The Effects of Self-Verbalizations on Phobic Anxiety

The modification of negative self-statements is one of the most frequently employed cognitive-behavioral interventions to alleviate phobic fear (for reviews on their effectiveness, see Dush, Hirt, & Schroeder, 1983; Eifert, 1984b; Eifert & Craill, 1989; Latimer & Sweet, 1984). It is therefore very surprising that, with very few exceptions (e.g., Zettle & Hayes, 1982), the conceptual status of such self-statements and the mechanisms underlying their effects have hardly been examined. Yet very important functions of language reside in the affective qualities of words. Although in some cases words and thoughts are merely concomitants of conditioned responses, in many other cases they are conditioned stimuli and responses. As noted earlier, thoughts and self-statements can come to function as (higher-order) UCSs capable of eliciting anxiety, but they can also be used to countercondition anxiety responses. In the social behavioral model, self-verbalizations are viewed as verbal stimuli produced by the individual. If they contain emotive labels, they will elicit affective responses and direct behavior. As all functions of affective word stimuli also apply to self-generated speech, it means that individuals can condition themselves through their own language responses.

These notions are also very helpful in overcoming a major source of disunity resulting from the distinction between *cognitive* and *noncognitive* variables. Not only is the distinguishing line hard to draw, but the distinction itself may be misleading. Much confusion could be overcome by avoiding the use of the terms as much as possible and by labeling and defining stimuli, processes, and responses more specifically and precisely. Although Wolpe's (1982) distinction between classically conditioned and cognitively based fears may have some use for selecting the appropriate intervention procedures, it could lead to the misunderstanding that cognitive processes belong to a domain that is not subject to biological rules. Even fears based on misinformation are a result of verbal classical conditioning in which certain events are associated with inappropriate and often negative emotive labels. Thus there may be different pathways to fear, but there is little reason to assume that there are two distinctly different processes underlying phobic anxieties. Differences may reside in the relative predominance of the particular behavioral repertoires that are involved but learning principles apply to all of them.

No matter how comprehensive and plausible a theory may seem, its final evaluation depends on the results of empirical studies testing it. In the following sections I will therefore present a summary of studies that have tested either directly or indirectly the basic assumptions of a social behavioral analysis of fear and treatment interventions derived from this framework.

Emotional Arousal and Self-Statements

Cognitive behavior therapists and social behaviorists alike assume that physiological arousal may be mediated or even caused by negative self-verbalizations. However, the relationship between self-statements and physiological arousal is quite complex and neither is straightforward as cognitive behavior therapists assume nor as automatic as one might be tempted to conclude from some language conditioning studies. For example, the conditioning of highly relevant negative self-verbalizations may produce considerable physiological arousal. Master and Gershman (1983) found that in high-relevance situations, "irrational" verbalizations led to greater physiological arousal than rational statements. On the other hand, Rogers and Craighead (1977) showed that neither minimally nor highly discrepant statements, but those that were moderately discrepant from current beliefs produced the highest physiological arousal. They also found that positive and negative statements produced similar levels of physiological arousal.

Effects of Language Conditioning on Conditioned Anxiety

I have been involved in two studies investigating the effects of language conditioning on conditioned anxiety responses. The first experiment (Eifert, 1984b) compared the effects of positive and negative self-verbalizations on the physiological, subjective-evaluative, and behavioral aspects of classically conditioned fear responses to slides of snakes. During language conditioning, these slides were paired with statements of either positive or negative affective meaning (higher-order UCS). Participants repeated these statements subvocally while the slides were on. The results showed a complete and rapid extinction of the galvanic skin response (GSR) in groups with positive verbalizations, whereas negative statements impeded extinction. However, when subjects could observe a living snake prior to language conditioning, negative verbalizations were unable to hamper GSR extinction. The affective evaluation of snakes on semantic differential rating scales improved in all groups with positive verbalizations and deteriorated in groups with negative statements. Although subjects in all groups with positive statements exhibited more approach behavior, this trend was not statistically significant.

In a procedurally similar second experiment (Eifert & Schermelleh, 1985), we specifically compared the conditioning effects of positive statements referring either to positive features of the phobic stimuli (snakes and rabbits) such as their beautiful skin color or describing approach responses (e.g., "I may soon touch the animal"). As was predicted from A-R-D theory, stimulus-referent statements, aimed at the verbal-emotional repertoire, facilitated extinction of the physiological response more than response-referent verbalizations. Although snakes were consistently rated more negatively than rabbits, their affective ratings improved significantly following language conditioning with both types of verbalizations. As response-referent statements relate directly to the verbal-motor repertoire, we expected them to lead to more approach behavior than stimulus-referent statements. However, this was not the case. It is quite conceivable that language conditioning may affect only responses to words, images, and symbols of the phobic animals— second signalling system abstractions—rather than responses to the real animals themselves; hence our failure to obtain significant improvements in approach behavior.

Both studies demonstrated that emotive language stimuli can affect the extinction of a conditioned physiological response. These results also qualify an argument frequently raised by proponents of "preparedness theory" (cf., Öhman et al., 1985) that conditioned physiological responses to fear-relevant stimuli (such as snakes) resist "cognitive" manipulation once they are acquired. According to social behavioral theory, cognitive stimuli will have an impact on existing conditioned responses if they are emotive language stimuli—and this is what we found. Moreover, fear-relevant stimuli could have more negative evaluative strength because of previous cultural learning rather than because of some "biological hardwiring." For instance, prior to our experiment, subjects were probably exposed to many language and vicarious conditioning trials in which the word or the sight of a snake was paired with negative affective verbal stimuli, such as *ugly, slimy,* and dangerous situations or scenes in movies and books. On the other hand, rabbits would have been more frequently associated with positive labels like *cute* and *cuddly.* In other words, fear-relevant stimuli become more salient than other stimuli through their frequent associations with aversive physical, verbal, and symbolic stimuli in the environment (Burgess et al., 1981). This is reflected in faster response acquisition and higher resistance to extinction. Finally, although such cultural preconditioning does not render language conditioning interventions ineffective, it does make counterconditioning more difficult (Tryon & Briones, 1985), and it means that a large number of conditioning trials over long periods of time may be necessary to overcome strong affective responses such as fear.

Semantic Conditioning Interventions

In the early seventies Hekmat and his associates tested the possibility of alleviating phobic anxiety through simple semantic conditioning interventions. These investigations as well as two interesting experiments by Evans and Weiss (1978) are discussed more fully in the following chapter by Hekmat. His early clinical studies followed closely the experimental procedure of the original attitude conditioning studies by Staats (1963; see also Staats, Chapter 2, and Burns, Chapter 5, this vol.) and had a somewhat mechanistic flavor, for instance, the word "snake" was paired with words like "gift" and "justice." Contemporary clients might rightfully question the appropriateness of such a procedure and have understandable problems of relating snakes to justice. It is therefore encouraging to note that over the years Hekmat and his associates (see Chapter 9, this vol.) have developed very sophisticated semantic conditioning interventions for anxiety. These techniques employ individually tailored and client-generated self-statements that have an obvious and clear thematic-semantic relationship to the feared situations—all of these factors have indeed been found to affect the effectiveness of language interventions (cf., Eifert, 1987). Apart from increasing the credibility and effectiveness of such interventions, these developments should also refute the common stereotype and criticism that therapy based on conditioning principles is necessarily mechanistic and impersonal.

A Paradigmatic Behavioral Framework for Cognitive-Behavior Therapy

The emergence of cognitive-behavioral interventions has divided the field of behavior therapy like no other development in its relatively short history. There is still considerable disagreement as to whether these interventions are really new and/or effective (e.g., Latimer & Sweet, 1984). "What appears to be needed, in addition to carefully conceived and conducted treatment outcome research, is the development of conceptual models . . . and theoretical systems to guide cognitive-behavioral procedures" (Kendall, 1984, p. 121). I believe that paradigmatic behaviorism could provide such a theoretical foundation and framework for cognitive behavior therapy because it provides the best account available for the basic mechanisms— based in extensive research—that underlie cognitive-behavioral and verbal psychotherapy methods. Moreover, its level-by-level analysis closely links interactions between affect, behavior, and cognition to basic learning principles and personality processes. That linkage could make it possible to dispense with the cognitive versus conditioning schism that has been so divisive in behavior therapy.

Meichenbaum (1977) pointed out that the various cognitive-behavioral treatments differ in terms of the relative emphasis placed on a formal logical analysis, the directiveness and forcefulness with which the therapeutic rationale and procedures are presented, and the relative reliance on adjunctive behavioral procedures. Based upon the social behavioral analysis of cognitive-behavioral interventions provided by Lohr and Hamberger (Chapter 7, this vol.), I will attempt to clarify the conceptual nature of such differences. Staats (1968a) suggested that a person's language repertoires (particularly labeling and reasoning) are learned and often constitute what is considered cognition: reasoning, problem solving, planning, hypothesizing, and so on. These activities involve interactions between several language repertoires and other subrepertoires. Frequently these subrepertoires are interactions between the basic behavioral repertoires as schematized in Figure 8.1.

Cognitive-behavioral interventions differ in the repertoires that they address and utilize in order to produce change. Purely language-based interventions, such as semantic conditioning, work largely through the verbal-emotional repertoire. Words or sentences elicit an affective response in the client, thereby changing the affective evaluation of the stimulus or event that the verbal stimuli refer to. At other times, words themselves do not elicit an affective response directly, but are merely used to produce a pleasant image which then elicits an affective response (cf., Hekmat, 1977). Any behavioral changes that follow from such interventions are believed to be mediated by a change in the affective response to the signified stimuli. Interestingly, semantic conditioning has never been regarded as a "cognitive" intervention even though it relies entirely on language and other symbolic activities. One can only speculate that this is because semantic conditioning is based on a conditioning framework, which for those who accept the cognition versus conditioning schism automatically means that it cannot be "cognitive."

In cognitive restructuring, client labeling and reasoning repertoires are changed through direct communication interactions with the therapist. The therapist challenges the appropriateness and em-

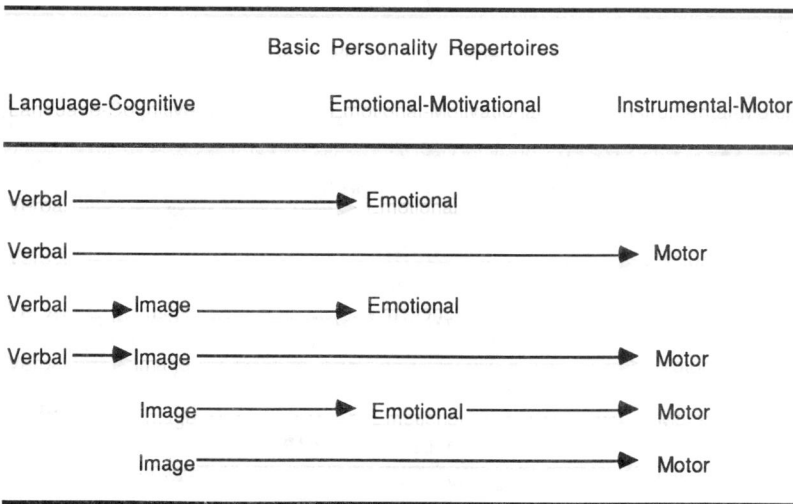

FIGURE 8.1 Examples of interactions between basic personality repertoires in cognitive-behavioral interventions.

pirical validity of client beliefs, appraisals, interpretations of situations and events, and the way information is categorized and processed ("cognitive styles"). Cognitive restructuring and self-instructional training programs usually combine a variety of performance-based and verbal-symbolic techniques that can be analyzed within social behavioral theory (e.g., Staats & Heiby, 1985). For instance, a reasoning or problem-solving act often includes (1) labeling of the event or situation, (2) sequences of verbal responses made to the labels, and (3) some final act elicited by the person's verbal processes (cf., Minke, Chapter 3, this vol.).

A close analysis of the standard procedure and variations of self-instructional training (Meichenbaum, 1977) reveals that the above three stages are integral parts of this technique. Clients are taught to emit self-statements that are incompatible with, and opposite in content to, the negative self-statements they have used previously. As the emotional value of labels affect client reasoning, fear, and overt behavior, the therapist assists the client in changing these labels. The principles of semantic counterconditioning and verbal reconditioning are employed in this stage. For instance, clients learn to label physiological arousal as a cue to employ coping skills rather than as a sign of an imminent panic attack. In addition, clients are instructed to use the verbal-motor repertoire to direct their overt behavior and speech in such a way that they can better cope with the feared situation (e.g., "one step at a time," "just think about what you have to do next"). Finally, reinforcing self-statements ("you did it, it worked") are used to maintain the newly acquired coping skills.

Although the interrelatedness of speech and thought is reflected in a great deal of overlap between language and reasoning (Staats, 1975; Vygotsky, 1962), inner speech is not just truncated external or subvocal speech ("speech minus sound") but filled with highly condensed meaning. Vygotsky's studies convinced him that language and thought undergo many qualitative changes as one turns into the other. These qualitative change processes should be carefully monitored by the therapist. After therapist and client agree on a specific set of statements, the client must learn and internalize these statements. During this internalization process, the client assigns personal meaning to these statements and may subsequently even forget the exact wording of the original statements. The client should therefore be asked to retransform this internalized speech into a specific set of overt statements when confronted with the feared situation in the presence of the therapist who can then monitor, and if necessary, change any recurrence of negative self-statements.

Critical Issues and Future Challenges

In this section, I will examine some critical conceptual and clinical issues arising from a paradigmatic behavioral framework for anxiety. I will also briefly comment on theoretical contributions and clinical findings from other lines of research that could serve to strengthen and expand the paradigmatic behavioral model of phobic anxiety and its treatment. Some of these issues represent formidable challenges for future research.

The Intricate Interface Between Affect, Behavior, and Cognition

Cognitive behavior therapists and social behaviorists alike have consistently argued that changing emotive labeling and reasoning will also change how clients feel and behave. Yet there is an extensive clinical literature examining the "desynchrony" of changes following the treatment of phobic anxiety (cf., Evans, 1986); this desynchrony refers to a lack of correspondence between changes in overt behavior, physiological arousal, and negative evaluations of the feared object or situations—with the latter often being the slowest to change. And, indeed, one of the most difficult clinical problems occurs not only if there is a time lag between, say, behavioral and affective changes, but if affective changes do not occur at all even though behavioral and/or cognitive changes have been accomplished (see Eifert, Craill, Carey, & O'Connor, 1988).

Although the primary function of affect is to predispose and prepare the individual for action (see Lang, 1984), a multitude of factors determines whether or not a negative evaluation of an object leads to avoidance behavior. Similarly, the exact relationships between different types of self-statements and overt behavior are not as clearcut as one might expect. Although there is a general tendency or predisposition to act in a way that corresponds with one's verbal and affective responses, positive statements do not always lead to approach behavior and negative statements do not always lead to avoidance behavior. We have recently examined the relationships between spontaneous self-verbalizations and overt behavior to a feared animal (Eifert &

Lauterbach, 1987) and found that subjects with a high level of learned resourcefulness (see Rosenbaum, Chapter 6, this vol.) approached a fear stimulus even in the presence of highly negative affective evaluations of that stimulus. As in our earlier reported studies, approach behavior was associated with a greater number of positive compared to negative statements: subjects approached fear stimuli as long as they had enough positive statements to compete with the negative ones. Studies investigating the effects of language conditioning on overt fear behavior have also produced somewhat mixed results. Most of Hekmat's studies (Chapter 9, this vol.) showed a significant decrease in avoidance behavior following semantic conditioning therapy. Other studies (e.g., Weiss & Evans, 1978) found only marginally significant changes following semantic conditioning, and our own studies failed to show significant changes, although the trend was in the predicted direction.

The Role of Affective Responses in Phobias

Rachman (1984) expressed his concern that the role of affect and emotional processing in fear reduction is still in need of explanation. He criticized cognitive therapists for viewing affect as postcognitive and for assuming that affective responses can always be changed through a process of rational reevaluation. This criticism is particularly valid for phobic anxiety which can be quite recalcitrant to verbal-symbolic interventions (Eifert & Craill, 1989).

It is often overlooked that while several researchers use a different terminology in their attempts to characterize the very nature of affective responses, their definitions are surprisingly similar. For instance, terms such as *affective judgments* (Zajonc, 1980), *evaluative responses* (Martin & Levey, 1978, 1985, 1987b), *primary appraisals* (R.S. Lazarus, 1984), and *emotional-attitudinal responses* (Staats, 1975) refer to the same type of response considered to be the most fundamental aspect of an emotion: they are nonreflective, instantaneous, subjective responses to salient environmental stimuli in terms of liked/disliked, pleasant/unpleasant, good/bad. If the eliciting stimulus is strong enough, peripheral physiological arousal, overt approach/avoidance behavior, and cognitive elaborations will follow the affective response to produce a complete emotional response. In other words, the affective response is a central nervous system response and the core and basis of what is generally termed emotion (Staats & Eifert, 1990).

The above approaches share a number of interesting similarities that serve to advance our understanding of the development and treatment of phobias. For instance, with regard to the involvement of affective responses in learning, Martin and Levey (1978) point out that the establishment and transfer of an affective (evaluative) response to a previously neutral stimulus is the carrier and central mechanism of classical conditioning: "Any stimulus event, *whether external or imaginary*, that evokes a positive or negative evaluation response can serve to classically condition that evaluation to previously neutral or negatively evaluated stimuli" (p. 82, italics added). This accounts for both the direct and indirect acquisition of phobic anxiety and is very much in line with social behavioral theory. Given the finding of Öst and Hugdahl (1981) that the majority of phobias are acquired by overt traumatic and/or semantic classical conditioning, it is quite conceivable that the establishment and transfer of a negative affective-evaluative response is not a by-product of conditioning, but a central aspect of the phobic response. Hence, therapy should be aimed at abolishing this response and as Rachman (1984) suggested, "given the imperfect influence of verbal cognitive operations on affect, attempts should be made to modify affective reactions more directly, using nonverbal means where possible, *e.g., music* (p. 582, italics added). In a series of experiments (Eifert, Craill, Carey, & O'Connor, 1988), we have begun to examine the conditioning potential of music, not only in establishing affective responses to neutral stimuli, but also in changing affective responses to feared animals by using positively evaluated ("liked") music as an adjunct to exposure therapy. Similarly, Levey and Martin (1987) have recently examined the need to modify affective responses and preferences and outlined the potential of deriving such treatment techniques from the evaluative conditioning theory—which is quite compatible with paradigmatic behaviorism—and their laboratory findings. This is also a fine example of the approach that used to be the defining characteristic and strength of behavior therapy: the application of findings from general experimental psychology.

The future success of all efforts to change affective responses will partly depend on whether we will be able to solve the formidable problem of measuring affective responses more adequately. We are currently faced with the dilemma that we can measure the experience of an affective response only by inferring its occurrence from overt behavior, self-report, and peripheral physiological changes. Rather than relying on these after-the-fact observations, more direct measures must be developed and tested; a promising example is the videotaping of changes in facial expressions, such as disgust, during behavior tests .

Credibility of Self-Statements

A problem that may occur in any cognitive-behavioral therapy of anxiety are discrepancies between clients' existing verbal-emotional repertoires and labels employed by the therapist. For instance, the therapist tries to associate more positive labels with the feared object or situation but the client's past learning often leads to extremely negative labeling of the fear stimuli which can actually counter the therapist's effort at "positive counterconditioning." Staats (1975) suggested that the same conditioning results whether the verbal stimuli are produced by oneself (the client) or by another person (the therapist), but it is not quite clear what will happen if these two sources are extremely discrepant. Is the therapist's conditioning effective only if the client can be prevented from emitting "countertherapeutic" language and thoughts, and is that possible at all? Marshall (1985) examined the timing of self-instructional training within an exposure program for acrophobic clients and concluded from his results that relabeling should be employed only after some initial anxiety reduction has occurred. At that stage positive labels and coping statements are less likely to be rejected, because they will be more in line then with what the client actually experiences. Similar to a desensitization approach, Craighead and Craighead (1980) suggested that a gradual shaping program might be most effective, starting with self-statements that are only moderately discrepant to existing ones. In conclusion, "faulty" self-statements should not and cannot be counterconditioned or replaced like a mechanic replaces faulty spark plugs (Coyne, 1982). To be maximally effective in alleviating anxiety, verbal-symbolic material used in semantic therapies and cognitive-behavioral interventions should be individualized, credible to the client, and not more than moderately discrepant to existing verbal repertoires.

What Type of Exposure Works and Why Does it Work?

The efficacy of behavioral treatments requiring some type of in vivo or imaginary exposure to the anxiety-provoking situation has been amply demonstrated. Exposure, however, is merely a description of what literally happens during therapy sessions. It is neither an explanation of the process(es) responsible for anxiety reduction nor does the term explain why some types and degrees of exposure are more important and effective than others. For instance, based on the results of a long-term clinical outcome study, Barlow, Craske, Cerny and Klosko (1989) concluded that it is essential for persons with panic disorder to be exposed to somatic (interoceptive) anxiety cues associated with panic rather than to the situations per se where the panic occurs: "These results suggest that we have a successful behavioral treatment for panic disorder, but leave questions on effective components and mechanisms of action unanswered"(p. 261).

In the case of simple phobias, too, I can safely conclude that exposure to the feared object is a very effective behavioral treatment, but I am much less certain as to why this is the case. Moreover, I have found in all my studies involving persons with animal phobias that there is a definite "breaking point" in a graduated exposure program: the moment a person touches the feared animal forthe first time. Successful exposure to the feared object requires more than merely approaching it, that is, walking toward it or looking at it. Unless individuals make *physical* contact with the feared object, they have not gone beyond the critical point: they still avoid the object, (often commenting that they will go as close as one foot but no further!). In other words, they still adhere to flight rather than fight. Barlow and his colleagues (1989) note that exposure-based treatments may prevent the escapist tendencies that are so characteristic of persons with anxiety disorders. I suggest one step further: in some cases, it may not be sufficient just to prevent escapist tendencies but to ensure "interactive approach" or "fight" behaviors. Such "full approach" behavior will allow the development of a sense of control that has increasingly more often been described as an essential change if a treatment is to be fully successful (cf., Barlow 1988).

In their paradigmatic behavioral theory of emotion, Staats and Eifert (1990) point out that one of the most important functions of an emotional response is to initiate approach or avoidance behavior on both an unlearned and a learned basis. I see fear as one of the most basic and important emotional responses and, in fact, most authors (cf., Barlow, 1988; Lang, 1984) agree that the primary biological function of fear is to elicit an appropriate behavioral response to avert harm. In the case of phobic persons the response is almost invariably a type of escape or avoidance of the fear-eliciting object. Learning to touch and handle the feared object, then, leads to the opposite behavioral tendency—approaching or "facing the enemy"—and, metaphorically, one could describe it as defeating ("beating") the dreaded enemy and perceived threat (the "aggressor"). In this sense, one could argue that physical contact changes the client from being the victim to being the one in control—particularly if the client initiates the contact and does not merely *re*-act. This conception is supported by the intriguing results of

Rachman and his associates (1988) who found that it was more the clients' sense of being in control than their overt behavior during sessions that mediated the outcome of treatment. I am currently exploring the function of this "getting in touch with the feared object" and why this contact is so important for clients. Although these notions are somewhat speculative at this stage, we must begin to ask and explore systematically what it is about exposure that works (at least most of the time) and why it works. Although there has recently been some renewed interest (see Barlow, 1988) in the processes of extinction and habituation, and the biological model of "toughening up" which refers to a decrease of noradrenaline through prolonged exposure, we do not seem to have made a great deal of progress since some of these processes were first mentioned more than half a century ago.

Conclusions

I have attempted to show in this chapter that empirical and clinical evidence neither justifies the treatment of cognitive variables as epiphenomena of conditioning nor supports the other extreme position of abandoning the conditioning paradigm altogether and declaring it moribund. The role of "cognitive variables" in conditioning is of a very complex nature and any simplistic, one-sided conclusions are unwarranted. There is an apparent necessity for a bridge-building paradigm to integrate the multitude of theories and treatments of anxiety. I believe social behaviorism can provide such a framework as it integrates simple conditioning models of fear, focusing on direct aversive conditioning, with complex higher-order forms of vicarious, semantic, and imagery conditioning.

Although the individual's learned labeling repertoire is important in mediating fear, it must be clearly recognized that verbal and symbolic stimuli are only one source of behavioral regulation—and in fear they may not even be the most powerful ones. Social behavioral theory postulates that emotive language stimuli have the same A-R-D functions as other physical stimuli, and studies have demonstrated that the principles of conditioning do apply to language and symbolic stimuli. At the same time, findings pointing to a desynchrony of fear changes and research on the interface between affect, behavior, and cognition (Izard, Kagan, & Zajonc, 1984) indicate that the functional relationships between central affective responses, peripheral physiological arousal, overt behavior, and the A-R-D functions of language are very complex; these interrelationships are far from fully understood and may not be quite as automatic and straightforward as social behavioral theory tends to assume. Similarly, Levis and Malloy (1982) pointed out that there are qualitative differences between language and other stimuli. The effects of language and other symbolic stimuli should be weaker as they are secondary or higher-order UCS; they cause no pain or tissue damage, reduce no primary drive, and so on. Similarly, Rachman (1981) referred to the limited potential of language in changing existing strong affective responses, even though language can be quite powerful in inducing or establishing affective responses. This is an interesting and very important distinction with implications that have not yet been fully investigated. If social behavioral theory is to accommodate such findings, it may have to be modified to allow for differential effects of language in fear acquisition and fear elimination.

If a comprehensive theory of phobic behavior is to be more than a general list of truisms, it must exactly specify how environment and personality variables interact to determine phobic behavior. In this sense, paradigmatic behaviorism has gone beyond the level of social learning theories. It explains the role of language repertoires in phobic anxiety and integrates cognitive-behavioral treatments of anxiety into a paradigmatic framework. Given the need for an integrative framework, it is therefore difficult to understand why social behaviorism has been largely ignored in (cognitive) behavior therapy. It accords language and reasoning processes their proper place in the etiology and treatment of phobic anxiety and offers a comprehensive higher-level conditioning and personality framework that circumvents divisive and separatistic controversies such as whether beliefs or behavior should be the proper focus in therapy. It should be apparent that a treatment program that disproportionately focuses upon one rather than both may be seriously limiting its own impact (Mahoney, 1977).

Since the late 1970s cognitive-behavioral theories and interventions for phobic anxiety have almost exclusively been conceptualized in some cognitive theory framework (cf,. Bandura, 1984; Beck & Emery, 1985). I have attempted to show, however, that language conditioning principles, such as extinction, counterconditioning, and the learning of new labeling and reasoning repertoires, are integral parts of cognitive-behavioral interventions for anxiety. The analysis of such interventions within the social behavioral paradigm enables us to incorporate systematically the findings of verbal and semantic conditioning studies into behavior therapy techniques, thereby refining them and, I hope, increasing their effectiveness. The current schism between cognitive and conditioning models and interventions is also unnecessary because what cognitive and behavior therapists actually do when they see a client is much more similar than what they say or think they are doing! Differences between the two approaches have been exaggerated and overemphasized, and are to no small extent due to differences in preferred terminology. A paradigmatic behavioral approach could help overcome these largely artificial differences and provide a bridge for rapprochement by reestablishing the links between basic experimental and applied clinical research.

9

Semantic Behavior Therapy of Anxiety Disorders: An Integrative Approach

Hamid Hekmat

Almost every psychologist, philosopher, and theologian has been preoccupied with ruminative discourses about the nature, source, and course of human anxiety. Anxiety has been a fertile ground for the growth of disparate, preparadigmatic theories in psychology. This has resulted in a variety of divergent theoretical propositions and a vast compendium of scattered, isolated treatment techniques, but we have not yet solved the puzzle of human anxiety.

In behavior therapy, artificial separations of cognition from behavior, semantic from affective domain, emotive from enacting processes have led to a proliferation of diversity at the expense of meaningful integration, unification, and rapprochement. Rather than exclusively advocating the primacy of cognition, behavior, or affect it will be more productive to delineate the interrelationships among these domains (cf., Eifert, 1987; Eifert & Craill, 1989) and develop conceptual schemes that can unify the field. Though our task of integration is a formidable one, it is less problematic to unify within behavior therapy than to espouse schemes for synthesizing the pluralistic perspectives of diverse schools of psychotherapy (see also Franks, 1988). Simply putting philosophical assumptions of one theory against the others is cumbersome, counterproductive, and in fact, highly divisive; nor is technical eclecticism desirable. However, it is quite beneficial to selectively choose aspects of each theory that can be meaningfully synthesized and derive from them clinical strategies that can have significant impact on reducing the suffering and discomforts of our clients.

Semantic behavior therapy is an integrative approach to behavior therapy that advocates the important role of language, meaning, and communication in understanding and treating behavior disorders. Theoretical principles of semantic behavior therapy are primarily derived from the paradigmatic behaviorism of Arthur Staats. Semantic behavior therapy stresses that behavior disorders may be acquired and maintained by higher-order semantic conditioning. It assumes that language and self-instructions are the principal, integrative components of complex semantic-affective-enacting processes that are partly determined by and interact with the individual's personality repertoires. Semantic behavior therapy also assumes that self-instructions can be conditioned to a host of physiological reactions elicited by a broad diversity of distal and proximal events. Furthermore, individuals who have acquired resourcefulness skills are expected to attenuate the discomfort of anxiety and cope more effectively with everyday stressors of modern life (see Rosenbaum, Chapter 6, this vol.).

In this chapter, I will provide a brief personal description of factors leading to the development of semantic behavior therapy. The pivotal role that language, meaning, and semantic processes play in the development of emotional disorders has already been reviewed in Chapter 7 by Lohr and Hamberger and Chapter 8 by Eifert. I will therefore concentrate on semantic perspectives regarding the etiology and treatment of anxiety disorders. In particular, I will delineate how semantic behavior therapy techniques such as semantic desensitization, instructional desensitization, and cue-controlled imagery are derived from the paradigmatic behaviorism framework theory and how these techniques can be clinically applied and presented. Finally, I will briefly discuss the importance of an effective therapeutic alliance and outline future directions in semantic behavior therapy.

Development of Behavior Therapy

I was introduced to Staats's theory as a graduate student in a clinical psychology program in California during the mid-sixties. My earliest research involved the application and extension of higher-order conditioning studies conducted by Staats and Staats

(1957, 1958). We were curious then about the relationship between semantic conditioning and avoidance behavior. We instructed college students to associate nonsense syllables as names of six large, dicelike wooden blocks (Phelan, Hekmat, & Tang, 1967). After subjects could write the nonsense syllable's name of different wooden blocks in two consecutive serious of random order presentation, we proceeded with semantic conditioning. For one of our experimental groups, the nonsense syllable "xeh" was paired with words with negative evaluation (i.e., dirty, disgusting, poison, ugly, etc.). After semantic conditioning was completed and its effects were measured by semantic differential scales, we asked subjects to select a block they liked the most to keep for the remainder of the experiment. We found that not only negative evaluative reactions could be conditioned to neutral nonsense syllables, as Staats and Staats (1957) had demonstrated, but, as Minke discusses in Chapter 3, once semantic conditioning was established, subjects' attitudes and motor reactions toward the wooden blocks were changed. Blocks that had acquired negative evaluations through semantic conditioning were avoided. When we examined the subjects' reaction in a postconditioning interview, we found that they were primarily "unaware" of the nature of the experiment. Subjects were offering us their own idiosyncratic hypothesis about why they chose a block. It was not because "xeh" was paired by negatively evaluated words, but because "yim" sounded better. In retrospect, our subjects acted as pointed out by Nisbett and Wilson (1977). They were unaware of our experimental procedure and were furnishing us only their "implicit causal theories" about why they chose certain blocks over others.

Being exposed to behavior therapy, especially studies of human fear reactions and methods of counterconditioning in behavior therapy used by Wolpe and others, I started to wonder about college students' avoidance reactions to negative "blocks," and its similarity and relevance to human attitudes, prejudices, and fear. Studies had already indicated (Lang & Lazovik, 1963) that avoidance was at least a component of human fear. Could human fear and anxiety reactions have been acquired by higher-order semantic conditioning? Could they be modified by higher-order semantic counterconditioning? As a graduate student in 1967, I explored the role of semantic counterconditioning processes in modifying human fear reactions, hoping to submit my experiments on semantic desensitization for my doctoral dissertation. However, I was advised to pursue a different line of integrative psychotherapeutic research for my dissertation (Hekmat, 1971b) since semantic interpretation of behavior therapy would not be a topic that would promote consensus among doctoral committee members. Undeterred however, I collected experimental data on semantic desensitization with the help of Dan Vanian and submitted them for publication in 1969; the article finally appeared after a 2-year publication lag in the *Journal of Consulting and Clinical Psychology* in 1971. The Hekmat and Vanian (1971) study demonstrated that higher-order negative evaluative reactions toward "snake" were present in snake phobics. The study also demonstrated that semantically based counterconditioning procedures in which pleasant words were paired with snakes by methods advocated by Staats and Staats (1957) were significant in reducing both the affective and motor components of fear.

Though I employed semantic counterconditioning procedures in the early seventies in order to experimentally test simple phobic reactions such as snake, spider, and rat phobias, I was dissatisfied with the early experimental procedures used to obtain the counterconditioning effect. I became progressively bored and satiated with the excessive pairing of stimulus words, sometimes as high as 120 times a session. My boredom susceptibility and its reciprocal effects on clients gradually diminished my enthusiasm for continuing with the early experimental desensitization procedures. I was looking for clinically refreshing techniques that would maximally involve the client in the treatment procedures and were more stimulating to the therapists as well. Staats's (1972) language behavior therapy article was a catalyst and provided me with significant insights into how to conduct such therapy. The article cited an earlier quotation by Staats that reads as follows:

> Composite sensory response that a group of words elicits may have reinforcing properties that each word does not have. Thus path, grass, stream, trees, may have as individual words relatively little reinforcement for a person. However, when put into a passage that elicits a composite sensory image of a country scene, the words may have much greater reinforcing properties. The reinforcement properties are elicited by composite sensory images not the words themselves. (Staats, 1968a, p. 504)

Rather than focusing on isolated pleasant or calm words, I proceeded in exploring sensory composites of visually relaxing scenes and self-instructions generated by them in therapy (Hekmat, 1977; Hekmat, Deal, & Lubitz, 1985: Hekmat, Lubitz, & Deal, 1984; Hekmat & Sage, 1981) thereby expanding the range of semantic behavior therapy techniques applicable to anxiety management. Before elaborating on further refinements and the development of more sophisticated semantic therapy interventions, I will briefly discuss in the following section the important role of semantic processes in anxiety.

The Role of Semantic Processes in Anxiety

Behavioristic theories of anxiety have been criticized for failure to provide explanatory accounts of why certain stimuli such as snakes, spiders, and rats are more "prepared" to form anxiety bonds through conditioning than others (i.e., curtains, pajamas, etc.). Though it is highly convenient to espouse evolutionary, biological, and phylogenetic theories that explain the "preparedness" of certain stimuli to accrue to anxiety (Öhman, Dimberg, & Öst, 1985; Seligman, 1971), the concept of "preparedness" is not without limitations and critics (Coyne & Gotlib, 1983; Delprato, 1980; Eysenck, 1987; McNally & Foa, 1986). Furthermore, the mere assertion or even finding that certain stimuli (snakes, spiders, etc.) are more prepared to establish associative bonds in anxiety reactions does not help us to determine the origin of preparedness.

Higher-order semantic conditioning process can explain why certain stimuli as compared to others are more ready to accrue associative bonds with anxiety (Burgess, Jones, Robertson, Radcliffe, Emerson, 1981; Eifert, 1984a; Eifert & Schermelleh, 1985; Hekmat, 1976; Maltzman & Boyd, 1984). Stimuli such as "snakes," "ugly people," and "spiders" that have already acquired negative connotative meaning through semantic conditioning are indeed more prepared to form conditioning bonds as compared to innocuous stimuli such as "curtains," and "wooden ducks" or positively evaluated ones such as "roses" and "pretty faces." In each instance, a prior semantic conditioning effect determines future conditioning reactions.

Nouns, adjectives, verbs, sentences, and phrases that are negatively evaluated are more prepared to be accrued to aversive events and form associative bonds through conditioning as compared to neutral or positively valued ones. Individuals who overtly or covertly have acquired prejudices toward some ethnic minorities are more prepared to develop anxiety reactions centered around the same ethnic group. Individuals displaying surplus negative evaluations toward cancer or AIDS are significantly more prepared to develop cancer phobia or AIDS phobia. A label such as "behavior modification" is generally evaluated more negatively than "humanistic education" (Woolfolk, Woolfolk, & Wilson, 1977). It is thus expected that it will be much easier to condition anxiety reactions to "behavior modification" than "humanistic education". The same principle holds true for covert and imaginal events. For example, the image of being confined in jail if paired with an aversive event such as shock or loud noise is more likely to elicit anxiety than the image of "being free," "smelling a rose," or "having fun at a party". Words such as "democracy," "freedom," "liberty," "justice," and "peace" are semantically conditioned to highly pleasant evaluative states that can interfere and thus render future reconditioning of anxiety to them futile. In general, stimuli that have already acquired negative affective-reinforcing-directive (A-R-D) value, regardless of whether they are proximal or distal, verbal or imaginal, overt or covert, are more "prepared" to serve as conditioned stimuli in aversive conditioning of emotional reactions. Also, a broad diversity of stimuli that elicit pleasant evaluations are significantly less "prepared" to serve as conditioned events in aversive classical conditioning.

Martin and Levey (1978, 1985, 1987b) have developed a conditioning paradigm that has significant heuristic and clinical implications. Their "evaluative conditioning" theory postulates that the transfer of "subjective evaluative responses" underlies a broad diversity of conditioning phenomena. They define an evaluative response as a characteristic reaction to environmental stimuli in terms of good/bad, disliked/liked, pleasant/unpleasant, which are "subjective" and "unique" to the individual. It is important to note that Martin and Levey do not define evaluative responses in terms of autonomic arousal, sensations, or motor behavior, but stress that evaluations are capable of being inferred from sensory, emotive and enacting modalities. Certain events such as a "pretty face," a "rose," a "friendly smile" immediately elicit pleasant evaluative reactions. Others such as pictures of "concentration camps," "battered people," and "starving children" readily elicit negative evaluative reactions. These evaluative responses, regardless of whether they are positive or negative, have primacy and control over subsequent behavior and emotions. The importance of evaluative conditioning processes for the acquisition of phobic fear has also been discussed in the preceding chapter by Eifert.

Learning about regularities of the environment is important for the survival of the organism. So individuals readily learn the "rules of consequence" (Martin & Levey, 1985). Language plays a prominent role in this learning for human beings. Self-instructions that acquire negatively evaluated consequences can, through A-R-D processes, influence an individual's avoidance reactions. Rules of consequence can be established even by a single conditioning trial when the unconditioned stimulus is an exceptionally negatively evaluated event that may have significant harmful consequences for an individual's well-being (Martin & Levey, 1978). Adaptive behavior mandates that individuals learn by inferences and extrapolations, cognitive summaries of a series of events, and rules governing them. "Rules of sequence" summarize experiences over an extended time and provide the basis for "scripts," "hypotheses," and "schemata" (Martin & Levey, 1985). Invariant features of environments are stored similar to maps or the letters of the alphabet and can become the basis for planning and action. Rules of sequence are usually learned gradually, and are contingent upon information, amenable to awareness, falsifiable, and essentially nonevaluative.

Borkovec (1983), in reacting to the notions of Martin and Levey, proposes that there are basically two types of emotional reactions to salient environmental events: immediate reactions and secondary reactions. The concept of immediate reactions described by Borkovec (1983) is very similar, if not identical, to Levey and Martin's evaluative response. Since immediate reactions occur rapidly in a period of less than a second after being exposed to salient events, mediational process cannot provide a theoretical account of their elicitation.

According to Borkovec (1983), immediate reactions, despite their emotional qualities, contain salient records of past conditioning, a stream of emotionally significant memories, a chain of associative thoughts and images along with their physiological, behavioral, and environmental consequences. He goes on to argue that we are rarely aware of our "immediate" or "evaluative" responses because secondary reactions elicited by their occurrence are rapid, automatic and shaped by environmental contingencies. The individuals who lack assertive skills are more likely to mask their immediate, evaluative reactions by socially desirable and yet deceptive mode of responding. For example, if someone has gone to considerable trouble knitting a sweater for them, they may, even though they may not like the sweater, display socially desirable responses by saying, "It's a fine sweater." Borkovec's (1983) article exemplifies another integrative, unifying, and liberalized reconceptualization of conditioning models, reinforcing the position that a paradigmatic reformulation of behaviorism—which should incorporate evaluative conditioning theory—has indeed significant promise for behavior therapy.

Semantic Behavior Therapy Interventions

Semantic behavior therapy applies to a broad diversity of anxiety management intervention programs. Among these are semantic desensitization, semantic sensitization, cue-controlled relaxation, cue-controlled imageries, cue-controlled instructions, instructional aversion relief, and instructional desensitization. In clinical interventions, an elaborate life history questionnaire as well as several self-report inventories are frequently administered at the outset of the treatment program. Patients receive self-monitoring instructions with examples during the first therapeutic session. Therapist's communication skills, empathy, and rapport building are considered extremely important. Equally important is for patients to become actively involved in their treatment program, to have clear conceptions of the parameters and goal of the treatment, their own assets, skills and resourcefulness. I think it is important for therapists to be supportive, caring, flexible, and problem centered. Because events in the environment are prime sources for patient's disturbances, it is important for both the therapist and client to become familiar with the client's milieu and identify supportive agents that may facilitate the client's improvement.

Semantic Desensitization

Semantic desensitization is a behavior therapy intervention that applies principles of semantic counterconditioning. The counterconditioning response is not the muscular relaxation that is traditionally used in behavior therapy. Instead, pleasant evaluative responses serve to counteract anxiety. Relaxing words, soothing self-instructions, and serene images are capable of eliciting a host of pleasant evaluative responses that can become bonded to anxiety-provoking events (Hekmat, 1972). The word *beautiful* stated by the therapist can serve as an inkblot facilitating the emergence of a broad diversity of pleasantly evaluated associative events.

Semantic Relaxation

In therapy, the clients may conjure up images of beautiful sunsets, vacation spots, oceans, and waves. Likewise, the word *relax* can in cold winter months elicit *warm* sensory cues associated with scenes such as *"I am watching the blaze of an open fire, sipping a glass of wine"*, or *"laying down on the beach and feeling the warmth of the sun"*. Words such as *calm, sunset, joy, gift, vacation, relax, fun, delight, happiness, peace, freedom, beauty,* and *success* are capable of visually evoking pleasant evaluative states. Scales that identify a client's preferences for reinforcing events (Cautela & Kastenbaum, 1967) and pleasant activities (Lewinsohn & Libet, 1972) can furnish therapists information that can facilitate the construction of the semantic relaxation hierarchy. In semantic desensitization, we frequently use scenes depicting the client's most preferred activities. Semantic relaxation can be achieved with imaginal enacting of sporting activities such as swimming, hiking, jogging, fishing, cycling, sailing, skiing, and so forth.

Scenes in which clients report experiencing serenity, calmness, peace of mind, unity with nature, universe and cosmos can also induce relaxation. These scenes not only have pleasant evaluative consequences for the client, but also are capable of facilitating experiential process that parallels those reported by Maslow (1968) in self-actualizing individuals.

Some clients verbalized preferences for scenes involving listening to music, having fun dancing, and singing. Visualization of musical events and their associative memories are capable of evoking pleasant evaluative states. Scenes in which individuals visualize loving or being loved by others, holding or being held, embracing or being embraced, praising or being praised, supporting or being supported by friends, partners, or significant others might also have beneficial effects in therapy. Scenes in which clients imagine dining in their most favorite restaurant, or drinking their most desirable beverage, or being highly delighted by their most preferred companion are also useful. Introverted clients may prefer scenes involving reading a book, working on a hobby, hiking, listening to their favorite music, and watching their favorite TV program by themselves. Extroverted people can enjoy scenes in which socializations play a dominant role such as having fun at parties, dances, or dating. Religious clients can conjure up a broad diversity of religious imageries.

Cue-elicited pleasant evaluative responses of the clients can be arranged in hierarchy. For example, the client may be asked to indicate which of the two scenes elicited by the word *relax* is more preferred: resting on the beaches of a fantastic island, or having meaningful conversation with a beautiful person. Pairwise comparisons can facilitate arrangements of pleasant scenes in a hierarchy. Pleasant evaluative scenes are usually rated on 0—100 Hedonic Evaluation Subjective Scale (HESS). Scenes with maximal hedonic values (i.e., the utmost pleasant, enjoyable, or relaxing ones) are assigned a numerical value of 100, those with minimal hedonic value are assigned a value of 0 (Hekmat, Lubitz, & Deal, 1984). Scenes rated 90 or higher on the HESS scale are those most suitable to include in the semantic desensitization intervention program. The procurement of 10 to 12 pleasantly evaluated scenes is usually sufficient with most clients.

Frequently, the semantically oriented behavior therapist engages the client on self-relaxation instructions while they imagine pleasant scenes. For example, if a client is describing that he or she is walking in the woods on a beautiful autumn day, the therapist inquires, "Do you feel the breeze? . . . What colors are the leaves? . . . Is the air fresh? . . . Do you smell its aroma? . . . Are you getting a relaxed feeling? . . . Are you relaxed? . . . Could you hold on to your feeling of relaxation? . . . Hold on to your pleasant sensations . . .". It is important that a dialogue be established to ensure that clients are actively involved in semantic relaxation. Clinical variants of semantic desensitization can be implemented by the addition of breathing relaxation, conditioned relaxation, progressive relaxation and its variants (Bernstein & Borkovec, 1973).

Semantic Anxiety Hierarchy

Semantic desensitization usually incorporates a Semantic Hierarchy of Anxiety Mediating-Stimuli (SHAMS). The SHAMS hierarchy consists of a progressively more aversive scene along with the client's self-instructions. It is assumed that as one ascends to progressively intense anxiety-provoking situations, the client's corresponding self-instructions also become increasingly more polarized, disturbed and negative. Anxious clients may engage themselves in different types of self-dialogues a week before the test as compared to the moment they are actually taking an examination.

It is important to explore self-instructions generated by different anxiety-provoking scenes and arrange them in a hierarchy. For example, a test-anxious young man may visualize the night before the examination and report experiencing tension. The therapist may react: "It is the night before the test, and you feel anxious . . . Tell me what you tell yourself to make yourself tense?" After recording the scene and their corresponding self-instructions, the therapist asks the client to rate the same scene on 0–100 subjective anxiety scale (SUDS) with higher numbers denoting maximal anxiety value. The therapist may then ask the clients to imagine the same scene with a different set of self-instructions. "It is the night before the examination. I won't let myself be overwhelmed by it . . .". The therapist may ask the client to rate the second scene from 0–100. The procedure is continued until the therapist and clients select about 12 anxiety-provoking scenes along with their corresponding self-instructions for semantic desensitization proper. The number of anxiety-provoking scenes are varied from client to client, depending on the nature of anxiety, their resourcefulness in handling tension, and the severity of their emotional problems.

In constructing SHAMS hierarchy, the therapist not only incorporates the anxiety-provoking situations, but also infuses them with their aversive consequences. For example, test-anxious clients may visualize being anxious on the GRE exam, obtaining a low score on the test, reporting their score to their friends, their advisors, their major professor, and their parents. Scenes that are too anxiety provoking may be rendered less threatening by several methods. This can include description of the scene with less details, elimination of sensory cues from the scene, suggestions that the scene can gradually become less anxiety provoking, blurry, and fade away. Imaginal transformation of the scene into progressively less disturbing events and use of less dramatic language in describing the scene can also reduce the anxiety value of the scene. It is also possible to conduct semantic desensitization with a hierarchy of progressively more disturbing self-verbalizations alone, without exposing the clients to anxiety-provoking imageries.

Symbolic exposure to reinforcing events as well as symbolic interactions with reinforcing resources are hypothesized to be of significant therapeutic value in reducing the client's anxiety. I frequently expose the client to the relaxing scenes in which they receive affection, approval, and acceptance from significant persons in their life. These symbiotic interactions not only provide symbolic gain of lost reinforcers, but can also elicit associative memories, images, and emotive states that can have soothing effects on the client. One may argue that symbiotic interactions with significant others through dialogues and imageries elicit pleasant evaluative reactions that can be contiguously bonded to anxiety-provoking events, and evoke a counterconditioning effect. By incorporating symbolic events into the relaxation scenes, semantic behavior therapy advances toward rapprochement with the psychodynamically oriented therapies.

It should be noted that in semantic desensitization, semantic relaxation scenes are contingent upon the termination of anxiety-provoking scenes. In contrast to emotive imageries techniques (Lazarus & Abramovitz, 1962), we keep the aversive and relaxing scenes contiguously associated and yet separate. Mastery over termination of anxiety-provoking imageries is considered an important skill and beneficial for clients. One may argue that clients' sense of mastery over their anxiety or resourcefulness in terminating anxiety-provoking events are reinforced covertly by imaginal relaxation events.

Finally, semantic relaxation scenes are usually rotated to prevent the semantic satiation effect (Hekmat, 1974; Hekmat & Lee, 1970). Since the semantic relaxation scenes often involve self-reinforcing verbalizations, mere exposure to the same scene may reduce the reinforcing values of the scene. Hekmat (1974), for example, showed that mere repetitions of a verbal reinforcer such as "mmm-hmm" reduced its pleasant evaluative connotation through "semantic satiation" and subsequently rendered it less potent in verbal conditioning. Semantic desensitization has been shown to be effective in a broad diversity of anxiety-based emotional, phobic, and anxiety reactions (Evans & Weiss, 1978; Hekmat, 1972, 1977; Hekmat, Deal, & Lubitz, 1985; Hekmat et al., 1984; Hekmat & Vanian, 1971; Sappington, Burleson, Studstill, Rice, Gordon, & Cornelison, 1982; Tryon & Briones, 1985).

Semantic Sensitization

Semantic sensitization is an aversive semantic behavior therapy technique that is primarily designed for treatment of long-term maladaptive behavior such as alcoholism, overeating, obsessional rumination, smoking, and pervasive anxiety that has failed to respond to nonaversive intervention. Semantic sensitization is usually implemented in three stages. First, after visually relaxing the client, the therapist constructs a semantic hierarchy of events leading to transgressions. Hierarchy constructions procedures are similar to those described from semantic desensitization. Sensitization hierarchies usually involve transgressional events and their corresponding self-instructions. Next, a hierarchy of Semantically Aversive Disturbing Events (SADE) is constructed. This hierarchy consists of usually 10 extremely aversive scenes rated 90 or higher on a 100-point scale. For alcoholic patients, semantically relevant words such as headaches, dizziness, brain damage, and vomiting can serve to elicit a broad variety of aversive images. Finally, the therapist proceeds by pairing progressively more difficult transgressional situations and their related self-instructions with aversive events in the SADE hierarchy. For example, assume that a patient with a drinking problem is invited to go to a bar to have a few drinks with an old friend. The therapist inquires, "When you were extremely tempted to go to the bar what kind of things did you say to yourself?" and the patient may reply, "A drink or two won't hurt." The therapist would then ask the client to visualize the same scene and then self-verbalize, "A drink or two doesn't hurt," followed immediately by imaginal evocation of harmful consequences for this transgression together with their corresponding self-instructions (i.e., "I see myself lying in bed and late for work...I am getting a headache and my headache is getting worse...My brain is getting damaged...The 'shit' is doing it to me").

Though semantic sensitization procedures appear on the surface to be highly similar to covert sensitization (Cautela, 1967), there are several theoretical and procedural differences between the two procedures. Cautela (1967) pioneered the development of a beneficial and rather widely used covert aversive conditioning procedure called covert sensitization that was primarily designed for the treatment of alcoholism, and eating and sexual disorders. First he relaxes his clients and asks them to visualize a transgressional scene ("you reach for a beer"). Transgressional scenes are followed by aversive imaginal consequences ("you puke") which in turn serve as covert cues for avoidance responses ("you run away from the bar"). Covert avoidance responses are in turn negatively reinforced by an "aversion relief" state ("you feel better").

Semantic sensitization differs from covert sensitization in several aspects. First, semantic sensitization is primarily derived from a classical semantic conditioning model, whereas Cautela's procedures are derived from a covert operant conditioning conceptualization. Despite the fact that Cautela did not initially conceptualize covert sensitization within an operant conditioning framework, he later conceded that covert sensitization was essentially a punishment procedure within the operant framework (Cautela, 1967, 1973). Second, in semantic sensitization, the presentation of an aversive scene is gradual, through a hierarchy; in covert desensitization, there is no hierarchy constructions and thus the procedures give the appearance of implosion and flooding. Third, in semantic sensitization, the therapist is less directive than in covert sensitization: clients are encouraged to be involved in their treatment and to emanate their own vivid images and self-instructions.

Fourth, semantic sensitization applies visual relaxation methods whereas covert sensitization applies muscular relaxation methods. However, variants of semantic sensitization may incorporate either progressive muscle relaxation training in conjunction with semantic relaxation. Fifth, covert sensitization procedures incorporate *aversion relief* and negative reinforcement procedures. In semantic sensitization, negative reinforcement procedures are not routinely used. However, procedural variations of semantic sensitization can incorporate aversion relief procedures. Semantic sensitization with aversion relief components may have the following sequence: semantic relaxation, exposure to transgressional hierarchy, aversive scenes, covert coping response and relief scene with pleasant self-instructions ("I feel better"). Both the aversive and relief scenes are semantically relevant.

Evans and Weiss (1978) established the prime importance of the issue of semantic relevance of the words applied in intervention programs. Thus, for the chocolate eater the word *pimple*, for a chain smoker the words *lung cancer*, for an alcoholic the words *brain damage* may be capable of eliciting semantically relevant self-instructions that can be used along with their imageries in semantic behavioral intervention programs. It should be noted that though semantically relevant procedures were used in later semantic behavior therapy interventions (Evans & Weiss, 1978; Hekmat, 1977; Weiss & Evans, 1978), semantic desensitization was effective in early studies that did not incorporate the principle of semantic relevance (Hekmat, 1971b; Hekmat & Vanian, 1971). Evaluative dimensions of meaning seem to be the prime dimension along which semantic sensitization or desensitization therapies are conducted. Additions of other dimensions such as passivity and activity may theoretically complicate the issues. For example, words that have high loading on the passive dimension of meaning (*relax, calm*) as well as those that are high on active components of meaning (*swimming, jogging, cycling*) are both capable of eliciting pleasant evaluative states that can be effectively used to semantically countercondition anxiety.

I have desensitized a client with performance anxiety who was apt to fall asleep through conventional relaxation procedures. Her favorite sports activity was skiing. She used scenes in which she was skiing down the slopes of the mountain. She viewed herself as an active person and her relaxation scenes were replete with a broad range of recreational activities. Sappington et al. (1982) demonstrated the effectiveness of semantic desensitizing along the potency dimension (i.e., performing "athletic feats"). To the extent that *potency* or *activity* dimensions of meaning elicit either pleasant evaluative states or emotive reactions with pleasant evaluative consequences, they can have beneficial effect in desensitization programs.

Cue-Controlled Techniques

Cue-controlled relaxation has been shown to be significantly effective in controlling anxiety (Grimm, 1980; Gurman, 1973; Russell, Miller, & June, 1975; Russell, Wise, & Strakoudakis, 1976). Cue-controlled procedures are clinically implemented by having the client relax and focus attention on breathing. The therapist proceeds by verbalizing a cue word (e.g., *relax*) that is paired in synchrony with the client's exhalation for a minimum of 5 pairings. The client is next instructed to continue pairing self-verbalized cue words with each exhalation of air for 15 times. A daily homework assignment is also administered. Patients completing these homework assignments typically whisper the cue word *relax* in synchrony with each exhalation at a frequency of 20 trials daily. The word *relax* will then become a cue capable of controlling the onset of anxiety. Not only can cues be conditioned to internal bodily processes, but they are also capable of eliciting covert self-instructions. Self-instructions such as "I am in control," or "I can handle my anxiety" can be conditioned to pleasant evaluative states evoked by the cue words.

A variation of this technique involves pairing a verbal stimulus *(relax, calm down)* with pleasant emotive scenes such as watching sunsets. Pleasant evaluative responses generated by visualizing relaxing scenes are conditioned to a verbal cue. Clinical methods for implementation of cue-controlled imageries are similar to those described in cue-controlled relaxation. After establishing conditioning reactions to a cue word, the clients are instructed to whisper the cue word in anxiety-provoking situations.

A cue may also be conditioned to a hierarchy of pleasant evaluative self-instructions. The therapist can elicit from the client a host of self-statements that can induce calm, serenity, comfort, and pleasant affective reactions. The client's self-statements are placed in a hierarchy. The clients are next relaxed. The therapist asks the clients to pair their cue words with pleasant items of the self-instruction hierarchy. The self-instruction hierarchy may also contain coping, mastery and self-efficacy instructions. The number of pairings, homework assignments, and other procedures for clinical implementation of cue-controlled instructions are similar to those described for cue-controlled relaxation.

Instructional Desensitization

Instructional desensitization is a semantic behavior therapy intervention that has basically two components: (1) semantic counterconditioning, and (2) verbal conditioning of coping self-instructions. In instructional desensitization, the sequential presentation of events are: a semantic anxiety hierarchy, semantic relaxation, coping self-instructions and visual reinforcement. The client and therapist construct and rehearse pleasant scenes conjugated with their corresponding self-instructions. This is followed by a construction of an anxiety hierarchy as described in semantic desensitization. Instructional desensitization proper involves pairing the self-instructional anxiety hierarchy with semantic relaxation. On the next trial, prerehearsed coping self-instructions are reinforced by pleasant imaged scenes.

Let us assume that a young male student is imagining a scene in which he is giving a speech to an audience of 30 students in a speech class. The client may visualize that during the course of his presentation a member of the audience starts to leave the class. An initial self-statement associated with anxiety-provoking imagery might be "I am driving people away with my lousy presentation." The therapist would expose the client to the anxiety-provoking scene for about 20 to 30 seconds and then ask the client to switch off the scene and relax by imagining "having fun on a date." The client is then instructed to hold on to the pleasant feelings generated by relaxation. Next, the therapist may proceed by saying: "Now I want you to tell yourself it does not matter what people do or think about what I say, I will relax and continue, the person is walking out probably because of a doctor's appointment." The coping self-instructions are immediately paired with visual relaxation. The client, for example, would imagine a scene (e.g., *receiving a gift*) and focus on the pleasant feeling and sensation evoked by it. Homework assignments are now routinely incorporated in both semantic and instructional desensitization instructions (Hekmat et al., 1984, 1985). During homework assignment, clients are instructed to immediately reinforce their resourceful behavior using their most preferred visually reinforcing scene. We explored the efficacy of instructional self-desensitization in the treatment of public speaking anxiety (Hekmat et al., 1985). Thirty speech-anxious clients were randomly assigned to one of the following groups: instructional desensitization, attention placebo group, no treatment waiting list control. The results indicated that instructional desensitization produced significant reductions in anxiety as measured by several behavioral and self-report measures of anxiety as compared to the controls. Furthermore, improvements in therapy were maintained on the follow-up and could not have been interpreted to be due to nonspecific treatment artifacts.

Therapist–Client Relationship

Behavior therapists can no longer relegate behavioral change entirely to the potency of their techniques at the expense of being impervious to interpersonal factors that are infused with their healing effect. It has been repeatedly shown that the therapist-client relationship is an "integral part" of behavior therapy (cf., Eifert, 1987; G.T. Wilson & Evans, 1977) and that interactions between the therapist and client are very important as good rapport fosters a favorable attitude toward therapy. Therapeutic caring resources such as empathy, warmth, genuineness, respect, permissiveness, trust, and support for the client seem essential for establishing rapport and facilitating behavior change in semantic behavior therapy. Therapists displaying a broad repertoire of therapeutic skill resources such as attending, focusing, reflecting, clarification, and communication skills are more likely to elicit pleasant evaluative states in their clients and thus enhance the likelihood of their recovery.

Empathy is a learned repertoire of interpersonal communication skills that facilitate the development of meaningful therapeutic relationships and promote clients' disclosure of intimate information. This learned resourcefulness enables them to be sensitive to others and show a greater appreciation of their clients' internal frame of reference. Therapists high in empathy attempt to envisage and perceive and communicate what their clients have gone through. They also tend to be low on neuroticism, personal discomfort, and other predictors of personal distress (Hekmat, Khajavi, & Mehryar, 1974; Hekmat, Khajavi, & Mehryar, 1975; Patterson, 1984). They show honesty, patience, warmth, openness, and candor in their therapeutic communications. Although events eliciting negative emotional states in the therapist may impede their empathic understanding of clients, these learned repertoires facilitate the interruption of negative emotional states that a therapist may experience. In other words, empathic therapists can effectively inhibit and block their dysfunctional negative reactions through learned personal resourcefulness. A paradigmatic behaviorism analysis of empathy thus suggests that therapist personality variables interact with, and are extensions of, semantic (verbal) therapeutic techniques. A recent analysis and review of this topic has also been conducted by Eifert (1987).

Conclusions

Psychologists from Freud to Pavlov, from Watson to Staats, have advocated the primacy of words, language, symbols, and meaning in understanding human emotional reactions. Language is an integral component of anxiety and plays a pivotal role in its development, maintenance, and amelioration. Semantic behavior therapy directly applies principles derived from language conditioning to the etiology and treatment of behavior disorders.

Semantic behavior therapy is a generic name for a broad diversity of semantic-conditioning-based behavior therapy interventions that are derived from the paradigmatic behaviorism of Arthur Staats. Semantic behavior therapy techniques such as semantic desensitization have been shown to be effective in the treatment of simple phobias, public-speaking anxiety, test anxiety, delay onset insomnia, and pain management. My students, colleagues, and I are currently in the process of exploring the efficacy of other semantic behavior therapy techniques presented in this chapter for the treatment of test anxiety and chronic pain. This is not sufficient, however, and we also need to test the clinical effectiveness of semantic behavior therapy for other behavior disorders.

Agoraphobia, social phobias, performance anxieties, sleep disturbances, eating, drinking, and sexual disorders, traumatic stress disorders, and psychophysiological reactions (e.g., tension headaches) provide a fertile ground for exploration, growth, and expansion. Equally important is to study semantic behavior therapy in comparative perspectives. Semantic behavior therapy intervention techniques need to be tested against standard methods of intervention such as systematic desensitization, in vivo exposure, flooding, and cognitive restructuring. Can we combine semantic behavior therapy intervention procedures with other cognitive or behavioral treatment procedures? Does combining two interventions induce a synergetic effect that makes them more efficacious than the individual components of treatment programs?

We also need to examine mechanisms of behavior change in semantic behavior therapy with greater precision and scrutiny. One may ask what role hierarchies serve in semantic desensitization therapy? Is semantic desensitization therapy as effective with an ascending rather than with a descending hierarchy, random order or no hierarchy at all? We can also address ourselves to the question of semantic relaxation and ask whether it is necessary and/or sufficient by itself? In other words, can we help clients by exposing them only to semantic relaxation? Does it make a difference if we incorporate Freudian symbolic components in the relaxation hierarchy? Does it make a difference if we incorporate efficacy components (i.e., success, potency, etc.)? Does adding experiential components such as those described by Maslow for self-actualizing individuals (i.e., autonomy, freedom, unity with nature) render relaxation more effective?

Most important, we need to continue to relate these questions and address ourselves to the issue of paradigmatic conceptualization in behavior therapy. Behavior therapy is currently flooded with a vast compendium of isolated intervention procedures and fluttered by fervid burgeoning of competing disparate preparadigmatic conceptualizations (cf., Fishman, Rotgers, & Franks, 1988). The time is ripe to abandon our polemics and achieve consensus by extending our efforts and expending our energies toward the productive development of paradigmatic conceptualizations in behavior therapy. Although this is an arduous and a long-term endeavor, the promise of greater clinical effectiveness that would result is a strong incentive.

Acknowledgments

The writer is indebted to Paul Schwieger for his invaluable comments. Special thanks go to Maureen and my daughter, Soraya, for her patience, care, and support throughout this project.

10

Depression: Classification, Explanation, and Treatment

Elaine M. Heiby
Arthur W. Staats

Etiology and classification of depressions have been controversial issues in clinical psychology since Kraepelin offered the first systematic approach to explaining and subtyping these disorders. Numerous contemporary hypotheses have been proposed and evaluated, but none have proven satisfactory. Much knowledge about depression has been developed in the past 20 years, but has yet to be integrated into a general theory. Instead, we see hypotheses abandoned when they fail to account for all cases of depression, and new, competing hypotheses are offered. These new hypotheses are often simply a restatement of old forgotten ideas.

The purpose of this chapter is to delineate guidelines for a classification schema based upon the paradigmatic behavioral unified theory of depression with both integrative value and heuristic implications. The classification of depression is important to the development of behavioral therapies for depression because different skill assets and deficits among depressed individuals suggest different targets for intervention in the reduction and prevention of depression. In addition, it is important for behavior therapists to acknowledge that communication with the larger psychological community involves the discussion of diagnostic categories. It is incumbent upon unified theorists to integrate the contributions of past clinical theory and research with behavioral principles and methods. It will be suggested that past classification systems have been in competition with each other, not attempting to accommodate findings from different areas of depression research. The paradigmatic behavioral theory, it will be argued, can promote the integration of past findings and provide a basis for developing a classification system that reflects current areas of knowledge regarding the symptomatology, etiology, effective treatment, and prevention for subtypes of depression.

Past Classification Attempts

Contemporary classification systems of depression can be divided into three types based on (a) family history of abnormal behavior, (b) hypothesized or empirically demonstrated etiology, and (c) symptomatology. First, a distinction among types of depression based upon a family history of the disorder has been proposed by Andreasen and Winokur (1979). This approach contends that bipolar disorder, along with depression secondary to other conditions (e.g., terminal cancer), can be identified and considered separately from unipolar depression. Unipolar depressions are further subtyped according to whether there is no family history of depression (nonfamilial), a family history of depression (pure), or a family history of substance abuse, antisocial personality, or hysteria (spectrum). Winokur (1979) maintains that this approach shows nonfamilial depression to be more severe than pure depression. He points to evidence that individuals exhibiting nonfamilial and pure types of depression are from a higher socioeconomic status and experience less parental divorce as children than those exhibiting spectrum types. To demonstrate the usefulness of this familial-based distinction, Winokur would need to provide evidence of differences in etiology and response to treatment; in our view, correlations—such as involving socioeconomic status—are not very informative, unless some closely reasoned theoretical connection is made that provides empirical expectations, such as social class influencing treatment strategies.

Classification systems based upon presumed or demonstrated differences in etiology include the well-known concepts of primary versus secondary (Munro, 1966) and the exogenous versus endogenous depressions. Primary depression is defined as a depression without a recent history involving prior (or concomitant) psychiatric or physical disorders; no assumption is made regarding particular antecedents. A depression that results from a psychiatric or physical disorder is considered to be secondary. Antecedents to secondary depression may include, for example, alcoholism, anxiety disorders, or chronic pain. According to this nosology, treatment for primary depression would focus on alleviating the depression, whereas treatment for secondary depression would also aim to eliminate the antecedent disorder. Evaluations of the primary-secondary distinction have resulted in mixed support for this classification system, partly, perhaps, because of differing definitions of secondary depression. Some investigators (e.g., Weissman, Pottinger, Kleber, Ruben, Williams & Thompson, 1977) have limited the antecedent disorders for secondary depression to drug abuse and schizophrenia, while others have included all psychiatric and medical disorders (e.g., Woodruf, Murphy, & Herjanc, 1967), which could result in classifying *all* depressions as secondary, due to the pervasiveness of medical illnesses. The latest revision of the *Diagnostic and Statistical Manual of Mental Disorders* (DSM-III-R) (American Psychiatric Association, 1987) classifies dysthymia (depressive neurosis) in terms of primary or secondary. This revision defines secondary depression as being related to *any* nonmood disturbance. The usefulness of the primary-secondary distinction hinges on the establishment of reliable criteria for secondary depression and the demonstration that possible etiological differences accurately predict onset, course, and response to treatment. With respect to the latter criterion, Munro (1966) did argue that one would expect, for example, treatment of depression associated with a limb amputation to include training focused on the effective use of a prosthetic device, whereas treatment for a depression associated with an obsessive-compulsive disorder may be more effective if it includes training in anxiety control. This still leaves the Munro system with no specific predictions for primary depression, which could involve a wide range of symptoms and possible etiological factors.

Another dichotomous, etiology-based classification system is the endogenous-exogenous distinction (e.g., Van Praag, Ulleman, & Spitz, 1965). This system, also referred to as the psychotic-neurotic distinction, is one of the more extensively investigated and is widely used by both researchers and clinicians. Endogenous depression is defined in terms of both etiology and symptomatology, with the presumed etiology involving unspecified physiological dysfunctions. Exogenous depression is assumed to be determined by any experience with the environment that may be identified as a precipitant. Often, the endogenous subtype is not defined biologically, but in terms of the *absence* of an identifiable precipitant, which is as logically problematic as attempting to prove the null hypothesis.

Because technical limitations prevent measurement of endogenous depression based strictly on biological etiology, there has been the practice of distinguishing endogenous and exogenous depression on the basis of symptoms. This has received some support from a number of factor-analytic studies (e.g., Rosenthal & Klerman, 1966), in which endogenous depression is characterized by more severe symptoms of terminal sleep disturbance, psychomotor retardation, weight loss, difficulty concentrating, depressed mood, and a lack of response to pleasant environmental events. Despite consistency in this clustering, it should be noted that the symptom category has not been consistently correlated to neuroendocrine and neurochemical studies of etiological factors in endogenous depression. Furthermore exogenous depression remains a heterogenous concept, defined in terms of the absence of the endogenous syndrome while still meeting established criteria for depression.

The usefulness of identifying the endogenous subtype is also supported by some evidence of a distinct response to treatment. Symptomatically measured endogenous depression predicts a positive response to physical treatment, including antidepressants (e.g., Rao & Coppen, 1979) and electroconvulsive shock therapy (e.g., Carney & Sheffield, 1972) although the success rate for antidepressants is often less than 50% (Kocsis, Frances, Voss, Mann, Mason, & Sweeney, 1988). Follow-up studies suggest that endogenous depression has a better long-term outcome, compared to other depressions (e.g., Paykel, Klerman, & Prusoff, 1974).

While, as indicated, there is not yet a universally accepted technology for measuring the hypothesized biological deficit in endogenous depression, one measurement device that has become popular is the dexamethasone suppression test (DST). The DST was developed to measure dysregulation of the hypothalamic-pituitary-adrenal (HPA) axis of the limbic system (Carroll, 1982) and is considered by many to be the best biological marker available for the identification of biologically based depression (Arana, Baldessarini, & Ornstein, 1985). Some studies have shown that depressed individuals with abnormal DST scores are more likely to respond to antidepressant treatment than are depressed individuals with normal DST scores (e.g., Arana et al., 1985). However, not all symptomatically defined cases of endogenous depression exhibit abnormal DST results (Heiby, Campos, Remick, & Keller, 1987). Therefore, the study of endogenous depression requires agreement upon a definition and concomitant method of measurement (e.g., symptoms vs. DST results), so that evidence of a biological subtype of depression can be cumulative.

The concept of exogenous depression, on the other hand, receives little support (Akiskal, Bitar, Puzantian, Rosenthal, & Parks, 1978). The diagnosis does not predict any specific etiology, course, or response to treatment, other than implying that these aspects distinguish it from endogenous depression. Attempts to identify a cluster of exogenous depression symptoms have failed to specify a homogeneous subtype (e.g., Kendell, 1968). Research evaluating the exogenous-endogenous classification system suggests that endogenous depression may represent one subtype, but that other subtypes remain to be identified.

The third type of classification system, based upon differences in symptomatology, is perhaps the most widely accepted. First discussed comprehensively by Leonhard (1979), it distinguishes between unipolar and bipolar depression, where bipolar includes the alternating occurrence of mania. Support for usefulness of this subtyping approach has been sought from areas of study investigating differences in symptomatology, genetic history, biological correlates, response to treatment, and course of the disorder. Bipolar depression has been distinguished from unipolar in terms of greater familial prevalence (Gershon, Bunney, Neckman, Van Erdewegh, & DeBauche, 1976) and a greater incidence in monozygotic, as opposed to dyzygotic, twins (Allen, 1976). Studies investigating the actual mechanism of genetic transmission of bipolar disorder, however, have yielded mixed results (e.g., Gershon et al., 1976). Studies searching for biological correlates of bipolar and unipolar subtypes (mostly investigating neurotransmitters) have also been inconclusive, perhaps due to the erroneous presumption that unipolar and bipolar forms of depression represent homogeneous subtypes (Akiskal, 1986).

The unipolar and bipolar categories do, in any event, show differences in course and response to treatment. Bipolar-depressed individuals are more likely to improve following lithium treatment, although not all bipolar cases respond favorably (Dunner, Goodwin, Gershon, Murphy, & Bunney, 1972). The severity of the bipolar disorder is greater in terms of earlier onset, more frequent episodes, greater social impairment (Angst, Bastrup, Grof, Hippius, Poldinger, & Weis, 1973) and a higher suicide rate (Dunner et al., 1972).

In conclusion, although the bipolar-unipolar classification system has received greater support than other nosologies, the distinction has limitations. Leonhard (1979) defines bipolar depression as depression with a history of mania, but at least one study indicates that some 28% of cases of mania are not accompanied by depression (Taylor & Abrams, 1973). This finding again suggests that bipolar depression may represent more than one subtype. A second limitation concerns the question of whether unipolar depression is a homogeneous disorder. One classification approach, Winokur's familial-based system (Andreasen & Winokur, 1979), has attempted to subtype unipolar depression, although problems with this system have already been indicated. Generally, however, research evaluating the unipolar-bipolar distinction has focused on identifying factors related to bipolar depression, but has offered no particular predictions regarding etiology and treatment of unipolar depression. This is a weakness of the classification system.

Overview of Current Classification Systems

Each contemporary classification system reviewed has made some contribution toward the classification of different types of depression. No one system, however, has offered a mechanism that accounts for the heterogeneity observed in the etiology and response to treatment in depression. The popular endogenous-exogenous system hypothesizes differing etiology and predicts treatment for the biologically versus environmentally determined depression. Leonhard's unipolar-bipolar system has led to the demonstration of a predictive usefulness for separating incidences of depression involving mania and suggests that bipolar disorders may have at least partial biological etiology. However, because no one system accounts for the variability within the syndrome of depression, it may be concluded that it is not adequate to propose a singular distinction between two major subtypes of depression. We will present an approach that recognizes subtypes of depression based on numerous potential etiologies. As others have suggested, ultimately *all* potential etiological factors in depression should be integrated, rather than seeking some isolated unitary cause (Craighead, 1980; Lewinsohn, Teri, & Hoberman, 1983). The paradigmatic behavioral theory of depression is the first attempt to provide an integration (Staats & Heiby, 1985). Past classification attempts have been presented in competition with each other and investigators of a particular system often ignore evidence that is not directly relevant to a unitary approach. For example, none of the traditional systems has proposed subtyping depression according to the interaction of "premorbid personality" (i.e., deficits in the behavior repertoires) and environmental precipitants, although a body of literature can be organized to support the role of these factors, as the present approach will indicate.

The role of a premorbid personality in depression was originally suggested by Hippocrates (Adams, 1939) and also outlined by early psychoanalysts, but the contemporary classification systems, in their lack of integration, evidence a strong atheoretical approach. The only theoretical assumption reflected in these systems is that some depressions have a biogenic etiology. Depressions resulting from environmental and personality factors are largely ignored, which is understandable because there has not been a heuristic framework with which to include such concerns. One consistent finding of research evaluating current classification systems is the usefulness of separating cases of depression that are distinctive in symptomatology, and may have at least a partial biological etiology (i.e., endogenous, which possibly includes bipolar). Studies attempting to identify the role of personality and environment in those types of depression have failed to delineate specific environmental or individual premorbid abnormalities (e.g., von Zerssen, 1982). But this can also be considered as a failure of the specific theories used, rather than the approach.

The failure to identify reliable environmental etiological factors is consistent with the search for genetic-biological determinants of endogenous and bipolar subtypes (e.g., Depue & Monroe, 1978). The possibility of an interaction between biological, environmental, and personality factors as an etiological model, however, has never been investigated. With the exception of Munro's (1966) attempt to identify subtypes in terms of premorbid or concomitant physical, or psychiatric disorders, the remaining cases of depression fall into a heterogenous "other" category (i.e., exogenous, unipolar). This "other" category actually represents *10 times* as many cases of depression as does the endogenous or bipolar categories (Boyd & Weissman, 1982). Now often referred to as Major Depressive Disorder in DSM III-R (American Psychiatric Association, 1987), unipolar exogenous depression may involve numerous subtypes (Craighead, 1980; Rapp & Fremouw, 1982; Staats & Heiby, 1985). Staats and Heiby provide one attempt to specify those subtypes.

The lack of predictive relevance for subtypes of unipolar depression in the current classification systems has been repeatedly pointed out by behaviorists (e.g., Kanfer & Saslow, 1969), but no completely adequate alternatives have been offered. Attempts to provide classification systems based on an operant functional analysis (e.g., Goldfried & Davison, 1976) have generated little theoretical, empirical, or applied interest. This is somewhat surprising since an operant functional analysis provides a framework to guide the focus of at least some treatment (e.g., suggesting depression results from the loss of reinforcement implies the manipulation of reinforcement contingencies in treatment). The problems with an operant functional analysis include failure to elucidate etiology (for prevention and treatment considerations) and the failure to delineate specific roles of personality variables that would predispose one to depression. Staats and Heiby (1985) have presented a theory, one of whose goals is the integration of findings relevant to the etiology of depression. This framework provides for specific prediction regarding both the etiology and treatment of numerous possible subtypes of depression. Proposed subtypes include consideration of the interaction of personality and environmental variables. The Staats–Heiby theory of depression will first be described and some relevant research noted. Implications and extensions of the theory for an elaborated classification system will then be delineated.

The Pardigmatic Behaviorism Theory of Depression

The paradigmatic behaviorism theory of depression (Staats & Heiby, 1985) differs from other attempts to explain etiology and predict response to treatment. First, the theory integrates findings from various sources of depression research, for example, findings from studies evaluating biogenic variables, psychoanalytic determinants, and social factors as well as findings from behavioristic studies. Second, the theory departs from those in the psychiatric literature by focusing on the role of variables that may account for the majority of cases of depression. Research and theory in the psychiatric literature have been primarily concerned with endogenous and bipolar depressions, which are in a small minority and involve the strongest suspicion of biogenic etiology. Third, the Staats–Heiby theory departs from prior behavioristic approaches to depression by including the concept of the etiological role of an abnormal personality. Fourth, the theory introduces the concept that the manic pole of bipolar depression is a cause in the etiology of depression. Fifth, the endogenous-exogenous difference is given specification and is considered as a continuous dimension, as Eysenck (1970) had proposed, not a typological variation. The Staats–Heiby theory is schematized in Figure 10.1.

In the diagram, the environmental influences occur at two points in the development of depression. In the first instance the environ-

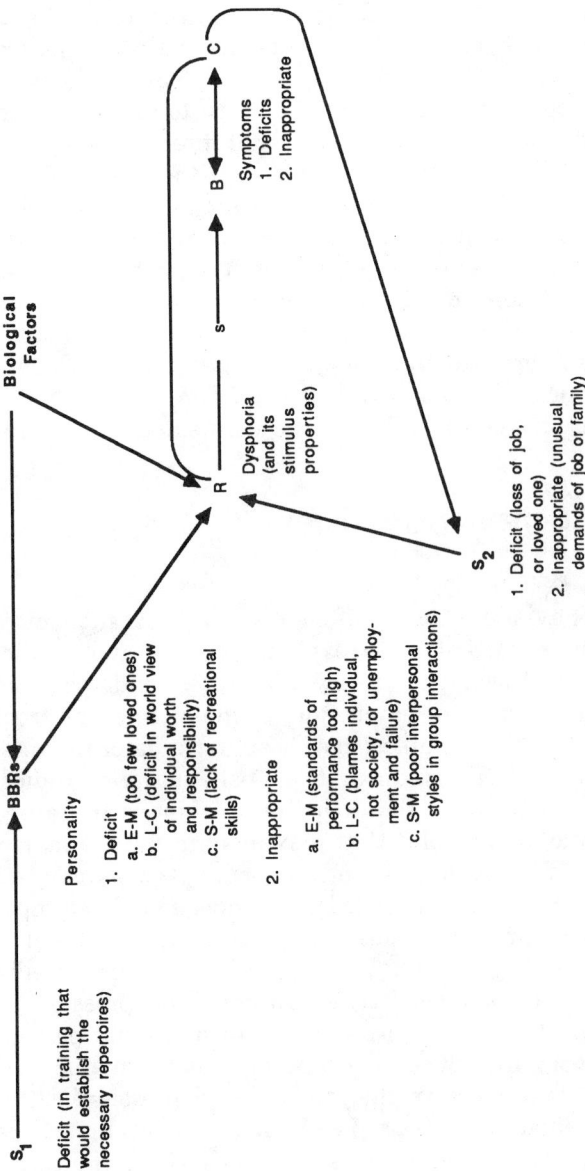

FIGURE 10.1 *Staats – Heiby Theory of Depression.* This figure illustrates the several proposed sites of causes and effects of depression. There are original learning conditions (S_1) that produce the three basic behavioral repertoires of personality; emotional-motivational (E-M), language-cognitive (L-C), and sensory-motor (S-M). The present life situation (S_2) may contain elements that by themselves or in interaction with the BBRs produce dysphoria (Rs). The dysphoric state produces the symptoms of depression (B). The consequences (C) of these symptoms may, in turn, affect the present life situation and elicit more dysphoria. Biological factors may directly influence the dysphoria or directly influence the BBRs. Examples of deficits and inappropriatenesses in the BBRs and S_2 are given in parentheses.

mental events are causes in the development of the individual's personality. As a consequence of experience the individual may develop very rich personality characteristics that have extensive adjustment value across a wide variety of environmental circumstances. Alternatively, the individual's personality may be deficient in important components, or, it may contain inappropriate components. The deficient and inappropriate aspects may be widespread and brought into play in a variety of environmental circumstances. As Figure 10.1 indicates, moreover, the environment also affects the individual as an etiological cause in the form of the present life circumstances. This would include any precipitating event, as well as the rest of the individual's life circumstances.

Centrally, as will be indicated, the subjective experience of dysphoria is a universal characteristic of the depression diagnosis. In paradigmatic behaviorism theory we consider it necessary to indicate the role of dysphoria in the syndrome. As shown in Figure 10.1, dysphoria is a consequence of the interacting effects of the individual's personality, and the individual's present life circumstances, depicted as S_2. On the other hand, the dysphoric state, along with the individual's personality and life situation, further acts as a determinant of the specific behaviors that the individual will display—that is, the various observable symptoms of depression.

Precipitating Environmental Variables

The etiological role of the environment has been cited in the clinical literature since Freud's (1933) treatise on depression in terms of a response to a real or an imagined object loss. The contemporary experimental literature has investigated the role of loss in terms of reductions in reinforcement (e.g., Ferster, 1973), "stressful" life events (e.g., Paykel, 1969), and other environmental factors that imply a loss of what can also be called pleasure sources, but refer more specifically to the nature of changes in the environment that result in such a loss. The traditional literature has also proposed that depression may function to obtain pleasure and secondary gain, and as a means of manipulating others in order to gain sympathy and attention (cf., Freedman, Kaplan, & Sadock, 1976). The contemporary behavioral counterpart to this notion is research evaluating the etiological role of environmental reinforcement of depression behavior (Ferster, 1973). The literature evaluating these environmental variables has produced a picture of mixed support. This is not surprising since investigations based on standard behaviorism conceptions customarily isolate an environmental variable without considering the environmental—personality interactions that might predict depression.

Nevertheless, there are important findings relevant to the present discussion. Environmental loss has been defined in terms of excessively low rates of reinforcement (ratio strain) and high rates of punishment (Ferster, 1973). These variables are still awaiting experimental investigation. Case studies (e.g., Moss & Boren, 1972), however, do provide anecdotal support for the role these variables may play in the onset of depression and suggest that further research may be promising. It has also been said that depression results from the loss conditions involved in response–outcome independence, or learned helplessness, where nondepressive, adaptive behavior ceases because it is not environmentally reinforced (Seligman, 1975). Such research (e.g., Miller & Seligman, 1975) has failed to demonstrate that this variable is related to depression (Heiby, 1979). Seligman and his colleagues (Abramson, Seligman, & Teasdale, 1978) have revised the learned helplessness hypothesis to include variables involving a cognitive concept by maintaining that attributional style is the critical determinant of depression. We will discuss the support for this revised hypothesis in the section on personality variables.

The analysis involving environmental losses that has received the greatest empirical support was proposed by both Ferster (1973) and Lewinsohn (1974). This involves the acquisition and maintenance of depressive behavior following a reduction in sources of environmental reinforcement which, in effect, places much of the individual's adaptive behavior on an extinction schedule. Case studies of depressed individuals commonly include descriptions of excessive complaining over losses and the failure to obtain pleasure and numerous correlational studies have indeed demonstrated that depressed individuals engage in fewer pleasurable activities than do nondepressed individuals (e.g., Lewinsohn & McPhillamy, 1974). Retrospective reports suggest that depressed individuals experience a reduction in reinforcement prior to the onset of the depression (e.g., Leff, Roatch, & Bunney, 1970). Other studies have demonstrated that severity of depression increases with a concurrent decrease in sources of reinforcement, and decreases with concurrent increases of such sources (e.g., Hammen & Glass, 1975). An environmental reduction in sources of reinforcement, however, does not always occasion depression and, in and of itself, is not a sufficient predictor (Hammen & Cochran, 1981; Lloyd, 1980). In a review of epidemiological factors related to depression, Hirshfield and Cross (1982) conclude that environmental loss 6 months prior to onset accounts for 25% of the variance in severity of symptoms and between 1 and 9% of the variance in *onset* of the disorder. Thus valuable but inconsistent research has been generated within the operant framework. Without a concept of personality, however, there is no explanation of why there are individual differences in response to the same environmental conditions of loss. The findings can be more useful when it is realized that environmental losses can interact with personality and thereby constitute an antecedent for depression onset, as will be indicated.

The role of environmental gain has been investigated by both Ferster (1973) and Lewinsohn (1974) who propose that depressive behavior is acquired and maintained by contingent environmental reinforcement. A person who attempts to obtain social support through depressive actions may become dependent on others to alleviate despondency through the provision of such special attention. There is correlational evidence that a depressive environment is characterized by an increase in the frequency of certain types of positive reinforcement, such as sympathy, but these reinforcers have not been related to specific contingencies controlling depressive behavior (e.g., Rehm & Plakosh, 1975; Sheslow & Erickson, 1975). Single subject reversal design studies have indicated that once the symptomatic behaviors of depression are extinguished, they can be reinstituted and maintained if followed by positive reinforcement (e.g., Liberman, 1970; Liberman & Raskin, 1971; Reisinger, 1972). Nevertheless, most of us live in social environments that provide for some contingent sympathy and attention following depressive behaviors without chronically exhibiting such behavior. Again, without a concept of personality, this individual difference is difficult to explain.

Personality Variables

In our theory, we advocate that personality must be included within an objective definition. Moreover, research has been conducted by psychoanalytic, trait-oriented, and behavioral researchers that can be interpreted to involve one or more of the three personality repertoires that constitute the personality theory of the present approach (see also Burns, Chapter 5, and Lohr and Hamberger, Chapter 7, this vol.).

The Sensory-Motor Repertoire

In the behavioral literature, numerous writers have hypothesized or demonstrated that dysfunctional social skills may render an individual depression prone (e.g., Lewinsohn, 1974). Studies comparing the quality of social skill in depressed and nondepressed individuals report mixed results. It is somewhat difficult to interpret these studies because so many different measures of social skills have been utilized. In the traditional literature, individuals exhibiting unipolar depression, compared to other psychiatric groups and non-psychiatric controls, have been found to reveal clinically deviant scores on the Minnesota Multiphasic Personality Inventory (MMPI) social introversion scale (Donnelley, 1976), be passive and unasser-tive (Riemann, 1967), and exhibit manipulativeness and hostility (Bibring, 1953). In the behavioral literature, depressed individuals have been found to exhibit a lower rate of speech during verbal interchanges, elicit fewer positive reactions from others (e.g., Libet & Lewinsohn, 1973), perform more ambiguous nonverbal communi-cation (Prakchin, Craig, Papgeorges, & Reith, 1977), and receive global ratings of greater dependency and lower social competence (Blatt, Quinlan, Chevron, McDonald, & Zuroff, 1982; Gotlib, 1982; Lewinsohn, Mischel, Chaplin, & Barton, 1980). This is what para-digmatic behaviorism theory would expect: deficits and inappro-priate aspects of such social skills result in little positive emotion elicitation and abundant negative emotion elicitation.

None of the above-mentioned studies, however, measured the level of social skill before the depression had begun, or after it has dissi-pated. Because depression is partly defined in terms of psychomotor retardation and decreased social activity, it is not surprising that depressed individuals appear less skilled than their nondepressed counterparts. Dysfunctional social skills cannot be a sufficient ante-cedent, or those with such deficiencies would be chronically de-pressed. It may be added that Tanner, Weissman, and Prusoff (1975) evaluated longitudinal data comparing social adjustment for two groups with a history of depression and found no relation between social skills and frequency of depression. Therefore, the evidence suggesting depressed individuals exhibit a dysfunctional sensory-motor repertoire is still somewhat weak.

Paradigmatic behaviorism theory suggests that this is the case because in manifestation, as well as in causative circumstances, depression is not a unitary disorder. Lack of social skills is only one of the various problems that may produce the negative affective conditions that underlie the symptoms of depression. Approaches that assume an oversimplified etiology, and that hypothesize the same causative agent in all patients, inevitably must produce con-fused and inconsistent findings. In addition, the paradigmatic be-haviorism theory predicts that other sensory-motor instrumental skills are potentially etiologic in depression. The theory suggests the instrumental skills involved in the work, education, and recreation repertoires are also worthy of investigation at more specific levels of analyses for their contributions to depression onset and maintenance under particular environmental circumstances.

The Language-Cognitive Repertoire

Research and theory on language-cognitive factors in depression have included variables regarding inappropriate causal attributions of unpleasant events, unrealistic expectations, and negative self-evaluations. What are called cognitive factors frequently include characteristics that would more appropriately be considered as emotional-motivational in paradigmatic behaviorism. Thus, the categorization of the literature is not always clearcut in these areas. Nevertheless, there are various lines of evidence implicating the language-cognitive repertoires. For example, depressed individuals engage in excessive self-criticism and experience excessive guilt (Blatt et al., 1982), are chronically pessimistic (Mendelson, 1967), have high aspirations (Matusseh & Feil, 1983), and report a low self-confidence (Wittenborg & Mower, 1977). These are aspects of language that have been analyzed in basic behavioral terms (Lohr & Hamberger, Chapter 7, this vol.; Staats, 1968a). Research that can be seen to involve some of the language-cognitive repertoires has been conducted by behavioral researchers at a more specific level of analysis. For example, Seligman and his colleagues (Abramson et al., 1978) revised the learned helplessness hypothesis by replacing the response-outcome-independence cause of depression with a cognitive variable involving inappropriate attributions regarding the cause of any real, or imagined, unpleasant experience. The revised hypothesis states that depression onset is a function of attributing all unpleasant events as being beyond one's own control, and caused by factors that are internal (one's own characteristics), stable (permanent), and global (generalizes to all unpleasant events). In other words, they hypothesize that persons become depressed when they assume responsibility for unpleasant events that are also believed to be uncontrollable. Again, the issue of why such persons are not chronically depressed is not addressed since their attribution characteristics are considered to be stable. Several studies have found depressed individuals are more likely to attribute unpleasant events to global, stable, and internal causes (e.g., Raps, Peterson, Reinhard, Abramson, & Seligman, 1982). Some studies report that only the internal attributions for failure are more likely in depressed persons (e.g., Nelson & Craighead, 1981). In a recent review of the evidence of etiologic factors in depression, Barnett and

Gotlib (1988) conclude there is little evidence supporting the role of cognitive dysfunctions prior to depression onset. This research has produced mixed results, however, which is what the present approach would expect when a complex disorder is considered in an oversimplified manner.

One study may be interpreted as evidence for the type of environment-personality interaction that has been described. Hammen and DeMayo (1982) found that some negative environmental events are more related to depression than are others. Undesirable events that the subject assesses as controllable were found to be more associated with depression than were negative events deemed to be beyond control. The depressed subjects attributed the former events to be self-caused (internal) and global. This is in contrast to undesirable events for which the subject reports no controllability. Undesirable not-controllable events were rated as equally upsetting, but due to external rather than internal causes, and these events were less associated with depression. Thus, self-blame (internal attributions) is more likely to occur if the event is undesirable and could have been affected by the subject. In other words, it is unlikely that depressed individuals make the attribution that Abramson et al. (1978) assume; otherwise they would take responsibility for such common events as poor weather, and this failure would be all encompassing. Instead, these data suggest that it is self-degradation for failure to prevent a controllable negative event that is characteristic of some depression. Additional research is necessary to study self-blame as a determinant of depression (cf., Coyne, Aldwin, & Lazarus, 1981; Peterson, Schwartz, & Seligman, 1981).

Beck (1967) has proposed variables that can be seen to involve the language-cognitive repertoire and hypothesized a "negative triad": depression is a function of a negative view of the self, the world, and the future. Again, as described by Eifert, Hekmat, Lohr and Hamberger, and others in this volume, these negative views can be explained in terms of language repertoires including labeling and self-labeling involving emotion-eliciting words (Staats, 1968a). These more inclusive negative views are purported to be maintained by several memory deficits that involve distorting environmental feedback in order to exaggerate the negative and ignore the positive. For Beck, the depression-prone individual fails to attend to events or feedback that contradicts those negative assumptions. The proposed habitual errors of logic include arbitrary inference, selective abstraction, overgeneralization, and personalization, as ways of lessening positive stimuli and increasing negative stimuli. Additional self-control hypotheses are related to Beck's (1967) notions.

Negative evaluations of one's performance and a failure to discriminate positive events are characteristics posited to be etiological factors to depression by a number of self-control theorists and researchers (Heiby, 1979; Jackson, 1972; Mathews, 1977; Rehm, 1977). What is called the self-control hypothesis suggests that language-cognitive deficits in evaluation and discrimination of positively valenced events may result in a dysfunctionally low frequency of self-reinforcement.

A low frequency of self-reinforcement is hypothesized to precede and partially contribute to depression. It has also been suggested that individuals who self-reinforce at a low frequency are relatively more dependent upon externally controlled contingencies, and so their adaptive functioning fluctuates according to sources of environmental reinforcement. Conversely, the individual with a high frequency of self-reinforcement exhibits more consistent adaptive functioning because functioning is not dependent upon changing environmental contingencies. At a descriptive level, the individual with a low frequency of self-reinforcement may appear to have a fluctuating sense of self-esteem and self-confidence, and may be predisposed to depression when environmental contingencies conducive to depression occur (Bandura 1969). Studies investigating the effect of low frequency of self-reinforcement per se will be reviewed in the next section, along with other variables of the emotional-motivational repertoire; first, the language-cognitive components of self-reinforcement will be considered below.

Both the Beck negative triad and the self-control literature provide consistent support for the hypothesis that individuals who are depressed exhibit concurrent negative expectations and a tendency to report fewer recent positive events than nondepressed persons. Numerous studies have shown that depressed individuals are more likely to rate their objectively comparable performance on experimental tasks as inferior (for a review, see Heiby, 1979). When asked to recall the frequency of recently experienced positive and negative outcomes on an experimental task, depressed individuals report a lower frequency of positive outcomes than did those who were not depressed (e.g., Gotlib, 1981). DeMonbreun and Craighead (1977) measured both immediate perception and recall of feedback, and found that depressed individuals negatively distort recall but are more accurate in reporting the frequency of immediate feedback. Perhaps the distortion involves errors of logic as Beck (1967) proposed, or perhaps it is inappropriate attention to and rumination over negative occurrences that inflate estimates of frequency of unpleasant events.

A few studies compared depressed and nondepressed subjects' estimates of positive events to the actual rate and found that depressed individuals do indeed report a lower frequency than do nondepressed individuals, but that the depressed subjects' estimates were more accurate and reflective of actual experience (e.g., Hoehn-Hyde, Schlottman, & Rush, 1982). These results suggest that the lower estimates of positive events reported by other researchers may be "low" by virtue of being more realistic than the estimates of the nondepressed individuals. In other words, depressed individuals may be lacking an adaptive skill of distorting the memory of recent events to exaggerate the positive. Jenkins and Ward (1965) demonstrated that nondepressed subjects identify a positive contingency for behavior when such a contingency is not actually operating. Unfortunately, no depressed subjects were evaluated in this study. Two studies have compared depressed to nondepressed subjects and found that the nondepressed subjects were more likely to report that success contingencies exist where there are none (Golin, Terrell, & Johnson 1977). This suggests that normative, nondepressed functioning is partly a correlate or consequence of distortion toward optimism. These various studies provide important findings, but they need integration into a coherent theoretical framework. Rosenbaum (Chapter 6, this vol.) provides an important explication of the language-cognitive repertoire in self-control that integrates research concerning information processing and process-regulating cognitions. This explication may prove useful in identifying specific language-cognitive deficits that render an individual vulnerable to depression. As Burns (Chapter 5, this vol.) has noted, there is overlap between the language-cognitive and the emotional-motivational personality repertoires (and the sensory-motor as well). For example, an important part of the language-cognitive system resides in the fact that there are many single words, and groups of words, that elicit emotional responses in the individual (Staats & Staats, 1958). Because the individual may use such words, he or she may provide self-stimulation that can elicit emotions of a positive or negative nature. When this is the case they may or may not function as reinforcing and directive (incentive) stimuli. Thus, the concept of self-reinforcement may be more usefully considered as the application of self-administered affective-reinforcing-directive stimuli, frequently of a verbal nature. Low and high frequency of self-reinforcement, a personal characteristic that has been employed in the present context, will now be considered as the application of a frequency of self-affective-reinforcing-directive (FSARD) stimulation.

Some people richly supply themselves with positive affective-reinforcing-directive (A-R-D) stimuli, while other people do not engage in this activity. A low frequency of self-produced A-R-D stimuli may be a consequence of learned negative self-evaluations, which may be associated with actual skill dysfunctions in the language-cognitive and sensory-motor repertoires that lead to negative self-labeling. On the other hand the negative self-evaluation may be independent of personal skill. For example, if parental values eschewed self-praise and equated such self-expression with boastfulness, then a developing individual may not acquire such self-language. This is what we call a low *frequency of self affective-reinforcing-directive language* (FSARD language).

There is consistent evidence that many depressed individuals exhibit a low FSARD language, and at least one study demonstrates that a low FSARD language can function as both an antecedent and a subsequent characteristic of depression. Depressed individuals exhibit a lower than normal frequency of self-produced affective-reinforcing-directive stimuli on a wide variety of experimental tasks (e.g., Rozensky, Rehm, Pry, & Roth, 1977) as well as in natural settings (Heiby, 1982). A low FSARD characteristic appears to be a generalized, as opposed to situational-specific, skill deficit, and is amenable to measurement by a self-report attitude scale (Heiby, 1982, 1983a, 1983c). Depressed individuals exhibiting low FSARD characteristics are not universally negative in evaluating and reinforcing the behaviors of others (Lobitz & Post, 1979), which suggests that such depressed individuals are inappropriate specifically in terms of *self*-evaluation and self-praise. Furthermore, low FSARD characteristics have been associated with general psychopathology, but deficits in recall of positive self-stimulation appear to be specific to depression (Gotlib, 1981).

As with all response-defined variables hypothesized to precede depression, most of the evidence has been derived from subjects who are already depressed, thus begging the question of whether the variable is a determinant or simply a symptom of depression. Two studies that the first author of this chapter has conducted, however, address the question of whether low FSARD characteristics actually precede depression onset. In an analogue study, Heiby (1983c) found that nondepressed subjects with a low FSARD stimulation exhibit a greater dysphoric reaction to a decrease in experimenter-controlled reinforcement than do nondepressed subjects with a high FSARD stimulation. This study provides evidence that low FSARD stimulation is not simply a symptom of depression, but may be exhibited without concomitant depressive symptoms. In the second study, it was found that persons exhibiting low FSARD stimulation are more likely to exhibit dysphoria than are persons exhibiting high FSARD stimulation when faced with similar naturally occurring environmental losses of reinforcement (Heiby, 1983b). Furthermore, this study found that some cases of depression occurred in people with low FSARD and high FSARD characteristics *without* environmental losses, suggesting that other determinants of depression were operating.

The data provided by these studies suggest that subtypes of depression exist that may be defined in terms of differences in etiological factors, and, perhaps, differences in response to treatment in the emotional-motivational aspects of personality. The interaction of conditions that result in an inappropriate low FSARD characteristic, along with a deficit in environmental sources of reinforcement, may result in one such subtype. Others have also recently suggested that subtypes according to whether the individual exhibits dysfunctional social skills or self-control skills may also prove useful in identifying etiology and selecting the most effective treatment (Blatt et al., 1982; Rehm, Fuchs, Roth, Kornblith, & Romano, 1979). A case study by Heiby (1986) describes four individuals for which depression decreased only when the treatment matched a presenting deficit in either social or self-control skills. A more recent report of 35 cases of depression in which six theoretically etiologic behavioral characteristics were measured suggested that *none* of these characteristics were deficit in *all* cases of depression (Heiby, 1989). Therefore, it can be argued that there may be numerous etiological subtypes of depression involving a range of behavioral deficits.

Implications for Classification

Unipolar Depressions

It is predicted from this theoretical framework that there exist numerous possible subtypes of unipolar depression. Many of these subtypes may be a function of interactions between personality and environmental factors. The classification system outlined accommodates the interactions of factors that have been demonstrated to account for some cases of depression. It also accommodates the variety of symptomatology and possible etiological factors, the heterogeneity of which is often lamented by those subscribing to any of the previously proposed classification systems. The taxonomy suggested by the Staats–Heiby theory furnishes a framework for investigating the possible etiologies, prevention strategies, and treatments for the majority of the cases of depression. Previous classification systems have contributed somewhat to the understanding of the less frequent so-called endogenous and bipolar disorders for which there is evidence developing to support the role of at least partial biological etiologies and treatment implications. The Staats—Heiby system facilitates the understanding of the "exogenous, unipolar, primary, and secondary" depressions for which there is little evidence, or theory, that gives reason for supposing an organic cause. The proposed paradigmatic behaviorism classification system thus provides a complement to the biologically based systems and has the flexibility to eventually accommodate the potential demonstration of interaction among personality, biological, and environmental factors. We will briefly indicate a theoretical framework within which this may be achieved.

The majority of possible subtypes proposed in the present analysis still require empirical confirmation. There is some evidence that the interaction of dysfunctionally low self-administration of positively valenced emotional stimuli (LFSARD) and a reduction in sources of environmental reinforcement may constitute one such subtype (Heiby, 1983b, 1983c). There is also evidence that cases of depression may be categorized according to the presence or absence of deficits in the language-cognitive repertoire (Rapp & Fremouw, 1982), as well as by degree of deficits in the sensory-motor (e.g., poor social skills) versus the language-cognitive and emotional-motivational repertoires (Blatt et al., 1982; Heiby, 1986). As another example, a direct determinant of depression may be general deficits in the individual's emotional-motivational system that make him or her vulnerable to losses of positive emotion elicitors in present life circumstances. Rose and Staats (1988) have recently shown that the composite score used in the Pleasant Events Schedule involves two variables: (1) the extent to which pleasant events are positive, and (2) the frequency of occurrence of these events. Moreover, some depressed people do not get enough pleasant events whereas others simply do not find "pleasant" events very positive regardless of their frequency. The paradigmatic behavioral analysis reveals two types of depression in this respect which require a different treatment approach. In order to develop a comprehensive classification system, all potential etiological factors must be considered.

The number of etiological subtypes remains an open question. For example, when a man with a sensory-motor repertoire deficit and consequent dependency experiences a major reduction in reinforcement as a result of losing his wife, one would expect this man to be depression prone particularly as he also faces additional problems caused by the lack of the skills necessary for everyday tasks such as shopping, cooking, or taking care of children. This same individual may not become depressed when faced with the environmental condition of ratio strain, such as when one's salaried work load increases, an area in which, let us say, the personality repertoire is very well developed. The point is that the sensory-motor (or any) deficit may be etiological under some environmental conditions while not under others. Similarly, the presence of yet other personality deficits may constitute the possibility of further etiological interactions. Dependency combined with the type of deficit in the emotional-motivational repertoire described above may interact in rendering an individual depression prone.

Endogenous Depression

The schematic model of depression shown in Figure 10.1 is also intended to incorporate the traditional endogenous-exogenous dichotomy. In the Staats–Heiby theory the general term *endogenous* refers to any independent variable that leads to or produces dysphoria, that is part of the person as distinguished from the external environment. Thus, for example, any deficit in the individual's personality repertoires that makes for an extreme and aberrant reaction to an environmental loss would be an endogenous depression. On the other hand, any metabolic aberration that affects the individual's personal adjustment in meeting life's problems can also be a cause of depression.

The theory provides a basis for understanding the findings with respect to the endogenous categorization. There are indications that biological variables may be involved. But the evidence is mixed, which is what would be expected if the gross category is actually produced by independent variables of a learned personality type, as well as of a biological type. We have conducted one study mentioned earlier (Heiby et al., 1987) that suggests that some symptomatically defined endogenously depressed persons who exhibit the expected biological marker on the dexamethasone suppression test have an average FSARD stimulation. In contrast, those who show no such biological deficits, do exhibit a dysfunctionally low FSARD stimulation. These findings are consistent with the sort of subtypes in depression that the Staats–Heiby theory predicts.

Eysenck (1970) suggested to view endogenous–exogenous distinction as a continuum rather than a dichotomy, but in the present theory the principle is that the two interact. Endogenous factors, whether biological or of a personality type, can be expected to have an environmental effect. For example, a medical problem will frequently incapacitate the individual, with a range of social repercussions. Conversely, precipitating environmental events can be expected typically to have effects upon the individual's biological functioning in a way that enters into the cause of depression. Most of the precipitating events, for example, involve losses that are physical stressors for the individual and can be expected to have physiological effects ranging from suppression of immune system efficacy, and consequent illnesses, to hypertension and the need for medication that further complicates the individual's life circumstances. This part of the theory is being advanced here only in preliminary form. The theory structure, however, does provide the basis for a wide ranging consideration of the endogenous-exogenous typology and the literature that underlies the typology.

Bipolar Depression

The Staats–Heiby theory can also incorporate bipolar depression into its framework. A strong feature of the traditional bipolar classification is that a biologically defined process is thought to be causal. The present theory hypothesizes that in addition to the depressed phase, the manic phase of bipolar depression can be seen to involve, at least in certain cases, the personality repertoires. Aside from biologically determined features, the individual's learning and experiential history can provide personality characteristics that evidence themselves as manic behavior. Someone, for example, who has learned grandiose self-descriptions and skillful styles of language (such as exaggeration, lying, and distortion), in the service of getting people to do as he or she wants, has acquired personality repertoires that initially may have significant positive environmental consequences. Such a person may successfully convince others to embark upon attractive but shaky ventures (e.g., investing financially in a high-risk project). Initial success can encourage elaboration of these actions in the individual, leading to additional positive developments and a progressive growth of euphoria and manic behavior.

The counterpart to our theory of depression, then, is a theory of the euphoric-manic state. The other components of the theory as shown in Figure 10.1 remain the same as those for depression, but the elicited emotional state is excessively positive instead of excessively negative. What makes this experience pathological is that the person's instrumental behaviors do not create lasting success, and while they may make the individual exceedingly happy, this is short lived. When the environmental success collapses, moreover, the individual enters the negative phase of the cyclical problem, because the collapse serves as the precipitating event for a depression. This process may occur in a way that is built on inadequate skills and unrealistic expectations. Or the process may occur where the individual has displayed great skill in constructing an important set of environmental events (e.g., becoming a Napoleon with mounting success) only to ultimately see the situation collapse with a consequent relegation to obscurity or worse. The important point here, however, is the extent to which the personality exaggerations of the individual result in environmental constructions that first induce euphoria but later collapse in a way that produces the precipitating social events of depression. This cannot be developed here but it outlines a part of the theoretical structure of paradigmatic behaviorism that needs to be developed more completely in the future to account for the bipolar typology.

Measurement and Research

There are existing instruments that have been proposed by various investigators to measure depression and etiological factors in depression. Of the latter, there are devices with demonstrated psychometric support available to measure, for example, reduction in environmental sources of reinforcement (The Unpleasant Events Schedule; Lewinsohn & Talkington, 1979) and a low frequency of self-administered affective-reinforcing-directive stimuli (The Self-Reinforcement Questionnaire; Heiby, 1982, 1983a).

One reason that research in depression is more prolific than for many other abnormal behaviors is that the definition and measurement of depression has met with greater agreement and standardization. The symptoms defining Major Depression Disorder in DSM III-R (American Psychiatric Association, 1987) represent the topography of general depressions that has been agreed upon by most researchers and clinicians (Lewinsohn, 1974). There are several types of psychometrically adequate assessment devices, including (1) self-report measures, such as the Beck Depression Inventory (Beck, 1967); (2) interview scales, such as the Research Diagnostic Criteria (Spitzer, Endicott, & Robins, 1978); and (3) behavioral observation checklists, such as the Behavior Rating Scale (Williams, Barlow, & Agras, 1972). These various scales yield a single score, and are highly intercorrelated, and are thus interchangeable for the general measure of the presence and intensity of any possible subset of depressive symptoms.

In order to identify specific etiological subtypes it will be necessary to provide more specific measures of presenting symptoms. It may be found, for example, that depression as a partial function of negative self-evaluation may also include an exaggeration of self-criticism, whereas depression as a partial function of inadequate social skills may be more marked by social withdrawal than by self-degradation. It remains an empirical question whether heterogeneity of symptoms represents differing etiology or some complex interaction of etiological factors with other aspects of personality. The research that supposedly suggests which deficits and inappropriate aspects of the environment and personality are etiological in depression remains suggestive because most studies have not been longitudinally prospective in nature. Measures are made on subjects who are already depressed, although some investigators instruct the subject to provide a retrospective, predepressed self-report. Such procedures risk confounding cause with consequence. Correlational evidence that depressed individuals are more likely to make internal attributions for failure (e.g., Nelson & Craighead, 1981), for example, may be demonstrating a refined definition of the symptoms of depression instead of pointing to etiological factors.

Since prospective research is usually prohibitively expensive, treatment studies represent an alternative, but less direct avenue of enquiring into etiological factors. The Staats–Heiby theory predicts that the most effective treatment for a particular incident of depression would be one that targets etiological factors. Thus, treatment comparison studies could evaluate the effects of remediation of deficits upon current depressions and prevention of future incidents. An additional concern of past research has been sample selection, in terms of the limits of generalization of results. Subjects are most often mildly depressed college students or severely depressed hospitalized patients, neither of which represent the general population. These studies have rarely included nondepressed psychiatric controls, so it is unknown whether the studied etiological factors are specific to depression or general psychiatric risk factors.

Studies evaluating the Staats–Heiby theory should not only avoid past mistakes but also consider specific questions raised by the theory itself. The basic assumption that dysphoria antecedes the remaining symptoms of depression requires confirmation. The acquisition and elicitation of the dysphoric response needs explication. The model maintains that dysphoria results from the interaction among personality, environmental, and biogenic variables. How the effects of such interactions cause dysphoria must be explored.

It is also necessary to investigate how each personality deficit (or inappropriate response pattern) is acquired. It has been shown, for example, that a deficit in self-reinforcement may result from modelling or direct training (Bandura, 1969). The parameters of each variable in the Staats–Heiby theory must also be established. The magnitude of losses of sources of reinforcement is an example of such needed parametric values. Once the etiology of subtypes of depression is established through prospective and treatment research, it should be possible to design and evaluate prevention strategies involving change in both personality repertoires and environmental predisposing factors. Demonstrating the effectiveness of prevention is the definitive illustration of the role played by hypothesized etiological conditions.

Conclusions

The usefulness of the proposed paradigmatic framework for developing an explanation, treatment or prevention strategy, and classification for each subtype of depression, has yet to be systematically tested. This examination will be based on its predictive accuracy and heuristic utility. The predictive accuracy of the personality and environmental variables proposed in the theory can begin to be empirically evaluated, given current psychometric technology. Advances in the use of self-report measures in the assessment of both personality (e.g., Kendall & Hollon, 1981) and environmental variables (e.g., Lewinsohn & Talkington, 1979) make it possible to undertake evaluation of these proposed etiological factors. It is likely that the consideration of numerous personality and environmental factors will account for more of the variance in depression than will the consideration of any one variable alone as Craighead (1980) has suggested. The theory, in addressing new information related to personality repertoires and environmental factors, thus provides a framework that embodies and encourages novel empirical findings. By including the concept of an abnormal personality, otherwise disparate findings regarding premorbidity to depression can be integrated.

It may be said that the theory underemphasizes biological factors in depression. Perhaps organic conditions can directly elicit dysphoria (or mania), regardless of prior learning history. Biological factors eventually may be shown to be direct determinants in some depressions (e.g., endogenous or bipolar) and interactive etiological factors in some or all of the remaining depressions (see Figure 10.1). For example, limbic and cortical neurotransmitter dysregulation may occasion a dysfunction of the hypothalamic-pituitary-adrenal (HPA) axis that, in turn, may directly result in a severe dysphoric (or manic) affective state regardless of adequate skills among the personality repertoires or a resourceful environment. In addition, it is feasible that an HPA dysregulation could result in a mild dysphoric (or manic) condition that occasions depression (mania) only among individuals who are also lacking in the personality repertoires and/or who face a detrimental environmental situation. It should be indicated that the theory includes biological factors in a way that has been absent in other behavioral theories. The Staats–Heiby theory presents a basis for bridging underlying behavioral and personality sources of knowledge. It also provides at least part of a basis for unifying biological and environmental variables. The extent to which this unification can be elaborated and supported remains for future developments. The theory is already equipped to accommodate findings that indicate the biological components that interact with both personality and environmental factors. There is nothing proposed in the paradigmatic behaviorism theory, moreover, that would preclude the integration of direct biological causes.

It is true that the basic tripartite personality theory of paradigmatic behaviorism (Staats, 1975) requires further specification. In each of the three personality repertoires there has been a series of studies conducted to specify each of the three personality repertoires, how each is learned, and how it functions in determining behavior. A great deal of work remains, however, in terms of this type of specification. The task is a very large one, and such work is basic to both the theory of depression and to the interests of behavioral assessment and behavior therapy. Nevertheless, the long observed heterogeneity in the study of depression has led to the failure of simplified, single-variable approaches. That our theory not only accommodates but predicts heterogeneity in depression provides us with some optimism that the paradigmatic behaviorism framework will promote a unified understanding of depression, and that this will deepen with further specification of its personality repertoires and the other variables indicated.

Our theory of depression differs from past attempts to account for this disorder in a number of ways. It differs from traditional approaches in psychiatry by focusing on the majority of depressions (i.e., the unipolar, exogenous cases). Psychiatric approaches have been primarily concerned with those depressions for which there is some, albeit *causally* inconclusive, evidence of biological involvement and treatment, as in the endogenous and bipolar types. It differs from the assumptions of standard behaviorism insofar as its notion of an abnormal personality is invested with causal power in addition to environmental determinants. It also stands in contrast to the cognitive theories by retaining the importance of environmental variables as they interact with cognitions, as well as by including personality variables of the emotional-motivational and sensory-motor repertoires. In fact, a major distinction between the present theory and social learning theories is the specification of what personality consists of, how it is learned, how it functions, on a broad basis. Furthermore, no other theory has included a functional role for dysphoria in the production of the other depressive symptomatology. The present theory focuses attention upon determinants of dysphoria that, in turn, lead to other symptoms of depression.

The Staats–Heiby theory of depression selectively incorporates into its structure the mixed, and sometimes conflicting contributions made by preceding explanations of depression, including elements from standard behaviorism, social learning theory, cognitive-behavioral strategies, psychoanalytic and trait-oriented approaches, and at least parts of the traditional biologically based findings. Prior approaches have assumed a unitary etiology and treatment for depression. By abandoning such an assumption, paradigmatic behaviorism theory attempts to make sense out of an otherwise confusing state of affairs. By including a personality, and environmental, and a biological level of theory, and the manner in which these interact with dysphoria (and mania), a theoretical structure is provided by which explanatory, closely-derived (vs. eclectic) unification is possible. Most importantly, the theory is heuristic. It has already stimulated published research and its broad purview promises much more. In view of the currently available knowledge and technology, we suggest that a general elaboration and evaluation of this approach is now both indicated and feasible.

Acknowledgment

Many thanks go to James D. Becker, Kapiolani Community College, for his editorial suggestions.

11

The Conceptual and Practical Evolution of Behavior Therapy with Children

Frances E. Wilson
Paolo Meazzini

Child behavior therapy constitutes a subset of behavior therapy with which it shares most of its distinguishing features. In fact, child behavior therapy has the same articulated framework as behavior therapy in general, including metatheoretical assumptions, basic working attitudes, heuristic models, and methodology. As a result of this common cultural background, behavior therapists and child behavior therapists conceptualize psychological events and problems in a way that differs, often markedly, from the viewpoint that once dominated child clinical psychology. In other words, behavior therapy allows one to supply different answers to fundamental questions for applied psychology such as: what is the essential class of events to study (behaviors vs. intrapsychic phenomena); why do psychological events and problems occur (organism—environment interaction vs. intrapsychic causality); and how is the intervention to be implemented (objective-operational vs. subjective methodology)?

Agreement on basic philosophical and practical issues such as these has provided child behavior therapists with a certain degree of intradisciplinary cohesion. Within the metatheoretical unity of behaviorism, however, there are various perspectives that have produced very different emphases in formulating clinical interventions. Among the major derivatives that come readily to mind are treatments based strictly on operant conditioning principles and the manipulation of cues and consequences, those emphasizing cognitive/verbal mediation of overt behavior (e.g., Meichenbaum, 1977, 1980), and educational methods designed to enhance the child's repertoire of skills (especially social and academic). There are also ecological models whereby social systems, such as the parent-child relationship, family, or peer group, are influenced to effect change in the child. Finally, there are interventions aimed at improving the child's physiological adaptation to the environment. In practice, child clinicians regularly intermix these strategies and move about among treatment foci within a single case. For example, a comprehensive treatment approach to childhood obesity demands some attention to physical health variables, child and family attitudes toward food and knowledge of nutrition, family mealtime practices, self-monitoring and self-control skills in the child, exercise patterns, parental relationships and how they impact reinforcement contingencies, enhancement of self-esteem and improvement in peer relationships, and so on. The enumeration of the classes of variables that yield specific methods for treating disorders like obesity is now relatively straightforward. However, with the exception of social behaviorism, there has been little theoretical work to elucidate the common conceptual rubric whereby all these elements (and their interaction) can be considered together, as a whole.

One of the proposed solutions to this increasingly perceived need for a comprehensive system for analyzing child behavior disorders has been to utilize the insights and findings of developmental psychology (cf., Gelfand & Peterson, 1985). Certainly, in our view, developmental considerations are a mandatory component of child behavior therapy. Unless, however, the rules for incorporating developmental psychology are more clearly defined, there is a risk that this orientation (with *its* own subsystems of loosely related approaches) will merely be added to existing tenets rather than integrated to form a global framework of the kind advocated by Staats in Chapter 2.

The childhood years are marked by rapid developmental changes that do have vast significance for the theory and implementation of child behavior therapy. First, the social influence of adult caregivers (usually parents) is initially very strong, but is then steadily superceded by both broader societal influences (e.g., peers and teachers) and more focused self-regulation. Second, there are periods of accelerated learning of cognitive skills, and this learning influences subsequent attainment in a hierarchical fashion (Staats, 1971a). A third, somewhat related implication is that during early phases of development the child's abilities to comprehend and cope with environmental and social complexities are limited. Fourth, motivational patterns (interests, needs, and social-emotional sophistication such as understanding one's own and others' feelings) change over time, together with still other modifications that are by-products of growth and development, such as physical strength, muscular coordination, and so forth. These are the central facets of child development, not specifically documented findings from child psychology, and they highlight the conceptual differences between the rationales of child and adult behavior therapy. Moreover, they have been incorporated within social behaviorism in a systematic way that will be illustrated in the remainder of this chapter.

Evolution of Child Behavior Therapy

Although the earliest behavioral case studies were of children (e.g., Jones, 1924; Watson & Rayner, 1920), the first textbook on child behavior therapy (Gelfand & Hartmann, 1968) was not published until the late sixties, and even then no more than 70 articles were cited. Since that time, however, the field has enjoyed tremendous growth, as evidenced by the number of journal submissions, textbooks, and conference symposia devoted to the topic, as well as the introduction in 1979 of a new journal *Child and Family Behavior Therapy*. Although most of the early experimental case studies focused on individuals with severe deficits in their behavioral repertoires (e.g., Ferster & DeMyer, 1962; Wolf, Risley, & Mees, 1964), contemporary child behavior therapy has been applied to a wide range of developmental problems in an ever wider variety of contexts. This rapid evolution reflects certain issues and attitudes within the field that require examination.

Professional Acceptance

A discipline such as child behavior therapy is embedded within a social and political climate that influences its character independent of theoretical guidance. Its essence is something like a *Weltanschauung*, a way of conceptualizing psychological events that has to do more with the perceptions, beliefs, and values of its scientific community than the laws, methods, and content areas of the enterprise. One such influence has been the need to secure professional acceptance which has had a considerable impact on the nature of the discipline.

The early pioneers were emphatic about the potency of their procedures and the supremacy of their approach. This disposition, however, was not altogether dishonorable. On the contrary, it was a necessity, instrumental in opening up new working space. This same self-assurance occurs at the beginning of any new scientific and cultural movement (Etzioni, 1964; Kuhn, 1962) and provides the impetus and resolve to surmount the inevitable criticism raised by the existing paradigms. Of course, this posture is no longer justifiable once a scientific working space has been conquered and is securely held. Some authorities have argued that child behavior therapists have now checked these doctrinaire leanings in favor of open-minded empiricism. Ross (1981), for instance, observed that "in a sense, the field has grown beyond its stage of missionary zeal and has embarked upon a mature self-scrutiny which a clearly established endeavor can afford" (p. 5).

However, because the early studies were most concerned with demonstrating that certain basic learning principles applied to child behavior, little attention was paid to the issue of evaluating the meaningfulness of the reported change. Social behaviorism (e.g., Staats, 1971a) suggested that the effective evaluation of intervention would require consideration of how changing one behavior in the child's repertoire would influence future development, how the behavior judged to be problematic or acceptable would reflect attitudinal consequences of the parents' own learning histories, and how "interventions" could be understood in terms of the natural *interactions* between children and their social environment. These important concepts gradually emerged as three broad considerations in the evaluation of clinical treatment. (1) As behaviors themselves are independent variables for other behaviors, the design of child behavior therapy requires consideration of the interrelationships among behaviors (Evans, Meyer, Kurkjian, & Kishi, 1988; Voeltz & Evans, 1982). (2) Both the selection of the target response for treatment (Wilson & Evans, 1983) and the social validity of the change in the child's repertoire (Voeltz & Evans, 1983) are judgments that require understanding of the affective value of the behavior to others (Evans & Wilson, 1983). (3) If interventions are artificial, rather than involving the redesign of the social ecology, the attitudes of parents and teachers toward these interventions have a major influence on how they will be implemented. This is often referred to as treatment acceptability and is really the contemporary refinement of the original issue of the professional acceptance of child behavior therapy.

Child Behavior Therapy: Applied Science or Technology?

It follows from the previous comments that the empirical evaluation of child behavior therapy cannot be separated from a comprehensive conception of children's behavioral development. This view is rather different from that of the early proponents of radical behavior modification (Baer, Wolf, & Risley, 1968), who saw the difference between basic research in animal behavior and applied, clinical analyses of socially relevant problems only in the immediate goals and variables under study. The methodology remained constant. Ironically, equating basic and applied research in this way enhanced child behavior modification's technological image, since radical behaviorists' basic research was itself not systematically derived from theory. Another popular position over the years has been that behavior change procedures derive directly from laboratory-based learning principles (cf., Eysenck, 1976; Ross, 1981), without ever delineating the rules of their application the way Minke does in Chapter 3. In fact, it can be argued that the overly simplistic application of laboratory-derived principles has resulted in the unnatural, age-inappropriate, and even dehumanizing intervention plans that are criticized in the next chapter.

Partly, perhaps, by recognizing that child behavior therapy has drawn on a disorderly set of principles, laws, and loose functional relationships, some interpreters of the field have persisted in asserting that behavior therapy is a technology rather than applied science (Erwin, 1978; A.A. Lazarus, 1971; London, 1972) and reflects the values of the modern technological society (Woolfolk & Richardson, 1984). According to London (1972), the claimed connection between behavior therapy and learning theory is groundless, being only a way of lending behavior therapy scientific credibility, or, more crudely, of embellishing it. This being true, the discipline would be merely technological, comprised of a set of procedures that can easily be modified by the results gradually accruing from their application. This description, although historically imprecise (Meazzini, 1983), contains more than a grain of truth, witness the recent growth of behavioral pediatrics, which was derived from clinical needs and social/professional circumstances, not theoretical or empirical advances. Although it is possible to try to catalogue what child behavior therapists do (cf., Bellack & Hersen, 1985), the exercise is completely antithetical to social behaviorism. It is not *what* is done, but *how* and *why* that set the paradigmatic behavioral child clinician apart. Thus psychiatric categories or standardized tests might be used in paradigmatic behavior therapy, but grounded in theories of response covariation (Evans, 1986) or basic behavioral repertoires (Burns, 1980; Nelson, 1980), not because of their popularity with the professional community.

Basic Attitudes of Child Behavior Therapists

A third feature of child behavior therapy's evolution that did not reflect simply translating the findings of basic research into practice is the set of working guidelines for analyzing and changing behavior. Some of these have remained relatively constant; for instance, child behavior therapists have always been interested in discovering the contextual factors that elicit and maintain the prosocial or maladaptive behaviors of children. This strong emphasis has been a sine qua non of effective behavior therapy and may be traced back to early American functionalism that so influenced the first generation of behaviorists (Meazzini & Bauer, 1984). On the other hand, the applied behavior analysis emphasis on the immediate antecedents and consequences of behavior has proved extremely superficial, and behavior modifiers have to be continually reminded that it is the *function* and the intent of the child's behavior that must be considered (e.g., Durand & Carr, 1985).

Another good illustration of an attitude that influences practice is the unit of analysis preferred by child behavior therapists. It is generally thought that behavioral scientists analyze behavior in molecular rather than the molar fashion once typical of Gestalt psychologists and now common to many cognitive psychologists. Actually, even the first behaviorists such as Watson never held a purely microanalytic attitude, being instead rather flexible and prone to choose the level of analysis that best fitted their research and intervention goals. These days behavioral researchers are engaged in assessing molar *entities* such as schools, communities, or families, as well as conducting fine-grained component analyses of, say, the self-injury that might be exhibited by a child with developmental disabilities. In a way, it is impossible to separate type of analysis from unit of analysis because even for global targets of intervention, the constituent elements of settings, persons, and events will be operationally defined and rendered accessible to some form of systematic observation in order to analyze functional relationships.

Therefore, regardless of the problem at hand, the child behavioral clinician will begin by defining, observing, and quantifying phenomena, and in eschewing subjective inference will necessarily appear molecular in comparison to proponents of other approaches. Despite differences in the intermediate forms of analysis, the ultimate treatment goals (e.g., promote well-being, or increase parent-child satisfaction) may be as global as those arrived at by nonbehavioral practitioners (Wilson & Evans, 1983). Identifying problematic behaviors rather than problematic children is also a critical perspective from which to understand that. Since children almost never self-refer, their supposed problems must be tied to parental perception and expectation at one level, just as they must be tied to direct parental influence and control at another. The careful work of Forehand and his associates (e.g., Forehand & McCombs, 1988) on the relationship between maternal depression and child functioning is a good example of the detail that must be considered in exposing the transactional nature of child and family influences.

Metatheoretical Assumptions of Child Behavior Therapy

Somewhat different from the attitudes we have mentioned, metatheoretical assumptions are deeply rooted beliefs that implicitly guide scientific research and are not easily analyzed by any scientific tool. With few exceptions, behavior therapists and child behavior therapists hold a very consistent set of beliefs, the chief of which are determinism, environmentalism, and a psychological model of deviance. We will discuss the first of these only briefly, give a little more attention to the second, and leave the commentary on the third to the next section, specifically describing the social behaviorism model of abnormal child behavior.

Determinism

Determinism is a belief that nature (including human nature) is an orderly set of phenomena, closely interconnected by a complicated network of temporal relationships, that, simply stated, are known as cause-effects. All behavioral scientists adhere to this basic tenet, but some hold strong deterministic assumptions (e.g., Skinner, 1953, 1974), whereas others espouse weak, probabilistic views. Opinions differ also between those who believe in one-way determinism, typical of most "second-generation" behaviorists (Staats, 1975), and those who hold a two-way or circular deterministic conviction that a class of events affects a second class of events that is in turn affected by the first. This second distinction may be of historical interest only, in that all present-day behavioral scientists would appear to accept what Bandura (1977b) called reciprocal determinism. In his 1971 textbook Staats described in considerable detail how the concept of behavioral interaction provided a consistent behavioral account of the emergence of the self-system in the child with its resultant self-determination.

Environmentalism

Environmentalism implies that human behavior is a product of the external conditions impinging upon the individual. The term *environment*, however, can be defined by at least three different ecological referents: (1) the *physical environment* that denotes the external, physical, climatic, and material properties of settings; (2) the *normative cultural environment* which is the very finely ingrained network of standards, values, rules, and customs that influence the behavior of individuals and groups; and (3) the social environment which encompasses all the interactions and relationships that occur between and among persons. The study of environmental attributes and their effects on behavior is becoming a productive point of convergence for behavioral scientists and ecological and environmental psychologists. Typologies and conceptual schemas such as the one developed by Moos (1973) and Insel and Moos (1974) have been applied to problems that are pertinent to child behavior therapy. For example, understanding how various physical and social dimensions of school environments contribute to student disruptiveness (Wiatrowski, Gottfredson, & Roberts, 1983) or how the physical environment promotes delinquency (Jeffrey, 1972) can be useful in designing effective interventions to be delivered in natural settings (O'Donnell, 1984).

The popular notions of psychosocial stress and stress-related illness arise from the assumption that aspects of one's broader social and cultural environment can be deleterious to physical and emotional well-being. Similarly, it has been suggested that psychological disorders can be the immediate result of societal and cultural norms and rules that are perceived as uncontrollable, oppressive, and unfair (Etzione, 1964). It could be that within the microcosm of the family, coercive interaction patterns, punitive discipline styles, and child behavior problems relate to the same phenomenon. Also, the data accumulating from ecobehavioral or psychosocial systems research perspectives (e.g., Wahler, 1980) indicate the importance of extrafamily parameters that may affect the functioning of parent-child dyads or parents' perceptions of children's behavior.

Person-to-person influences are apparent in all forms of social persuasion, including psychotherapy, and a significant contribution of behavior therapy has been to make explicit the influence of one's behavior on the behavior of others. Early parent-training programs exemplified this belief, since the intent was to modify child behavior by first changing the behavior of their most relevant and immediate educational agents. However, such ideas and methods need to be updated, because even though parents can be taught to observe child behavior accurately (Wilson, Parrish, Mace, Kolko, & Kalsher, 1985), and to use contingency management strategies appropriately (Patterson, Cobb, & Ray, 1973), and although their implementation of these skills can be measured and monitored (Weitz, 1981), parent training has not been uniformly successful (e.g., Bernal, Klinnert, & Schultz, 1980). Fortunately, there is a developing trend toward identifying distal setting events and determining the relevant response classes to be studied in parent-child training. Comprehensive systems analyses of multiple components of family and child social environments are also being performed to elucidate the range of variables that can affect treatment outcome (e.g., Wahler & Graves, 1983). Recent attention to the reciprocal influences in adult—child interactions and adult-mediated treatments (Emery, Binkoff, Houts, & Carr, 1983) also suggest the serious limitations of unidirectional parent-training models.

Paradigmatic Behaviorism and Child Clinical Psychology

In the two preceding sections, concepts were considered that are consistent with paradigmatic behaviorism but not derived directly from it. These concepts are really the assumptions under which social behaviorism originally emerged as a system, so in a way they are the universals of any perspective than can be considered behavioral. Staats's explication of social behaviorism laid out certain more specific principles having direct significance for the derivation of child behavior therapy procedures—those principles having special relevance to children will be considered in this next section.

Model of Abnormal Child Behavior

Definitions of abnormal behavior invariably reflect the interplay between the subject's stream of behaviors and society, which evaluates all subjects via its agents (Goffman, 1963; Ullmann & Krasner, 1969). The immediate consequence of this evaluative process is that the labeling of behaviors as deviant or abnormal will vary according to prevailing societal norms and rules. Amidst this complexity, efforts to define and classify psychological disorders regularly appear (e.g., Yule, 1981). Most taxonomic proposals, however, are the expression of a medical nosology rather than a psychological model. One way of eliminating this medical bias is to specify descriptive criteria that are as free as possible from any intrapsychic diagnostic model or psychiatric framework. The rudimentary system first advanced by Staats in 1963 is a good example of such an effort.

Behavioral taxonomies, which have been strongly influenced by operant principles, usually contain three different criteria for classification: frequency, duration, and amplitude. Thus, deviant behaviors are those displayed at abnormal (either too little or too much) rates, durations and intensities as defined by the socially recognized norm. As also discussed by Léduc, Dumais, and Evans in the next chapter, Staats's (1963) proposal accommodated these quantitative parameters but also simultaneously considered the topographical characteristics of behavior, that is, the specification of behaviors as deficient or inappropriate. "Deficient" refers to the fact that individual behaviors and skills comprising the basic behavioral repertoires may be displayed at rates, durations, or intensities inadequate to the situation. "Inappropriate" in this context refers to behaviors that do not comply with the normative expectations commensurate with the physical or interpersonal environment in which they occur. This may be due to the topographical characteristic of atypical behavior (e.g., self-injury), or to excesses in the above quantitative dimensions. If for no other reason, the ideas are noteworthy in that they complete the symmetry of a single model of personality, abnormal behavior, and its development.

Furthermore, the interactive, interdependent nature of personality repertoires within this classification system means that behaviors do not have to be fitted arbitrarily into mutually exclusive categories. Echolalia, for example, is the expression of primary deficits in a number of specific skills within the language-cognitive repertoire. There are also collateral deficits within the other two repertoires (e.g., attentional skills) that together produce behavior highly inappropriate in all environments. To the degree that there are multiple deficits within and across elemental skills (personality repertoires) the behavior will be judged abnormal in more and more settings. Parents are most likely to seek help for child behavior problems that are publicly visible (Thomas, Chess, & Birch, 1968), indicating their sensitivity to these mismatches between child behaviors and environments. Thus even though it is often necessary to focus on discrete skill deficits as intermediate targets, the ultimate purpose of treatment is to reduce the discrepancy between the target behavior and the normative environmental expectations (which are always in flux).

If child development is the hierarchical attainment of basic behavioral repertoires via interaction with the environment, there is no need to consider age per se as central to the evaluation and classification of behavior. Failure to achieve developmental milestones by the expected ages may be just as easily interpreted as skills deficits. So, behaviors entirely natural to the very young child (e.g., mouthing objects, repetitive vocalizations, drooling) acquire negative valence if exhibited later on because they represent deficits vis-à-vis the prevailing sociocultural norms. Even for the toddler these behaviors represent skills deficits (e.g., learning the discrimination between edible and inedible), but they would not typically warrant intervention unless other factors (e.g., oral-motor handicaps, environmental deprivation) were also present to preclude the usual sequence of learning processes.

Cumulative-Hierarchical Learning and Child Development

Human development may be understood as a progressive interaction between two different classes of events. One class is comprised of the maturational processes that develop from within the child, whereas the other denotes all transactions between child and environment that make up the context of learning. No psychologist denies the existence and importance of either class of events, but disagreement among developmental psychologists has long existed as to the proportional significance to be attributed to one class or the other. Biologically oriented psychologists view maturation as the primary factor affecting human development, whereas learning theorists attach greater importance to the role of organism—environment interactions. This particular controversy seems almost to have gone beyond the usual realm of scientific argument, as it is probably closely related to one's Weltanschauung. The criticisms of maturational theories raised by Staats (1971a, 1973) will be summarized next, to illustrate the major contrasts between the biological and the paradigmatic behavioral views of child development.

Maturational, or stage theories, have been found wanting on the grounds that they oversimplify and only superficially address important issues such as the *mechanism* by which change occurs. More revealing, however, is the contention that there is virtually no biological evidence to support sequential stages of development. Stage theories also rely on notions of fixed development, or "readiness" that have not been verified empirically. In fact, cognitive skills that should be learned at a certain age, according to the stage position, can actually be learned much earlier, provided the child's learning is carefully planned (Engelmann, 1983; Staats, 1971a). By emphasizing maturational processes, the biological theories may also have obscured understanding of child learning, orienting research toward less educationally relevant goals. Finally, allegiance to stage theories can easily lead one into a logical trap in which age is regarded as an independent variable, whereas it is really only a continuum by which elapsed time is measured.

Behavioral child psychologists conceptualize human development primarily as successive interdependent learning processes. Staats (1968a) coined the term *cumulative hierarchical learning* to refer to the process by which a child masters more-and-more complex skills. According to the theory, the results of these learning sequences accrue one on the other and thereby enable children to master increasingly difficult tasks. Consequently, children learn how to learn and gradually extend their mastery to novel tasks, hence accelerating their speed of cognitive attainment (Staats, 1973).

In our view, this level of theory construction could be enhanced by greater conceptual clarity and better terminological precision (i.e., what is the definition of a complex skill and what exactly is meant by an accelerated rate of acquisition?). And in order to assess the heuristic value of the cumulative-hierarchical model, there needs to be an emphasis on stating specific predictions that can be empirically tested. In this regard it is useful to consider questions such as: how would the theory explain the ease with which a child may accomplish one task such as discriminating same from different in pictorial representations or labeling pictures of objects, and the difficulty the same child displays, despite identical environmental conditions for learning, in making auditory discriminations among speech sounds or in learning the concepts of bigger versus smaller? Could neuropsychological theories of brain behavior relationships or models of human perceptual development explain such phenomena more parsimoniously, or can the tenets of these approaches be elegantly integrated within paradigmatic behaviorism? It is not that competing theories exist that do a better job of prediction or explanation, overall, but if paradigmatic behaviorism is to be billed as a general framework for the integration and synthesis of knowledge of human development, there is still work to be done.

The Study of Intelligence

Another factor contributing to the distinction between behavioral and traditional child psychology relates to the manner in which intelligence is defined and measured. Whereas traditional psychometricians (e.g., Jensen, 1980) view intelligence as basically inherited and measure it by means of normative tests, behavioral psychologists view it as a complex set of skills that develop in conformity with learning principles and laws. At the basis of this scientific dispute lies a metatheoretical clash regarding the role of environment versus innate characteristics. Belief in the latter means that intelligence functions as an independent variable, whereas among behavioral psychologists it is regarded as a dependent variable. Paradigmatic behaviorism, as a third alternative, integrates and exploits the advantages of both points of view.

The theory defines intelligence as the network of functional skills (Basic Behavioral Repertoires—BBRs) learned according to the combined principles of classical and operant conditioning, and, once acquired, they become independent variables that can affect future behavior and skill acquisition. Children can successfully develop the relevant composite skills found on IQ tests so long as they are given the proper learning experiences (Staats & Burns, 1981). Research of this nature is important for documenting that children do not learn fixed and stereotyped sets of responses, but functional skills that can be applied to a host of different tasks. In terms of assessment methodology, standard tests of intelligence need not be discarded provided their meaning and underlying philosophy are reinterpreted in accordance with the theory (Burns, Chapter 5, this vol.; Nelson, 1980). Essentially, normative tests measure previous knowledge, almost exclusively from the language-cognitive system, and a limited number of problem-solving skills thought to be important for additional academic attainment and which have, therefore, been traditionally labeled "intelligent." The validity of any such test, therefore, depends upon the integrity of the relationship between the behavioral samples elicited by the instrument and the child's behavioral universe. Hence, the more similar the sample is to the universe, the more valid is the test—for further discussion see Chapter 5.

The tremendous importance of this approach for clinical behavior therapy is that it consists almost entirely in arranging opportunities for child clients to acquire new skills. Even where the goal is ostensibly the extinction of an inappropriate response, such as a fear of dogs, the desired outcome is a series of new competencies, such as discriminating between safe and unsafe interactional patterns with dogs, self-control of escape behaviors, and the proper care and attention that pets require. Similarly, a child who is socially withdrawn will require an environment that permits social contact and may require specific communication and other interactional skills, including positive emotional attitudes toward peer friendships. Children considered to differ in intelligence actually differ in the degree to which they have prior repertoires of the basic behavioral skills. Thus, the design of intervention will be greatly influenced by the deliberate or implicit assessment of these BBRs. A socially withdrawn child with an extensive adult vocabulary may need to acquire positive attitudes toward peers that will in turn modulate reliance on an overly sophisticated and negative conversational repertoire. However, a child designated as mentally retarded may have positive peer attitudes but have limited verbal skills for initiating interactions. Interpreted this way, "intelligence" becomes a critical factor in designing interventions, but not because some children are labelled mentally retarded and therefore require a different approach to treatment.

The Concept of Personality

The study of personality has been marked by long-standing disputes, since in this subject matter—more than any other—psychologists have organized themselves into discordant clans: psychoanalytic, psychometric, and behavioral. Early behaviorists (e.g., Thorndike, 1908; Watson, 1924) originally conceptualized personality as the sum of behaviors that a person is able to emit in different situations and at different moments. This notion was subsequently adopted by Skinner (1953) and most operant psychologists. The predominant theme within the behavioral tradition has been that trait-oriented "personality tests" have minimal utility as they represent attempts to measure hidden metaphysical dimensions, and are at best descriptive. Conversely, behavioral evaluations tend to be isomorphic with manifest events and typically consist of repeated observations across time and situations. The greater the number of observations, the greater the likelihood of understanding behavioral tendencies of the child. Predictions may then be made about future behavior in the same settings. There is an annoying paradox, however, in that both stability and inconsistency may be found in any given subject's behavior.

As has been discussed in Chapters 5 and 6, Staats's solution to this paradox forms the personality level of his theory, consisting of the following premises. (1) Personality is essentially an organized collection of acquired skills (the BBRs). (2) For descriptive convenience, not psychological reality, one can think of three major systems: the emotional–motivational, the sensory-motor, and the language–cognitive. (3) The BBRs exert reciprocal influences within the organism and are also simultaneously involved in reciprocal exchanges with the environment. (4) Thus personality is formulated as both a dependent and an independent variable, capable of exhibiting both cause and effect (see also Figures 5.1 and 5.2, Chapter 5, this vol.).

The implications for child behavior therapy are considerable. One of the major ones is that certain experiences in childhood, such as bonding and attachment or method of toilet training, are not singled out as essential, universal determinants of later personality, since the theory emphasizes the totality of antecedent interchanges among the developing repertoires and the environment. On the other hand, the theory makes it clear that a variety of early experiences, such as sexual abuse, physical neglect, death of a parent, parental divorce, and so on, will significantly alter later development. Whether the effect is general (e.g., the sexually abused child has negative verbal and emotional attitudes conditioned to all intimate relationships) or specific (e.g., the sexually abused child becomes promiscuous because sexual activity is established as a major behavior for eliciting approval and acceptance) will depend entirely on the exact learning circumstances, the BBRs already established, and subsequent opportunities to learn new skills. Thus it would be difficult if not impossible to generalize about the effects of early sexual abuse on later behavior, but it is clear that development will be altered and that an analysis of the individual child's attitudes, verbal representations, and so on, can guide both preventative and subsequent treatment.

Another implication is that no one particular set of behaviors can be singled out as more important than another in some absolute sense. Bandura (1977a) has placed central importance on self-efficacy beliefs, which implies that this is a highly generalized response, influencing behavior in every domain. However even the more limited element from the emotional–motivational system—perceptions of the child's own competence—can be seen to be specific to different BBRs, such as motor, language, and social skills (Harter, 1983). Similarly, in Western culture there is selective attention given to skill acquisition within the sensory-motor system for young children (i.e., walking, self-help) that shifts to language and cognitive attainment once the child reaches 5 or 6 years of age and enters the formal educational milieu. Less obvious, but equally important in terms of personality development, is the fact that in the emotional–motivational system, self-perception of competence is acquired through both success and failure experiences interpreted through parental evaluation, social praise based on an external standard, and the child's experience of achievement based on self-reward (Amato & Ochiltree, 1986). Staats (1971a) provided a detailed analysis of how parental reinforcement for effort rather than outcome, semantic conditioning via parental instructions ("try to win"), and children's own repertoire of beliefs and standards (attributions) regarding the causes of their success, all interact to determine motivation. This perspective is fundamentally different from the simplistic operant principle that external reinforcement contingencies determine performance.

Implications for Child Behavior Therapy

It would be impossible in one chapter to spell out all the implications of these broad theoretical assumptions for the conceptualization and treatment of childhood behavior problems. Thus we will highlight a few that seem most noteworthy in view of the way in which clinical child behavior therapy has traditionally been presented.

Indirect Intervention

Perhaps the most important implication is the manner in which social behaviorism's personality theory provides a framework for the design of indirect interventions. At an ecological level, for example, consider children who are unpopular and socially isolated. Such children might be thought of as having deficient social skill repertoires, so the conventional clinical judgment is to teach social skills. A more complex model of the interrelated variables, however, predicts an equally effective intervention directed toward the child's peers. For instance, Parish (1974) associated positive adjectives with the names of children who were the object of social biases and aggression from primary school children. He sought to change the other students' labeling repertoires and thereby change their evaluative attitudes. The results revealed not only a dramatic change in the attitudes of the class members, but also compatible prosocial behavioral changes—as one would predict from affective-reinforcing-directive (A-R-D) principles.

Meazzini (1977) designed a behavioral intervention to increase time spent studying three academic subjects by a junior high school student. After baseline assessment, differential reinforcement procedures were implemented and were then followed by a token reinforcement system that was gradually faded. The results provided evidence for the superiority of the token system over differential reinforcement, which in turn was superior to no treatment. These findings are not unusual; they result from the application of well-established contingency principles. But another dependent variable, one less commonly reported in these types of studies, was also measured. This was the student's attitudes toward the three subject areas, which were assessed before and after treatment to determine whether enhanced achievement would be associated with positive attitude change. The results confirmed this to be the case. In addition, a significant decrease in the frequency of family quarrels was observed. A personality framework theory accounts for collateral changes such as these and covariations among responses (e.g., changes in attitudes and studying behavior) because it delineates the kinds of interactions that take place "within persons" as well as between persons and environments.

Indirect interventions are especially important for serious but low frequency behaviors. These are often not detected until some time after the action has been initiated by the child (e.g., fire-setting). Such behaviors generally relate either directly or indirectly to deficits in the child's repertoire of more appropriate skills (Meyer & Evans, 1989). The kinds of deficits that need to be considered can be illustrated by one of our recent cases of a 9-year-old boy with a mild handicap. The presenting complaint was that his mother had, on a number of occasions, found him dressed up in her underwear. An analysis of the setting events, occasions, and functions of this behavior, as well as the child's own verbal attributions, suggested a range of deficits (what Staats has called the downward spiral of hierarchical learning). These included: (1) emotional–motivational deficits both in the environment (lack of expressions of warm feelings by his parents) and in his own repertoire (low self-esteem attributable to recent school failure); (2) language–cognitive problems (his expression of the rationale for not engaging in the behavior was in terms of "God not liking it" rather than the principle that it violated others' rights and privacy; and (3) instrumental deficits, such as poor social skills, limited peer interactions, and lack of recreational opportunities. Intervention was successfully focused on these deficits rather than on the low-frequency excess behavior itself and its supposed reinforcing consequences.

Multiple Functions

The analysis of complex response relationships at the developmental level of theory makes it obvious that response components have multiple functions. The increasingly popular types of "cognitive behavior therapy" with children (e.g., Craighead, Meyers, Wilcoxon-Craighead, & McHale, 1983; Kendall, 1981) are little more than downward extensions from adult cognitive therapies and presume that the major function of inner speech is self-regulatory. However, as Lohr and Hamberger detail in Chapter 7, language has denotative as well as connotative properties, and other functions in addition. Thus it is equally "cognitive" to ensure that derogatory verbal labels are not used by peers of children with handicaps when attempting to arrange the social integration that will enhance learning opportunities for both disabled and nondisabled children.

Similarly, it is language repertoires that provide the crucial communicative skills necessary for disabled and nonhandicapped children to interact effectively (Putallaz & Gottman, 1982). Following similar reasoning, cognitive information concerning medical procedures can serve to reduce a child's anxiety before surgery. However, the effect depends on the verbal coping and reasoning skills already in the child's repertoire, and whether the materials presented ensure attention to the relevant features of the information (e.g., Melamed, 1983). Through direct and semantic conditioning, words come to have powerful influence over emotional expression, physiological change and medical symptoms, and the regulation of physiological functioning (eating, toileting) required by society (Staats, 1975).

Multiple, Simultaneous Intervention Strategies

It is now generally recognized (Evans, 1989) that intervention design, in clinical practice, rarely involves the single variable manipulations that are typically described in the applied behavior analysis literature. It follows directly from social behaviorism that interventions would inevitably be multifaceted, which in turn imposes interesting problems for the evaluation of specific treatments, such as contingency management. Note that there is a difference between treatment being presented as a package (which may contain many elements that are similar for each child client) and being multifaceted. The latter simply means that if a child exhibits even a relatively simple behavioral excess, individual treatment plans contain a variety of components relevant to the specific child's circumstances. For instance, in the case of phobic anxiety over dogs, clinical treatment might include: positive relabeling; rational information ("the dog is barking like that to tell his owner that you are outside"); modeling fearless behavior by parents; teaching coping strategies ("stay calm"); effective interaction skills ("pet the dog like this, don't make sudden movements"); ecological strategies to expose the child to safe dogs and avoid potentially fierce dogs; imaginal flooding; skills for taking care of a dog. These are not alternative treatments from which one is selected. All these features are woven into a naturalistic whole.

Assessment has two major purposes, within this framework. One of these is the mapping out of the system of variables (including skill deficits) that influences the child's problem behavior (cf., Evans, 1985) in order to design the various foci for intervention. Burns elaborated on this purpose in Chapter 5. The second major purpose is to understand the reciprocal interactions relevant to the child so that a structure can be created whereby intervention is carried out. To illustrate the latter necessity, consider the commonly used indirect intervention strategy of "parent training" we have already touched upon. Usually, this may be thought of as enhancing parental behavior management skills. Such skills, however, are supported partly by their effectiveness in changing the child's behavior, and partly by the parent's own social network and motivational BBR (Wahler, 1980). Rondal (Chapter 4, this vol.) explains how certain natural interaction patterns provide an effective instructional environment for learning language, and we may presume that the same applies to all the other elements of the BBRs. Thus intervention design involves understanding of the conditions that maintain naturally effective parenting. If the parents of a child with severe disabilities feel embarrassed taking him or her to public places, they will not follow verbal suggestions to increase learning opportunities through community involvement. Conversely, if the barriers are in the form of time, energy, social support, or knowledge of the resources available, there will be equal resistance to change, but for entirely different reasons.

Conclusions

We began this chapter with a consideration of the most general metatheoretical assumptions of a behavioral perspective and then examined some of the specific features of Staats's social behaviorism as it relates to the analysis and treatment of childhood behavior problems. Considerable theoretical integration becomes possible if the constructs used are general, for instance, identifying "language," "social skills," or "academic skills" as all equated with BBRs that interact with one another. This is in contrast to the way the current research literature is organized, in which the investigator interested, say, in teaching problem-solving skills to delinquent teenagers makes little contact with the researcher evaluating self-monitoring in students with Down's syndrome. The practicing clinician, working directly with the child and the family, also compartmentalizes, sometimes having too little knowledge of, for instance, the individual's peer influences at school. When these traditional content areas are viewed under a common rubric, professional distinctions between educational or school psychology and clinical behavior therapy seem to be quite artificial. Most of behavior therapy with children can be reduced to one form or another of skill acquisition, with the design of intervention essentially being decisions as to which skill, in which context, and through which medium of indirect influence will produce ongoing benefits. The most valuable intervention is the one having the greatest continued implications for the child's long-term development and welfare.

With so much theoretical and practical emphasis thus converging on response relationships and the organization of individual repertoires (personality), it seems essential that studies of new phenomena for child behavior therapy (e.g., preventive health maintenance for children) move beyond the traditional single-variable research designs of behavior modification. Imposing old and limited methodologies on a wider and wider range of children's needs does not represent meaningful progress, only expansion. The critical feature of paradigmatic behaviorism is not that it necessarily generates novel treatments, but that it provides a framework within which a variety of seemingly different approaches can be integrated. We have suggested some very general dimensions whereby the explanatory constructs of the theory, especially those involving development, can guide the behavioral clinician in the conceptualization and management of any aspect of children's behavior.

Having such a broad, encompassing approach makes it a little difficult to see how social behaviorism per se can be evaluated. Like other general metatheories the assumptions will be valued to the extent that they guide the behavior of clinicians in ways that prove constructive and efficacious. For us there seems to be tremendous potential in an approach that does not proscribe essential features of childhood, in the way, for instance, a radical operant position might do. Equally important, social behaviorism allows this flexibility without compromising the essential features of behaviorism, a problem that seems to be occurring more frequently in the field as child behavior therapists accept the medically oriented categories and constructs of psychiatry and traditional child psychopathology. However, if the tenets of the approach are very general (e.g., the prediction that there will be numerous treatment avenues to achieve a given clinical outcome), then confirming their specific contribution provides an interesting empirical challenge.

12

Social Behaviorism, Rehabilitation, and Ethics: Applications for People with Severe Disabilities

Aimee Léduc
Alfred Dumais
Ian M. Evans

From the time of the original developments in behavior therapy there has been intense debate over the ethical issues surrounding treatment. There are numerous reasons for this interest. The most obvious is that in the early days, behavioral interventions appeared to represent a greater degree of control and manipulation over the client than was advocated, at least, in other major schools of psychotherapy. Behavior therapy became highly sensitive to accusations of coercion and denial of freedoms which were for a long time a focal point of the popular reaction to radical behaviorism (Skinner, 1969, 1974). Another important factor contributing to ethical concerns was that behavior therapy was demonstrably potent. As it became recognized that behavior therapy really could effect change, the concept of effectiveness had to be revised to include such considerations as the desirability of the change.

A third factor in the ethical debate has been behavior therapy's grounding in basic science and its reliance on empirical research as the standard for judging outcome. The rather simplistic self-perception that behavior therapists were just humble scientists guided only by their objective data tended to ignore the importance of the term *value* in the concept of evaluation. Outcome research as evaluation requires two independent judgments: what the treatment produces *and* whether these effects are desirable, appropriate, or worthwhile (Voeltz & Evans, 1983). This issue became really apparent only in the early seventies when Davison startled his audience at an Association for the Advancement of Behavior Therapy convention by arguing (in his presidential address) that the common practice of offering aversion therapy to alter sexual preference in homosexual men was ethically wrong. His argument was based partly on the procedure, but even more forcefully on the implicit assumption inherent in such treatment that homosexual preferences were intrinsically undesirable and in need of change. At the time many people felt that Davison was quite wrong in raising value judgments in a field that was trying to establish itself as an objective science.

Only a few years later, however, behavior modification was said to be "finding its heart" (Wolf, 1978) and social judgment, both of treatment plans (Kazdin, 1980) and the nature of the outcome, became increasingly recognized as an essential component of evaluation (Kazdin, 1977a). Values become particularly critical considerations in the design of rehabilitation programs for those with the least capability for self-advocacy and for participating actively in the selection of their own therapeutic goals. Thus individuals with severe disabilities, such as those with chronic psychiatric problems or those with significant mental retardation, are especially vulnerable to intervention plans that fail to take the full range of their needs into account. Behavior modification with such individuals has, therefore, come into increasing conflict with changing values and standards of service delivery and public policy. As we will show in this chapter, a sophisticated conceptual foundation, such as social behaviorism, is able to anticipate and incorporate ethical issues.

Behavior Modification in Institutional Settings

In the previous chapter, Wilson and Meazzini argued that the early demonstrations in behavior modification were concerned with proving the general applicability of behavioral principles given the domination of the conceptual illness models of psychiatry. Staats's

(1957a) early analysis of the abnormal speech of an individual labeled schizophrenic heralded the initial clinical studies using reinforcement and extinction principles to change the behavior of patients in psychiatric hospitals (e.g., Ayllon & Michael, 1959). Many of these classic studies focused on rearranging contingencies of social reinforcement (e.g., Haughton & Ayllon, 1965), but the changes produced were typically limited to isolated single target behaviors that made little or no difference to the clients' actual circumstances (Evans & Scotti, 1989). What they contributed, however, was support for the theoretical assumptions of a sociobehavioral model, in contrast to the medical model, and confirmation of the powerful, probably harmful, contingencies existing in institutional settings. However the broader treatment conclusion drawn was not a demand for deinstitutionalization, but the need for greater alteration of contingencies via intensive staff training.

Nevertheless, the *meaningfulness* of behavior change programs in institutions was first discussed in this context. By the end of the sixties, when Franks (1969) produced his excellent review of behavior therapy's status, Davison (1969) was able to provide a detailed critique of the institutional treatment studies on the basis of the kinds of results that were being achieved. Most of the other chapter authors in that volume were content merely to document the general efficacy of behavioral approaches. It was partially as a result of this challenge over the clinical significance of the changes being achieved in institutions that token economies became more widely used. Ayllon and Azrin (1968) introduced the system as a wardwide program at Anna State Hospital, and the use of token economies became steadily more widespread and sophisticated (Kazdin, 1977b, 1982).

A variety of outcome studies were carried out on token economies (e.g., Atthowe & Krasner, 1968; Baker, Hall, Hutchison, & Bridge, 1977; Boothe, Stephens, Ronald, & Matson, 1978; Fullerton, Cavner, & McLaughlin-Reidel, 1978; Rostow & Smith, 1975; Winkler, 1970). While ratings of general improvement in skills and other positive behaviors were the most commonly used outcome criteria, there was some indication that the programs did result in movement to community placements. Zeldow (1976) reported, however, that the token economy program reduced inappropriate behaviors but the clients did not want to return to the community. This result could be predicted on the basis of affective-reinforcing-directive (A-R-D) principles if the reinforcements are artificially concentrated in the institutional setting rather than the natural environment.

The outcomes for token economy programs have been compared

directly to traditional hospital care, with favorable results generally reported (e.g., Fraser, McLeod, Begg, Hawthorne, & Davis, 1976; Gripp & Magaro, 1971; Heap, Boblitt, Moore, & Hord, 1970; Schwartz & Bellack, 1975). However, follow-up after discharge from the hospital was less satisfactory (e.g., Birky, Chambliss, & Wasden, 1971), indicating the central importance of instruction in daily living skills taking place in the normalized and community settings where the skills would be needed. Broadening the programs to include the interpersonal and communication skills emphasized in milieu therapy (Lehman & Ritzler, 1976) might improve outcomes somewhat (Greenberg, Scott, Pisa, & Friesen, 1975; Last, Giaor, Lowental, Klein, & Hebrew, 1978; Olson & Greenberg, 1972). However, the fact that behavior modification and milieu therapy could be contrasted really reflects the narrow focus that had become a feature of behavioral programs. For instance, Paul and Lentz (1977) compared milieu and "social learning" token economy programs. The latter was superior to the milieu approach or the traditional hospital program on various criteria, but the supposedly nonbehavioral treatments included both instruction in functional skills as well as the provision of support in the period following discharge. Paradigmatic behaviorism's theory of abnormal behavior reveals how such elements can and should be integral parts of any comprehensive rehabilitation program. We will review the major elements of this theory and then present an institutional case study illustrating the problems of a behavioral program that did not attend to the broader questions of meaningful change.

Paradigmatic Behaviorism and Abnormal Behavior

Social (paradigmatic) behaviorism's theory of abnormal behavior was touched upon by Staats in Chapter 2 and was further elaborated by Burns (Chapter 5) and Heiby and Staats (Chapter 10; see also Staats & Heiby, 1985); an account of the theory in French has been provided by Levesque and Léduc (1982). The organizational scheme is based on an assumption—one widely used in behavior therapy generally—that only two categories are necessary to classify abnormal behaviors: behaviors critical to individual adjustment which are absent from the repertoire (deficit behaviors), and behaviors detrimental to adjustment (inappropriate behaviors). Since personality is viewed as being made up of interacting systems (emotional-motivational, language-cognitive, and sensory-motor), deficit behavior and inappropriate behavior can be found in each of these three systems. Thus, for example, in the case of someone diagnosed as schizophrenic, flat affect would be considered a deficit behavior and uncontrollable laughter an inappropriate behavior in the emotional-motivational system. In the language-cognitive system, thought-disordered speech illustrates a deficit, and paranoid delusions illustrate inappropriate responding. In the instrumental system, abnormal behavior might consist of deficits in work skills, and inappropriate responses could be ones such as coercive aggression.

It is interesting to note that in recent years, researchers in schizophrenia who follow an experimental psychopathology approach have found it useful to make the distinction between positive and negative symptoms in schizophrenia (e.g., Andreasen & Grove, 1986). Positive symptoms are inappropriate behaviors and negative symptoms are deficit behaviors. These authors do not, however, make reference to Staats's taxonomy, nor do they specifically distinguish between types of basic behavioral repertoires. Thus it remains to be seen if some rapprochement between the two theories will prove useful. In reference to individuals having severe intellectual handicaps, other writers (e.g., Evans & Meyer, 1985) have stressed the term *excess* behavior rather than "inappropriate," since it is a more neutral term and emphasizes how inappropriateness is really a social judgment, greatly influenced by the A-R-D system of the person making the judgment. It is also important to realize that excess and deficit behaviors interact, according to a variety of organizational principles. For instance, excess behavior may be the reciprocal of a deficit behavior, in that the individual acquires an undesirable form of responding that serves the same function as an unlearned skill in the same basic behavioral repertoire (BBR) (Evans, Meyer, Kurkjian, & Kishi, 1988). Alternatively, Staats suggested the concept of behavioral competition, in which the acquisition of one skill may be the causal factor preventing the acquisition of another, perhaps superior or more socially desirable, response.

Just as there are deficit and inappropriate behaviors, so there can be deficit and inappropriate environmental conditions that facilitate the learning and maintenance of abnormal behavior. This is why an individual's learning history plays such a central role in the understanding of personality repertoires and specific abnormal behaviors. Deficit and inappropriate behavior and environments interact. A child who is not toilet trained, for instance, might not be accepted into a preschool program that would enhance language-cognitive learning. Consequently this child might eventually enter a formal educational system with a less well developed repertoire of verbal self-control skills, making it harder to learn both socially accepted toileting behavior and tactics for dealing with teasing by peers for toileting accidents.

Another major social mechanism whereby inappropriate behaviors result in deficit environments is that of institutionalization. Staats, as others have done, argues that when conceptualized from the perspective of learning opportunities, large residential institutions are clearly deficit environments for acquiring everyday living skills. In operant-oriented behavior modification, training direct care staff to shape and reinforce self-help and other basic skills became a major professional endeavor, but it was less often realized that the institutional environment failed to provide the opportunities to practice these skills in their ecological context, so that clients were often unable to initiate functional, independent activities in new settings. In operant theory, this was typically interpreted as a problem of generalization of the skill to a new situation. It is more likely, however, that the important components of the skill, such as initiation, solving problems that might arise, and terminating the activity correctly (Evans, Brown, Weed, Spry, & Owen, 1987), were never acquired by the clients in the artificial training environment. Similarly, the types of behaviors considered important to target were often basic self-help skills. Valuable as these might be for independent functioning, leisure, social, and communicative skills are equally important for a normalized life-style. In Chapter 4, Rondal describes the types of social interactions that are necessary for the acquisition of language. Institutional settings can create such conditions only if social relationships exist between the staff and the clients, and these relationships were never the focus of behavior modification training.

Similarly, social behaviorism's concept of reciprocal influence points to the importance of the attitudes of direct care staff, which can be influenced by a variety of factors including the behavior of the clients. The attitudes of staff in many institutions are made more negative by the presence of both inappropriate (e.g., aggression) and deficit (e.g., lack of grooming) behaviors. In the poignant account of Anne McDonald (Crossley & McDonald, 1980), who was institutionalized at 3 years of age as severely handicapped, it is clear that deficits in her instrumental BBR (due to athetoid cerebral palsy) led professionals to assume deficits in her language-cognitive and emotional-motivational systems, although her functioning in these systems was essentially intact. She later described very incisively how the staff's dehumanizing neglect of her as a person was determined by her limited instrumental repertoire. Similarly, parents who label excess behaviors in highly negative terms are, through A-R-D principles, going to be more likely to find the child exhibiting such behaviors as punishing and may seek institutional placement as an escape activity. The literature on expressed emotion toward people diagnosed as schizophrenic by family members indicates that negative attitudes mediate subsequent criticism, punishment, or neglect (e.g., Leff & Vaughn, 1981; Vaughn & Leff, 1976). This in turn influences the degree to which the former patient is able to adjust to family and community life. Empirical support for this general phenomenon comes from numerous areas. For instance, when parents are depressed—perhaps for reasons quite unrelated to their children's behavior—they tend to label their children's behavior more negatively than it deserves (Griest, Forehand, Wells, & McMahon, 1980).

The hierarchical concept of learning suggests that gaining all the skills required for adult life takes a long time. The acquisition of one skill is the basis for the acquisition of more complex skills, which in turn allows the acquisition of still more elaborate skills. The process lends itself to an analogy with a race, which can take a positive upward direction or resemble a downward spiral. The societal consequences for the early acquisition of desirable skills are substantial. Society in general, and the group to which the individual belongs, offer extensive rewards to the "winner" of the race. The more rapid acquisition of developmental and academic skills results in better grades, scholarships, honors, success in organized sports and so on. Such rewards will contribute to the maintenance and practice of these skills and thus make it easier to learn more complex ones. The individual can continue to create conditions even more favorable for learning highly complex behaviors. The downward spiral, conversely, is the opposite of this, with failure experiences and low levels of social reinforcement perhaps contributing to low self-esteem and limited motivational repertoires that are analyzed by researchers into depression (see Heiby and Staats, Chapter 10, and Rosenbaum, Chapter 6, this vol.).

It might be noted that the heavy concentration of the societal reward system in favor of achievement and success results in people with excess behaviors or limited competencies typically having very low status, and little positive attitudinal/evaluative significance to others. Even if the attitudinal value of a person with a handicap is positive, it may be an undesirable attitude, such as sympathy. As Staats (1975) pointed out: "There is also a strong cultural characteristic of giving special privilege to individuals who are ill or who suffer some handicap. Someone who is labelled mentally ill also fits into this category. The special treatment given such individuals, however, may simply be another circumstance in which the individual is reinforced for undesirable behaviors" (p. 271). Thus recent emphases on normalization, the integration of persons with developmental disabilities into the social mainstream (e.g., Lakin & Bruininks, 1985), and the consequent enhancement of attitudes (Voeltz, 1982), reflect trends in social policy and service provision that are fully compatible with paradigmatic behavior therapy. However, behavior therapy in general, by focusing so much on individual interventions, has had little impact on these policies. In fact, it could be argued that traditional behavior modification has fostered negative evaluative attitudes toward persons with disabilities by supporting intervention techniques that are demeaning and unacceptable for nonhandicapped persons, such as some forms of physical punishment.

Implications for Treatment

From this brief overview of the theory, several implications should be apparent for the design of intervention programs for people whose abnormal behavioral repertoires have results in hospitalization or other forms of institutional placement. Principles of the A-R-D system, for instance, point to the importance of personnel participating in positive interactions with the clients. This will enhance caregivers' positive attitudinal value and thus make more salient their reinforcing and directive functions. Punishment and deprivation must be avoided for the opposite reason (Evans, in press). Conversely, for caregivers to provide effective learning opportunities, the clients must have positive attitudinal value for them. The skills necessary for social interaction, however, can be acquired only in the natural learning opportunities afforded by genuine relationships and friendships, which almost invariably require contact with nonhandicapped peers. Planned rehabilitative treatments should be directed at teaching skills in all three personality systems. The elimination of inappropriate behavior should be achieved by remedying the deficits in the individual's repertoires. Therefore the direct reduction of an excess behavior should be an objective only in emergency situations or when such behaviors completely prevent the filling of the deficits (Meyer & Evans, 1989).

Moreover, social behaviorism requires a careful analysis of the individual's history—a link with traditional personality theory quite different from some behavioral stances concentrating almost exclusively on current behavior. The principles relating to the inter-action between deficit and excess behaviors and deficient and inap-propriate environments suggest that a rehabilitation program be implemented in the normal environment in order to prevent the learning of new excess behaviors and the accumulation of greater deficits. It is therefore desirable to execute treatment programs in the community settings in which the skills will be required (e.g., Falvey, 1986). The following case study in organizational change will illustrate how these principles of effective treatment can and should be translated to practices representing important values.

A Case Study in Organizational Behavior Change

The Original Program

In the early seventies, the Robert Giffard Hospital Center in Que-bec launched a behavior modification program, grounded in a stand-ard operantly oriented token economy system. The program was first made available to 48 men, over 80% of whom were diagnosed as schizophrenic, with an average length of hospitalization at the Center of 10 years. The program expanded quite rapidly: within a year it was extended to another 70 male residents and a year after that it was offered to the women residents of the hospital. Although the program was a standard token economy of the kind already reviewed, there were certain conceptual assumptions that influ-enced its flavor. The chief of these was the supposition that many patients had become chronic residents because they were being rein-forced for choosing to live in the hospital. Such a conception led to the design of interventions involving programmed discomfort in or-der to convince the clients to leave the institution. The value of the token rewards and the prices of the backup reinforcers were such that the most active client would never be able to afford more than two-thirds of his or her desired objects. The less active person, of course, was even further limited and deprived of basic commodities.

In the initial phase of the program the learning objectives were to increase self-help skills, participate in some leisure activities, and to try to establish a permanent motivational system that would sustain such behaviors, this being arranged through the pro-grammed discomfort. The purpose of the second phase was to de-velop work skills and also to be able to administer the artificial budgeting required by the token economy. The third phase concentrated on teaching more independent vocational skills. In addition to the overall program there were individually designed treatments aimed at modifying specific excess behaviors not included in the more general intervention plan. After completing the three phases, a resident could be discharged directly into the outside world or move into a resource facility for smoothing the transition from the institutional environment to the community.

The Controversy

After a few years, a Five Year Report on the operations of the Behavioral Module—as the program was called—was released. This report triggered a serious professional and administrative controversy when it was seriously attacked by the attending physician of the program. The criticisms confounded two quite unrelated themes. One of these was the professional rivalry between psychology and psychiatry. The physician could not accept that his role in the program had been limited to that of a consultant. The other was an ethical concern regarding the treatment of the clients. The physician claimed that the program was dehumanizing to the residents, and the programmed discomfort in particular was quite unacceptable. Unfortunately, an ideological quarrel then arose between those favoring a medical model and those supporting a behavioral model, the conflict being fueled by the power struggle between the psychologists and the psychiatrists. About one year later, the section head of the Behavioral Module was advised by the administration that admissions would be frozen and that a committee was being created charged with the independent evaluation of the program. Once the committee was formed, the unfreezing of admissions was announced, however, the number of patients in the program continued to decline because no one was willing to refer patients to the Module.

After some months, Léduc, Dumais, and Grunberg submitted the report of the evaluative committee formed to investigate the behavioral program. We will not go into the details of the quantitative analysis here, but it was interesting that in purely statistical terms the program appeared to have had some benefits. During the 7 years of its existence 330 residents had participated in the program. Out of this number, 144 (44%) could be rated as significantly improved. During these same years, 80 clients (27%) returned to independent community living; these results are comparable to those reported by other token economy programs pursuing similar objectives. Despite its relative efficacy, however, the evaluation committee agreed that the methods used were unacceptable, particularly as reflected by the standards of the Quebec community. We were especially critical of the deprivation procedures used in the programmed discomfort stages of Phase 1 and the punishment procedures used for individual behavior problems, typically involving response cost and isolation time-out. These intrusive procedures are also contrary to patients' rights as protected by the Canadian Act on the Protection of the Mentally Ill, and, of course, similar legal protections have emerged in the United States (Grunberg, 1976). It would probably be fair to say that applied behavior analysts in the United States have resented and rejected these statutory protections of legal rights as they seemed to undermine therapeutic efforts that were well intentioned and designed to benefit patients in the long term. A similar attitude was expressed by the behavioral psychologists at the Robert Giffard Hospital.

The committee proposed that a new behavioral program be designed, based on principles of social behaviorism. Social behaviorism was chosen because it has the encompassing theoretical structure needed to guide ethical treatment decisions. An especially appealing feature of Staats's perspective was its ability to integrate apparently competing perspectives. The approach of the psychiatrists at the hospital was based on psychodynamic theory, with its emphasis on the influence of internal structures, whereas the original approach of the psychological program was elementary behaviorism, with its emphasis on symptomatic treatment. Staats (1975) suggests the importance of internal response mechanisms, the necessity for a personality level of theory, and an integration of verbal-cognitive and emotional-motivational behaviors, allowing some reconciliation of otherwise very different conceptions of abnormal behavior.

The New Program

Organizational Aspects

Recognizing the affective value of words, the old name Behavioral Module, which had become so aversive to many, was dropped for the new program which accepts 50 clients*, both men and women. Con-

---

*Editors' note: Léduc and Dumais used the charming term *beneficiary* to refer to the recipients of their revised program. We have changed this to the dryer term *client* which will be more familiar to readers. It is worth mentioning that in the early development of behavior therapy most authors made special attempts to use more neutral, less derogatory terms to refer to their "beneficiaries," and to avoid labeling

trary to the vast ward of the previous program, the clients live in small groups in units resembling family dwellings as much as possible. There are 23 staff members, consisting of monitors, educators, nurses, administrators, and a programming advisor. Regardless of professional background, each person's major role is to facilitate learning by the clients. Each of them is a tutor for a few clients and responsible for the attainment of the program objectives; they do not have any office or room to which they can retire. In-service training in principles of social behaviorism has been provided.

To ensure the ethical quality of the treatment program, a fairly complex supervisory structure was established. Each family unit has a team head who coordinates intervention plans. Together with the division head, an assistant, the programming advisor, the attendant physician, and sometimes an outside consultant, they constitute the Quality Control Committee responsible for the management of the program. An advisory board, called the Programming Committee, deals with general policies, and also includes the senior administrators of the program as well as the first two authors of this chapter.

Program Objectives and Components

The main objective of the program is to increase the clients' autonomy and positive adjustment, and thus improve their quality of life. It involves, to the greatest extent possible, training deficit behaviors and thus eliminating inappropriate behaviors. Occasionally, certain behaviors are first reduced and subsequently the behavior deficits are filled. In this regard, Evans and Meyer (1985) have proposed that deceleration of an excess behavior should be the primary treatment goal only when the behavior is life threatening. This ethical guideline is supported by research demonstrating that the single most important criterion for reducing an undesirable behavior endorsed by both professional and lay judges is that "the behavior is dangerous to self or others" (Voeltz, Evans, Freedland, & Donellon, 1982). In all cases, a second objective of the program is the reinstatement of the client as an independent member of society. Each client has an individual rehabilitation plan, based on an assessment

---

the person rather than the behavior. But with behavior therapists increasingly identifying with medical practitioners, the use of medical diagnostic terminology is once again common. Where possible we have tried to edit out such labels as "phobics," "depressives," or "the retarded," all of which seem to be out of keeping with social behaviorism's recognition of the emotional significance of labels.

that includes a detailed case history. Time is spent identifying, with the client, his or her interests and skills in living, working, and recreation, both at the cognitive (e.g., reading) and instrumental (e.g., basic self-help skills) levels. Goals in these areas are set up with the client to increase motivation in a natural way. The second phase of the plan involves the careful definition of the steps needed to achieve the objectives, in comparison to the skills the client already has in these areas. The third stage consists of specific teaching strategies and procedures to remedy the skill deficits.

This approach incorporates three important principles of program design for people with severe disabilities. The first of these is that goal setting follows a "top-down" strategy, rather than the developmental tactic of identifying important skills as those that are next on the normative developmental sequence (a bottom-up strategy). Following this logic, Brown and his colleagues (e.g., Brown, Nietupski, & Hamre-Nietupski, 1976) have emphasized how important it is to conduct an ecological inventory of the skills that will be needed by the future as well as the current environment of the individual. Goals are then set on the basis of the discrepancy between the skills the client has at present and those that will be needed in the next environment. In the new program, therefore, the staff in each family unit identify a core program based on the minimum skills that an adult must have in order to be autonomous (Léduc, 1980).

The second principle is that the skills needed will cover a wide range of domains. Staats's BBR concept comprises three major psychological domains, and everyday skills always incorporate all three. At the practical level, there are loose criteria for classifying skills, for instance, the environments in which the skills will be necessary, such as home, work, and the community. A common classification system is self-management skills (the sorts of things that if you could not do them yourself someone else would have to do them for you), work skills (the activities that are designated by someone else), and leisure/recreation skills (those activities one engages in solely for enjoyment) (Evans et al., 1987). The Robert Giffard Hospital program identified domains on the basis of the client's role as producer, consumer, citizen, and participant in recreation. In one family unit, for instance, the core program constitutes daily activities (making meals) and weekly activities (care of clothes). The skills connected with the producer role in this group are mainly represented by housekeeping activities, and the consumer role by shopping. For recreation there are activities such as watching television, going to the movies, going bowling, and so on.

Discussion, planning, and group decision making help to prepare for the citizen role. The exact way the domains are divided seems less important than the fact that some representative skills are drawn from each of them.

The third principle represented by the new program is that of the importance of functional skills. This has become of central concern in the education of people with the most severe intellectual handicaps (see, e.g., Falvey, 1986). The essence of the argument is that by attempting to teach severely handicapped individuals so-called prerequisite skills for more complex tasks, the individual learns, if at all, isolated general behaviors that do not allow meaningful participation in the community. For example, someone might learn how to match shapes and colors, or sort objects, but not acquire any useful job skills that would ensure later competitive employment. Critics counterargue that all complex skills are made up of underlying components and these subroutines must be acquired before more elaborate skills can be acquired. However, it is possible that these components can be acquired within the context of instruction on specific tasks, since effort to teach severely handicapped people a general underlying ability such as matching, eye-hand coordination, and so on, has so often resulted in individuals improving on tests of these behaviors but not going on from there to demonstrate actual functional competencies.

Social behaviorism would propose that this debate is not an either/or matter. As Wilson and Meazzini describe in Chapter 11 on child development, it follows from the concept of cumulative-hierarchical learning that there are component skills, that, once acquired, make learning other behaviors possible. Reading, for example, which itself is made of such underlying elements as attention, eye tracking, and a prior symbolic system (Léduc, 1988), makes possible a wide range of other activities, including leisure reading for enjoyment, following directions to operate unfamiliar machinery such as a washing machine, or reading street signs and directions for community participation. At any point in time it would seem that the skill acquired should have some immediate benefit as well, and it is this opportunity to use the new skill that makes it functional and thus meaningful. In many cases, as Staats has pointed out, it is a social contingency that determines the benefits accrued from a skill, and thus it becomes possible to engineer social and physical environments where a given form of a skill is not mandatory. For instance, a person for whom learning to read might be extremely difficult, it would be possible to substitute symbols that would allow him or her to follow directions. This is the essence of social and environmental adaptations or prostheses. Thus the new program also emphasized academic skills that would tend to have particular relevance for the clients. This included a basic literacy course at a local educational facility (which also provided social opportunities for more natural social contacts), and a course in preparation for employment.

A final important feature of the rehabilitation program was to enable clients to live outside the hospital as soon as possible. During the second year of the program a house was obtained in a local neighborhood and the direct care staff were seen more as tutors preparing the clients for community living. Obviously, the move toward community care rather than large institutional residences is not a policy that is driven by social behaviorism. Deinstitutionalization represents a major international movement that has responded to humanitarian, legal, and moral concerns for the rights of people with emotional and intellectual disabilities. This is despite the fact that politicians have frequently used these concerns to justify large-scale deinstitutionalization programs as a convenient cost-cutting measure without preparing the persons concerned for life in the community and without providing resources for adequate backup facilities.

In any case, paradigmatic behaviorism encompasses various principles that provide a psychological rationale in support of these rights and in this way suggests strategies that would ensure their successful implementation. For instance, arguments in favor of institutionalization might suggest that people with mental retardation would be protected from exploitation, but in social behaviorism this concern would be expressed as a need to remedy a client's skill deficits in safety procedures, self-protection, and self-advocacy. Or, as another example, community care is thought to lead to social isolation, which suggests that, in accordance with A-R-D principles, negative attitudes result in avoidance behavior. As clients with severe disabilities become consumers (e.g., shoppers), neighbors, and citizens, their reinforcing potential will change negative and stereotyped attitudes.

Evaluating the New Program

Annual evaluations were carried out over the first few years of the new program and the major findings will be highlighted in this section. Some of the demographic features of the clients served were as follows: There were 30 men and 18 women, ranging in age from 10 to 58, with a mean of 36 years. With respect to education level,

14 of the clients had had no schooling, 14 had attended elementary school, and 20 had a high school education or above. They had been hospitalized at the center for an average of 10.6 years. Schizophrenia was the diagnosis given to 26 of the group, 17 were labelled mentally retarded, and 5 were given other diagnostic labels (e.g., manic depressive psychosis).

One of the outcome measures used was derived from a detailed interview with each client to investigate their perceptions of the quality of their lives. All of the clients reported that they enjoyed the variety of the work activities, the community and recreational experiences, and the choices offered by the program. They stressed the atmosphere of trust and understanding and appreciated the group discussions in which everyone was able to express a point of view. Although they were happy with the distribution into smaller family units, they complained about the housekeeping duties, feeling that there were too many and that they were too closely supervised.

A variety of criteria were developed in order to measure functional skill improvement objectively. Of special importance were (1) discharge from the hospital and return to the family or other natural living arrangement, (2) placement in a community residence outside the hospital, (3) transfer into a living unit working on more advanced goals, and (4) estimates of ability to live a more independent life. Ratings of improvement had to demonstrate high levels of agreement among the raters. Composite ratings of overall improvement in the clients were calculated, and subdivided into three groups: greatly improved, fairly improved, and unchanged. Out of the 48 clients evaluated, 16 (37%) were classified as greatly improved, 12 (28%) as fairly improved, and 15 (35%) were rated as unchanged. The most improved clients tended to be diagnosed as mentally retarded with a relatively short period of hospitalization. The moderately improved client was typically a poorly educated man diagnosed as schizophrenic with a long history of hospitalization. Schizophrenic women who had been in the hospital for the longest time (more than 12 years) showed the least gain. For the most improved clients the areas of greatest progress, in order of importance, were: basic self-help skills, vocational skills, social skills, behavior during community activities, inappropriate behaviors, and citizenship skills. In a direct comparison with another unit of the hospital having similar goals but not using systematic behavioral methods, the number of improved clients was significantly lower in the traditional program.

In his evaluation report, Dumais concluded that the program was producing excellent results. He also noted the positive atmosphere in the program units, the naturally occurring social contingencies, the emphasis on individual programming for each client, and the cohesion among the staff. In a later evaluation period, the percentages of clients showing great or fair improvement increased further. The unchanged clients continued to be the longer-stay, better-educated women labelled schizophrenic. During the second evaluation period, the most significant improvements were in areas such as increased contact with family of origin and recreational/leisure skills and participation.

Issues in Policy and Practice

Misuse of Behavioral Principles

The case study of how an entire program could be reorganized on the basis of social behaviorism illustrates that the manner in which behavioral principles are translated into practice, and the range of principles considered, influences the style, philosophy, and ethics of clinical behavior therapy. Evaluating programs thus goes beyond the simple matter of the "acceptability" of a given intervention (Witt, Elliott, & Martens, 1984) or the "social validity" of the outcomes. Expanded outcome criteria can perhaps help in discovering when a program, based only on the contingency management concepts of applied behavior analysis, becomes detrimental to the participants and contains undesirable professional practices and attitudes. In another interesting case study, criteria relating to program atmosphere provided important information in evaluation.

This example was carefully documented by the New York State Commission on Quality of Care for the Mentally Disabled (1987). They reported on a facility called Opengate, a small residential facility for about 30 adults. One client's intervention involved earning tokens for periods of silence and then being able to use them to purchase time to talk; for another woman screaming behavior resulted in her being bound hand and foot in a restraint chair with a helmet over her head. A behavioral intervention plan involving contingent ammonia and water spray was introduced for one person's self-stimulatory behaviors on the first day he was admitted; in other words, less intrusive methods were neither considered nor tried. As the Commission commented:

> In each of the four case records examined, Opengate had moved beyond using a single aversive to reduce a maladaptive behavior to the use of

multiple aversives. This phenomenon demonstrated the reinforcing nature of the aversives on the person administering them. The absolute power of the staff and the reciprocal powerlessness of the client, combined with the apparent success of aversives in reducing the targeted behaviors, easily leads to the "more is better" way of thinking. As commonly recognized, aversives are potentially reinforcing to the person administering them. (p. 9)

As a result of the Commission's enquiry a new director for Opengate was hired and the staff reeducated in "sound pedagogical principles, behavior modification through positive reinforcement, and the building of open and trusting relationships between staff and residents...Those professionals who could or would not abandon punitive treatment measures were terminated." In a subsequent review by the Commission, "residents' behaviors were continuing to respond to the emphasis on skill-building, the focus on appropriate behavior and the sense of being valued which came from interacting with caring staff."

In recent years within behavior modification circles a major controversy has erupted over the continued use of aversive interventions involving physical punishment. Advocates opposed to the use of punishment with clients having severe disabilities (e.g., Evans & Meyer, 1985; LaVigna & Donnellan, 1986) have made the argument on a number of grounds: empirical (punishment is effective only for the short-term control of behavior rather than producing lasting clinical benefits); legal (severely handicapped persons cannot give informed consent); and clinical (use of punishment indicates a lack of understanding of the function of the excess behavior and its antecedents). Social behaviorism principles, however, emphasize the reciprocal relationships between a client's behavior and the response of the environment. As can be seen from the Opengate example, the sanctioned use of aversive interventions by care staff influenced the behavior of the staff and their attitudes. The design of interventions thus also influences the kinds of interactions that clients will experience, independent of the formal treatment protocol being in effect at a given moment.

Social Integration

A similar argument can be made about other standards in social policy. Perhaps because traditional behavior modification has been too literal in its translation of principles from the operant conditioning laboratory, behavioral clinicians have tended to see institutional settings as relatively easily controlled environments. Thus there has been a great emphasis over the years on staff training, and much less interest in strategies for eliminating large residential facilities entirely. For instance, behavioral programs for autistic children often are conducted in highly structured lab schools, rather than blended into the local public school system (mainstreaming). Paradigmatic behaviorism makes it rather clear, however, that abnormal and deficit environments cannot be designed that duplicate the reciprocal influence of the normalized environment.

This is well illustrated in the area of social skills training by comparing the Robert Giffard Hospital program described to the detailed social skills training program presented by Monti, Corriveau, and Curran (1982). These authors have developed and evaluated very specific methods and target behaviors for teaching social skills, such as starting conversations, giving compliments, and being assertive. These are valuable procedures that can be incorporated into any overall rehabilitation program, but it is equally the responsibility of behavior therapists to consider other important elements of programming. Of special importance, for example, is the actual amount of contact afforded a client and his or her opportunities to have significant relationships and friendships rather than general social skills. Acceptance in the local community might be critical for the maintenance of learned social behaviors. Alternatively, the attainment of a marketable work skill, irrespective of one's social competence, would be necessary to gain competitive employment, which in turn would yield other social contacts and reinforcing opportunities likely to impact the individual's emotional-motivational repertoire. Paradigmatic behaviorism fosters bringing together these programmatic elements under a common theoretical rubric. And because the program we described was not successful with every client, we accept the need to learn more about the specific response deficits of those individuals showing the least improvement. Liberman, Neuchterlein, and Wallace (1982) have provided an interesting account of how social skills training can be geared to specific response deficits that might be characteristic of schizophrenia. These can be both content specific (strategies for coping with stress may be more important than dating skills) and method specific (if clients with schizophrenia are easily distracted by irrelevant cues, the training setting should be uncluttered).

Individualizing Programs

The need to learn more about specific response deficits raises a fundamental issue for designing meaningful programs for individuals. Clearly each person is unique, having highly varied learning histories and patterns of experience and environmental interaction. Does that mean that it is impossible or undesirable to generalize about clients? We tend to think that people with mental retardation, or with chronic psychiatric histories, or with disabilities due to age, head trauma, or physical handicap are not fundamentally different from other people, in that their needs and rights are the same. It is a fundamental tenet of a behavioral perspective that the characteristics that render some people "disabled" are the features for which society has the greatest responsibility to provide remedies. The commonalities mean that individuals, no matter how severely handicapped, have the same right as anyone else to the common opportunities that encourage self-determination for work, pleasure, and quality of life.

The tendency to categorize should thus occur at a level of theory. For instance, the right of a person with severe disabilities to make choices would seem to be a necessary generalization to make; how to foster that right for an individual with severe intellectual impairment then becomes an individualized issue. Generalizations at other levels are inconsistent with a behavioral theory, for example, the recent tendency to refer to people who have deficits in intellectual repertoires and the emotional-motivational BBRs as people with "dual diagnoses". This merely creates another meaningless category. Obviously, someone who has been placed in an institutional environment could exhibit the characteristics of depressed behavior according to the sort of principles Heiby and Staats outlined in Chapter 10. Some self-injurious or aggressive behavior is motivated by fear similar to phobic anxiety. Thus there is a considerable degree of consistency across areas that have traditionally represented different professional bailiwicks. The pattern of deficits revealed by someone with a closed head injury might be very different from those of an individual with a developmental disability; however, the treatment generalizations (and thus the standards for services) will be quite similar. Family reactions and feelings, following different expectancies altered at different points in time, might be different in form, but the need to consider the impact of those feelings for the disabled person is common.

Conclusions

In this chapter we have described a general program for patients who have been long-term residents in a mental hospital setting. We have emphasized the contrast between this program, designed according to a social behaviorism perspective on abnormal behavior, and an earlier program that was based on more traditional behavior management principles. Although the redesign of the behavior therapy program at the Robert Giffard Hospital Center was guided by paradigmatic behaviorism, it must be recognized that many of the elements of the new program are practiced in many other hospital programs. The therapeutic communities alluded to at the beginning of this chapter often contained elements of interpersonal problem solving through group discussion. The development of functional, daily living competencies described for the hospital program also represents one of the most significant curricular innovations in current work on preparing students with severe handicaps for social integration (e.g., Horner, Meyer, & Fredericks, 1986). In community psychology there has long been an interest in providing other family members with the skills and attitudes needed to assist the reintegration of institutionalized persons, or to prevent institutionalization in the first place. Deinstitutionalization is a major national policy goal. Social skills training programs have become widespread.

Thus one needs to consider what, if any, unique elements are provided by attending to an underlying theoretical conceptualization such as social (paradigmatic) behaviorism. In our view the major contribution lies in the integration of numerous separate intervention strategies, clinical techniques, and social policies under one conceptual umbrella. Specifically, the model followed helps clarify how variables previously studied in isolation—such as staff attitudes, ward atmosphere, remedial educational programs, work skill development, self-esteem—can and should be logically interrelated.

There is much professional consensus that training in natural community environments is critical for long-term, meaningful lifestyle changes in persons considered chronic mental patients (e.g., Brown, 1982) or individuals with severe mental retardation (e.g., Falvey, 1986). To create a full program of rehabilitation outside the residential institution requires major changes in social policy and political decisions to ensure financial reimbursement is contingent upon the development of small, family-style residences in neighborhood communities for those people whose deficit repertoires will continue to necessitate support. Such structures, of course, do not in themselves guarantee that the environments will foster further rehabilitation and serve to contribute to the upward spiral of cumulative-hierarchical learning. However, they do seem to provide a better infrastructure for creating such conditions. In this chapter we have attempted to show how intricately behavior therapy is tied to social policy. Staats's theoretical contributions effectively demonstrate how a more unified, multilevel behavioral analysis can sensitize the clinician to the complexities of clients' needs and the social systems within which we all operate.

IV

Conclusions

13

A Critical Appraisal of Paradigmatic Behaviorism's Contribution to Behavior Therapy

Ian M. Evans
Georg H. Eifert
Sheila A. Corrigan

In this final chapter we will attempt to integrate some of the preceding contributions and place them in the context of a critical evaluation of a paradigmatic approach to behavior therapy. It would seem to be an opportune time in the development of behavior therapy to conduct such an evaluation. Various commentators (e.g., Ross, 1985) have noted that the upward climb of behavior therapy—if we may be permitted a vinelike metaphor—has slowed relative to its extensive lateral growth. Behavior therapy has established its grip on virtually every aspect of clinical and educational application and has sent off shoots and runners in many new directions (cf. Franks, 1987). Behavioral medicine is probably the best example of the lateral type of growth, since although there is a nonbehavioral version (health psychology), behavioral medicine clearly represents the most robust and energetic form of innovation and progress in the association of the medical and behavioral sciences (Foreyt, 1987). It also typifies the lateral growth in another way. Behavioral medicine is largely atheoretical and has few conceptual roots in behavior therapy, although some behavioral principles and techniques (such as positive reinforcement, shaping, discrimination training, etc.) have been applied in a number of settings. It is also arguable that this is true of almost all other areas of application as well. There is a certain irony that in order to encourage theoretical interests again, a group of members of the Association for the Advancement of Behavior Therapy (AABT) recently found it necessary to establish a special interest group devoted to theoretical concerns.

In this chapter we will also discuss some fundamental questions that need to be addressed in judging Staats's contribution; they are (1) whether a conceptual position that includes many different behavioral constructs is really an integration of these constructs and thus more than just a general eclectic position; (2) whether the amalgamation of other principles is sufficiently unique to be identifiable as a specific theory, or merely the restatement of generally agreed-upon ideas; and (3) whether the paradigmatic position offers any testable insights. With some reservations, we think the answers to all of these questions is in the affirmative; the various chapters in this book reveal these points quite clearly, and we will elaborate the reasons for our judgment in this final chapter.

The Role of Conditioning in Behavior Therapy

It is easy to bemoan the fading interest in theory in behavior therapy, but much harder to explain how theory in general advances the field and how paradigmatic behavior theory, derived from and based on social behaviorism, could make a unique contribution. To do so, it might be quite useful to take a practical example, and we will select school dropout, which was not mentioned in any of the previous chapters, but happens to be an interest of one of us. There is no behavioral theory of school dropout, but if we were to construct one it would almost certainly be a psychological theory. In other words, the concepts of relevance for understanding, predicting, and intervening with this phenomenon would be related to individual influences. Other levels of theory are perfectly possible; for instance, a socioeconomic theory might identify the forces that create employment opportunities for youth without high school diplomas—which is clearly one "cause" of dropout—or the clash of cultural expectations between schools as institutions and certain family and neighborhood systems. While not all irrelevant to behavioral theory, these broader variables would have to be translated to individual differences, so that a specific job opportunity, let us say, could be thought of as a more potent reinforcement than attending school. Thus the behavior of an individual student could be explained by simple reinforcement principles. This level of analysis is valued in behavior theory since it encourages interaction with other psychological constructs. For instance, in regard to the concept of individual differences we would have to explain why not every child is reinforced by the offer of a minimum wage position. This would lead us in turn to such constructs as willingness or ability to delay gratification, or attributions about the financial opportunities afforded by completion of school.

The Analysis of Individual Cases on the Basis of General Theory

To say that behavior theory is at the level of the individual or psychological influences is not the same as saying that it is at an idiographic level, that of the individual case. The behavioral assessment and therapy for an individual student who is about to drop out of school might certainly reveal a totally unique set of contributing factors. Examples that come to mind are that the student might be depressed, so that the desire to quit school is a secondary aspect of a more central internal adjustment difficulty. Individual analysis might suggest that the student is quite happy at school but is involved in a negative family situation; threatening to leave school is then a means of attacking or getting back at demanding and domineering parents. Neither of these possibilities could have been predicted by more general sociological or economic constructs. And assuming these analyses to be approximately correct, a behavior theorist would not want to generalize them to all dropout situations. In fact, part of the success of behavior therapy at the individual level is that it is not overly dependent upon some a priori theory about the causes of a phenomenon. Instead our causal model is around general principles of influence.

What are these assumptions that go into the analysis of the individual case on the basis of a general principle? Certainly one is a loose environmental influence position. Fortunately, we do not have anyone proposing that dropping out of school is a disease for which genetic causes should be sought—one good reason for selecting dropout rather than alcoholism as the construct for analysis. Another assumption, closely related, is that we are influenced by our learning histories, and a third is that under the appropriate environmental and social circumstances, anyone is capable of anything. We recognize that dropping out is a behavior and that the "dropout" is a fictional label for an individual. Thus in behavior theory we would predict that even exemplary students from ideal social backgrounds could become school dropouts, since the phenomenon is not an independent pathology but a pattern of behavior. Finally, another important assumption is that there are interactions among behaviors within the individual. In this respect the behavioral position is compatible with systemic theories of multiple and interacting sources of influence.

It should be noted that the above comments are in accordance with paradigmatic behaviorism, but they are neither uniquely related to it nor do they constitute a theory in the formal sense. What we are referring to is a systemic position, a set of metatheoretical assumptions that are general principles of behavior that accomodate the uniqueness of individuals without having to adopt a wholly idiographic position. In order to understand Staats's contribution, it is instructive to consider conditioning as a principle in this light. Everyone would agree that conditioning—and for now let us restrict the discussion to classical conditioning—has played an enormous conceptual and explanatory role in the history and practice of behavior therapy. But go back, for a moment, to our discussion of dropping out of school. Was classical conditioning ever mentioned as a causal or explanatory process? Obviously it was not. Nor was it mentioned anywhere in the implications for treatment—neither in regard to providing an intervention for the individual nor for designing a prevention program to reduce the tendency to drop out for a group of students. If, however, we had selected a specific phobia to discuss, including a discrete school phobia leading to a refusal to go to school, then it is quite possible that we would look to classical conditioning as a highly relevant causal mechanism for why one person would have a strong emotional reaction in the presence of a harmless object or situation that would produce no anxiety or fear at all in the vast majority of people. It is certainly logical to think that the explanation for a person's fearing a harmless insect or a perfectly safe elevator might be akin to the mechanism whereby a dog drools at the sight of an inedible object, such as a food dish.

Much of early behavior therapy, therefore, was focused on phenomena such as these and still does so, despite the fact that specific phobias represent a tiny fraction of the emotional problems of our society. In Staats's presentation of behavior therapy, however, he did not propose that "irrational" fears and phobias could be thought of as a direct result of an inadvertent classical association between a neutral stimulus and a fear-eliciting unconditioned stimulus (UCS). Staats would not deny that such events are possible and were some traumatic event to occur in close temporal contiguity with the neutral stimulus, then he would probably argue that the neutral stimulus might well become a conditioned stimulus (CS) for fear. There is no suggestion, however, that this was a common or probable occurrence and so the explanation of phobic anxiety must be found somewhere in the symbolic or verbal conditioning experiences of the individual.

The Inadequacies of Simple Separate Conditioning Models

It did not take the behavior therapy field very long to recognize that simple conditioning analogues were not good explanations for most complex human fears (Rachman, 1977), which, of course, came as no surprise to Staats and other social behaviorists, who never thought they were. The objections to a simple conditioning interpretation have been presented at great length by many different authors and boil down to one major concern: the theory does not fit the facts, neither the obvious clinical observations nor the more formal research studies. Having reached that conclusion the field responded in a variety of ways. One was to abandon general behavior theory altogether, another was to abandon conditioning concepts (e.g., Meichenbaum, 1977), and a third was to rescue the basic classical conditioning position by a variety of extensions and additions to the original analogy (e.g., Rachman, 1980).

One of the logical problems of abandoning conditioning models for explaining phobic behavior is that it leaves uncertain the role of conditioning theory in the design of treatment. At least two therapeutic strategies were derived from classical conditioning and seemed useful even if the original cause of the problem was not in accord with a conditioning interpretation. These two treatment strategies are systematic desensitization, which is based on classical extinction, and some variants of aversion therapy, which are based on the attempt to condition a fear response to a stimulus whose valence for the client is too positive (e.g., alcohol or a fetish). Note that the issue for the moment is not whether these techniques work or not, simply the consistency of a behavior therapy theory that repudiates a conditioning model in one context without seriously questioning its value in another. Of course, many behavior therapists did just that. Those that were totally abandoning any pretence at having a behavioral theory were also strong advocates of treatment approaches that were described as being "cognitive," or finding cognitive explanations for treatments that were originally derived from conditioning principles. For the social behaviorist, as simple classical conditioning was not itself a direct explanation, there was nothing to protest about; also as verbal processes were of special importance, it stood to reason that verbal treatments would be specially important. Thus cognitive therapy seemed to be a revolution without a cause!

As we said earlier, behavior therapy has always been very focused on those clinical phenomena that seemed to recapitulate experimental phenomena like classical conditioning. In other words, in its research and treatment efforts the field tended to concentrate on those behaviors that embody the classical conditioning paradigm particularly well. In a moment we will consider clinical phenomena that have little or nothing to do with classical conditioning and see what behavior therapy has done with them. Before doing so, however, it is necessary to consider another conditioning concept that has dominated behavior therapy and that is instrumental or operant conditioning. Thinking of problem behaviors as operants—functional activities that are unfortunately under the control of some aberrant reinforcement schedule—has been a principle of enormous conceptual power within behavior therapy. The notion leads directly to intervention design, it keeps exotic behavior like schizophrenic speech or trichotillomania out of the realm of disease and squarely within a natural psychological science. Yet in its power and its generality also lies its weakness: reinforcement explains all and thus nothing. As with phobias and classical conditioning, early behavior therapy quite understandably focused on phenomena that revealed the ubiquity of reinforcement very well. Some of the behaviors that came to clinical attention were those that were being maintained by contingencies of social and material reinforcement. Furthermore, even if the behavior of interest was not an operant maintained by reinforcement, it could still be quite sensitive to the influence of some new contingency. Thus if one had access to sufficiently potent rewards, it was possible to bring all sorts of clinical behavior under operant control. Note that we did not say "effective cure," but only that behaviors were manipulable by suitable contingencies.

Because of this, it has been a little harder to show that the simple analogy with a laboratory operant did not fit the facts of behavior any better than the classical conditioning paradigm did. People have never really decided that a reinforcement interpretation of common clinical phenomena is wrong. Those that abandoned behavioral theories altogether simply abandoned operant principles at the same time. You will not typically hear a cognitive theorist explain any aspect of depression by reference to reinforcement. It is very interesting to note that even though there have been numerous articulate attacks launched against classical conditioning theories of clinical phenomena (e.g., Bandura, 1978a), there have been no similar challenges rendered against operant conditioning. It just seems to be ignored, treated as though it were totally irrelevant. So we have the very odd situation in behavior therapy that there is one group of theorists and therapists who, one would have to say, are totally committed to a general operant perspective, and another group of professionals—in ostensibly the same field—who completely ignore operant principles and give them minimum significance in the discussion of treatment or of the explanatory etiologies (causes) of the problems.

To those of us who are social behaviorists, this represents a very strange situation indeed. Early on in the development of his theory, Staats (1963) made it very clear that both respondent and operant conditioning principles would need to be incorporated into any comprehensive model of behavior using a learning theory and conditioning framework, as behavior therapy was purporting to do. He also demonstrated the value of a theory that explained the interaction between the three functions of salient stimuli (i.e., affective, reinforcing, and behavior directive). We believe that this was a major theoretical insight, not so much because it was necessarily correct, but because it showed how two rather different traditions within the first and second generation of learning theory needed to come together if they were to ever have any impact beyond explaining the behavior of rats in boxes and mazes. Was this insight unique to Staats or did many other major theorists make a similar point? We think that whereas many people accepted both classical and operant principles—evidenced, for example, in the wide-spread acceptance of Mowrer's two-factor theory of fear acquisition and maintenance—there was no integration, especially not at the metatheoretical level.

For many years, behavior therapy has been quite polarized, with a group of behavior therapists maintaining strong metatheoretical, intellectual, and conceptual ties to Skinner and to standard operant theory. Not that operant theory has not become increasingly complicated. Reinforcement theory gained its momentum from its wonderful simplicity. One of us (I.E.) still remembers as a graduate student listening to Skinner give a colloquium on schizophrenia at the Maudsley in the late sixties. There were many behaviorally sophisticated psychiatrists in the audience, in addition to psychologists and other researchers investigating behavioral genetics, and he can recall vividly their amazement when Skinner argued that schizophrenia was basically a matter of reinforcement contingencies. Even until quite recently it was still possible to read in behavior therapy texts Ferster's theory of reinforcement to explain autistic children's behavior. One does not have to deny the significance of reinforcement for explaining behavior to recognize that such accounts are totally divorced from reality, and yet they can be seriously entertained and pursued, probably well into the contemporary era. On the other hand, if contemporary researchers exploring the speech, language, and information-processing characteristics of people labelled schizophrenic or autistic were to have the bridging theory Staats advocates in Chapter 2, interesting treatment implications would be offered to those who are trying to find the best ways to teach such individuals new and useful skills.

An interesting question that follows from these arguments is how one can use the fundamentally important concept of reinforcement without saying silly things about complex human behavior disorders. It is our opinion that Staats's theory did just that, as described in the 1963 work *Complex Human Behavior*. It did so because it translated the principles more or less reasonably and because it developed the principles further to account for the peculiarities of human behavior. Radical behaviorists that translate the principles directly give the false impression that there is a direct correspondence between a rat pressing a lever for food and, say, a child repeating a behavior because his parents laughed at it the first time. Through learning history, some child might interpret the laughter as ridicule, and so the reinforcer has to be defined functionally, and thus circularly. On the other hand, as a result of a long experience of verbal control, the parent can stop the behavior by saying, "OK, Johnny, it was funny the first time, but please don't do it again," and in many cases the behavior will just stop. So other principles determine whether the simple reinforcement principle will be overridden or not. Perhaps the Skinnerian purist can derive all sorts of higher-order principles to explain the human situation, but typically they do not do so within behavior therapy. This is illustrated in the Chapter 12 by Léduc, Dumais, and Evans in which they show how reasonable operant principles can result in inappropriate treatment if they are translated into clinical practice too literally.

Are Conditioning Models in Behavior Therapy Moribund?

In the previous sections, we have outlined some of the factors that, probably in combination, have been responsible for the decline and perceived inadequacy of conditioning models in behavior therapy:

(1) theoretical and practical problems of the simple conditioning models and their limited explanatory and application value; and (2) the emerging general cognitive Zeitgeist or "cognitive revolution" (Baars, 1986) in psychology in response to radical and simple behaviorist theories and research in which covert phenomena received too often only token attention. Does all this mean, however, that conditioning models are moribund? In the following sections we will continue to argue that we do not consider conditioning models have outlived their usefulness for behavior therapy—provided these models are conceptualized at the human level of functioning rather than the basic animal learning theory level, and provided the literal and simplistic transfer of basic principles to treatment techniques is avoided. In other words, conditioning principles need to be subjected to a careful translation and extension process before they can be adequately applied to the emotional and behavioral problems of human beings. In addition, conditioning models themselves have changed considerably over the last 20 years and are no longer simplistic mechanistic accounts of behavior (cf., Dickinson, 1987; Eysenck, 1987; Mackintosh, 1983; Martin & Levey, 1987a, 1987b).

The inadequacies of simple separate conditioning models as well as the controversy between conditioning and information-processing positions indicate that there is a real necessity for a more comprehensive bridge-building paradigm to explain and treat psychological dysfunctions. If this is to be more than a general list of truisms, however, it must exactly specify how environment and personality variables interact to determine problem behavior. In this sense, paradigmatic behaviorism has gone beyond the level of other social learning theories. It explains the role of emotion, language, and behavior repertoires in a wide variety of behaviors, and as it is primarily oriented toward human behavior, it accords language and reasoning processes their proper place in the etiology and treatment of psychological dysfunctions. Social behaviorism could therefore integrate cognitive-behavioral treatments within a paradigmatic framework and form the basis for the development of new techniques, too. Given the widely recognized need for an integrative framework, it is in some ways difficult to understand why social behaviorism has been largely ignored in behavior therapy. The authors in this book have argued that the conceptual status of behavior therapy could be advanced by the adoption of a paradigmatic behavioral framework that circumvents not only divisive and separatistic theoretical disputes but also clinical controversies such as whether beliefs, "distorted cognitions," or overt motor behavior should be the proper focus in therapy. These artificial dichotomies have unnecessarily separated the field of behavior therapy as evidenced by several series of articles and rebuttals in a number of major journals.

Integrating Conditioning with Other Conceptual Advances: The Major Challenge for a Unified Paradigmatic Behavior Therapy

The most significant, but also divisive, conceptual development in behavior therapy has been the introduction of various ideas and concepts from *information-processing theory.* We use that term rather than *cognitive psychology,* which is unfortunately rather vague and ambiguous. Behavior therapists started to use the term *cognitive* and *cognitive behavior therapy* when they really meant *verbal*—a position Staats explained very well in his 1972 paper on language behavior therapy. If, for instance, we try to teach a hyperactive child a self-control skill by instructing him or her to say things such as "go slow," "take your time," and so on, this is using language repertoires to regulate motor behavior. The processes involved have been described in considerable detail by Staats in numerous writings (see also Burns, Chapter 5, this vol.). Similarly, if we argue that a client's mood will be influenced by saying to him or herself "life is not worthwhile" or "I am a failure," we are again using previously acquired connections between these words (as CSs) and emotional responses. Assumptions regarding these sorts of processes abound in contemporary behavior therapy.

The arguments are completely different, however, if we try to understand the information processing, or cognitive processing, that underlies such phenomena. For example, we could try to explain the phenomenon of depression by conceptualizing different ways in which people acquire and retain information about their experiences. Imagine two persons at a party: they are exposed to a great deal of information—their own feelings, their own thoughts and spoken remarks, the other people at the party, how these people responded to them, and the kinds of things that were said.

One possible individual difference might be the way in which the depressed individual and the nondepressed individual perceive a remark, such as "nice clothes." This comment might be perceived as a compliment and elicit a positive emotional response, or as an insult (received as "you don't usually dress nicely") and thus elicit a negative emotion. Another difference might be in selective attention—of all the things that were said to the individual, the most salient comment was "nice clothes." There would also be individual differences in the encoding or the storage in memory of all these experiences as one is obviously not going to be able to store every tiny detail of these complex experiences. Thus one might store the few more negative events, or one might store the few positive events.

Or, even more complicated, one might store the negative events in a dysphoric file, such that the next time one was in a depressed mood, one would be most likely to remember those negative events, and vice versa. Later, perhaps at the end of the evening, one might think back over the evening and selectively rehearse various events that happened. For instance, if you had spilled your drink on the host's best outfit you might go over that event in your mind and such cognitive rehearsals of events have an important impact on what is later recalled. Finally, some weeks later, there might be individual differences in what information about the party you were able to retrieve from memory; regardless of what information had been stored, you might have a selective tendency to retrieve only negative events.

Loosely, we have presented here a variety of "cognitive" concepts surrounding depression. Any or all of these processes might be implicated, but the entire set depends on certain presumptions about cognitive processes, that we can reasonably use these models of attention, storage, rehearsal, and retrieval of information to explain clinical phenomena. The advantage of doing so is that there is an extensive body of theorizing and research in experimental psychology around these various topics and cognitive phenomena. Although this theoretical work has some limitations in relevance because information-processing studies have in the past rarely paid attention to individual differences, more recent research has begun to deal with the storage and retrieval of emotional experiences (Clark & Teasdale, 1985). In fact, quite a considerable amount of research has been conducted on mood-state-dependent learning and recall (Blaney, 1986; Bower, 1987). In addition, the approach has a number of well-developed research paradigms for investigating verbal and affective memory that have been used to good effect by clinical researchers (e.g., Teasdale, 1983) interested in the differences between individuals with certain clinical features and those without.

Another type of information-processing analysis refers to the relationship between an emotion and the performance of some task. There are many clinical situations in which the expression of anxiety as an emotional or autonomic behavior results in decrements in performance, whether it is the ability to perform well in a test or the ability to maintain an erection. In traditional behavior theory, anxiety interferes with performance mostly through a mechanism whereby autonomic arousal motivates escape and avoidance behavior and that behavior is antithetical to performing the task. In some situations the autonomic arousal that constitutes the emotional expression also results in direct interference. For instance, muscular tension makes it harder to speak and the autonomic pathways involved in fear or anxiety are inhibitory of autonomic pathways necessary to maintain sexual responses. Information-processing views are somewhat different. In the case of sexual anxiety, for example, Barlow and his colleagues argue that the reason for anxiety interfering with sexual arousal is that anxiety—by means of a mechanism not clearly specified—results in a redistribution of attention, so that the individual now attends to irrelevant cues and stimuli, including those from his or her autonomic nervous system such as heart pounding and shortness of breath. It is this shift in attention from erotic cues to irrelevant internal cues that results in the loss of sexual excitation, almost as though the person were no longer in a sexual situation at all. A similar account is given of test anxiety in which the attention to the internal experience of anxiety, and thoughts related to failure rather than to the content of the test result in difficulty in recall of previously learnt materials or in some other interference with performance.

The question we wish to consider is not the correctness or incorrectness of these various ideas, but how they fit into a general paradigmatic theory of behavior therapy. This question is difficult because it is clear that these theories come from a different paradigm: information-processing rather than stimulus-response (S-R) learning theory. Can these concepts be translated into the terms and concepts used in Staats's theory and by other writers within social behaviorism? Or should social behaviorism be modified in some way so that it can be incorporated within information processing? Or could there even be a third alternative, that is, the development of a new theoretical framework requiring that both conditioning and information processing be modified in order to be integrated with other important conceptual advances into a new superordinate structure? Regardless of the answer to these questions we hope that this book has at least convinced the reader that some form of rapprochement is necessary, otherwise a huge amount of research and theorizing in classical conditioning and its role in complex human behavior is simply lost—

deleted from scientific concern because the ideas are deemed irrelevant to the alternative paradigm. Conversely, if the information-processing viewpoint should not gain a majority support, these rather interesting and potentially most useful ideas remain totally unutilized by much of behavior therapy. Let us therefore attempt a rapprochement. It is encouraging, indeed, to note some developments toward this goal in the experimental animal-conditioning field (Mackintosh, 1983) and in the human field as well (e.g., Martin & Levey, 1985, 1987b) although, unfortunately, in the clinical literature itself such attempts have either been very rare or not very successful (Franks, 1988).

Unlike the Skinnerian position that has consistently eschewed intervening response variables, social behaviorism, like other expanded behavioral theories, allows for a great deal of processing to take place between a stimulus input and a response output. The Staatsian concept of basic behavioral repertoires provides a complete substrate to learned behavioral mechanisms which subsequently mediate all other interactions between the organism and the environment. Sensory, perceptual, and attentional mechanisms are in fact presumed in any behavioral theory, but they are simply bypassed in the attempt to explain a behavior such as fear of snakes. The part of the phenomenon that is of interest is how the sight of a snake comes to elicit fear, not how the person comes to be able to perceive an object and identify it as a snake. It is assumed, however, that such a process must occur as a prerequisite. Some parts of information processing are thus taken for granted and presupposed but simply not represented in the theory as such. The really critical issue arises when a proposed mechanism that is central in social behaviorism is replaced or substituted for by an information-processing model: in other words, when verbal encoding, storage, and retrieval of information are used as an alternative conceptualization to conditioning to explain changes in performance as a result of experience.

Many theorists over the years have been interested in replacing the mechanistic associationism of classical conditioning with a cognitive perspective. For example, when a dog salivates at the sound of a bell that has been paired with food, conditioning is the name we give to the phenomenon; it is not really an explanation of why it should be. On the other hand, if we say that the dog salivates because he "knows" or "has developed an expectancy" that food is about to come, then we have merely given another label to the phenomenon but not advanced our explanation either. We might, however, explain the facts of conditioning by reference to a cognitive process, such as memory, without being circular, and increasingly animal learning theory is attending to such cognitive processes (cf., Mackintosh, 1983). This is not necessarily a challenge to social behaviorism since the phenomenon of conditioning is used to explain other complex events—such as why a Vietnam veteran might drop to the ground when he hears a car backfiring. Similarly, we might be able to take other cognitive processes and use conditioning concepts to explain them. We are left with the odd situation in which we have conditioning theorists using conditioning to explain some cognitive events, and cognitivists using cognitive concepts to explain conditioning. In his thoughtful analysis of the value of current animal conditioning and learning theory for behavior therapy, Dickinson (1987) raises similar points, but even more interestingly, his conclusions show how compatible *contemporary* conditioning theory and social behavioral theory seem to be—particularly if we were to extend Dickinson's use of the term *cognitive* to *verbal-cognitive:*

> Conditioning cannot be understood without reference to cognitive processes. . . . The contemporary (conditioning) approach recognizes a role for representations and beliefs about predictive and causal relationships even in the case of animal conditioning. This is important because it means that the conditioning model is not necessarily at variance with the increasing recognition of the role of mental processes in psychiatric disorders. The contemporary model allows for the idea that inappropriate and maladaptive beliefs may well have arisen through a conditioning experience and that such beliefs may be changed through conditioning procedures. . . . Secondly, conditioning is neither a simple nor well-understood process; the last 20 years have revealed complexities and subtleties that transcend any simple reinforcement mechanism. . . . Whether or not this richer framework can provide a rational basis for the development of more effective therapeutic procedures remains an open question; at the very least, the contemporary approach stands a better chance of matching up to the complex cognitive and behavioral profiles observed in the clinic than did traditional reinforcement theory. (pp. 77–78)

It is quite possible that there are some aspects of an event that are best accounted for by simple association principles in which cognitive mediation is not required, whereas other aspects of the same event could be best accommodated for by information processing. An example might be the trauma of a rape experience from which the victim is now experiencing anxiety in dark situations—a conditioned negative emotional response—something that the individual might recognize as irrational. She also might have a complex verbal and imaginal memory of the experience, which, when recalled, makes her feel angry and which changes her perception of men. These latter processes could probably also be accounted for in conditioning terms, but the account would be tortuous and convoluted. An information-processing or cognitive account might be more parsimonious and have interesting treatment implications as well. For example, to reduce the fear response to the dark as a conditioned emotional response, one might be disposed to attempt in vivo desensitization or flooding, whereas to rebuild her trust in men it might be possible to use a program of verbal reasoning that would allow the person to make better discriminations between dangerous and gentle men. Such verbal reasoning might be quite an effective way of modifying a verbal categorization problem.

Martin and Levey (1985, 1987a, 1987b) have also recently developed what they call "an axis for integrating conditioning and cognition theory." They argue that some aspects of behavior are best accounted for by associative conditioning models—for instance, behavior that is under direct stimulus control and regulated by "rules of sequence" such as preferences, likes and dislikes, and so on—whereas other aspects of behavior (e.g., awareness, abstractions of reality) are guided by mental representations of knowledge ("rules of consequence") that are best accounted for by information-processing concepts and models: "Behavioral theory has gone a long way toward defining external determinants in its analysis of stimulus control and stimulus-response relationships, and contemporary conditioning theory is now moving inward to shift some of the external control of behavior to mediating internal representations of events" (Martin & Levey, 1987a, p. 150). Based on this analysis, these authors suggest that there are three levels at which maladaptive behavior can be approached: (1) the level of classically conditioned affective responses; (2) the level of cognitive structure in which the rules of sequence are summarized; (3) the level of planned strategies that involves the action component and is based on knowing the consequences of sequences of actions. Treatment methods and combinations should be based on an assessment of which level is primarily involved in a particular maladaptive behavior.

Does all this sound horribly like eclecticism that we have tried to get away from in behavior theory for so long? In Chapter 2 Staats has attempted to distinguish between eclecticism and bridging theories. Let us return to the rape victim as an example of how we might explain different reactions to such an experience. One possible reaction to such an experience is to blame oneself—victims have reported that they think they may have enticed the attacker in some way, or caused him to come on to her. This reasoning could result from the recurrent exposure to such statements in the media and/or having heard such statements being made by a particularly forceful person, such as a parent, husband, or police officer.

Alternatively, the person might blame herself because that is a characteristic of her verbal reasoning as a result of depression and low self-esteem. The latter habits would be ones that could be traced back to childhood experiences, with obvious implications for treatment. The generality would have to be that prior learned ways of responding to events would influence the psychological consequences of rape, independent of the exact circumstances of the violent incident itself. The onus would be on those who study rape to see (1) whether there were any data roughly supporting the position outlined, and (2) to place the reasoning or theorizing around rape in the context of other mechanisms from other areas of study, such as, in this case, the depression literature. A person who is prone to depression might be expected to respond to rape experiences in predictable ways. On the other hand, the trauma of a rape might be sufficient to make a person depressed regardless of her prior cognitive style because the rape episode enacts the circumstances that create cognitive vulnerability for depression.

Finally, it is important to realize that conditioning principles always represented only a *metaphor* for behavior therapy. We have explained earlier in this chapter that social behaviorism provides a vehicle for translating basic principles, rather than supporting the view that a given clinical phenomenon, or a given behavioral treatment, is literally identical to the laboratory procedure referred to as classical conditioning. A major contribution of the paradigmatic position is that part of our theory building must contain conceptual rules for how basic research is to be translated to meaningful applications (see also Minke, Chapter 3, this vol.). Multiple levels of theory permit a variety of different avenues of explanation, which can be seen in Rondal's Chapter 4 on language learning. If language is a function of learning history, early environmental experiences result in both direct effects (such as traumatic experience) and indirect effects (shaping the nature and content of one's language repertoire). Only the systematic inclusion of learning, developmental, and personality levels of theory could allow behavior therapy to draw on the resources of psychology as a science.

Let us now turn our attention to another crucial issue which is how well paradigmatic behaviorism can respond to new conceptual and empirical advances that have not come from social behaviorism and the basic traditions of learning theory. In most chapters in this collection the major theoretical connections are made to Staats's writings, not to other empirical or theoretical advances in psychology—something that Staats has been very critical of in the work of other scholars.

Paradigmatic Behaviorism's Contribution to New Knowledge

If paradigmatic behaviorism represents a framework theory for behavior therapy—as most authors of this book have asserted—then it becomes an essential task to evaluate the theory's contribution to new knowledge. We have argued a number of times, at conference symposia and other occasions, that while a given presentor's approach or data were compatible with social behaviorism, they were not uniquely derived from that framework. This enormous generality of the paradigm, and its ability to incorporate much of the general rubric of behavior therapy, may partially account for Staats's perception that he has not been afforded proper credit for various theoretical ideas. It may also account for the perception by many in the field that there is nothing particularly novel or unique about social behaviorism. For example, at a recent colloquium at the State University of New York at Binghamton, Peter Campos, a student of Heiby and Staats, presented a paradigmatic integration of various behavioral theories of depression. The response from one senior professor in the audience was that if *that* was paradigmatic behaviorism, then he, like Moliére's character who discovered he had been speaking prose all the time, had been a paradigmatic behaviorist without realizing it.

These challenges are worth taking up in some detail since they may determine whether the conceptual position adopted in this book will end an interesting sideshow in the ongoing carnival of behavior therapy, or will really serve to gather the unruly and motley group together and shape their future direction. The issues to consider seem to be (1) does integration of different theoretical or conceptual perspectives result in new insights and treatments and what novel perspectives have emerged from social behaviorism in behavior therapy, if any? and (2) what are the other benefits of having a general framework theory, such as avoiding redundancy of ideas, making other research literatures relevant for the clinician, and so on?

New Insights, Perspectives, and Treatments

Some of the preceding chapters have provided ample evidence that some novel concepts and treatments are emerging. These developments are particularly obvious in the work on anxiety and depression, and there are treatment implications that arise from this and much of the other work presented in this book.

Anxiety

There are two major principles in the multilevel theory of anxiety and its cognitive-behavioral treatment which, although not completely new, are novel in their combination: (1) a central emotional response is at the core of some types of phobias; this proposition has led to new ways of changing that basic affective component of phobic anxiety in a more direct fashion through nonverbal means such as positively evaluated music (Eifert, Craill, Carey, & O'Connor, 1988); and (2) this emotional response can be acquired not only directly through aversive classical conditioning but also indirectly through language-symbolic experiences. In other words, although sufficient, it is not necessary for an individual to have an actual traumatic experience to develop a phobia. The association of inappropriate or negative emotion-eliciting verbal-symbolic stimuli with objects or situations is sufficient for those objects to acquire aversive properties and may explain the puzzle of phobias with no history of overt aversive conditioning. For instance, agoraphobic clients constantly pair negative thoughts and verbal stimuli with images of panic and disaster in potentially frightening situations so that they do not need to have direct reconditioning experiences to remain phobic and continue to avoid these situations. They may condition themselves by providing their own verbal-symbolic stimuli that elicit negative responses. These views have led to the development of new concepts and treatment strategies for the treatment of anxiety that are aimed at changing the language repertoires of phobic persons (see Hekmat, Chapter 9, this vol.).

A paradigmatic behavioral account of clinical problems relates and integrates the basic forms of direct classical conditioning (e.g., fainting in a crowded, stuffy bus) with the specifically human types of learning involving language and imagery. When the two mechanisms are truly linked in a multilevel approach—each accorded its proper place—they make divisive controversies between the "scientific camps" of traditional conditioning theorists and cognitive therapists superfluous and help to create greater unity in the field.

Depression

Another important contribution of paradigmatic behaviorism to the understanding and treatment of clinical problems has been achieved in the area of depression (Heiby & Staats, Chapter 10, this vol.;

Staats & Heiby, 1985). Central in this theory is the concept of dysphoria as the negative emotional state that in turn elicits the behavioral and physiological symptoms of depression. The state occurs as a consequence of an interaction between the individual's environmental situation (especially in terms of losses of positive emotional stimulation or the occurrence of negative emotional stimuli) and the individual's personality repertoires (especially the emotional-motivational system). The theory also stipulates ways that biological factors (e.g., biochemical imbalances) enter into the etiology of depression and how these factors may combine with psychological deficits such as low levels of self-esteem and self-reinforcement to produce depression.

Moreover, the theory includes a classification scheme that recognizes that there are multiple possible subtypes of depression based on numerous potential etiological factors. For example, the Pleasant Events Schedule, used in measuring depression, lumps together the frequency of pleasant events and the strength of their pleasantness (Lewinsohn & Libet, 1972). The more detailed paradigmatic behaviorism theory, however, predicts subtypes of depression: some individuals feel strongly about positive emotional events but experience those events infrequently, whereas others experience the events infrequently but care little about the events as such. Research shows that this typology differentially predicts depression (Rose & Staats, 1988) and that different clinical treatment is effective with these different subtypes (Heiby, 1989). Heiby's study also demonstrates the close relationship that should exist between research on psychopathology and treatment—a relationship that is possible when the analysis of psychopathology is made in terms of principles that specify the interaction of particular environmental influences and person variables.

An important reason that the principles involving emotional conditioning have frequently not been seen as basic in depression is that dysphoria does not have the specific, immediate, ephemeral characteristics of an emotional response. For such reasons Heiby and Staats have differentiated emotional responses from emotional states, as they should be, but that differentiation does not imply separate and independent processes. Rather, the emotional state has been described as a conglomeration of stimulus circumstances that in their complexity produce a deep, pervasive, lasting negative emotional responding or state (Rose & Staats, 1988; Staats & Eifert, 1990). This theoretical formulation suggests further analysis of the circumstances that serve to differentiate discrete negative emotional responses to specific stimuli, such as in simple phobias, from negative emotional states, such as in generalized anxiety or stress, and the continuing, pervasive dysphoric state of a depressed individual. Paradigmatic behaviorism's theories of anxiety and depression begin to provide a framework within which such analyses can be made.

Other Benefits of a General Framework Theory

It seems that one of the most important benefits of the approach presented in this book is that a general framework theory reduces unnecessary conflict between nonopposing positions. As we have indicated already, another great advantage is that in some cases the framework theory allows useful concepts and principles to be retained when other newer concepts emerge. There are many ideas in psychology that are not really wrong, they simply fall into disuse and out of favor. This fashionlike, faddish tendency in psychology seems like a terrible waste of time and resources and is ultimately detrimental to the development of psychology into a unified science. The best example is that of classical conditioning. There a great many facts known about this phenomenon and most of these facts cannot easily be accounted for by other cognitive interpretations. Thus a position that allows one to retain some concept like classical conditioning while at the same time recognizing the many areas in which classical conditioning does not provide an adequate explanation is a very valuable contribution.

It should also be recognized that a function of framework theory is to incorporate many complex phenomena under one simpler conceptual rubric. The framework theory allows. different theoretical constructs to be preserved, but does that serve a simplification function? Are previously unrelated events now perceived as part of a general principle, or are they merely classifiable within a category, so that concepts are amassed but never integrated into one or two superordinate or higher-order constructs? We believe that paradigmatic behaviorism can provide such higher-order constructs as a result of the hierarchical nature and different levels of its theory construction approach. This can help behavior therapists interrelate the various aspects of a client's problem in a similar hierarchical fashion (e.g., biological aspects, conditioning, verbal reasoning, personality).

It should also be noted that behavior therapy already has a few higher-order constructs, some of which have been illustrated in the preceding chapters—for instance, with respect to psychopathology. To give an example, bulimia is a behavior pattern that shares some conceptual similarity with obsessive compulsive behavior, in that a behavior becomes a powerful habit because it is negatively reinforced by anxiety reduction. Or, to take another example, children who are considered emotionally disturbed probably do not have disturbed emotions but have learned a variety of inappropriate behaviors and have failed to learn a variety of appropriate others. These inappropriate and deficit aspects of the child's personality can be assessed to provide important information for intervention programs. All this may not sound as precise as thinking of such children as belonging to a separate category, but it does allow for the integration of a vast variety of "treatment" strategies that have been suggested for children in general (Wilson & Meazzini, Chapter 11, this vol.).

There is another way in which integration through generalization provides novel principles. Staats and other chapter authors in this volume have pointed out that specialization within clinical behavior therapy has typically occurred at the level of clinical phenomena. But if certain common processes are reported within each of these different areas, then a general principle emerges that could be extended to entirely new areas. For example, in their chapter on children's behavior, Wilson and Meazzini mentioned the work of Dodge. His studies suggested that children who were considered hyperaggressive differed from other children in the way they interpreted the behavior of their peers. Aggressive children perceived peers' behavior as having hostile intent—this would obviously be an additional principle to the important consideration mentioned in Chapter 3 that aggressive behavior is a function of reinforcement. Is this process conceptually akin to someone with phobic anxiety perceiving a stimulus such as a dog as being dangerous or hostile? Or similar to the observations in the depression literature that some people judge situations as negative? Our position is that within a framework theory these represent a common process. This process can then be applied, in a way that has not been done before, to the influence on caregivers' reactions of their perceptions of the behavior of people in institutions, or to behavioral medicine and the different ways in which patients perceive their own internal stimuli (symptoms).

Thus a primary test of the heuristic value of the framework theory is its ability to stimulate additional theoretical and empirical elaboration. We have exemplified this with the paradigmatic behavioral accounts of anxiety and depression where the multilevel theory provides conceptual elements that range from biological knowledge, through behavioral principles, and into personality. Consequently, this theory can be more detailed than most presently used theories in behavior therapy which do not include these various levels but are restricted to one or two levels at most, and thus are less rich in concepts and principles with which to face the task of analyzing the various clinical phenomena. We believe that the contributions in this book have demonstrated that a paradigmatic behavioral formulation has heuristic value in behavior therapy and indicates new directions of research.

Integrating the Role of Language and Affect in Behavior Therapy

Several authors (e.g., Barlow, 1988; Eifert, 1987; Rachman, 1984) have recently expressed their concern that the role of affect in therapeutic change is still in need of explanation. It is indeed interesting that despite the extensive basic research on classical conditioning, contemporary behavioral clinical psychology has not dealt well with emotions. A central reason is that radical behaviorism has never granted emotions (and thus classical conditioning) a causal role in the determination of behavior—and consequently has not been interested in treatment methods directed toward changing emotions, notwithstanding that this is exactly what is involved in much behavior therapy treatment. Although the present cognitive-behavioral approaches postulate a link between cognitive activities and emotions, these formulations do not provide the bridging theory that would connect them with basic behavioral analyses of emotions and language. The multilevel paradigmatic behavioral theory of emotions provides a basis for understanding the acquisition of emotional dysfunctions through primary as well as specifically human forms of learning—such as language learning and observational learning—as well as why it is important to treat emotions in solving behavior problems.

Cognitive-behavioral approaches in particular have been criticized for viewing emotion as postcognitive and for assuming that emotions can always be changed through a process of rational reevaluation. As indicated above, some of these criticisms could be overcome within a paradigmatic behavioral framework. On the other hand, although the individual's learned labeling repertoire is important in mediating affect and behavior, it must also be clearly recognized that verbal and symbolic stimuli are only one source of behavioral regulation—and in many instances they may not even be the most powerful ones. Paradigmatic behavioral theory postulates that emotive language stimuli have the same affective-reinforcing-directive

(A-R-D) functions as other physical stimuli, and studies have demonstrated that the principles of conditioning do apply to language and symbolic stimuli. At the same time, a growing body of research (Izard, Kagan, & Zajonc, 1984) indicates that the functional relationships between central affective responses, peripheral physiological arousal, overt behavior, and language are very complex, far from fully understood, and they may not be quite as automatic and straightforward as social behaviorist theory and cognitive behavior therapists tend to assume. For instance, Levis and Malloy (1982) pointed out that there are qualitative differences between language and other stimuli. Language and other symbolic stimuli should have weaker effects as they are secondary or higher-order UCSs that cause no pain or tissue damage, reduce no primary drive, and so on. Even though emotions can be quite effectively generated and maintained by verbal-symbolic means, language and symbolic stimuli are much less effective when it comes to changing existing strong affective responses (Eifert, 1987; Rachman, 1981, 1984). This is an interesting and very important distinction with implications that have not yet been fully investigated. If social behaviorist theory is to accommodate such findings, it may have to be modified to allow for differential effects of language in the acquisition versus treatment of emotional dysfunctions.

Paradigmatic Behaviorism: Dogma or Applied Science?

Many of the comments in this chapter are intended to caution against turning paradigmatic behaviorism into some kind of dogma. Its viability as a unifying paradigm will depend on its openness to refinement, modification, and change in view of findings and theoretical arguments by other researchers who work within related, but what they consider, different models. An example are information-processing models of phobic anxiety and depression. Science is made by human beings. Other relevant findings, theories, and models cannot merely be subsumed under the rubric of paradigmatic behaviorism. So when paradigmatic behaviorists talk about integrating and relating other models and findings, they must not be seen to mean "swallowing" them! Staats (1983b) himself cautioned against adopting such a reductionistic approach and outlined the need for a bridging type of theory. In the process of such integrative efforts paradigmatic behavioral theory will also have to be modified and refined.

Moreover, whether paradigmatic behaviorism will indeed be adopted as a unifying framework will also depend on three other factors that are not completely independent from each other:

1. The results of future empirical studies rigorously testing the applicability of social behavioral principles to explain the acquisition and treatment of behavioral and emotional dysfunctions;
2. The willingness and readiness of the behavior therapy field to reconsider its original learning, social, and general experimental psychology bases in order to refine and develop them further, and last, but by no means least,
3. An honest and genuine commitment to unification: we feel very strongly about this point because we have at times been under the distinct impression that whereas there is a lot of talk about integration and greater unity—with "integrative" theories of all kinds being presented in journals and at conferences—not many psychologists are *really* much in favor of integration of ideas for fear it might reduce their own preeminence! We believe that this problem cannot be overcome just by verbal/written appeals to the scientific community but only by redefining originality as involving more than the creation of ever more "new" (= different) concepts and terms for the same phenomena. In addition, professional and financial incentives must be provided for linking findings and concepts and for building bridges between minitheories that were previously unrelated but aim to explain the same phenomena.

Hence, the overriding issue for the future of behavior therapy— and for clinical psychology—is how information derived from basic research is to be assimilated in a usable form. We have emphasized a number of times that basic research findings cannot just be translated into therapeutic techniques or insights into the problems presented by clients. Research paradigms or methodologies need to be varied and expanded—one of the advantages of the contemporary interest in information processing is that novel experimental paradigms have become available for use with clinical phenomena and with clients. The interaction among levels of research benefits the basic science as well. This is nicely illustrated in a recent study by one of our students, Adria DiBenedetto. She was using a semantic interference procedure to investigate the emotional impact of words on people with obsessive-compulsive disorder. One research subject, who was of course also a clinical patient, stopped halfway through simply reading the list of relevant words (in a Stroop-type test) and broke down in tears, refusing to continue because the words she was reading aroused such intense anxiety. Experimental psychologists interested in the relationship between emotion and cognition rarely have such powerful, ecologically valid conditions in their studies (see Neisser, 1976).

Finally, we cannot and do not want to make a conclusive (let alone definitive) statement regarding the unification potential of paradigmatic behaviorism for behavior therapy. The authors of the various chapters have basically presented their case for such a potential, and we have outlined some of the promises of but also challenges facing paradigmatic behaviorism in its claim to provide a unifying framework for behavior therapy. The time is certainly ripe for integration and unification in behavior therapy, and as the title of Ross's (1985) AABT Presidential Address suggests, "it is time to stop standing still and form a more perfect union." We are inclined to agree with Franks (1988) who believes that unification is not possible at this stage across different systems of psychotherapy which he describes as a nebulous and totally unintegrated nonentity. On the other hand, in behavior therapy, as a conceptually and methodologically consistent approach to therapy, "unification becomes a meaningful proposition . . . The unique strength of behavior therapy did not and does not rest upon its technical and therapeutic achievements, impressive as they may be. Its strength lies in the development of a flexible, yet rigorous, approach which can be used to advance our general understanding and interpretation in the area of mental health" (p. 26).

In that spirit, but also in much the same way that the famous German playwright Bertolt Brecht refused to write an end—happy or sad—for his dramas, leaving the end open and telling the viewer "to go home and find his own ending," we would like to conclude this book by saying, "Now reader, make up your own mind!"

References

Abramson, L. Y., Seligman, M. E. P., & Teasdale, J. D. (1978). Learned helplessness in humans: Critique and reformulation. *Journal of Abnormal Psychology, 87*, 49–74.

Adams, F. (Ed.) (1939). *The genuine works of Hippocrates.* Baltimore, MD: Williams & Wilkins.

Agras, W. S., Sylvester, D., & Oliveau, D. (1969). The epidemiology of common fears and phobias. *Comparative Psychiatry, 10*, 151–156.

Akiskal, H. S. (1986). A developmental perspective on recurrent mood disorders: A review of studies in man. *Psychopharmacology Bulletin, 22*, 579–586.

Akiskal, H. S., Bitar, A. H., Puzantian, V. R., Rosenthal, T. L., & Parks, W. W. (1978). The nosological status of neurotic depression. *Archives of General Psychiatry, 35*, 756–766.

Allen, M. G. (1976). Twin studies of affective illness. *Archives of General Psychiatry, 33*, 1476–1478.

Alloy, L. B., & Abramson, L. Y. (1979). Judgment of contingency in depressed and nondepressed students: Sadder but wiser? *Journal of Experimental Psychology: General, 108*, 441–485.

Allport, G. W., Vernon, P. E., & Lindzey, G. (1951). *Study of values* (rev. ed.). Boston: Houghton Mifflin.

Amato, P. R., & Ochiltree, G. (1986). Family resources and the development of child competence. *Journal of Marriage and the Family, 48*, 47–56.

American Psychiatric Association. (1987). *Diagnostic and Statistical Manual of Mental Disorders* (3rd ed., rev.). Washington, DC: Author.

Andreasen, C., & Winokur, G. (1979). Newer experimental methods for classification of depression. *Archives of General Psychiatry, 36*, 447–452.

Andreasen, C., & Grove, W. M. (1986). Thought, language, and communication in schizophrenia: Diagnosis and prognosis. *Schizophrenia Bulletin, 12*, 348–359.

Angst, J., Bastrup, P., Grof, H., Hippius, H., Poldinger, W., & Weis, P. (1973). The course of monopolar depression and bipolar psychoses. *Psychiatrica Neurologia et Neurochirurgia, 76*, 489–500.

Arana, G. W., Baldessarini, R. J., & Ornstein, M. (1985). The dexamethosone suppression test for diagnosis and prognosis in psychiatry. *Archives of General Psychiatry, 42,* 1193–1204.

Atkinson, M. (1982). *Explanations in the study of child language development.* New York: Cambridge University Press.

Atthowe, J. M., & Krasner, L. (1968). Preliminary report on the application of contingent reinforcement procedures (token economy) on a "chronic" psychiatric ward. *Journal of Abnormal Psychology, 73,* 37–43.

Ayllon, T., & Azrin, N. H. (1968). *The token economy: A motivational system for therapy and evaluation.* New York: Appleton-Century-Crofts.

Ayllon, T., & Michael, J. (1959). The psychiatric nurse as a behavioral engineer. *Journal of the Experimental Analysis of Behavior, 2,* 323–334.

Baars, B. J. (1986). *The cognitive revolution in psychology.* New York: Guilford.

Baer, D. M. (1976). The organism as host. *Human Development, 19,* 87–98.

Baer, D. M., Wolf, M. M., & Risley, T. R. (1968). Some current dimensions of applied behavior analysis. *Journal of Applied Behavior Analysis, 1,* 91–97.

Baker, C., & Battison, R. (Eds.) (1980). *Sign language and the deaf community: Essays in honor of William C. Stokoe.* Washington, DC: National Association of the Deaf.

Baker, R., Hall, J. N., Hutchison, K. O., & Bridge, G. (1977). Symptom changes in chronic schizophrenic patients on a token economy: A controlled experiment. *British Journal of Psychiatry, 131,* 381–393.

Ban, P. K. (1979). *Descriptions of stuttered and fluent response patterns: An electromyographic investigation.* Unpublished doctoral dissertation, University of Hawaii, Honolulu.

Ban, P. K., & Minke, K. A. (1984). The use of generalization gradients for the study of mediational processes. *Journal of General Psychology, 110,* 115–128.

Bandura, A. (1969). *Principles of behavior modification.* New York: Holt, Rinehart and Winston.

Bandura, A. (1971). *Psychological modeling.* Chicago: Aldine-Atherton.

Bandura, A. (1977a). Self-efficacy: Toward a unifying theory of behavior change. *Psychological Review, 84,* 191–215.

Bandura, A. (1977b). *Social learning theory.* Englewood Cliffs, NJ: Prentice-Hall.

Bandura, A. (1978a). Reflections on self-efficacy. *Advances in Behaviour Research and Therapy, 1,* 237–269.

Bandura, A. (1978b). The self-system in reciprocal determinism. *American Psychologist, 33,* 344–358.

Bandura, A. (1984) Recycling misconceptions of perceived self-efficacy. *Cognitive Therapy and Research, 8,* 231–255.

Bandura, A., & Perloff, B. (1967). Relative efficacy of self-monitored and externally imposed reinforcement systems. *Journal of Personality and Social Psychology, 7,* 111–116.

Bandura, A., & Schunk, D. H. (1981). Cultivating competence, self-efficacy, and intrinsic interest through proximal self-motivation. *Journal of Personality and Social Psychology, 41*, 586–598.

Bandura, A., & Walters, R. H. (1959). *Adolescent aggression*. New York: Ronald.

Bandura, A., & Walters, R. H. (1963). *Social learning and personality development*. New York: Holt, Rinehart and Winston.

Barlow, D. H. (1988). *Anxiety and its disorders*. New York: Guilford.

Barlow, D. H., Craske, M. G., Cerny, J. A., & Klosko, J. S. (1989). Behavioral treatment of panic disorder. *Behavior Therapy, 20*, 261–282.

Barlow, D. H., Hayes, S. C., & Nelson, R. O. (1984). *The scientist-practitioner*. New York: Pergamon.

Barnett, P. A., & Gotlib, I. H. (1988). Psychosocial functioning and depression: Distinguishing among antecedents, concomitants, and consequences. *Psychological Bulletin, 104*, 97–126.

Bayes, R. (1980). *Una introduccion al metodo scientifico en psicologia*. Barcelona: Editorial Fontanella.

Beck, A. T. (1967). *Depression: Clinical, experimental, and theoretical aspects*. New York: Harper & Row.

Beck, A. T. (1976). *Cognitive therapy and the emotional disorders*. New York: International University Press.

Beck, A. T., & Emery, G., with R. L. Greenberg. (1985). *Anxiety disorders and phobias: A cognitive perspective*. New York: Basic Books.

Bellack, A. S. (1983). Recurrent problems in the behavioral assessment of social skill. *Behaviour Research and Therapy, 21*, 29–42.

Bellack, A. S., & Hersen, M. (Eds.) (1985). *Dictionary of behavior therapy techniques*. New York: Pergamon.

Bellack, A. S., & Hersen, M. (Eds.). (1988). *Behavioral assessment: A practical handbook* (3rd ed.). New York: Pergamon.

Bellack, A. S., & Morrison, R. L. (1982). Interpersonal dysfunction. In A. S. Bellack, M. Hersen, & A. E. Kazdin (Eds.), *International handbook of behavior modification and therapy* (pp. 717–747). New York: Plenum.

Bem, D. J. (1972). Constructing cross-situational consistencies in behavior: Some thoughts on Alker's critique of Mischel. *Journal of Personality, 40*, 17–26.

Bem, D. J., & Funder, D. C. (1978). Predicting more of the people more of the time: Assessing the personality of situations. *Psychological Review, 85*, 485–501.

Berkowitz, L., & Knurek, D. A. (1969). Label-mediated hostility generalization. *Journal of Personality and Social Psychology, 13*, 200–206.

Bernal, M. E., Klinnert, M. D., & Schultz, L. A. (1980). Outcome evaluation of behavioral parent training and client centered parent counseling for children with conduct problems. *Journal of Applied Behavior Analysis, 13*, 677–691.

Bernstein, D. A., & Borkovec, T. D. (1973). *Progressive relaxation training*. Champaign, IL: Research Press.

Bersh, P. (1980). Eysenck's theory of incubation: A critical analysis. *Behaviour Research and Therapy, 18*, 11–17.

Bever, T. G. (1970). The cognitive basis for linguistic structures. In J. R. Hayes (Ed.), *Cognition and the development of language* (pp. 279–362). New York: Wiley.

Bibring, E. (1953). The mechanism of depression. In P. Greenacre (Ed.), *Affective disorders*. New York: International Universities Press.

Bijou, S. W. (1957). Patterns of reinforcement and extinction with young children. *Child Development, 28,* 47–54.

Birky, H. J., Chambliss, J. E., & Wasden, R. (1971). A comparison of residents discharged from a token economy and two traditional psychiatric programs. *Behavior Therapy, 2,* 46–51.

Bitterman, M. E., Reed, P. C., & Kubala, A. L. (1953). The strength of sensory preconditioning. *Journal of Experimental Psychology, 46,* 178–182.

Blaney, P. H. (1986). Mood and memory: A review. *Psychological Bulletin, 99,* 229–246.

Blatt, S. J., Quinlan, D. M., Chevron, E. S., McDonald, C., & Zuroff, D. (1982). Dependency and self-criticism: Psychological dimensions of depression. *Journal of Consulting and Clinical Psychology, 50,* 113–124.

Boothe, D., Stephens, R. M., Ronald, M., & Matson, J. L. (1978). Long-term effects of a simple contingency management program with chronic psychiatric patients. *Psychological Reports, 42,* 282.

Borkovec, T. D. (1978). Self-efficacy: Cause or reflection of behavioral change? *Advances in Behaviour Research and Therapy, 1,* 163–170.

Borkovec, T. D. (1983). The evaluative CR, cognitions and the role of awareness. *Advances in Behaviour Research and Therapy, 4,* 197–199.

Bower, G. H. (1987). Commentary on mood and memory. *Behaviour Research and Therapy, 25,* 443–455.

Bowlby, J. (1977). The making and breaking of affectional bonds: Etiology and psychopathology in the light of attachment theory. *British Journal of Psychiatry, 130,* 201–210.

Boyd, J. H., & Weissman, M. M. (1982). Epidemiology. In E. Paykel (Ed.), *Handbook of affective disorders* (pp. 109–125). New York: Guilford.

Bridgman, P. W. (1936). *The nature of physical theory.* Princeton: Princeton University Press.

Brogden, W. J. (1947). Sensory pre-conditioning of human subjects. *Journal of Experimental Psychology, 37,* 527–539.

Brown, L., Nietupski, J., & Hamre-Nietupski, S. (1976). The criterion of ultimate functioning and public school services for the severely handicapped student. In M. A. Thomas (Ed.), *Hey, don't forget about me: Education's investment in the severely, profoundly, and multiply handicapped* (pp. 2–15). Reston, VA: Council for Exceptional Children.

Brown, M. (1982). Maintenance and generalization issues in skills training with chronic schizophrenics. In J. P. Curran & P. M. Monti (Eds.), *Social skills training: A practical handbook for assessment and treatment* (pp. 230–246). New York: Guilford.

Brown, R. (1973). *A first language.* Cambridge, MA: Harvard University Press.

Buium, N., Rynders, J., & Turnure, J. (1974). Early maternal linguistic environment of normal and Down syndrome language-learning children. *American Journal of Mental Deficiency, 79*, 52–58.

Burgess, I. S., Jones, L. M., Robertson, S. A., Radcliffe, W. N., & Emerson, E. (1981). The degree of control exerted by phobic and non-phobic verbal stimuli over the recognition behaviour of phobic and non-phobic subjects. *Behaviour Research and Therapy, 19*, 233–243.

Burns, G. L. (1980). Indirect measurement and behavioral assessment: A case for social behaviorism psychometrics. *Behavioral Assessment, 2*, 197–206.

Burns, G. L. (1988). Radical and paradigmatic behaviorism: Alternative theory construction methodologies. *Behavior Analysis, 23*, 66–72.

Burns, G. L., & Farina, A. (1987). Physical attractiveness and self-perception of mental disorder. *Journal of Abnormal Psychology, 96*, 161–163.

Buss, A. R. (1977). The trait-situation controversy and the concept of interaction. *Personality and Social Psychology Bulletin, 3*, 196–201.

Camp, B. W. (1977). Verbal mediation in young aggressive boys. *Journal of Abnormal Psychology, 86*, 145–153.

Cardoso-Martins, C., & Mervis, C. B. (1985). Maternal speech to prelinguistic children with Down syndrome. *American Journal of Mental Deficiency, 89*, 451–458.

Carlson, C. G. (1971). Extinction of conditioned meaning (Doctoral dissertation, University of Hawaii, 1970). *Dissertation Abstracts International, 31*, 6922B.

Carney, M. W., & Sheffield, B. F. (1972). Depression and the Newcastle scales: Their relationship to Hamilton's scale. *British Journal of Psychiatry, 121*, 35–40.

Carroll, B. J. (1982). Use of the dexamethasone suppression test in depression. *Journal of Clinical Psychiatry, 43*, 44–48.

Carver, C. S. (1979). A cybernetic model of self-attention processes. *Journal of Personality and Social Psychology, 37*, 1251–1281.

Carver, C. S., & Scheier, M. F. (1982). An information-processing perspective on self-management. In P. Karoly & F. H. Kanfer (Eds.), *Self-management and behavior change: From theory to practice*. New York: Pergamon.

Cautela, J. (1967). Covert sensitization. *Psychological Reports, 20*, 459–468.

Cautela, J. (1973). Covert processes and behavior modification. *Journal of Nervous and Mental Disease, 157*, 27–36.

Cautela, J. R., & Kastenbaum, R. (1967). A Reinforcement Survey Schedule for use in therapy, training and research. *Psychological Reports, 20*, 1115–1130.

Chafe, W. (1970). *Meaning and the structure of language*. Chicago: University of Chicago Press.

Chomsky, N. (1965). *Aspects of a theory of syntax*. Englewood Cliffs, NJ: Prentice-Hall.

Chomsky, N. (1980). *Rules and representations*. New York: Columbia University Press.

Clark, D. M., & Teasdale, J. D. (1985). Constraints on the effects of mood on memory. *Journal of Personality and Social Psychology, 48,* 1595–1608.

Cofer, C. N., & Foley, J. P. (1942). Mediated generalization and the interpretation of verbal behavior: I. Prolegomena. *Psychological Review, 49,* 513–540.

Collette, M. A. (1979). Dyslexia and classic pathognomic signs. *Perceptual and Motor Skills, 48,* 1055–1062.

Collette-Harris, M. A., & Minke, K. A. (1978). A behavioral experimental analysis of dyslexia. *Behaviour Research and Therapy, 16,* 291–295.

Coyne, J. C. (1982). A critique of cognitions as causal entities with particular reference to depression. *Cognitive Therapy and Research, 6,* 3–13.

Coyne, J. C., Aldwin, C., & Lazarus, R. S. (1981). Depression and coping in stressful episodes. *Journal of Abnormal Psychology, 90,* 439–447.

Coyne, J. C., & Gotlib, I. H. (1983). The role of cognition in depression: A critical appraisal. *Psychological Bulletin, 94,* 472–505.

Craighead, L. W., & Craighead, W. E. (1980). Implications of persuasive communication research for the modification of self-statements. *Cognitive Therapy and Research, 4,* 117–134.

Craighead, W. E. (1980). Away from a unitary model of depression. *Behavior Therapy, 11,* 122–128.

Craighead, W. E., Meyers, A. W., Wilcoxon-Craighead, L., & McHale, S. M. (1983). Issues in cognitive-behavior therapy with children. In M. Rosenbaum, C. M. Franks, & Y. Jaffe (Eds.), *Perspectives on behavior therapy in the Eighties* (pp. 234–261). New York: Springer.

Critchley, M. (1970). *The dyslexic child.* London: Redwood.

Cross, T., Morris, J., & Nienhuys, T. (1980). *Linguistic feedback and maternal speech: Comparisons of mothers addressing hearing-impaired children.* Unpublished manuscript, University of Melbourne, Victoria, Australia.

Crossley, R., & McDonald, A. (1980). *Anne's coming out.* London: Penguin Books.

Danaher, B. G., & Thoresen, C. E. (1972). Imagery assessment by self-report and behavioral measures. *Behaviour Research and Therapy, 10,* 131–138.

Davison, G. C. (1969). Appraisal of behavior modification techniques with adults in institutional settings. In C. M. Franks (Ed.), *Behavior therapy: Appraisal and status* (pp. 220–278). New York: McGraw-Hill.

Delprato, D. J. (1980). Hereditary determinants of fear and phobias: A critical review. *Behavior Therapy, 11,* 79–103.

DeMonbreun, B. G., & Craighead, W. E. (1977). Distortion of perception and recall of positive and neutral feedback in depression. *Cognitive Therapy and Research, 1,* 311–329.

Depue, R. A., & Monroe, S. N. (1978). The unipolar-bipolar distinction in the depressive disorders. *Psychological Bulletin, 85,* 1001–1029.

Dollard, J., Doob, L. W., Miller, N. E., Mowrer, O. H., & Sears, R. R. (1939). *Frustration and aggression.* New Haven, CT: Yale University Press.

Dollard, J., & Miller, N. (1950). *Personality and psychotherapy.* New York: McGraw-Hill.

Donnellan, A. M., Mirenda, P. L., Mesaros, R. A., & Fassbender, L. L. (1984). Analyzing the communicative functions of aberrant behavior. *Journal of the Association for Persons with Severe Handicaps, 9,* 201–212.

Donnelly, E. F. (1976). Cross-sectional and longitudinal comparisons of bipolar and unipolar depressed groups on the MMPI. *Journal of Consulting and Clinical Psychology, 44,* 233–237.

Dunner, D. L., Goodwin, F. K., Gershon, E. S., Murphy, D. L., & Bunney, W. E. (1972). Excretion of 17–OHCS in unipolar and bipolar depressed patients, *Archives of General Psychiatry, 26,* 360–363.

Durand, V. M., & Carr, E. G. (1985). Self-injurious behavior: Motivating conditions and guidelines for treatment. *School Psychology Review, 14,* 171–176.

Dush, D. M., Hirt, M. L., & Schroeder, H. (1983). Self-statement modification with adults: A meta-analysis. *Psychological Bulletin, 94,* 408–422.

Eastman, C., & Marzillier, J. S. (1984). Theoretical and methodological difficulties in Bandura's self-efficacy theory. *Cognitive Therapy and Reseach, 8,* 213–229.

Eaves, L., Eysenck, H. J., & Martin, N. (1989). *Genes, culture and personality.* New York: Academic Press.

Egolf, D., Shames, G., Johnson, P., & Kaspisin-Burelli, A. (1972). The use of parent-child interaction patterns in therapy for young stutterers. *Journal of Speech and Hearing Disorders, 2,* 222–232.

Eifert, G. H., (1984a). Cognitive behaviour therapy: A critical evaluation of its theoretical-empirical bases and therapeutic efficacy. *Australian Psychologist, 19,* 179–191.

Eifert, G. H. (1984b). The effects of language conditioning on various aspects of anxiety. *Behaviour Research and Therapy, 22,* 13–22.

Eifert, G. H. (1985). Bridging the gap between conditioning theory and cognitive psychology to integrate "traditional" and "cognitive" behavior therapy. *The Cognitive Behaviorist, 7,* 2–8.

Eifert, G. H. (1987). Language conditioning: Clinical issues and applications in behavior therapy. In H. J. Eysenck & I. M. Martin (Eds.) *Theoretical foundations of behavior therapy.* (pp. 167–193). New York: Plenum.

Eifert, G. H., Craill, L., Carey, E., & O'Connor, C. (1988). Affect modification through evaluative conditioning with music. *Behaviour Research and Therapy, 26,* 321–330.

Eifert, G. H., & Craill, L. (1989). The relationship of affect, behaviour, and cognition in behavioural and cognitive treatment of depression and phobic anxiety. *Behaviour Change, 6,* 96–103.

Eifert, G. H., & Lauterbach, W. (1987). Relationships between overt behavior to a fear stimulus and self-verbalizations measured by different assessment strategies. *Cognitive Therapy and Research, 11,* 169–183.

Eifert, G. H., & Schermelleh, K. (1985). Language conditioning, emotional instructions, and cognitions in conditioned responses to fear-relevant and fear-irrelevant stimuli. *Journal of Behavior Therapy and Experimental Psychiatry, 16,* 101–110.

Ellis, A. (1962). *Reason and emotion in psychotherapy.* New York: Lyle Stuart.

Ellis, A. (1979). A note on the treatment of agoraphobics with cognitive modification versus prolonged exposure in vivo. *Behaviour Research and Therapy, 17,* 162–164.

Ellis, A. (1983). The philosophic implications and dangers of some popular behavior therapy techniques. In M. Rosenbaum, C. M. Franks, & Y. Jaffe (Eds.), *Perspectives on behavior therapy in the eighties* (pp. 138–151). New York: Springer.

Emery, R. E., Binkoff, J. A., Houts, A. C., & Carr, E. G. (1983). Children as independent variables: Some clinical implications of child-effects. *Behavior Therapy, 14,* 398–412.

Engelmann, S. (1983). Piaget et la didattica: Promessa o delusione? *Psicologia e Scuola, 16,* 6–12.

Ervin-Tripp, S. (1964). Imitation and structural change in children's language. In E. Lenneberg (Ed.), *Directions in the study of language.* Cambridge, MA: Massachusetts Institute of Technology Press.

Erwin, E. (1978). *Behavior therapy: Scientific, philosophical, and moral foundations.* New York: Cambridge University Press.

Etzioni, E. (1964). *Modern organization.* Englewood Cliffs, NJ: Prentice-Hall.

Evans, I. M. (1976). Classical conditioning. In M. P. Feldman & A. Broadhurst (Eds.), *Theoretical and experimental bases of the behaviour therapies* (pp. 73–112). London: Wiley.

Evans, I. M. (1985). Building systems models as a strategy for target behavior selection in clinical assessment. *Behavioral Assessment, 7,* 21–32.

Evans, I. M. (1986). Response structures and the triple response mode concept in behavioral assessment. In R. O. Nelson & S. C. Hayes (Eds.), *Conceptual foundations of behavioral assessment* (pp. 131–155). New York: Guilford.

Evans, I. M. (1989). A multi-dimensional model for conceptualizing the design of child behavior therapy. *Behavioural Psychotherapy, 17,* 237–251.

Evans, I. M. (in press). Teaching personnel to use state-of-the-art nonaversive alternatives for dealing with problem behavior. In A. P. Kaiser & C. McWhorter (Eds.), *Preparing personnel to work with persons who are severely handicapped.* Baltimore, MD: Paul H. Brookes.

Evans, I. M., Brown, F. A., Weed, K. A., Spry, K. M., & Owen, V. (1987). The assessment of functional competencies: A behavioral approach to the evaluation of programs for children with disabilities. In R. J. Prinz (Ed.), *Advances in behavioral assessment of children and families* (Vol. 3, pp. 195–239). Greenwich, CT: JAI Press.

Evans, I. M., & Litz, B. T. (1987). Behavioral assessment: A new theoretical foundation for clinical measurement and evaluation. In H. J. Eysenck & I. M. Martin (Eds.), *Theoretical foundations of behavior therapy* (pp. 331–351). New York: Plenum.

Evans, I. M., & Meyer, L. H. (1985). *An educative approach to behavior problems: A practical decision model for intervention with severely handicapped learners.* Baltimore, MD: Paul H. Brookes.

Evans, I. M., Meyer, L. M., Kurkjian, J. A., & Kishi, G. S. (1988). An evaluation of behavioral interrelationships in child behavior therapy. In J. C. Witt, S. N. Elliott, & F. N. Gresham (Eds.), *Handbook of behavior therapy in education* (pp. 189–215). New York: Plenum.

Evans, I. M., & Scheuer, A. D. (1987). Analyzing response relationships in childhood aggression: The clinical perspective. In D. C. Crowell, I. M. Evans, & C. R. O'Donnell (Eds.), *Childhood aggression and violence: Sources of influence, prevention and control* (pp. 75–94). New York: Plenum.

Evans, I. M., & Scotti, J. R. (1989). Defining meaningful outcomes for persons with profound disabilities. In F. Brown & D. Lehr (Eds.), *Persons with profound disabilities: Issues and practices* (pp. 83–107). Baltimore, MD: Paul H. Brookes.

Evans, I. M., & Weiss, A. R. (1978). Process studies in language conditioning: II. The role of semantic relevance in conditioning negative emotional responses. *Journal of Behavior Therapy and Experimental Psychiatry, 9,* 121–124.

Evans, I. M., & Weld, E. M. (1989). Evaluating special education programs: Process and outcome. In D. Biklen, D. Ferguson, & A. Ford (Eds.), *Schooling and disability* (pp. 232–255). Chicago: University of Chicago Press.

Evans, I. M., & Wilson, F. E. (1983). Behavioral assessment as decision making: A theoretical analysis. In M. Rosenbaum, C. M. Franks, & Y. Jaffe (Eds.), *Perspectives on behavior therapy in the eighties* (pp. 35–53). New York: Springer.

Eyberg, S. M. (1980). Eyberg Child Behavior Inventory. *Journal of Clinical Child Psychology, 9,* 27.

Eyberg, S. M., & Matarazzo, R. G. (1980). Training parents as therapists: A comparison between individual parent-child interaction training and parent group didactic training. *Journal of Clinical Psychology, 36,* 492–499.

Eyberg, S. M., & Robinson, E. A. (1982). Parent-child interaction training: Effects on family functioning. *Journal of Clinical Child Psychology, 11,* 130–137.

Eysenck, H. J. (1959). Learning theory and behaviour therapy. *Journal of Mental Science, 105,* 61–75.

Eysenck, H. J. (1960). *Behavior therapy and the neuroses.* London: Pergamon.

Eysenck, H. J. (1967). *The biological basis of personality.* Springfield, IL: Charles C. Thomas.

Eysenck, H. J. (1970). The classification of depressive illnesses. *British Journal of Psychiatry, 117,* 241–250.

Eysenck, H. J. (1976). Behavior therapy: Dogma or applied science? In M. P. Feldman & A. Broadhurst (Eds.), *Theoretical and experimental basis of behaviour therapy* (pp. 333–363). London: Wiley.

Eysenck, H. J. (1981). *A model for personality.* New York: Springer.

Eysenck, H. J. (1982). Neobehavioristic (S-R) theory. In G. T. Wilson & C. M. Franks (Eds.), *Contemporary behavior therapy: Conceptual and empirical foundations* (pp. 205–276). New York: Guilford.

Eysenck, H. J. (1987). The role of heredity, environment, and "preparedness" in the genesis of neurosis. In H. J. Eysenck & I. M. Martin (Eds.), *Theoretical foundations of behavior therapy* (pp. 379–402). New York: Plenum.

Eysenck, H. J., & Rachman, S. (1965). *The causes and cures of neurosis.* London: Routledge & Kegan Paul.

Falvey, M. A. (1986). *Community-based curriculum: Instructional strategies for students with severe handicaps.* Baltimore, MD: Paul H. Brookes.

Farina, A., Burns, G. L., Austad, C., Bugglin, C. S., & Fischer, E. H. (1986). The role of physical attractiveness in the community readjustment of psychiatric patients. *Journal of Abnormal Psychology, 95,* 139–143.

Farina, A., Fischer, E. H., Sherman, S., Smith, W. T., Groh, T., & Mermin, P. (1977). Physical attractiveness and mental illness. *Journal of Abnormal Psychology, 86,* 510–517.

Fay, W. H., & Schuler, A. L. (1980). *Emerging language in autistic children.* Baltimore, MD: University Park Press.

Ferster, C. B. (1973). A functional analysis of depression. *American Psychologist, 28,* 857–870.

Ferster, C. B., & DeMyer, M. K. (1962). A method for the experimental analysis of the behavior of autistic children. *American Journal of Orthopsychiatry, 32,* 89–98.

Finch, G. (1938). Hunger as a determinant of conditional and unconditional salivary response magnitude. *American Journal of Physiology, 123,* 379–382.

Finley, J. R., & Staats, A. W. (1967). Evaluative meaning words as reinforcing stimuli. *Journal of Verbal Learning and Verbal Behavior, 6,* 193–197.

Fishman, D. B., Rotgers, F., & Franks, C. M. (Eds.). (1988). *Paradigms in behavior therapy: Present and promise.* New York: Springer.

Forehand, R., & McCombs, A. (1988). Unraveling the antecedent-consequence conditions in maternal depression and adolescent functioning. *Behaviour Research and Therapy, 26,* 399–405.

Foreyt, J. P. (1987). Behavioral medicine. In G. T. Wilson, C. M. Franks, P. C. Kendall, & J. P. Foreyt (Eds.) *Review of behavior therapy* (Vol. 11, pp. 154–186). New York: Guilford.

Fraley, L. E., & Vargas, E. A. (1986). Separate disciplines: The study of behavior and the study of the psyche. *The Behavior Analyst, 9,* 47–59.

Franks, C. M. (Ed.). (1969). *Behavior therapy: Appraisal and status.* New York: McGraw-Hill.

Franks, C. M. (Ed). (1983). Review of [Industrial Behavior Modification and Organizational Behavior Management.] *Child & Family Behavior Therapy, 5,* 68–70.

Franks, C. M. (1987). Behavior therapy: An overview. In G. T. Wilson, C. M. Franks, P. C. Kendall, & J. P. Foreyt (Eds.), *Review of behavior therapy* (Vol. 11, pp. 1–39). New York: Guilford.

Franks, C. M. (1988). Unifying psychology with special reference to clinical psychology. *International Newsletter of Uninomic Psychology, 5,* 25–27.

Fraser, D., McLeod, W. L., Begg, J. C., Hawthorne, J. H., & Davis, P. (1976). Against the odds: The results of a token economy program with long-term psychiatric patients. *International Journal of Nursing Studies, 13,* 55–63.

Freedman, A. M., Kaplan, H. I., & Sadock, B. J. (1976). *Modern synopsis of comprehensive textbook of psychiatry/II.* Baltimore, MD: Williams & Wilkins.

Freud, S. (1933). *The complete introductory lectures on psychoanalysis.* New York: Norton.

Fulker, D. W. (1981). The genetic and environmental architecture of psychoticism, extraversion and neuroticism. In H. J. Eysenck (Ed.), *A model for personality.* New York: Springer.

Fullerton, D. T., Cavner, J. J., & McLaughlin-Reidel, T. (1978). Results of a token economy. *Archives of General Psychiatry, 35,* 1451–1453.

Furrow, D., Nelson, K., & Benedict, H. (1979). Mother's speech to children and syntactic development: Some simple relationships. *Journal of Child Language, 2,* 423–442.

Gelfand, D. M., & Hartmann, D. P. (1968). *Child behavior analysis and therapy.* New York: Pergamon.

Gelfand, D. M., & Peterson, L. (1985). *Child development and psychopathology.* Beverly Hills, CA: Sage.

Gershon, E. S., Bunney, W. E., Neckman, J. F., Van Erdewegh, M., & DeBauche, B. A. (1976). The inheritance of affective disorders: A review of data and hypotheses. *Behavior Genetics, 6,* 227–261.

Goffman, E. (1963). *Stigma.* New York: Doubleday.

Goldfried, M. R. (1980). Psychotherapy as coping skills training. In M. J. Mahoney (Ed.), *Psychotherapy process: Current issues and future directions* (pp. 89–119). New York: Plenum.

Goldfried, M. R., & Davison, G. C. (1976). *Clinical behavior therapy.* New York: Holt, Rinehart & Winston.

Goldfried, M. R., & Merbaum, M. (1973). A perspective on self-control. In M. R. Goldfried & Merbaum (Eds.), *Behavior change through self-control* (pp. 3–34). New York: Holt, Rinehart & Winston.

Goldfried, M. R., & Sprafkin, J. (1974). *Behavioral personality assessment.* Morristown, NJ: General Learning Press.

Golin, S., Terrell, F., & Johnson, B. (1977). Depression and the illusion of control. *Journal of Abnormal Psychology, 86,* 440–442.

Golin, S., Terrell, F., Weitz, J., & Drost, P. L. (1979). The illusion of control among depressed patients. *Journal of Abnormal Psychology, 88,* 454–457.

Gotlib, I. H. (1981). Self-reinforcement and recall: Differential deficits in depressed and nondepressed psychiatric inpatients. *Journal of Abnormal Psychology, 90,* 521–530.

Gotlib, I. H. (1982). Self-reinforcement and depression in interpersonal interaction: The role of performance level. *Journal of Abnormal Psychology, 91,* 3–13.

Gray, B. B., & England, G. (Eds.). (1969). *Stuttering and the conditioning therapies.* Monterey, CA: The Monterey Institute for Speech and Hearing.

Grayson, J. B., & Borkovec, T. D. (1978). The effects of expectancy and imagined response to phobic stimuli on fear reduction, *Cognitive Therapy and Research, 2,* 11–24.

Greenberg, D. J., Scott, S. B., Pisa, A., & Friesen, D. D. (1975). Beyond the token economy: A comparison of two contingency programs. *Journal of Consulting and Clinical Psychology, 43,* 498–503.

Griest, D. L., Forehand, R., Wells, K. C., & McMahon, R. J. (1980). An examination of differences between nonclinic and behavior-problem clinic-referred children and their mothers. *Journal of Abnormal Psychology, 89,* 497–500.

Grimm, L. G. (1980). The evidence for cue-controlled relaxation. *Behavior Therapy, 11,* 283–293.

Gripp, R. F., & Magaro, P. A. (1971) A token economy program evaluation with untreated control ward comparisons. *Behaviour Research and Therapy, 9,* 137–149.

Grunberg, F. (1976). Les grandes contestations juridiques de l'antipsychiatrie aux Etats-Unis. *L'union medicale du Canada, 105,* 935–941.

Guay, P. F. (1971). *The effect of the attitudinal value of social stimulus on imitation and sociometric choice: A test of the A-R-D theory.* (Tech. Rep. No. 11), Honolulu: University of Hawaii, Department of Psychology.

Guess, D., Sailor, W., Rutherford, G., & Baer, D. M. (1968). An experimental analysis of linguistic development: The productive use of morphemes. *Journal of Applied Behavior Analysis, 1,* 297–306.

Guralnick, M. (Ed.). (1978). *Early intervention and the integration of handicapped and nonhandicapped children.* Baltimore, MD: University Park Press.

Gurman, A. S. (1973). Treatment of a case of public speaking anxiety by in vivo desensitization and cue-controlled relaxation. *Journal of Behavior Therapy and Experimental Psychiatry, 4,* 51–54.

Gutmann, A., & Rondal, J. A. (1979). Verbal operants in mothers' speech to nonretarded and Down's syndrome children matched for linguistic level. *American Journal of Mental Deficiency, 83,* 446–452.

Hamberger, L. K., & Lohr, J. M. (1980). Relationship of relaxation training to the controllability of imagery. *Perceptual and Motor Skills, 51*, 103–110.

Hamilton, S. A. (1988). Behavioral formulation of verbal behavior in psychotherapy. *Clinical Psychology Review, 8*, 181–194.

Hammen, C. L., & Cochran, S. E. (1981). Cognitive correlates of life stress and depression in college students. *Journal of Abnormal Psychology, 90*, 23–27.

Hammen, C. L., & DeMayo, R. (1982). Cognitive correlates of teacher stress and depressive symptoms: Implications for attributional models of depression. *Journal of Abnormal Psychology, 91*, 96–101.

Hammen, C. L., & Glass, D. (1975). Depression, activity, and evaluation of reinforcement. *Journal of Abnormal Psychology, 84*, 718–721.

Harms, J. Y., & Staats, A. W. (1978). Food deprivation and conditioned reinforcing value of food words: Interaction of Pavlovian and instrumental conditioning. *Bulletin of the Psychonomic Society, 12*, 294–296.

Harter, S. (1983). Developmental perspectives on the self-system. In P. H. Mussen (Ed.). *Handbook of child psychology* (pp. 275–385). New York: Wiley.

Hartmann, D. P., Roper, B. L., & Bradford, DC (1979). Some relationships between behavioral and traditional assessment. *Journal of Behavioral Assessment, 1*, 3–21.

Haughton, E., & Ayllon, T. (1965). Production and elimination of symptomatic behavior. In L. P. Ullmann & L. Krasner (Eds.), *Case studies in behavior modification* (pp. 94–98). New York: Holt, Rinehart & Winston.

Heap, R. F., Boblitt, W. E., Moore, C. H., & Hord, J. E. (1970). Behavior-milieu therapy with chronic neuropsychiatric patients. *Journal of Abnormal Psychology, 76*, 349–354.

Heiby, E. M. (1979). Conditions which occasion depression: A review of three behavioral models. *Psychological Reports, 45*, 683–714.

Heiby, E. M. (1982). A self-reinforcement questionnaire. *Behaviour Research and Therapy, 20*, 397–401.

Heiby, E. M. (1983a). Assessment of frequency of self-reinforcement. *Journal of Personality and Social Psychology, 44*, 1304–1307.

Heiby, E. M. (1983b). Depression as a function of the interaction of self- and environmentally controlled reinforcement. *Behavior Therapy, 14*, 430–433.

Heiby, E. M. (1983c). Toward the prediction of mood change. *Behavior Therapy, 14*, 110–115.

Heiby, E. M. (1986). Social versus self-control deficits in four cases of depression. *Behavior Therapy, 17*, 158–163.

Heiby, E. M. (1989). Multiple skill deficits in depression. *Behaviour Change, 6*, 76–84.

Heiby, E. M., Campos, P. E., Remick, R. A., & Keller, F. D. (1987). Dexamethasone suppression and self-reinforcement correlates of clinical depression. *Journal of Abnormal Psychology, 96,* 70–72.

Hekmat, H. (1971a). Extraversion, neuroticism, and verbal conditioning of affective self-disclosures. *Journal of Counseling Psychology, 18,* 25–31.

Hekmat, H. (1971b). Reinforcing values of interpretations and reflections in a quasi-therapeutic interview. *Journal of Abnormal Psychology, 77,* 25–31.

Hekmat, H. (1972). The role of imagination in semantic desensitization. *Behavior Therapy, 3,* 223–231.

Hekmat, H. (1974). Three techniques for reinforcement modification: A comparison. *Behavior Therapy, 5,* 541–548.

Hekmat, H. (1977). Semantic behavior therapy: Unidimensional or multidimensional. *Behavior Therapy, 8,* 805–809.

Hekmat, H., Deal, R., & Lubitz, R. (1985). Instructional desensitization: A semantic behavior treatment of anxiety disorder. *Psychotherapy: Theory, Research and Practice, 22,* 273–280.

Hekmat, H., Khajavi, F., & Mehryar, A. (1974). Psychoticism, neuroticism, and extraversion: The personality determinants of empathy. *Journal of Clinical Psychology, 30,* 559–561.

Hekmat, H., Khajavi, F., & Mehryar, A. (1975). Some personality correlates of empathy. *Journal of Consulting and Clinical Psychology, 43,* 89.

Hekmat, H., & Lee, Y. B. (1970). Conditioning of affective self-references as a function of semantic meaning of verbal reinforcers. *Journal of Abnormal Psychology, 76,* 427–433.

Hekmat, H., Lubitz, R., & Deal, R. (1984). Semantic desensitization: A paradigmatic intervention approach to anxiety disorders. *Journal of Clinical Psychology, 40,* 463–466.

Hekmat, H., & Sage, R. (1981). Semantic densensitization treatment of insomnia. *International Newsletter of Social Behaviorism, 1,* 20–24.

Hekmat, H., & Theiss, M. (1971). Self-actualization and modification of affective self-disclosures during a social conditioning interview. *Journal of Counseling Psychology, 18,* 101–105.

Hekmat, H., & Vanian, D. (1971). Behavior modification through covert semantic desensitization. *Journal of Consulting and Clinical Psychology, 36,* 248–251.

Hewett, F. M. (1965). Teaching speech to an autistic child through operant conditioning. *American Journal of Orthopsychiatry, 35,* 927–936.

Hilgard, E. R. (1948). *Theories of learning.* New York: Appleton-Century-Crofts.

Hiroto, D. S., & Seligman, M. E. P. (1975). Generality of learned helplessness in man. *Journal of Personality and Social Psychology, 31,* 311–327.

Hirshfield, R. M., & Cross, C. K. (1982). Epidemiology of affective disorders. *Archives of General Psychiatry, 39,* 35–46.

Hoehn-Hyde, D., Schlottman, R. S., & Rush, A. J. (1982). Perception of social interactions in depressed psychiatry patients. *Journal of Consulting and Clinical Psychology, 50,* 209–212.

Horner, R. H., Meyer, L. M., Fredericks, H. D. (1986). *Education of learners with severe handicaps: Exemplary service strategies.* Baltimore, MD: Paul H. Brookes.

Horton, L. E. (1970). Generalization of aggressive behavior in adolescent delinquent boys. *Journal of Applied Behavior Analysis, 3,* 205–211.

Hugdahl, K. (1981). A three-systems-model of fear and emotion: A critical analysis. *Behaviour Research and Therapy, 19,* 75–85.

Hull, C. L. (1943). *Principles of behavior.* New York: Appleton-Century.

Hull, C. L. (1952). *A behavior system.* New Haven, CT: Yale University Press.

Huttenlocher, J., & Higgins, E. T. (1971). Adjectives, comparatives, and syllogisms. *Psychological Review, 78,* 487–504.

Hymes, D. (1974). *Foundations in sociolinguistics.* Philadelphia: University of Pennsylvania Press.

Ikenaga, C. S. (1982). *A latency analysis of linear syllogistic reasoning.* Unpublished master's thesis, University of Hawaii, Honolulu.

Insel, P. M., & Moos, R. H. (1974). Psychological environments: Expanding the scope of human ecology. *American Psychologist, 29,* 179–188.

Israel, A. C. (1978). Some thoughts on correspondence between saying and doing. *Journal of Applied Behavior Analysis, 11,* 271–276.

Izard, C., Kagan, J., & Zajonc, R. (Eds.). (1984). *Emotion, cognition, and behavior.* Cambridge, England: Cambridge University Press.

Jackson, B. (1972). Treatment of depression by self-reinforcement. *Behavior Therapy, 3,* 298–307.

Jackson, D. N., & Paunonen, S. V. (1980). Personality structure and assessment. *Annual Review of Psychology, 31,* 503–551.

Jeffrey, C. R. (1972). *Crime prevention through environmental design.* Beverly Hills, CA: Sage.

Jenkins, H. M., & Ward, W. C. (1965). Judgment of contingency between responses and outcomes. *Psychological Monographs: General and Applied, 79,* (1, Whole No. 594).

Jenkins, J., & Palermo, D. (1964). Mediation processes and the acquisition of linguistic structure. *Monographs of the Society for Research in Child Development, 29,* (Whole No. 92).

Jensen, A. R. (1980). *Bias in mental testing.* New York: Free Press.

Johnston, J. M., & Pennypacker, H. S. (1971). A behavioral approach to college teaching. *American Psychologist, 26,* 219–244.

Jones, M. C. (1924) The elimination of children's fears. *Journal of Experimental Psychology, 7,* 382–390.

Kanfer, F. H., & Gaelick, L. (1986). Self-management methods. In F. H. Kanfer & A. P. Goldstein (Eds.), *Helping people change* (3rd ed., pp 238–245). New York: Pergamon.

Kanfer, F. H., & Hagerman, S. M. (1985). Behavior therapy and the information processing paradigm. In S. Reiss & R. R. Bootzin (Eds.), *Theo-*

retical issues in behavior therapy (pp. 3–33). New York: Academic Press.

Kanfer, F. H., Karoly, P., & Newman, A. (1975). Reduction of children's fear of the dark by competence-related and situational threat-related verbal cues. *Journal of Consulting and Clinical Psychology, 43,* 251–258.

Kanfer, F. H., & Saslow, G. (1969). Behavioral diagnosis. In C. M. Franks (Ed.), *Behavior therapy: Appraisal and status* (pp. 417–444). New York: McGraw-Hill.

Kanfer, R., & Zeiss, A. M. (1983). Depression, interpersonal standard setting, and judgments of self-efficacy. *Journal of Abnormal Psychology, 92,* 319–329.

Karoly, P., & Dirks, M. J. (1977). Developing self-control in preschool children through correspondence training. *Behavior Therapy, 8,* 398–405.

Kazdin, A. E. (1977a). Assessing the clinical or applied importance of behavior change through social validation. *Behavior Modification, 1,* 427–452.

Kazdin, A. E. (1977b). *The token economy.* New York: Plenum.

Kazdin, A. E. (1978). Conceptual and assessment issues raised by self-efficacy theory. *Advances in Behaviour Research and Therapy, 1,* 177–185.

Kazdin, A. E. (1980). Acceptability of alternative treatments for deviant child behavior. *Journal of Applied Behavior Analysis, 13,* 259–273.

Kazdin, A. E. (1982). The token economy: A decade later. *Journal of Applied Behavior Analysis, 15,* 431–445.

Keller, F. S. (1974). Ten years of personalized instruction. *Teaching of Psychology, 1,* 4–9.

Kelley, M. J. (1987). Hormones and clinical anxiety: An imbalanced neuromodulation of attention. In H. J. Eysenck & I. M. Martin (Eds.), *Theoretical foundations of behavior therapy* (pp. 403–432). New York: Plenum.

Kendall, P. C. (1981). Cognitive interventions with children. In B. B. Lahey & A. E. Kazdin (Eds.), *Advances in Clinical Child Psychology,* (Vol. 4, pp. 53–85). New York: Plenum

Kendall, P. C. (1984). Cognitive processes and procedures. In G. T. Wilson, C. M. Franks, K. D. Brownell, & P. C. Kendall (Eds.), *Annual Review of Behavior Therapy,* (Vol.8, pp. 120–155). New York: Guilford.

Kendall, P. C., & Braswell, L. (1985). *Cognitive-behavioral therapy for impulsive children.* New York: Guilford.

Kendall, P. C., & Hollon, S. D. (Eds.) (1981). *Assessment strategies for cognitive-behavioral interventions.* New York: Academic Press.

Kendell, R. E. (1968). *The classification of depressive illnesses.* London: Oxford University Press.

Kenrick, D. T., & Braver, S. L. (1982). Personality: Idiographic and nomothetic: A rejoinder. *Psychological Review, 89,* 182–186.

Kirchner, E. P. (1970). The vividness of connotative adjectives and their paired-associate learning. *Psychonomic Science, 19,* 83–85.

Kirkland, K. (1978). Frequency of dependent measures in two non-behavioral journals. *The Behavior Therapist, 1*, 14.

Kleinknecht, R. (1982). The origins and remission of fear in a group of tarantula enthusiasts. *Behaviour Research and Therapy, 20*, 437–443.

Koch, S. (1981). The nature and limits of psychological knowledge: Lessons of a century qua "science." *American Psychologist, 36*, 257–269.

Kocsis, J. H., Frances, A. J., Voss, C., Mann, J. J., Mason, B. J., & Sweeney, J. (1988). Imipramine treatment for chronic depression. *Archives of General Psychiatry, 45*, 253–257.

Krantz, D. S., & Deckel, W. A. (1983). Coping with coronary heart disease and stroke. In T. G. Burish & L. A. Bradley (Eds.), *Coping with chronic disease: Research and applications* (pp. 85–112). New York: Academic Press.

Krauskopf, C. K. (1978). Comment on Endler and Magnusson's attempt to redefine personality. *Psychological Bulletin, 84*, 280–283.

Kruglanski, A. W. (1980). Lay epistemo-logic-process and contents. *Psychological Review, 87*, 70–87.

Kruglanski, A. W., & Klar, Y. (1985). Knowing what to do: On the epistemology of actions. In J. Kuhl & J. Beckman (Eds.). *Action control: From cognition to behavior*. New York: Springer-Verlag.

Kuhn, T. S. (1962). *The structure of scientific revolutions*. Chicago: University of Chicago Press.

Lakin, K. C., & Bruininks, R. H. (Eds.) (1985). *Strategies for achieving community integration of developmentally disabled citizens*. Baltimore, MD: Paul H. Brookes.

Landau, R. J., & Goldfried, M. R. (1981). The assessment of schemata: A unifying framework for cognitive, behavioral, and traditional assessment. In P. C. Kendall & S. D. Hollon (Eds.), *Assessment strategies for cognitive-behavioral interventions* (pp. 363–399). New York: Academic Press.

Lang, P. J. (1977). Imagery in therapy: An information processing analysis of fear. *Behavior Therapy, 8*, 862–886.

Lang, P. J. (1984). Cognition in emotion: Concept and action. In C. Izard, J. Kagan, & R. Zajonc, (Eds.), *Emotion, cognition, and behavior* (pp. 192–226). Cambridge, England: Cambridge University Press.

Lang, P. J., & Lazovik, A. D. (1963). Experimental desensitization of a phobia. *Journal of Abnormal and Social Psychology, 66*, 519–525.

Langer, E., Blank, A., & Chanowitz, R. (1978). The mindlessness of ostensibly thoughtful action: The role of placebic information in interpersonal interaction. *Journal of Personality and Social Psychology, 36*, 635–642.

Last, U., Giaor, M., Lowental, U., Klein, H., & Hebrew, U. (1978). A token economy in the framework of a hospital therapeutic community: Practice and psychosocial implications. *Mental Health and Society, 5*, 200–214.

Latimer, P. R., & Sweet, A. (1984). Cognitive vs. behavioral procedures in cognitive-behavior therapy: a critical review of the evidence. *Journal of Behavior Therapy and Experimental Psychiatry, 15*, 9–22.

Lauterbach, W. (1979). Learning plus: Towards a multifactorial theory of phobias. *Journal of Behavior Therapy and Experimental Psychiatry, 10*, 25–28.

LaVigna, G. W., & Donnellan, A. M. (1986). *Alternatives to punishment: Solving behavior problems with non-aversive strategies.* New York: Irvington.

Lazarus, A. A. (1971). *Behavior therapy and beyond.* New York: McGraw-Hill.

Lazarus, A. A., & Abramovitz, A. (1962). The use of "emotive imagery" in the treatment of children's phobias. *Journal of Mental Science, 108*, 191–195.

Lazarus, R. S. (1984). On the primacy of cognition. *American Psychologist, 39*, 124–129.

Lazarus, R. S., & Folkman, S. (1984). *Stress, appraisal, and coping.* New York: Springer.

Léduc, A. (1980). Les competences minima qu'un adulte doit avoir acquis pour etre autonome. *Apprentissage et Socialisation, 3*, 180–190.

Léduc, A. (1988). A paradigmatic behavioral approach to the treatment of a "wild" child. *Child & Family Behavior Therapy, 9*, 1–16.

Lefcourt, H. M. (1982). *Locus of control: Current trends in theory and research* (2nd ed.). Hillsdale, NJ: Erlbaum.

Leff, J., Roatch, J. F., & Bunney, W. E. (1970). Environmental factors preceding the onset of severe depression. *Psychiatry, 33*, 293–311.

Leff, J., & Vaughn, C. (1981). The role of maintenance therapy and relatives' expressed emotion in relapse of schizophrenia: A two-year follow-up study. *British Journal of Psychiatry, 139*, 102–104.

Lehman, A., & Ritzler, B. (1976). The therapeutic community inpatient ward: Does it really work? *Comprehensive Psychiatry, 17*, 755–761.

Leifer, J. S., & Lewis, M. (1984). Acquisition of conversational response skills by young Down syndrome and nonretarded young children. *American Journal of Mental Deficiency, 88*, 610–618.

Leonhard, K. (1979) [Untitled]. In R. Robins (Ed.), *The classification of endogenous psychoses* (R. Berman, Trans.). New York: Irvington.

Levesque, M., & Léduc, A. (1982). L'apprentissage du comportement anormal dans le cadre du behaviorisme social. *Apprentissage et Socialisation, 5*, 196–209.

Levey, A. B., & Martin, I. M. (1987). Evaluative conditioning: A case for hedoic transfer. In H. J. Eysenck & I. M. Martin (Eds.), *Theoretical foundations of behavior therapy* (pp. 113–131). New York: Plenum.

Levis, D. J., & Malloy, P. F. (1982). Research in infrahuman and human conditioning. In G. T. Wilson & C. M. Franks (Eds.), *Contemporary behavior therapy: Conceptual and empirical foundations* (pp. 65–118). New York: Guilford.

Lewinsohn, P. M. (1974). A behavioral approach to depression. In R. Friedman & M. Katz (Eds.), *The psychology of depression: Contemporary theory and research.* New York: Wiley.

Lewinsohn, P. M., & Libet, J. (1972). Pleasant events, activity schedules, and depressions. *Journal of Abnormal Psychology, 79,* 291–295.

Lewinsohn, P. M., & McPhillamy, D. (1974). The relationship between age and engagement in pleasant activities. *Journal of Gerontology, 41,* 258–261.

Lewinsohn, P. M., Mischel, W., Chaplin, W., Barton, R. (1980). Social competence and depression: The role of illusory self-perceptions. *Journal of Abnormal Psychology, 89,* 203–212.

Lewinsohn, P. M., Steinmetz, J., Larson, D., & Franklin, J. (1981). Depression related cognitions: Antecedent or consequence? *Journal of Abnormal Psychology, 90,* 213–219.

Lewinsohn, P. M., & Talkington, J. (1979). Studies on the measurement of unpleasant events and relations with depression. *Applied Psychological Measurement, 3,* 83–101.

Lewinsohn, P. M., Teri, L., & Hoberman, H., (1983). Depression: A perspective on etiology, treatment, and life span issues. In M. Rosenbaum, C. M. Franks, & Y. Jaffe (Eds.), *Perspectives on behavior therapy in the eighties* (pp. 155–183). New York: Springer.

Liberman, R. P. (1970). Behavioral approaches to family and couple therapy. *American Journal of Orthopsychiatry, 40,* 106–118.

Liberman, R. P., Nuechterlein, K. H., & Wallace, C. J. (1982). Social skills training and the nature of schizophrenia. In J. P. Curran & P. M. Monti (Eds.), *Social skills training: A practical handbook for assessment and treatment* (pp. 183–214). New York: Guilford.

Liberman, R. P., & Raskin, D. E. (1971). Depression: A behavioral formulation. *Archives of General Psychiatry, 24,* 525–533.

Libet, J., & Lewinsohn, P. M. (1973). Concept of social skill with special reference to the behavior of depressed persons. *Journal of Consulting and Clinical Psychology, 40,* 304–312.

Lindsley, O. R. (1956). Operant conditioning methods applied to research in chronic schizophrenia. *Psychiatric Research Reports, 5,* 140–153.

Lloyd, C. (1980). Life events and depressive disorders reviewed. *Archives of General Psychiatry, 37,* 529–535.

Lobitz, W. C., & Post, R. D. (1979). Parameters of self-reinforcement and depression. *Journal of Abnormal Psychology, 88,* 33–41.

Lohr, J. M. (1976). Concurrent conditioning of evaluative meaning and imagery. *British Journal of Psychology, 76,* 353–358.

Lohr, J. M., & Rookey, C. (1982, November). *The effect of relaxation training and level of fear upon controllability of fearful and neutral imagery.* Paper presented at the Sixteenth Annual Convention of the Association for Advancement of Behavior Therapy. Los Angeles, CA.

London, P. (1972). The end of ideology in behavior modification. *American Psychologist, 27,* 913–920.

Lovaas, O. I., Berberich, J. P., Perloff, B., & Schaeffer, B. (1966). Acquisition of imitative speech by schizophrenic children. *Science, 151,* 705–707.

Lumsdaine, A. A. (Ed.) (1961). *Student response in programmed instruction* (Publication 943) Washington, DC: National Research Council.

Luria, A. R. (1961). *The role of speech in the regulation of normal and abnormal behavior.* New York: Liveright.

MacDonald, J. D. (1982). Communication strategies for language intervention. In D. P. McClowry, A. M. Guilford, & S. O. Richardson (Eds.), *Infant communication: Development, assessment, and intervention.* (pp. 107–124). New York: Grune & Stratton.

Mackintosh, M. J. (1983). *Conditioning and associative learning.* Oxford, England: Oxford University Press.

MacMillan, D. L. (1972). Paired-associate learning as a function of explicitness of mediational set by EMR and non-retarded children. *American Journal of Mental Deficiency, 76,* 686–691.

Maestas y Moores, J. (1980). *A descriptive study of communication modes and pragmatic functions used by three prelinguistically, profoundly deaf mothers with their infants one to six months of age in their homes.* Unpublished doctoral dissertation, University of Minnesota, Minneapolis.

Magnusson, D., & Endler, N. S. (Eds.) (1977). *Personality at the cross-roads: Current issues in interactional psychology.* Hillsdale, NJ: Erlbaum.

Mahoney, M. J. (1977). Reflections on the cognitive learning trend in psychotherapy. *American Psychologist, 32,* 5–13.

Mahoney, M. J. (1982). Psychotherapy and human change processes. In J. H. Harvey & M. M. Parks (Eds.), *Psychotherapy research and human behavior change* (pp. 77–122). Washington, DC: American Psychological Association.

Maltzman, I., & Boyd, G. (1984). Stimulus significance and bilateral SCRs to potentially phobic pictures. *Journal of Abnormal Psychology, 93,* 41–46.

Manly, P. C., McMahon, R. J., Bradely, C. F., & Davidson, P. O. (1982). Depressive attributional style and depression following childbirth. *Journal of Personality and Social Psychology, 91,* 245–254.

Marks, I. M. (1977). Phobias and obsessions: Clinical phenomena in search of laboratory models. In J. D. Maser & M. E. P. Seligman (Eds.), *Psychopathology: Experimental models* (pp. 175–213). San Francisco: Freeman.

Marks, I. M. (1987). *Fears, phobias and rituals.* Oxford, England: Oxford University Press.

Marshall, N., Hegrenes, J., & Goldstein, S. (1973). Verbal interactions: Mothers and their retarded children versus mothers and their nonretarded children. *American Journal of Mental Deficiency, 77,* 415–419.

Marshall, W. L. (1985). The effects of variable exposure in flooding therapy. *Behavior Therapy, 16,* 117–135.

Martin, I. M., & Levey, A. B. (1978). Evaluative conditioning. *Advances in Behaviour Research and Therapy, 1,* 57–102.

Martin, I. M., & Levey, A. B. (1985). Conditioning, evaluations and cognitions: An axis for integration. *Behaviour Research and Therapy, 23,* 167–175.

Martin, I. M., & Levey, A. B. (1987a). Knowledge, action, and control. In H.

J. Eysenck & I. M. Martin (Eds.), *Theoretical foundations of behavior therapy* (pp. 133–152). New York: Plenum.

Martin, I. M., & Levey, A. B. (1987b). Learning what will happen next: Conditioning, evaluation, and cognitive processes. In G. Davey (Ed.), *Cognitive processes and Pavlovian conditioning in humans* (pp. 57–81). New York: Wiley.

Maslow, A. H. (1968). *Toward a psychology of being* (2nd ed.). New York: Van Nostrand Reinhold.

Master, S., & Gershman, L. (1983). Physiological responses to rational-emotive self-verbalizations. *Journal of Behavior Therapy and Experimental Psychiatry, 14,* 289–296.

Mathews, C. O. (1977). A review of behavioral theories of depression and a self-regulation model for depression. *Psychotherapy: Theory, Research and Practice, 14,* 79–85.

Matusseh, P., & Feil, W. (1983). Personality attributes of depressive patients. *Archives of General Psychiatry, 40,* 783–790.

McGrath, J. E. (1976). Stress and behavior in organizations. In M. D. Dunnette (Ed.), *Handbook of industrial and organizational psychology* (pp. 1351–1395). Skokie, IL: Rand McNally.

McNally, R. J., & Foa, E. B. (1986). Preparedness and resistance to extinction to fear-relevant stimuli: A failure to replicate. *Behaviour Research and Therapy, 24,* 529–535.

McNeil, D. (1970). *The acquisition of language.* New York: Harper & Row.

Meazzini, P. (1977). Analisi esperimentale di un caso di underachievement scolastico trattato dei genitori mediante contrattazione delle contingenze. *Formazione e Cambiamento, 2,* 24–49.

Meazzini, P. (1983). La terapia e modificazione del comportamento: Un' introduzione storico-epistemologica. In P. Meazzini (Ed.), *Trattato teoritico-pratico de terapia e modificazione del comportamento.* Pordenone, Italy: Erip.

Meazzini, P., & Bauer, B. (1984). La terapia e modificazione del comportamento: Una rivoluzione mancata? *Giornale Italiano di Scienza e Terapia del Comportamento, 1,* 2–17.

Meichenbaum, D. (1977). *Cognitive-behavior modification: An integrative approach.* New York: Plenum.

Meichenbaum, D. (1980). Cognitive behavior modification with exceptional children: A promise yet unfulfilled. *Exceptional Education Quarterly, 1,* 83–88.

Meichenbaum, D. (1986). Cognitive behavior modification. In F. H. Kanfer & A. P. Goldstein (Eds.), *Helping people change* (3rd ed., pp. 346–380). New York: Pergamon.

Meichenbaum, D., & Cameron, R. (1982). Cognitive behavior therapy. In G. T. Wilson & C. M. Franks (Eds.), *Contemporary behavior therapy: Conceptual and empirical foundations* (pp. 310–338). New York: Guilford.

Meichenbaum, D., & Gilmore, J. B. (1984). The nature of unconscious processes: A cognitive-behavioral perspective. In K. S. Bowers & D. Meichenbaum (Eds.), *The unconscious reconsidered* (pp. 273–298). New York: Wiley.

Meichenbaum, D., & Goodman, J. (1971). Training impulsive children to talk to themselves: A means of developing self-control. *Journal of Abnormal Psychology, 77*, 115–126.

Melamed, B. G. (1983). The effects of preparatory information on adjustment of children to medical procedures. In M. Rosenbaum, C. M. Franks, & Y. Jaffe (Eds.), *Perspectives on behavior therapy in the eighties* (pp. 344–362). New York: Springer.

Merluzzi, T. V., Glass, C. R., & Genest, M. (Eds.). (1981). *Cognitive assessment*. New York: Guilford.

Metzl, M. (1978, August). *Teaching parents to stimulate their infants as a strategy for enhancing infant development*. Paper presented at the First International Congress for the Study of Child Language, Tokyo, Japan.

Meyer, L. H., & Evans, I. M. (1986). Modification of excess behavior: An adaptive and functional approach for educational and community contexts. In R. H. Horner, L. H. Meyer, & H. D. Fredericks (Eds.), *Education of learners with severe handicaps: Exemplary service strategies.* (pp. 315–350). Baltimore, MD: Paul H. Brookes.

Meyer, L. H. & Evans, I. M. (1989). *Non-aversive intervention for behavior problems: A manual for home and community*. Baltimore, MD: Paul H. Brookes.

Miller, G. A. (1962). *Psychology: The science of mental life*. New York: Harper & Row.

Miller, N. E. (1948). Studies of fear as an acquired drive: I. Fear as motivation and fear-reduction as reinforcement in the learning of new responses. *Journal of Experimental Psychology, 38*, 89–101.

Miller, N. E. (1959). Liberalization of basic S-R concepts: Extensions to conflict behavior, motivation and social learning. In S. Koch (Ed.), *Psychology: A study of a science* (Vol. 2., pp. 196–292). New York: McGraw-Hill.

Miller, N. E., & Dollard, J. (1941). *Social learning and imitation*. New Haven, CT: Yale University Press.

Miller, R. C., & Berman, J. S. (1983). The efficacy of cognitive behavior therapies: A quantitative review of the research evidence. *Psychological Bulletin, 94*, 39–53.

Miller, W. R., & Seligman, M. E. (1975). Depression and learned helplessness in man. *Journal of Abnormal Psychology, 84*, 228–236.

Mineka, S. (1979). The role of fear in theories of avoidance learning, flooding, and extinction. *Psychological Bulletin, 86*, 985–1010.

Mineka, S. (1987). A primate model of phobic fears. In H. J. Eysenck & I. M. Martin (Eds.), *Theoretical foundations of behavior therapy* (pp. 81–111). New York: Plenum.

Minke, K. A. (1980). Behavioral engineering. In L. P. Ince (Ed.), *Behavioral psychology in rehabilitation medicine* (pp. 3–22). Baltimore, MD: Williams & Wilkins.

Minke, K. A. (1986). Toward a general theory of behavior: Two-level vs.

multilevel theory methodology. *International Newsletter of Social Behaviorism, 6*, 3–8.

Minke, K. A. (1987). A comparative analysis of modern behaviorism's general theories: Unification through generational advance. In A. W. Staats & L. Mos (Eds.), *Annals of Theoretical Psychology* (Vol. 5, pp. 315–343). New York: Plenum.

Minke, K. A. (1988). *Unit mastery instructor's guide to accompany psychology and life.* Glenview, Ill.: Scott, Foresman.

Minke, K. A., & Heard, W. G. (1964). *The development of hand-eye coordination in a brain damaged child.* Paper presented at the meeting of the Southwestern and Rocky Mountain Division of the American Association for the Advancement of Science, Lubbock, TX.

Mischel, W. (1968). *Personality and assessment.* New York: Wiley.

Mischel, W. (1969). Continuity and change in personality. *American Psychologist, 24*, 1012–1018.

Mischel, W. (1972). Direct versus indirect personality assessment: Evidence and implications. *Journal of Consulting and Clinical Psychology, 38*, 319–324.

Mischel, W. (1973). Toward a cognitive social learning reconceptualization of personality. *Psychological Review, 32*, 252–283.

Mischel, W. (1974). Processes in delay of gratification. *Advances in Experimental Social Psychology, 7*, 249–292.

Mischel, W. (1977). On the future of personality assessment. *American Psychologist, 32*, 246–254.

Mischel, W. (1979). On the interface of cognition and personality: Beyond the person-situation debate. *American Psychologist, 34*, 740–754.

Mischel, W. (1983). Delay of gratification as process and person variable in development. In D. Magnusson & V. P. Allen (Eds.), *Interactions in human development* (pp. 149–165). New York: Academic Press.

Mischel, W. (1984). Convergences and challenges in the search of consistency. *American Psychologist, 39*, 351–364.

Mischel, W., & Moore, B. S. (1973). Effects of attention to symbolically presented rewards on self-control. *Journal of Personality and Social Psychology, 28*, 172–179.

Moerk, E. (1972). Principles of interaction in language learning. *Merrill-Palmer Quarterly, 18*, 229–257.

Moerk, E. (1975). Verbal interactions between children and their mothers during the preschool years. *Developmental Psychology, 11*, 788–794.

Moerk, E. (1980a, May). *The LAD was a lady.* Paper presented at the meeting of the Western Psychological Association, Honolulu, HI.

Moerk, E. (1980b). Relationship between parental input frequencies and children's language acquisition: A reanalysis of Brown's data. *Journal of Child Language, 7*, 1–14.

Monti, P. M., Corriveau, D. P., & Curran, J. P. (1982). Social skills training for psychiatric patients: Treatment and outcome. In J. P. Curran & P. M. Monti (Eds.), *Social skills training: A practical handbook for assessment and treatment* (pp. 215–243). New York: Guilford.

Moore, B. S. (1977). Cognitive representation of rewards in delay of gratification. *Cognitive Therapy and Research, 1*, 73–83.

Moore, B. S., Mischel, W., & Zeiss, A. (1976). Comparative effects of the reward stimulus and its cognitive representation in voluntary delay. *Journal of Personality and Social Psychology, 34*, 419–424.

Moores, D. (1978). *Educating the deaf: Theory and practice.* Boston: Houghton Mifflin.

Moores, D., & Maestas y Moores, J. (1982). La communication totale. In J. A. Rondal & X. Seron (Eds.), *Troubles du langage: Diagnostic et réducatien.* Brussels, Belgium: Mardaga.

Moos, R. H. (1973). Conceptualizations of human environments. *American Psychologist, 28*, 652–665.

Moss, G. R., & Boren, J. J. (1972). Depression as a model for behavioral analysis. *Comprehensive Psychiatry, 13*, 581–590.

Mowrer, O. H. (1947). On the dual nature of learning—a re-interpretation of "conditioning" and "problem solving." *Harvard Educational Review, 17*, 102–148.

Mowrer, O. H. (1954). The psychologist looks at language. *American Psychologist, 9*, 660–694.

Mowrer, O. H. (1960). *Learning theory and the symbolic processes.* New York: Wiley.

Munro, A. (1966). Some familial and social factors in depressive illness. *British Journal of Psychiatry, 112*, 429–441.

Murray, E. J., & Foote, F. (1979). The origins of fear of snakes. *Behaviour Research and Therapy, 17*, 489–493.

Neisser, U. (1976). *Cognition and reality.* San Francisco: Freeman.

Nelson, K. (1977). Facilitating children's syntax acquisition. *Developmental Psychology, 13*, 107–109.

Nelson, R. E., & Craighead, W. E. (1977). Selective recall of positive and negative feedback, self-control behaviors and depression. *Journal of Abnormal Psychology, 86*, 379–388.

Nelson, R. E., & Craighead, W. E. (1981). Tests of a self-control model of depression. *Behavior Therapy, 12*, 123–239.

Nelson, R. O. (1980). The use of intelligence tests within behavioral assessment. *Behavioral Assessment, 2*, 417–423.

Nelson, R. O., & Evans, I. M. (1968). The combination of learning principles and speech therapy techniques in the treatment of noncommunicating children. *Journal of Child Psychology and Psychiatry, 9*, 111–124.

Nelson, R. O., & Hayes, S. C. (Eds.). (1986). *Conceptual foundations of behavioral assessment.* New York: Guilford.

Nelson, R. O., Hayes, S. C., Felton, J. L., & Jarrett, R. B. (1985). A comparison of data produced by different behavioral assessment techniques with implications for models of social skill inadequacy. *Behaviour Research and Therapy, 43*, 1–11.

Nerenz, D. R., & Leventhal, H. (1983). Self-regulation theory in chronic illness. In T. G. Burish & L. A. Bradley (Eds.), *Coping with chronic disease: Research and application* (pp. 13–37). New York: Academic Press.

New York State Commission on Quality of Care for the Mentally Disabled (1987). *Abusing the unprotected: A study of the misuse of aversive behavior modification techniques and weaknesses in the regulatory structure.* Albany, NY: Author.

Newport, E. L., Gleitman, H., & Gleitman, L. R. (1977). Mother, I'd rather do it myself: Some effects and non-effects of maternal speech style. In C. E. Snow & C. A. Ferguson (Eds.), *Talking to children: Language input and language acquisition* (pp. 109–149). Cambridge, England: Cambridge University Press.

Nisbett, R. E., & Wilson, T. D. (1977). Telling more than we can know: Verbal reports on mental processes. *Psychological Review, 84,* 231–259.

Nunally, J. C., Duchnowski, A. J., & Parker, R. K. (1965). Association of neutral words with rewards. *Journal of Personality and Social Psychology, 1,* 270–274.

O'Donnell, C. R. (1984). Behavior community psychology and the natural environment. In C. Franks (Ed.), *New developments in behavior therapy* (pp. 495–524). New York: Haworth.

Ohman, A., Dimberg, U., & Öst, L. G. (1985). Animal and social phobias: Biological constraints on learned fear responses. In S. Reiss & R. R. Bootzin (Eds.), *Theoretical issues in behavior therapy* (pp. 123–175). New York: Academic Press.

Olson, R. P., & Greenberg, D. J. (1972). Effects of a contingency-contracting and decision-making group with chronic mental patients. *Journal of Consulting and Clinical Psychology, 38,* 376–383.

Osgood, C. E. (1953). *Method and theory in experimental psychology.* New York: Oxford University Press.

Osgood, C. E. (1971). Where do sentences come from? In D. D. Steinberg & L. H. Jakobovits (Eds.), *Semantics* (pp. 497–529). London: Cambridge University Press.

Osgood, C. E., Suci, G. J., & Tannenbaum, P. A. (1967). *The measurement of meaning.* Urbana: University of Illinois Press.

Öst, L. G. (1989). One-session treatment of specific phobias. *Behaviour Research and Therapy, 27,* 1–7.

Öst, L. G., & Hugdahl, K. (1981). Acquisition of phobias and anxiety response patterns in clinical patients. *Behaviour Research and Therapy, 19,* 439–447.

Overmier, B. J., & Lawry, J. A. (1979). Pavlovian conditioning and the mediation of behavior. In G. H. Bower (Ed.), *The psychology of learning and motivation* (Vol. 13, pp. 1–55). New York: Academic Press.

Page, M. M. (1969). Social psychology of a classical conditioning of attitudes experiment. *Journal of Personality and Social Psychology, 11,* 177–186.

Paivio, A. (1971). *Imagery and verbal processes.* New York: Holt, Rinehart & Winston.

Palkes, H., Stewart, M., & Kahana, B. (1968). Porteus maze performance of hyperactive boys after training in self-directed verbal commands. *Child Development, 39,* 817–829.

Parish, T. (1974). The conditioning of racial attitudes in children. *Perceptual and Motor Skills, 39,* 704–714.

Parish, T. S., Shirazi, A., Lambert, F. (1976). Conditioning away prejudicial attitudes in children. *Perceptual and Motor Skills, 43,* 907–912.

Patterson, C. H. (1984). Empathy, warmth and genuineness in psychotherapy: A review of reviews. *Psychotherapy: Theory, Research and Practice, 21,* 431–438.

Patterson, C. J., & Mischel, W. (1976). Effects of temptation-inhibiting and task-facilitating plans on self control. *Journal of Personality and Social Psychology, 33,* 209–217.

Patterson, G. R., Cobb, J. A., & Ray, R. S. (1973). A social engineering technology for retraining the families of aggressive boys. In H. E. Adams & I. P. Unikel (Eds.), *Issues and trends in behavior therapy* (pp. 121–165). Springfield, IL: Charles C. Thomas.

Paul, G. L., & Lentz, R. J. (1977). *Psychosocial treatment of chronic mental patients: Milieu versus social-learning programs.* Cambridge, MA: Harvard University Press.

Paykel, E. S. (1969). Life events and depression. *Archives of General Psychiatry, 21,* 753–560.

Paykel, E. S., Klerman, G. L., & Prusoff, G. A. (1974). Prognosis of depression and the endogenous-neurotic distinction. *Psychological Medicine, 4,* 57–64.

Perin, C. T. (1942). Behavior potentiality as a joint function of the amount of training and degree of hunger at time of extinction. *Journal of Experimental Psychology, 30,* 93–113.

Peterson, C., Schwartz, S. M., & Seligman, M. E. (1981). Self-blame and depressive symptoms. *Journal of Personality and Social Psychology, 41,* 253–259.

Phelan, J. G., Hekmat, H., & Tang, T. (1967). Transfer of verbal conditioning to non-verbal behavior. *Psychological Reports, 20,* 979–986.

Phillips, L. W. (1958). Mediated verbal similarity as a determinant of the generalization of a conditioned GSR. *Journal of Experimental Psychology, 55,* 56–62.

Prakchin, K. M., Craig, K., Papgeorges, D., & Reith, C. (1977). Nonverbal communication deficits and responses to performance feedback in depression. *Journal of Abnormal Psychology, 86,* 224–234.

Putallaz, M., & Gottman, J. (1982). Conceptualizing social competence in children. In P. Karoly & J. J. Steffen (Eds.), *Improving children's competence: Advances in child behavior analysis and therapy* (Vol. 1, pp. 159–189). Lexington, MA: D. C. Heath.

Pylyshyn, Z. W. (1973). What the mind's eye tells the mind's brain: A critique of mental imagery. *Psychology Bulletin, 80,* 1–24.

Rachman, S. (1977). The conditioning theory of fear acquisition. *Behaviour Research and Therapy, 15,* 375–387.

Rachman, S. (1980). Emotional processing. *Behaviour Research and Therapy, 18,* 51–60.

Rachman, S. (1981). The primacy of affect: Some theoretical implications. *Behaviour Research and Therapy, 19,* 279–290.

Rachman, S. (1984). A reassessment of the "primacy of affect". *Cognitive Therapy and Research, 8,* 579–584.

Rachman, S., Craske, M., Tallman, K., & Solyom, C. (1986). Does escape behaviour strengthen agoraphobic avoidance? A replication. *Behavior Therapy, 17,* 366–384.

Rao, V. A., & Coppen, A. (1979). Classification of depression and response to Amitripline therapy. *Psychological Medicine, 9,* 321–325.

Rapp, S. R., & Fremouw, W. J. (1982, November). *Empirical subtypes of unipolar depression: An examination of three contemporary models of depression.* Paper presented at the annual meeting of the Association for Advancement of Behavior Therapy, Los Angeles, CA.

Raps, C. S., Peterson, C., Reinhard, K. E., Abramson, L. Y., & Seligman, M. E. (1982). Attributional style among depressed patients. *Journal of Abnormal Psychology, 91,* 102–108.

Razran, G. H. (1939). A quantitative study of meaning by a conditioned salivary technique. *Science, 90,* 89–90.

Reber, A. (1973). On psycholinguistic paradigms. *Journal of Psycholinguistic Research, 2,* 289–319.

Redden, E. M., Tucker, R. K., & Young, L. (1983). Psychometric properties of the Rosenbaum Schedule for Assessing Self-Control. *The Psychological Record, 33,* 77–86.

Rehm, L. P. (1977). A self-control model of depression. *Behavior Therapy, 8,* 787–804.

Rehm, L. P. (1984). Self-management therapy for depression. *Advances in Behaviour Research and Therapy, 6,* 83–98.

Rehm, L. P., Fuchs, C. Z., Roth, D. M., Kornblith, S. J., & Romano, J. M. (1979). A comparison of self-control and assertion skills treatments of depression. *Behavior Therapy, 10,* 429–442.

Rehm, L. P., Mattei, M. L., Potts, S., & Skolnick, M. (1974, December). *Effects of practice, emotional content and relaxation on vividness and latency of imagery.* Paper presented at the Eighth Annual Convention of the Association for Advancement of Behavior Therapy. Chicago, IL.

Rehm, L. P., & Plakosh, P. (1975). Preference for immediate reinforcement in depression. *Journal of Behavior Therapy and Experimental Psychiatry, 6,* 101–103.

Reichle, J., & Karlan, G. (1985). The selection of an augmentative system in communication intervention: A critique of decision rules. *Journal of the Association for Persons with Severe Handicaps, 10,* 146–156.

Reisinger, J. (1972). The treatment of "anxiety depression" via positive reinforcement and response cost. *Journal of Applied Behavior Analysis, 5,* 125–130.

Rescorla, R. A., & Solomon, R. L. (1967). Two-process learning theory:

Relationships between Pavlovian conditioning and instrumental learning. *Psychological Review, 74*, 151–182.

Richards, P. S. (1985). Construct validation of the Self-Control Schedule. *Journal of Research in Personality, 19*, 208–218.

Riemann, F. (1967). *Grundformen der Angst.* Munich, West Germany: Reinhardt.

Risley, T. R., & Hart, B. (1968). Developing correspondence between saying and doing: Teaching children to share and praise. *Journal of Applied Behavior Analysis, 1*, 267–281.

Robinson, D. M., & Robinson, H. B. (1976). *The mentally retarded child.* New York: McGraw-Hill.

Robinson, E. A., Eyberg, S. M., & Ross, A. W. (1980). The standardization of an inventory of child conduct problem behavior. *Journal of Clinical Child Psychology, 9*, 22–28.

Rogers, T., & Craighead, W. E. (1977). Physiological responses to self-statements. *Cognitive Therapy and Research, 1*, 99–120.

Rondal, J. A. (1978a). Developmental sentence scoring procedure and the delay-difference question in language development of Down's syndrome children. *Mental Retardation, 16*, 169–171.

Rondal, J. A. (1978b). Maternal speech to normal and Down's syndrome children matched for mean length of utterance. In C. Meyers (Ed.), *Quality of life in severely and profoundly mentally retarded people: Research foundations for improvement* (pp. 193–266). Washington, DC: American Association on Mental Deficiency.

Rondal, J. A. (1978c). Patterns of correlation for various language measures in mother–child interactions for normal and Down's syndrome children. *Language and Speech, 21*, 242–252.

Rondal, J. A. (1980). Fathers' and mothers' speech in early language development. *Journal of Child Language, 7*, 353–369.

Rondal, J. A. (1981). On the nature of linguistic input to language-learning children. *International. Journal of Psycholinguistics, 21*, 75–107.

Rondal, J. A. (1983). *L'interaction parent—enfant et la construction du langage.* Brussels, Belgium: Mardaga.

Rondal, J. A., Harrod, M., & Charlier, M. (1985). *Adult–child interaction and the process of language acquisition.* New York: Praeger.

Rondal, J. A., & Henrot, F. (1984). *Le langage des signes.* Brussels, Belgium: Mardaga.

Rose, G. D., & Staats, A. W. (1988). Depression and the frequency and strength of pleasant events: Exploration of the Staats–Heiby theory. *Behaviour Research and Therapy, 26*, 489–494.

Rose, R. J., & Ditto, W. B. (1983). A developmental-genetic analysis of common fears from early childhood to adolescence. *Child Development, 54*, 361–368.

Rosenbaum, M. (1980a). Individual differences in self-control behaviors and tolerance of painful stimulation. *Journal of Abnormal Psychology, 89*, 581–590.

Rosenbaum, M. (1980b). A schedule for assessing self-control behaviors:

Preliminary findings. *Behavior Therapy, 11*, 109–121.

Rosenbaum, M. (1983). Learned resourcefulness as a behavioral repertoire for the self-regulation of internal events. In M. Rosenbaum, C. M. Franks, & Y. Jaffe (Eds.), *Perspectives on behavior therapy in the eighties* (pp. 54–73). New York: Springer.

Rosenbaum, M., & Ben-Ari, K. (1985). Learned helplessness and learned resourcefulness: Effects of noncontingent success and failure on individuals differing in self-control skills. *Journal of Personality and Social Psychology, 48*, 198–215.

Rosenbaum, M., & Ben-Ari Smira, K. (1986). Cognitive and personality factors in the delay of gratification of hemodialysis patients. *Journal of Personality and Social Psychology, 49*, 357–364.

Rosenbaum, M., Franks, C. M., & Jaffe, Y. (Eds.). (1983). *Perspectives on behavior therapy in the eighties.* New York: Springer.

Rosenbaum, M., & Hadari, D. (1985). Personal-efficacy, external locus of control and perceived contingency of parental reinforcement among depressed, paranoid, and normal subjects. *Journal of Personality and Social Psychology, 49*, 539–547.

Rosenbaum, M., & Jaffe, Y. (1983). Learned helplessness: The role of individual differences in learned resourcefulness. *British Journal of Social Psychology, 22*, 215–225.

Rosenbaum, M., & Palmon, N. (1984). Helplessness and resourcefulness in coping with epilepsy. *Journal of Consulting and Clinical Psychology, 52*, 244–253.

Rosenbaum, M., & Rolnick, A. (1983). Self-control behaviors and coping with seasickness. *Cognitive Therapy and Research, 7*, 93–98.

Rosenthal, S. H., & Klerman, G. L. (1966). Content and consistency in the endogenous depressive pattern. *British Journal of Psychiatry, 112*, 471–481.

Ross, A. O. (1981). *Child behavior therapy.* New York: Wiley.

Ross, A. O. (1985). To form a more perfect union: It is time to stop standing still. *Behavior Therapy, 16*, 195–204.

Ross, E. S., & Karoly, P. (1977, December). *Verbal self-control in children: An investigation of mother-child communication patterns.* Paper presented at the Eleventh Annual Meeting of the Association for Advancement of Behavior Therapy, Atlanta, GA.

Rostow, C. D., & Smith, C. E. (1975). Effects of contingency management of chronic patients on ward control and behavioral adjustment. *Journal of Behavior Therapy and Experimental Psychiatry, 6*, 1–4.

Rotter, J. B. (1954). *Social learning and clinical psychology.* Englewood Cliffs, NJ: Prentice Hall.

Rotter, J. B. (1960). Some implications of a social learning theory for the prediction of goal directed behavior from testing procedures. *Psychological Review, 67*, 301–316.

Rozensky, R. H., Rehm, L. P., Pry, G., & Roth, D. M. (1977). Depression and self-reinforcement behavior in hospitalized patients. *Journal of Behavior Therapy and Experimental Psychiatry, 8*, 31–34.

Rushton, J. P., Jackson, D. N., & Paunonen, S. V. (1981). Personality: Nomothetic or idiographic? A response to Kenrick and Stringfield. *Psychological Review, 81,* 582–589.

Russell, R. K., Miller, D. E., & June, L. N. (1975). A comparison between group systematic desensitization and cue-controlled relaxation in the treatment of test anxiety. *Behavior Therapy, 6,* 172–177.

Russell, R. K., Wise, F., & Strakoudakis, J. P. (1976). Treatment of test anxiety by cue-controlled relaxation and systematic desensitization. *Journal of Counseling Psychology, 23,* 563–566.

Russell, W. A., & Storms, L. H. (1955). Implicit verbal chaining in paired-associate learning. *Journal of Experimental Psychology, 49,* 287–293.

Ryback, D., & Staats, A. W. (1970). Parents as behavior therapy technicians in treating reading deficits (dyslexia). *Journal of Behavior Therapy and Experimental Psychiatry, 1,* 109–119.

Sandin, B., & Chorot, P. (1989). The incubation theory of fear/anxiety: Experimental investigation in a human laboratory model of Pavlovian conditioning. *Behaviour Research and Therapy, 27,* 9–18.

Sappington, A. A., Burleson, R., Studstill, L., Rice, J., Gordon, J., Cornelison, K. (1982). Reduction of avoidance behavior through the semantic conditioning of a self-related target stimulus. *Cognitive Therapy and Research, 6,* 315–323.

Sato, K. Y. (1987). *A delineation of the relative effects of affect and lexical marking in linear syllogistic reasoning.* Unpublished master's thesis, University of Hawaii, Honolulu.

Schwartz, J., & Bellack, A. S. (1975). A comparison of a token economy with standard inpatient treatment. *Journal of Consulting and Clinical Psychology, 43,* 107–108.

Seligman, M. E. P. (1971). Phobias and preparedness. *Behavior Therapy, 2,* 307–320.

Seligman, M. E. P. (1975). *Helplessness: On depression, development and death.* San Francisco: W. H. Freeman.

Seligman, M. E. P. (1981). A learned helplessness point of view. In L. P. Rehm (Ed.), *Behavior therapy for depression: Present status and future directions.* New York: Academic Press.

Seligman, M. E. P., Abramson, L. Y., Semmel, A., & von Bayer, C. (1979). Depressive attributional style. *Journal of Abnormal Psychology, 88,* 242–247.

Shatz, M., & Gelman, R. (1973). The development of communication skills: Modifications in the speech of young children as a function of listener. *Monographs of the Society for Research in Child Development, 38,* (5, Serial No. 152).

Sheslow, D., & Erickson, M. (1975). Analysis of activity preference in depressed and nondepressed college students. *Journal of Counseling Psychology, 22,* 329–332.

Sidman, M. (1960). *Tactics of scientific research.* New York: Basic Books.

Siegel, G. (1967). Interpersonal approaches to the study of communication disorders. *Journal of Speech and Hearing Disorders, 32,* 112–120.

Silverstein, A. (1973). Acquired pleasantness and conditioned incentives in verbal learning. In D. E. Berlyne & K. B. Madsen (Eds.), *Pleasure, reward, preference* (pp. 177–226). New York: Academic Press.

Simons, A. D., Lustman, P. J., Wetzel, R. D., & Murphy, G. E. (1985). Predicting response to cognitive therapy of depression: The role of learned resourcefulness. *Cognitive Therapy and Research, 7,* 93–98.

Sinclair, H. (1982). Some recent trends in the study of language development. *International Journal of Behavioral Development, 5,* 413–431.

Skinner, B. F. (1938). *The behavior of organisms.* New York: Appleton.

Skinner, B. F. (1950). Are theories of learning necessary? *Psychological Review, 57,* 193–196.

Skinner, B. F. (1953). *Science and human behavior.* New York: Macmillan.

Skinner, B. F. (1957). *Verbal behavior.* New York: Appleton-Century-Crofts.

Skinner, B. F. (1966). What is the experimental analysis of behavior? *Journal of the Experimental Analysis of Behavior, 9,* 213–218.

Skinner, B. F. (1969). *Contingencies of reinforcement.* New York: Appleton-Century-Crofts.

Skinner, B. F. (1974). *About behaviorism.* New York: Knopf.

Sloane, H. M., & MacAulay, B. D. (Eds.). (1968). *Operant procedures in remedial speech and language training.* Boston: Houghton Mifflin.

Slobin, D. (1973). Cognitive prerequisites for the development of grammar. In C. Ferguson & D. Slobin (Eds.), *Studies of child language development* (pp. 175–208). New York: Holt, Rinehart & Winston.

Slobin, D. (1982). Universal and particular in the acquisition of language. In E. Wanner & L. Gleitman (Eds.), *Language acquisition: The state of the art* (pp. 128–170). New York: Cambridge University Press.

Smith, T. V. G. (1979). *Cognitive correlatives of response to a behavioral weight control program.* Unpublished doctoral dissertation, Queen's University, Kingston, Ontario, Canada.

Solarz, A. K. (1960). Latency of instrumental responses as a function of compatibility with the meaning of eliciting verbal signs. *Journal of Experimental Psychology, 59,* 239–245.

Solomon, R. L., & Wynne, L. C. (1954). Traumatic avoidance learning: The principles of anxiety conservation and partial irreversibility. *Psychological Review, 61,* 353–385.

Spitzer, R. L., Endicott, J., & Robins, E. (1978). Research diagnostic criteria: Rationale and reliability. *Archives of General Psychiatry, 35,* 773–782.

Staats, A. W. (1957a). Learning theory and "opposite speech." *Journal of Abnormal and Social Psychology, 55,* 268–269.

Staats, A. W. (1957b). Verbal and instrumental response hierarchies and their relationship to problem-solving. *American Journal of Psychology, 70,* 442–446.

Staats, A. W. (1961). Verbal habit families, concepts, and the operant conditioning of word classes. *Psychological Review, 68,* 190–204.

Staats, A. W. (1963). *Complex human behavior.* (with contributions by C. K. Staats). New York: Holt, Rinehart & Winston.

Staats, A. W. (Ed.). (1964). *Human learning*. New York: Academic Press.

Staats, A. W. (1968a). *Learning, language and cognition*. New York: Holt, Rinehart & Winston.

Staats, A. W. (1968b). Social behaviorism and human motivation: Principles of the attitude-reinforcer-discriminative system. In A. G. Greenwald, T. C. Brock, & T. M. Ostrom (Eds.), *Psychological foundations of attitudes* (pp. 33–66). New York: Academic Press.

Staats, A. W. (1969). Experimental demand characteristics and the classical conditioning of attitudes. *Journal of Personality and Social Psychology, 11*, 187–192.

Staats, A. W. (1970). A learning-behavior theory: A basis for unity in behavioral-social science. In A. R. Gilgen (Ed.), *Contemporary scientific psychology* (pp. 183–239). New York: Academic Press.

Staats, A. W. (1971a). *Child learning, intelligence and personality*. New York: Harper & Row.

Staats, A. W. (1971b). Linguistic-mentalistic theory versus an explanatory S-R learning theory of language development. In D. I. Slobin (Ed.), *The ontogenesis of grammar* (pp. 103–152). New York: Academic Press.

Staats, A. W. (1972). Language behavior therapy: A derivative of social behaviorism. *Behavior Therapy, 3*, 165–192.

Staats, A. W. (1973). Behavior analysis and token reinforcement in educational behavior modification and curriculum research. In C. E. Thoresen (Ed.), *Behavior modification in education* (pp. 115–150). Chicago: University of Chicago Press.

Staats, A. W. (1974). Behaviorism and cognitive theory in the study of language: A neopsycholinguistics. In R. L. Schiefelbusch & L. L. Lloyd (Eds.), *Language perspectives: Acquisition, retardation, and intervention* (pp. 615–646). Baltimore, MD.: University Park Press.

Staats, A. W. (1975). *Social behaviorism*. Homewood, IL.: Dorsey Press.

Staats, A. W. (1980). Behavioral interaction and interactional psychology theories of personality: Similarities, differences, and the need for unification. *British Journal of Psychology, 71*, 205–220.

Staats, A. W. (1981). Social behaviorism, unified theory, unified theory construction methods, and the zeitgeist of separatism. *American Psychologist, 36*, 239–256.

Staats, A. W. (1983a). Paradigmatic behaviorism: Unified theory for social-personality psychology. In L. Berkowitz (Ed.), *Advances in experimental social psychology* (Vol. 16, pp. 126–179). New York: Academic Press.

Staats, A. W. (1983b). *Psychology's crisis of disunity: Philosophy and method for a unified science*. New York: Praeger.

Staats, A. W. (1986). Behaviorism with a personality: The paradigmatic behavioral assessment approach. In R. O. Nelson & S. C. Hayes (Eds.), *Conceptual foundations of behavioral assessment* (pp. 244–296). New York: Guilford.

Staats, A. W. (1987). Unified positivism: Philosophy for a unification psychology. In A. W. Staats & L. P. Mos (Eds.), *Annals of theoretical psychology* (Vol. 5, pp. 11–54). New York: Plenum.

Staats, A. W. (1988a). Paradigmatic behaviorism, unified positivism, and paradigmatic behavior therapy. In D. B. Fishman, R. Rotgers, and C. M. Franks (Eds.), *Paradigms in behavior therapy: Present and promise* (pp. 211–253). New York: Springer.

Staats, A. W. (1988b). Skinner's theory and the emotion-behavior relationship: Incipient change with major implications. *American Psychologist, 43,* 747–748.

Staats, A. W., Brewer, B. A., & Gross, M. C. (1970). Learning and cognitive development: Representative samples, cumulative-hierarchical learning, and experimental-longitudinal methods. *Monographs of the Society for Research in Child Development, 35* (8, Serial No. 141).

Staats, A. W., & Burns, G. L. (1981). Intelligence and child development: What intelligence is and how it is learned and functions. *Genetic Psychology Monographs, 104,* 237–301.

Staats, A. W., & Burns, G. L. (1982). Emotional personality repertoire as cause of behavior: Specification of personality and interaction principles. *Journal of Personality and Social Psychology, 43,* 873–881.

Staats, A. W., & Butterfield, W. H. (1965). Treatment of nonreading in a culturally-deprived juvenile delinquent: An application of reinforcement principles. *Child Development, 36,* 925–942.

Staats, A. W., & Eifert, G. H. (1990). A paradigmatic behaviorism theory of emotions: A basis for unification. *Clinical Psychology Review, 10,* 1–40.

Staats, A. W., & Fernandez-Ballesteros, R. (1987). The self-report in personality measurement: A paradigmatic behaviorism approach to psychodiagnostics. *Evaluacion Psicological [Psychological Assessment], 3,* 151–190.

Staats, A. W., Finley, J. R., Minke, K. A., & Wolf, M. M. (1964). Reinforcement variables in the control of unit reading responses. *Journal of the Experimental Analysis of Behavior, 7,* 139–149.

Staats, A. W., Gross, M. C., Guay, P. F., & Carlson, C. G. (1973). Personality and social systems and attitude-reinforcer-discriminative theory: Interest (attitude) formation, function and measurement. *Journal of Personality and Social Psychology, 26,* 251–261.

Staats, A. W., & Hammond, W. W. (1972). Natural words as physiological conditioned stimuli: Food-word elicited salivation and deprivation effects. *Journal of Experimental Psychology, 96,* 206–208.

Staats, A. W., & Heiby, E. (1985). Paradigmatic behaviorism's theory of depression: Unified, explanatory, and heuristic. In S. Reiss & R. R. Bootzin, (Eds.), *Theoretical issues in behavior therapy* (pp. 279–330). New York: Academic Press.

Staats, A. W., & Lohr, J. M. (1979). Images, language, emotions, and personality: Social behaviorism's theory. *Journal of Mental Imagery, 3,* 85–106.

Staats, A. W., Minke, K. A., & Butts, P. (1970). A token-reinforcement remedial reading program administered by black instructional technicians to backward black children. *Behavior Therapy, 1,* 331–353.

Staats, A. W., Minke, K. A., Finley, J. R., Wolf, M. M., & Brooks, L. O. (1964). A reinforcer system and experimental procedure for the laboratory study of reading acquisition. *Child Development, 35,* 209–231.

Staats, A. W., Minke, K. A., Goodwin, W., & Landeen, J. (1967). Cognitive behavior modification: "Motivated learning" reading treatment with sub-professional therapy technicians. *Behaviour Research and Therapy, 5,* 283–299.

Staats, A. W., Minke, K. A., Martin, C. H., & Higa, W. R. (1972). Deprivation-satiation and strength of attitude conditioning: A test of attitude-reinforcer-discriminative theory. *Journal of Personality and Social Psychology, 24,* 178–185.

Staats, A. W., & Staats, C. K. (1958). Attitudes established by classical conditioning. *Journal of Abnormal and Social Psychology, 57,* 37–40.

Staats, A. W., & Staats, C. K. (1959). Effect of number of trials on the language conditioning of meaning. *Journal of General Psychology, 61,* 211–223.

Staats, A. W., Staats, C. K., & Crawford, H. L. (1962). First-order conditioning of a GSR and the parallel conditioning of meaning. *Journal of General Psychology, 67,* 159–167.

Staats, A. W., Staats, C. K., & Heard, W. G. (1961). Denotative meaning established by classical conditioning. *Journal of Experimental Psychology, 61,* 300–303.

Staats, A. W., Staats, C. K., Schutz, R. E., & Wolf, M. M. (1962). The conditioning of reading responses using "extrinsic" reinforcers. *Journal of the Experimental Analysis of Behavior, 5,* 33–40.

Staats, A. W., & Warren, D. R. (1974). Motivation and three-function learning: Deprivation-satiation and approach-avoidance to food words. *Journal of Experimental Psychology, 103,* 1191–1199.

Staats, C. K., & Staats, A. W. (1957). Meaning established by classical conditioning. *Journal of Experimental Psychology, 54,* 74–80.

Stampfl, T. G., & Levis, D. J. (1967). Essentials of implosive therapy: A learning-theory-based psychodynamic behavioral therapy. *Journal of Abnormal Psychology, 72,* 496–503.

Strong, E. K., Jr. (1952). *Vocational interest blank for men.* Stanford, CA: Stanford University Press.

Suppe, F. (1977). *The structure of scientific theories.* Urbana, IL.: University of Illinois Press.

Taine, H. (1876). Note sur l'acquisition du langage chez les enfants et dans l'espece humaine. *Revue Philosophique, 1,* 23 ff.

Tanner, J., Weissman, M., & Prusoff, B. (1975). Social adjustment and clinical relapse in depressed outpatients. *Comprehensive Psychiatry, 16,* 547–556.

Taylor, M., & Abrams, R. (1973). Manic states: A genetic study of early and late affective disorders. *Archives of General Psychiatry, 28,* 656–658.

Taylor, S. E. (1983). Adjustment to threatening events: A theory of cognitive adaptation. *American Psychologist, 38,* 1161–1173.

Teasdale, J. D. (1983). Negative thinking in depression: Cause, effect, or reciprocal relationship. *Advances in Behaviour Research and Therapy, 5,* 3–25.

Thomas, A., Chess, S., & Birch, H. G. (1968). *Temperament and behavior disorders in children.* New York: New York University Press.

Thomas, D. R. (1974). The role of adaptation-level in stimulus generalization. In G. H. Bower (Ed.), *The psychology of learning and motivation* (Vol. 8, pp. 91–145). New York: Academic Press.

Thomas, D. R., & Thomas, D. H. (1974). Stimulus labeling, adaptation-level, and the central tendency shift. *Journal of Experimental Psychology, 103,* 896–899.

Thorndike, E. L. (1908). *Educational psychology.* New York: Lemerck-Brechner.

Torgerson, S. (1979). The nature and origin of common phobic fears. *British Journal of Psychiatry, 134,* 343–351.

Trapold, M. A., & Winokur, S. W. (1967). Transfer from classical conditioning and extinction to acquisition, extinction, and stimulus generalization of a positively reinforced instrumental response. *Journal of Experimental Psychology, 73,* 517–525.

Trayman, R. N., & Witte, K. L. (1976). The effects of modifying color-meaning concepts of racial concept attitudes in five- and eight-year-old children. *Journal of Experimental Child Psychology, 21,* 165–174.

Tryon, W. W. (1974). A reply to Staats' "Language behavior therapy: A derivative of social behaviorism." *Behavior Therapy, 5,* 273–276.

Tryon, W. W., & Briones, R. G. (1985). Higher-order semantic counterconditioning of Filipino women's evaluations of heterosexual behaviors. *Journal of Behavior Therapy and Experimental Psychiatry, 16,* 125–131.

Turner, C. W., & Layton, J. F. (1976). Verbal imagery and connotation as memory induced mediators of aggressive behavior. *Journal of Personality and Social Psychology, 33,* 755–763.

Ullmann, L. P., & Krasner, L. A. (1969). *A psychological approach to abnormal behavior.* New York: Prentice-Hall.

Van Praag, H. M., Ulleman, A. M., & Spitz, J. C. (1965). The vital syndrome interview. *Psychiatrica, Neurologia et Neurochirurgia, 68,* 329–346.

Vaughn, C., & Leff, J. (1976). The influence of family and social factors on the course of psychiatric illness. *British Journal of Psychiatry, 129,* 125–137.

Voeltz, L. M. (1982). Effects of structured interactions with severely handicapped peers on children's social attitudes. *American Journal of Mental Deficiency, 86,* 380–390.

Voeltz, L. M., & Evans, I. M. (1982). The assessment of behavioral interrelationships in child behavior therapy. *Behavioral Assessment, 4,* 131–165.

Voeltz, L. M., & Evans, I. M. (1983). Educational validity: Procedures to evaluate outcomes in programs for severely handicapped learners. *Journal of the Association for the Severely Handicapped, 8,* 3–15.

Voeltz, L. M., Evans, I. M., Derer, K. R., & Hanashiro, R. (1983). Targeting excess behavior for change: A clinical decision model for selecting priority goals in educational context. *Child & Family Behavior Therapy, 5,* 17–35.

Voeltz, L. M., Evans, I. M., Freedland, K., & Donellon, S. (1982). Teacher decision making in the selection of educational programming priorities for severely handicapped children. *Journal of Special Education, 16,* 179–198.

von Zerssen, D. (1982). Personality and affective disorders. In E. Paykel (Ed.), *Handbook of affective disorders* (pp. 212–228). New York: Guilford.

Vygotsky, L. A. (1962). *Thought and language.* New York: Wiley.

Wachtel, P. (1973). Psychodynamics, behavior therapy, and the implacable experimenter: An inquiry into the consistency of personality. *Journal of Abnormal Psychology, 82,* 324–334.

Wachtel, P. (1977). *Psychoanalysis and behavior therapy.* New York: Basic Books.

Wachtel, P. (1987). *Insight and action.* New York: Academic Press.

Wahler, R. G. (1980). The insular mother: Her problems in parent-child treatment. *Journal of Applied Behavior Analysis, 13,* 207–219.

Wahler, R. G., & Graves, M. G. (1983). Setting events in social networks: Ally or enemy in child behavior therapy? *Behavior Therapy, 14,* 19–36.

Warren, D. R. (1978). *The language conditioning of attitudes: Two interpretations.* Unpublished doctoral dissertation, University of Hawaii, Honolulu.

Waters, W. F., & McDonald, D. G. (1973). Autonomic response to auditory, visual and imagined stimuli in a systematic desensitization context. *Behaviour Research and Therapy, 11,* 577–585.

Watson, J. B. (1924). *Behaviorism.* New York: Norton.

Watson, J. B. (1930). *Behaviorism* (rev. ed.). Chicago: University of Chicago Press.

Watson, J. B., & Rayner, R. (1920). Conditioned emotional reactions. *Journal of Experimental Psychology, 3,* 1–12.

Weerts, T. C., & Lang, P. J. (1978). Psychophysiology of fear imagery: Differences between focal phobia and social performance anxiety. *Journal of Consulting and Clinical Psychology, 46,* 1157–1159.

Weiss, A. R., & Evans, I. M. (1978). Process studies in language conditioning: I. Counterconditioning of anxiety by "calm" words. *Journal of Behavior Therapy and Experimental Psychiatry, 9,* 115–119.

Weissman, M. M., Pottinger, M., Kleber, H., Ruben, H. L., Williams, D., & Thompson, W. D. (1977). Symptom patterns in primary and secondary depression. *Archives of General Psychiatry, 34,* 854–862.

Weitz, S. E. (1981). A code for assessing teaching skills of parents of developmentally disabled children. *Journal of Autism and Developmental Disorders, 12,* 13–24.

Wexler, K., & Culicover, P. W. (1980). *Formal principles of language acquisition.* Cambridge, MA: Massachusetts Institute of Technology Press.

Wiatrowski, M. D., Gottfredson, G., & Roberts, M. (1983). Understanding behavior disruption: Classifying school environments. *Environment and Behavior, 15,* 53–77.

Williams, J. C., Barlow, D. H., & Agras, W. S. (1972). Behavioral measurement scale of depression. *Archives of General Psychiatry, 27,* 330–333.

Williams, J. E., & Edwards, C. D. (1969). An explanatory study of the modification of color and racial concept attitudes in preschool children. *Child Development, 40*, 737–750.

Wilson, F. E., & Evans, I. M. (1983). The reliability of target behavior selection in behavioral assessment. *Behavioral Assessment, 5*, 33–54.

Wilson, F. E., Parrish, J. M., Mace, F. C., Kolko, D. J., & Kalsher, M. J. (1985, November). *Training parents in observational skills.* Paper presented at the meeting of the Association for Advancement of Behavior Therapy, Houston, TX.

Wilson, G. T. (1978). Cognitive behavior therapy: Paradigm shift or passing phase? In J. P. Foreyt & D. P. Rathjen (Eds.), *Cognitive behavior therapy: Research and application* (pp. 7–32). New York: Plenum.

Wilson, G. T., & Davison, G. C. (1971). Process of fear reduction in systematic desensitization. *Psychological Bulletin, 76*, 1–14.

Wilson, G. T., & Evans, I. M. (1977). The therapist-client relationship in behavior therapy. In A. S. Gurman & M. M. Razin (Eds.), *Effective psychotherapy* (pp. 544–565). New York: Pergamon.

Wilson, G. T., & Franks, C. M. (Eds.) (1982). *Contemporary behavior therapy: Conceptual and empirical foundations.* New York: Guilford Press.

Winkler, R. C. (1970). Management of chronic psychiatric patients by a token reinforcer system. *Journal of Applied Behavior Analysis, 3*, 47–55.

Winokur, G. (1979). Unipolar depression: Is it divisible into autonomous subtypes? *Archives of General Psychiatry, 36*, 47–52.

Witt, J. C., Elliott, S. N., & Martens, B. K. (1984). Acceptability of behavioral interventions used in classrooms: The influence of amount of teacher time, severity of behavior problem, and type of intervention. *Behavior Disorders, 9*, 95–104.

Wittenborg, J. R., & Mower, S. (1977). Persisting personalities among depressed women. *Archives of General Psychiatry, 34*, 968–971.

Wolf, M. M. (1978). Social validity: The case for subjective measurement, or how applied behavior analysis is finding its heart. *Journal of Applied Behavior Analysis, 11*, 203–214.

Wolf, M. M., Risley, T. R., & Mees, H. (1964). Application of operant conditioning procedures to the behavior problems of an autistic child. *Behaviour Research and Therapy, 1*, 305–312.

Woll, S. (1978). *The best of both worlds? A critique of cognitive social learning theory.* Unpublished manuscript, California State University, Fullerton, CA.

Wolpe, J. (1950). Need-reduction, drive-reduction, and reinforcement: A neurophysiological view. *Psychological Review, 57*, 19–26.

Wolpe, J. (1982). *The practice of behavior therapy* (3rd ed.). New York: Pergamon.

Woodruf, R. A., Murphy, G. E., & Herjanc, M. (1967). The natural history of affective disorders: I. Symptoms of 72 patients at the time of index hospital admission. *Journal of Psychiatric Research, 5*, 255–263.

Woodward, W. R. (1982). The "discovery" of social behaviorism and social learning theory, 1870–1980. *American Psychologist, 37,* 396–410.

Woolfolk, A. E., Woolfolk, R. L., & Wilson, G. T. (1977). A rose by another name: Labeling bias and attitudes toward behavior modification. *Journal of Consulting and Clinical Psychology, 45,* 184–191.

Woolfolk, R. L., & Richardson, F. C. (1984). Behavior therapy and the ideology of modernity. *American Psychologist, 39,* 777–786.

Wulbert, M., Inglis, S., Kriegsmann, A., & Mills, B. (1975). Language delay and associated mother-child interactions. *Developmental Psychology, 11,* 61–70.

Yule, W. (1981). The epidemiology of child psychopathology. *Advances in Clinical Child Psychology, 4,* 2–51.

Zajonc, R. (1980). Feeling and thinking: Preferences need no inferences. *American Psychologist, 35,* 151–175.

Zajonc, R. (1984). On the primacy of affect. *American Psychologist, 39,* 117–123.

Zeldow, P. B. (1976). Some antitherapeutic effects of the token economy: A case in point. *Psychiatry, 39,* 318–324.

Zettle, R. D., & Hayes, S. C. (1980). Conceptual and empirical status of rational-emotive therapy. In M. Hersen, R. Eisler, & P. M. Miller (Eds.), *Progress in behavior modification* (Vol. 9, pp. 123–166). New York: Academic Press.

Zettle, R. D., & Hayes, S. C. (1982). Rule-governed behavior: A potential theoretical framework for cognitive-behavioral therapy. In P. C. Kendall (Ed.), *Advances in cognitive-behavioral research and therapy* (Vol. 1, pp. 76–118). New York: Academic Press.

Index

Author Index

Abramovitz, A., 211
Abrams, R., 224
Abramson, L.Y., 141,143,146,230, 233,234
Adams, F., 226
Agras, W.S., 175,242
Akiskal, H.S., 224
Aldwin, C., 234
Allen, M.G., 224
Alloy, L.B., 141,146
Amato, P.R., 262
Andreasen, N.C., 221,225,272
Angst, J., 224
Arana, G.W., 223
Atkinson, M., 89
Atthowe, J.M., 270
Austad, C., 106
Ayllon, T., 270
Azrin, N.H., 270

Baars, B.J., 301
Baer, D.M., 41,81,251
Baldessarini, R.J., 223
Ban, P.K., 69–70,75,79
Bandura, A., 4,13,22,29,33,38,41,47, 62,102,103,128,129,132,133, 138–139,141,142,144,146,148, 158,177,178,179–180,181,199,235, 244,254,261,299
Barlow, D., 58,196,197,198,242,304,314
Barnett, P.A., 233
Barton, R., 141,232
Bastrup, P., 224
Battison, R., 96
Bauer, B. 252
Bayes, R., 45
Beck, A.T., 36,135,142,160,161,163,178, 199,234,235,242
Begg, J.C., 271
Bellack, A.S., 99,123,251,271
Bem, D.J., 102
Ben-Ari Smira, K., 133,145,146,147

Benedict, H., 89
Berberich, J.P., 81
Berkowitz, L., 168
Berman, J.S., 154,182
Bernal, M.E., 255
Bernstein, D.A., 210
Bersh, P., 176
Bever, T.G., 83
Bibring, E., 232
Bijou, S.W., 28
Binkoff, J.A., 255
Birch, H.G., 256
Birky, H.J., 271
Bitar, A.H., 224
Bitterman, M.E., 166
Blaney, P.H., 303
Blank, A., 134
Blatt, S.J., 232,233,238,239
Boblitt, W.E., 271
Boothe, D., 270
Boren, J.J., 230
Borkovec, T.D., 169,180,181,207,210
Bower, G.H., 302
Bradely, C.F., 143
Bradford, D.C., 99
Braswell, L., 158
Braver, S.L., 102
Brewer, B.A., 33,37
Bridge, G., 270
Bridgman, P.W., 17
Briones, R.G., 189,212
Brogden, W.J., 166
Brooks, L.O., 72
Brown, F.A., 273
Brown, L., 380
Brown, M., 288
Brown, R., 87–88,92
Brownell, K.D.
Bruininks, R.H., 275
Bugglin, C.S., 106
Bunney, W.E., 224,230
Burgess, I.S., 183,189,205

Burleson, R., 212
Burns, G.L., 8,33,38,40,42,48,98–125,
    179,189,231,236,252,259,265,271,302
Buss, A.R., 103
Butterfield, W.H., 79
Butts, P., 79,113,114

Cameron, R. 6,178
Camp, B.W., 156
Campos, P.E., 223,309
Cardoso-Martins, C., 94
Carey, E., 193,195,310
Carlson, C.G., 79,107
Carney, M.W., 223
Carr, E.G., 252,255
Carroll, B.J., 223
Carver, C.S., 130,136,142
Cattell, R.B., 106
Cautela, J.R., 209,213
Cavner, J.J., 270
Chafe, W., 92
Chambliss, J.E., 271
Chanowitz, R., 134
Chaplin, W., 141,232
Charlier, M., 86
Chess, S., 256
Chevron, E.S., 232
Chomsky, N., 7–8,38,83,86,108
Chorot, P., 176
Clark, D.M., 302
Cobb, J.A., 255
Cochran, S.E., 230
Cofer, C.N., 21,34
Collette, M.A., 63–65,79
Collette-Harris, M.A., 64,113–114
Coppen, A., 223
Cornelison, K., 212
Corrigan, S.A., 293–317
Corriveau, D.P., 286
Coyne, J.C., 182,196,205,234
Craig, K., 232
Craighead, L.W., 196
Craighead, W.E., 142,187,196,225,226,
    233,235,243,244,264
Craill, L., 178,182,186,193,195,201,310
Craske, M., 175,196
Crawford, H.L., 35,67
Critchley, M., 64
Crossley, R., 273
Culicover, P.W., 83,89
Curran, J.P., 286

Danaher, B.G., 169
Davidson, P.O., 143
Davis, P., 271
Davison, G.C., 76,169,226,269,270
Deal, R., 204,210,212

DeBauche, B.A., 224
Deckel, W.A., 138
Delprato, D.J., 205
DeMayo, R., 234
DeMonbreaun, B.G., 235
DeMyer, M.K., 249
Depue, R.A., 226
DiBeneditto, A., 316
Dimberg, U., 175,205
Dirks, M.J., 157
Dollard, J., 22,28,49,63,69
Donellon, S., 279,285
Donnellan, A.M., 96
Doob, L.W., 63
Drost, P.L., 146
Dumais, A., 11,43,120,256,268–289,300
Dunner, D.L., 224
Durand, V.M., 252
Dush, D.M., 186

Eastman, C., 181,182
Edwards, C.D., 168
Egolf, D., 91
Eifert, G.H., 9–10,48,75–76,118,157,
    168,173–200,201,202,205,206,
    217,234,293–317
Elliott, S.N., 284
Ellis, A., 135,160,161,163,178–179
Emerson, E., 183,205
Endicott, J., 242
Endler, N.S., 38,102
Engelmann, S., 258
England, G., 81
Erickson, M., 231
Ervin-Tripp, S., 84
Erwin, E., 6,251
Etzioni, E., 250,254
Evans, I.M., 9,16,43,81,109,119,121–122,
    128,174,189,193,194,212,214,217,
    250,252,253,256,263,264,265,
    268–269,270,272,273,275,279,280,
    285,293–317
Eyberg, S.M., 115,117
Eysenck, H.J., 8,42,106,154,174,176,
    179,181,182,184,205,226,240,251,301

Falvey, M.A., 276,281,288
Farina, A., 106
Fassbender, L.L., 96
Fay, W.H., 96
Feil, W., 233
Felton, J.L., 123
Fernandez-Ballesteros, R., 40,42,112
Ferster, C.B., 229,230,231,249
Finch, G., 32
Finley, J.R., 34,70,72
Fischer, E.H., 106

Fishman, D.B., 219
Foa, E.B., 205
Foley, J.P., 21,34
Folkman, S., 141
Forehand, R., 253,274
Foreyt, P.J., 293
Frances, A.J., 223
Franklin, J., 143
Franks, C.M., 37,201,219,270,293,305,317
Fraser, D., 271
Fredericks, H.D., 288
Freedland, K., 279
Freedman, A.M., 229
Fremouw, W.J., 226,239
Freud, S., 19–20,25,62,106,217,218,229
Friesen, D.D., 271
Fuchs, C.Z., 238
Fullerton, D.T., 270
Furrow, D., 89

Gaelick, L., 128,129,132,136,142,144
Gelfand, D.M., 248,249
Gelman, R., 86
Genest, M., 99
Gershman, L., 187
Gershon, E.S., 224
Giaor, M., 271
Gilmore, J.B., 131,153
Gleitman, H., 87
Gleitman, L.R., 87
Goffman, E., 255
Goldfried, M.R., 42,76,130–131,144,148,
    164,185,226
Goldstein, S., 92
Golin, S., 146,236
Gordon, J., 212
Gotlib, I.H., 205,232,234,235,237
Gottfredson, G., 254
Gottman, J., 264
Graves, M.G., 255
Gray, B.B., 81
Grayson, J.B., 169
Greenberg, D.J., 271
Griest, D.L., 274
Grimm, L.G., 214
Gripp, R.F., 271
Grof, H., 224
Gross, M.C., 33,37,107
Grove, W.M., 272
Grunberg, F., 277,278
Guay, P.F., 107
Guess, D., 81
Guralnick, M., 96
Gurman, A.S., 214
Gutmann, A., 93

Hadari, D., 146

Hall, J.N., 270
Hamberger, L.K., 9,107,110,153–172,
    173,185,190,202,231,233,234,264
Hammen, C.L., 230,234
Hammond, W.W., 32,122
Hamre-Nietupski, S., 280
Harms, J.Y., 32,34,70
Harrod, M., 86
Hart, B., 157
Hartmann, D.P., 99,100,249
Haughton, E., 270
Hawthorne, J.H., 271
Hayes, S.C., 39,58,99,123,179,186
Heap, R.F., 271
Heard, W.G., 79,165
Hebrew, U., 271
Hegrenes, J., 92
Heiby, E.M., 10,25,119,143,159,192,
    220–246,271,274,287,310,311
Hekmat, H., 9,110,189,191,194,201–219,
    234,310
Henrot, F., 94
Herjanc, M., 222
Hersen, M., 99, 251
Hewett, F.M., 81
Higa, W.R., 32,67,122
Higgins, E.T., 75
Hilgard, E.R., 28
Hippius, H., 224
Hippocrates, 226
Hiroto, D.S., 146
Hirshfield, R.M., 230
Hirt, M.L., 186
Hishinuma, E., 57
Hoberman, H., 225
Hoehn-Hyde, D., 236
Hollon, S.D., 99,118,244
Hord, J.E., 271
Horner, R.H., 288
Horton, L.E., 62–63,79
Houts, A.C., 255
Hugdahl, K., 174,195
Hull, C.L., 17,20,25,27,28,30,48,49
Hutchison, K.O., 270
Huttenlocher, J., 75

Ikenaga, C.S., 75,76,78,79
Inglis, S., 91
Insel, P.M., 254
Israel, A.C., 157
Izard, C., 198,315

Jaffe, Y., 146
Jarrett, R.B., 123
Jeffrey, C.R., 254
Jenkins, J., 84
Jensen, A.R., 259

Johnston, J.M., 79
Jones, L.M., 183
Jones, M.C., 205,249
June, L.N., 214

Kagan, J., 198,315
Kahana, B., 157
Kalsher, M.J., 255
Kanfer, F.H., 128,129,130,132,136,142,
    144,148,156,226
Kaplan, H.I., 227
Karlan, G., 96,97
Karoly, P., 156,157
Kaspisin-Burelli, A., 91
Kastenbaum, R., 209
Kazdin, A.E., 60,181,269,270
Kendall, P.C., 99,118,158,190,244,264
Kendell, R.E., 224
Kenrick, D.T., 102
Khajavi, F., 217
Kirchner, E.P., 167
Kirkland, K., 101
Kishi, G.S., 250,272
Klar, Y., 135,136
Kleber, H., 222
Klein, H., 271
Kleinknecht, R., 175
Klerman, G.L., 223
Klinnert, M.D., 255
Knurek, D.A., 168
Kocsis, J.H., 223
Kolko, D.J., 255
Kornblith, S.J., 238
Kraepelin, E., 220
Krantz, D.S., 138
Krasner, L.A., 255,270
Krauskopf, C.K., 103
Kriegsmann, 91
Kruglanski, A.W., 135,136
Kubala, A.L., 166
Kuhn, T.S., 250
Kurkjian, J.A., 250,272

Lakin, K.C., 275
Lambert, F., 168
Landau, R.J., 164,185
Landeen, J., 79,114
Lang, P.J., 165,169,186,193,197,203
Langer, E., 134
Larson, D., 143
Latimer, P.R., 154,178,182,186,190
Lauterbach, W., 176,184,194
LaVigna, G.W., 285
Lawry, J.A., 32
Layton, J.F., 168
Lazarus, A.A., 211,234,251
Lazarus, R.S., 141,195

Lazovik, A.D., 203
Leduc, A., 11,119,256,268–289,300
Lee, Y.B., 212
Lefcourt, H.M., 142–143
Leff, J., 230,274
Lehman, A., 271
Leifer, J.S., 93
Lentz, R.J., 271
Leonhard, K., 224,225
Leventhal, H., 141
Levesque, M., 271
Levey, A.B., 68,180,195,196,206,207,301,
    305,307
Levis, D.J., 169,199,315
Lewinsohn, P.M., 141,143,148,209,225,
    230,231,232,242,244,311
Lewis, M., 93
Liberman, R.P., 231,286
Libet, J., 209, 232, 311
Lindsley, O.R., 28
Lloyd, C., 230
Lobitz, W.C., 237
Lohr, J.M., 9,107,110,153–172,173,185,
    190,202,231,233,234,264
London, P., 251
Lovaas, O.I., 81
Lowental, U., 271
Lubitz, R., 204,210,212
Luria, A.R., 156

MacAulay, B.D., 81
Mace, F.C., 255
Mackintosh, M.J., 301,305,306
MacPhillamy, D., 230
Maestas y Moores, J., 94
Magaro, P.A., 271
Magnusson, D., 38,102
Mahoney, M.J., 38,131,154,178,
    182,199
Malloy, P.F., 199,315
Maltzman, I., 205
Manly, P.C., 143
Mann, J.J., 223
Marks, I.M., 175,176
Martens, B.K., 284
Marzillier, J.S., 181,182
Maslow, A., 209,218
Mason, B.J., 223
Master, S., 187
Matarazzo, R.G., 115
Mathews, C.O., 235
Matson, J.L., 270
Mattei, M.L., 169
Matusseh, P., 233
McCombs, A., 253
McDonald, A., 273
McGrath, J.E., 140

McHale, S.M., 264
McLaughlin-Reidel, T., 270
McLeod, W.L., 271
McMahon, 143,274
McNally, R.J., 205
McNeil, D., 83
Meazzini, P., 10,247–267,269,281,313
Mees, H., 81,249
Mehryar, A., 217
Meichenbaum, D., 6,131,144,148,153,
    158,164,178,185,190,192,248,297
Melamed, B.G., 264
Merbaum, M., 130–131
Merluzzi, T.V., 99
Mervis, C.B., 94
Mesaros, R.A., 96
Metzl, M., 94
Meyer, L.M., 250,263,272,275,279,285,
    288
Meyers, A.W., 264
Michael, J., 270
Miller, G.A., 84
Miller, N.E., 27,165
Mills, B., 91
Mineka, S., 176–177
Minke, K.A., 7,32,53,57–79,113–115,
    122,192,203,251,308
Mirenda, P.L., 96
Mischel, W., 38,40–41,99,101,102,103,
    132,141,157,170,232
Moerk, E., 85,87–88
Monroe, S.N., 226
Monti, P.M., 286
Moores, D., 94
Moos, R.H., 254
Morris, J., 95
Morrison, R.L., 123
Moss, G.R., 230
Mower, S., 233
Mowrer, O.H., 21,27–28,34,63,84,165,299
Munro, A., 221,222,226

Neckman, J.F., 224
Neisser, U., 317
Nelson, K., 58,87
Nelson, R.O., 81,89,99,118,123,142,233,
    243,252,259
Nerenz, D.R., 141
Newman, A., 156
Newport, E.L., 87
Nienhuys, T., 95
Nietupski, J., 280
Nisbett, R.E., 203
Nuechterlein, K.H., 286

O'Connor, C., 193, 195,310
O'Donnell, C.R., 254

Ochiltree, G., 262
Öhman, A., 175,189,205
Oliveau, D., 175
Olson, R.P., 271
Ornsteen, M., 223
Osgood, C.E., 21,28,34,84
Öst, L.G., 173,175,205
Overmier, B.J., 32
Owen, V., 273

Page, M.M., 68
Paivio, A., 167
Palermo, D., 84
Palkes, H., 157
Palmon, N., 145,146,147
Papgeorges, D., 232
Parish, T.S., 168,262
Parks, W.W., 224
Parrish, J.M., 255
Patterson, G.R., 217,255
Paul, G.L., 271
Paunonen, S.V., 102
Pavlov, I., 29,32,217
Paykel, E.S., 223,229
Pennypacker, H.S., 79
Perloff, B., 81,158
Phelan, J.G., 203
Phillips, L.W., 166
Piaget, J., 108
Pisa, A., 271
Plakosh, P., 231
Poldinger, W., 224
Post, R.D., 237
Pottinger, M., 222
Potts, S., 169
Prakchin, K.M., 232
Prusoff, G.A., 223,232
Pry, G., 237
Putallaz, M., 264
Puzantian, V.R., 224
Pylyshyn, Z.W., 169

Quinlan, D.M., 232

Rachman, S., 174,175,177,183,195,198,
    199,297,314,315
Radcliffe, W.N., 183,205
Rapp, S.R., 226,239
Raps, C.S., 233
Raskin, D.E., 231
Ray, R.S., 255
Rayner, R., 249
Razran, G.H., 21,34
Reber, A., 82
Redden, E.M., 145
Reed, P.C., 166
Rehm, L.P., 140,142,169,231,235,237,238

Reichle, J., 96,97
Reinhard, K.E., 233
Reisinger, J., 231
Reith, C., 232
Remick, R.A, 223
Rescorla, R.A., 27
Rice, J., 212
Richards, P.S., 145
Richardson, F.C., 251
Riemann, F., 232
Risley, T.R., 81,157,249,251
Ritzler, B., 271
Roatch, J.F., 230
Roberts, M., 254
Robertson, S.A., 183,205
Robins, E., 242
Rogers, T., 106,187
Rolnick, A., 145
Romano, J.M., 238
Ronald, M., 270
Rondal, J.A., 7,38,81–97,108,118,155,
    265,273,308
Rookey, C., 169
Roper, B.L., 99
Rosenbaum, M., 8,109–110,126–149,
    194,202,274
Rostow, C.D., 270
Rotgers, F., 219
Roth, D.M., 237,238
Rotter, J.B., 28,102–103
Rozensky, R.H., 237
Ruben, H.L., 222
Rush, A.J., 236
Rushton, J.P., 102
Russell, R.K., 214
Russell, W.A., 214
Rutherford, G., 81

Sadock, B.J., 229
Sage, R., 204
Sailor, W., 81
Sandin, B., 176
Sappington, A.A., 212,214
Saslow, G., 226
Sato, K.Y., 57,78
Schaeffer, B., 81
Scheier, M.F., 130,136
Schermelleh, K., 175,188,205
Scheuer, A.D., 121
Schlottman, R.S., 236
Schroeder, H., 186
Schuler, A.L., 96
Schultz, L.A., 255
Schunk, D.H., 132
Scott, S.B., 271
Scotti, J.R., 270
Sears, R.R., 63

Seligman, M.E.P., 139,143,146,175,230,
    233,234
Semmel, A., 143
Shames, G., 91
Shatz, M., 86
Sheffield, B.F., 223
Sheslow, D., 231
Shirazi, A., 168
Sidman, M., 45,61
Siegel, G., 91–92
Silverstein, A., 71
Simons, A.D., 147
Sinclair, H., 83
Skinner, B.F., 7–8,17,20–21,25,27,28–29,
    30,31,32,45–46,48,49,66,82,84,92,
    109,154,253,260,268,299,300,305
Skolnick, M., 169
Sloane, H.M., 81
Slobin, D., 83,85
Solarz, A.K., 68
Solomon, R.L., 27
Solyom, C., 175
Spitz, J.C., 222
Spitzer, R.L., 242
Sprafkin, J., 42
Spry, K.M., 273
Staats, A.W., 4–5,7–8,9,10,12–13,14–54,
    57,58,61,62,64–65,66,67,68,69,70,72,
    76,79,81,82,84,87,90,96–97,98–99,103,
    105,107 *et seq.*, 119,122,127, *et seq.*,
    142,143,154,155,159,164,165,166,
    168,173,178,181,185,186,189,190,
    192,194,196,197,202,203,204,217,
    218,220–246,250,253 *et seq.*, 269 *et
    seq.*, 278,280,281,287,294,296–297,
    300 *et seq.*
Staats, C.K., 34,67,165,203,204,236
Stampfl, T.G., 169
Steinmetz, J., 143
Stewart, M., 157
Storms, L.H., 21
Strakoudakis, J.P., 214
Studstill, L., 212
Sweeney, J., 223
Sweet, A., 154,178,182,186,190
Sylvester, D., 174

Tadaki, S., 57
Taine, H., 85
Talkington, J., 242,244
Tallman, K., 175
Tang, T., 203
Teasdale, J.D., 230,302
Teri, L., 225
Terrell, F., 146,236
Thomas, D.H., 69,70
Thomas, D.R., 256

Thompson, W.D., 222
Thoresen, C.E., 169
Thorndike, E.L., 27,29,48,49,260
Trapold, M.A., 71
Trayman, R.N., 168
Tryon, W.W., 189,212
Tucker, R.K., 145
Turner, C.W., 168

Ulleman, A.M., 222
Ullmann, L.P., 255

Van Erdewegh, M., 224
Van Praag, H.M., 222
Vanian, D., 204,212,214
Vaughn, C., 274
Voeltz, L.M., 119,121,128,250,269,275, 279
von Zerssen, D., 226
Vygotsky, L.A., 156,192

Wachtel, P. 47,102
Wahler, R.G., 254,255,265
Wallace, C.J., 286
Walters, R.H., 22,29,33,62
Ward, W.C., 236
Warren, D.R., 32,34,68,122
Wasden, R., 271
Waters, W.F., 169
Watson, J.B., 16,17,21,29,37,48,109, 126–127,217,249,252,260
Weed, K.A., 273
Weerts, T.C., 169

Weis, P., 224
Weiss, A.R., 189,194,212,214
Weissman, M.M., 222,226,232
Wells, K.C., 274
Wetzel, R.D., 147
Wexler, K., 83, 89
Wiatrowski, M.D., 254
Wilcoxon-Craighead, L., 264
Wilson, F.E., 10,247–267,269,281,313
Wilson, G.T., 217
Winkler, R.C., 270
Wise, F., 214
Witt, J.C., 284
Witte, K.L., 168
Wittenborg, J.R., 233
Wolf, M.M., 72,81,249,251,269
Woll, S., 22
Wolpe, J., 4,28,187,203
Woodruf, R.A., 222
Woolfolk, A.E., 205
Woolfolk, R.L., 205,251
Wulbert, M., 91
Wynne, L.C., 27

Young, L., 145
Yule, W., 256

Zajonc, R., 195,198,315
Zeiss, A.M., 142,170
Zeldow, P.B., 270
Zettle, R.D., 39,179,186
Zuroff, D., 232

Subject Index

A-R-D theory, 12,32,67,70–71,73–74, 108,109,115,206–207,237,270,275
Abnormal behavior:
  child's; model of, 255–257 and paradigmatic behaviorism, 271–276
  verbal-cognitive repertoires and, 163–164
Abnormal psychology, 42–43,123
  level of paradigmatic behaviorism, 42–43
Acquired-distinctiveness-of-cues hypothesis, 69–70
Adaptive behavior, 207
ADC hypothesis, 69–70
Adult behavior therapy: see Behavior therapy
Advances in Behaviour Research and Therapy, 180
Affective-cognitive-behavioral assessment: see Personality and behavioral assessment
Affective-reinforcing-directive theory: *see* A-R-D theory
Aggression, 62–63
Agoraphobia, 177,185
AIDS, 205
Allport-Vernon-Lindsey Study of Values, 108
American Psychologist, 13
Analog stimulus situations, 115
Animal learning:
  laboratory, 33,50
  theory, 20–21,29
Anxiety, 310
  acquisition and treatment, 183–190
  and language, 217–218
  and language conditioning, 188–189
  phobic: see Phobic anxiety
  semantic behavior therapy: *see* Semantic behavior therapy of anxiety disorders

  social learning perspectives of, 177–182
  three-system models of, 181
triple-response-mode concept of, 174
Association for Advancement of Behavior Therapy (AABT), 294
  convention, 269
Attributional style, 143
Autism, 43
Aversive unconditioned stimulus (USC), 174

Basic behavioral repertoire (BBR), 39,47,110–111,128–129,259,260,280
  assessment of original learning of, 113–114
  hierarchical ordering of, 12
  image-motor, 110
  image-word, 110
  and imagery representation, 164–168
  interaction, 103–106
  various labeling, 110
  verbal-emotional, 109
  verbal-motor, 109
  word-image, 110
Basic learning theory level of paradigmatic behaviorism, 27–33
Beck Depression Inventory, 242
Behavior Therapy, 128
Behavior Rating Scale, 242
Behavior therapists:
  for children, 252–253
  practicing; needs of, 49–50
  therapist–client relationship, 216–217
  training of, 51
Behavior therapy, 10
  applications with severely handicapped people: see Handicapped people
  changes in nature of, 3–4
  of children: *see* Child behavior therapy

Behavior therapy *(cont.)*
  cognitive interpretations of behavior,
    59
  and conditioning, 294–302,302–309
  conditioning models; inadequacies,
    297–300
  constants of, 4
  development of, 202–205
  exposure, 196–198
  individual cases analyzed on basis of
    general theory, 295–297
  language and affect, integration of
    role of, 314–315
  nature of, 15
  and paradigmatic behaviorism,
    3–13,293–317
  and part-to-whole method, 20
  philosophical underpinnings, 16–17
Behavioral assessment:
  assumed causes of behavior, 100
  current trends, 121–125
  defined, 100
  inference from behavioral sample,
    101–102
Behavioral Assessment and *Journal of*
  Psychopathology and Behavioral
  Assessment, 99
Behavioral covariation, 121–122
Behavioral engineer, 58–59
Behavioral interaction, 38
Bipolar depression, 224–225,241–242
Bridging theory, 24–25,41

Canadian Act on the Protection of the
  Mentally Ill, 278
Cancer, 205
Catharsis theory of aggression, 62–63
Child behavior therapy, 10,247–267
  determinism, 253–254
  environmentalism, 254–255
  evolution of, 249–253
  indirect intervention, 262–263
  metatheoretical assumptions, 253–255
  multiple functions, 264–265
  professional acceptance of, 249–250
  therapists, attitudes of, 252–253
  viewed as applied science or technol-
    ogy, 251–252
Child clinical psychology, 255–262
  abnormal behavior, model of, 255–257
  intelligence, study of, 259–260
  personality, concept of, 260–262
Child development: cumulative-
    hierarchical learning and, 257–258
  level of paradigmatic behaviorism,
    37–38
  milestones, 257

  stage theories, 257–258
Child and Family Behavior Therapy, 249
Children, 272–273
  see also Child behavior therapy;
    Child clinical psychology; Child
    development
  acquisition of cognitive repertoires,
    72–73
  basic behavioral repertoires of, 105
  hearing-impaired, language acquisi-
    tion by, 94–95
  labeling skills, development, 110
  language-delayed, 91
  mentally retarded: *see* Mentally
    retarded children
  motor skills, 111
  nonverbal; language acquisition by,
    81–82
  parent–child verbal interaction: *see*
    Parent–child verbal interaction
Cognititive repertoires, language-based,
  171
Cognitive interpretations of behavior,
  59
Cognitive Therapy and Research, 3
Cognitive repertoires, acquisition in
  young children, 72–73
Cognitive-behavior therapy, 10,153–172
  for dysfunctions, 153–173
  language repertoires, 155–164
  paradigmatic behavioral framework
    for, 190–193
  repertoires, 191
Complex Human Behavior, 4,36,300
Conceptual vacuum, 179
Conditioned response (CR), 174
Conditioned stimulus (CS), 174
Conditioning:
  and behavior therapy, 294–302,302–
    309
  models: *see* Conditioning models
Conditioning models, 6,300–302
  Boulder model, 7
  simple and separate; inadequacies of,
    297–300
Conditioning theory, 177
Consciousness versus unconsciousness:
  conscious deliberation, 131
  schematic representations, 134
  and self-regulation, 130–131
Cue-controlled techniques of relaxation,
  214–215
Cumulative-hierarchical learning
  perspective, 33,96–97

Deaf children: *see* Hearing-impaired
  children

Defense mechanisms, 163
Denial, 136,138
Depression, 10,36–37,220–246,310–312
  Beck Depression Inventory, 242
  bipolar, 224–225, 241–242
  classification, 220–225,238–242
  current classification systems, 225–227
  and dysfunctional social skills, 232
  endogenous, 222–224, 240–241
  environmental influences, 227,229–231
  exogenous, 222–224
  language-cognitive repertoire, 233–238
  measurement and research, 242–244
  paradigmatic behaviorism theory of, 227–238
  and personality, 229,231
  primary, 221–222
  psychotic–neurotic distinction, 222–224
  secondary, 221–222
  and self-regulation, 143,148
  and self-reinforcement, 235
  and sensory-motor repertoire, 231–233
  Staats–Heiby theory of, 220–246,228
  unipolar, 221, 224–225, 238–240
Deprivation, 31
Desensitization, 208
  instructional, 215–216
Determinism, 253–254
Developmental psycholinguistics, 82
Dexamethasone suppression test (DST), 223
Diagnostic and Statistical Manual of Mental Disorders, 7,119,222,242
  Major Depressive Disorder, 226,242
Dogs, 185–186,260
Down syndrome children: *see* Mentally retarded children
DSM-III-R: *see* Diagnostic and Statistical Manual of Mental Disorders
Dynamics of Anxiety and Hysteria, 8
Dysfunctional behavior,
  language repertoires in, 155–164
Dyslexia, 63–65
Dysphoria, 229,243–244
Dysthymia, 222

Emotional behavior:
  arousal and self-verbalizations, 187
  image-produced reactions, 168,169
  language control of, 158–161
Emotional response, 31, 67–68
  emotional-attitudinal, 194

  unconditioned, 174
Emotional-motivational personality
  system, 107–108
  assessment of, 114–116
Empathy, 217
Endogenous depression, 240–241
Endogenous-exogenous distinction: *see*
  Psychotic–neurotic distinction
Engineer, behavioral, 58–59
Environment:
  and behavior-environment interactions, assessment of, 113,120–121
  and child behavior therapy, 254–255
  and depression, 227,229–231
Epilepsy, 147
Evaluative responses, 194
Exposure, effective, 196–198
Eyberg Child Behavior Inventory, 117

Fear, 175
  and social competence, 122–125
  triple-response-mode concept of, 121–122
  two-factor theory of fear acquisition and maintenance, 299
Framework theories:
  benefits of, 312–314
  characteristics of, 50
  eclectic combinations, 22–23
  multilevel theory, 23–26
  paradigmatic behaviorism as, 43–52
  part-to-whole method, 19–22
  types of, 19–26
Frequency of self-affective-reinforcing-directive (FSARD), 236–238
Functional behavior repertoires, 74

Galvanic skin response (GSR), 188
Goals, 132
Guilford–Zimmerman Temperament Survey, 117

Handicapped people:
  abnormal behavior and paradigmatic behaviorism, 271–276
  behavior modification in institutional settings, 269–271
  organizational behavior change; case study, 276–284
  and rehabilitation, 268–289
  statutory protections, 278
  treatment, implications for, 275–276
Hearing-impaired children, language acquisition by, 94–95
Hedonic Evaluation Subjective Scale (HESS), 209–210
Helplessness, 146

Heuristic function of theory, 45–49
Hierarchical theory, 53
  role in semantic behavior therapy,
    218
Human learning theory level of
  paradigmatic behaviorism, 33–37
Hypothalamic-pituitary-adrenal (HPA)
  dysfunction, 245

Image-verbal repertoire, 167
Imagery:
  and basic behavioral repertoires,
    164–168
  and phobic anxiety, 184–186
  repertoires, 168–171
Incubation, process of, 176
Indirect intervention and child behavior
  therapy, 262–263
Indirect observation, 66–67,79
Information-processing theory, 302
  and self-regulation, 129–130
Institutional settings, behavior modification in, 269–271
Intelligence:
  acquisition of linked to language
    learning, 90
  study of, 259–260
Interactive viewpoint of language
  acquisition, 85–91
Interlevel theory: *see* Bridging theory
Intervention strategies:
  indirect, 262–263
  simultaneous and multiple, 264–265

*Journal of Consulting and Clinical
  Psychology*, 204

Labeling repertoires, 118,161–162
Language, 81–97
  acquisition: *see* Language acquisition
  and affect, 314–315
  and anxiety, 205,206,217–218
  disorders: *see* Language disorders and
    intervention
  emotional functions of, 35
  emotional word learning, 36
  importance of, 10
  intervention: *see* Language disorders
    and intervention
  and learning, 34
  phobic anxiety and, 183–184
  repertoires: *see* Language repertoires
  self-verbalizations, 186–187
  speech anxiety, 163
  speech fluency in stuttering, 74–75
  studies modifying emotional and
    connotative meaning of words, 9

theory of, 24
  unit-image words, 166
Language acquisition:
  associationist position, 84
  content approach, 82
  general paradigms of, 82–85
  home environment, importance of,
    95–96
  intelligence linked to, 90
  interactive viewpoint, 85–91
  learning theory analysis combined
    with theories of, 84
  parent–child verbal interaction, 86–
    87
  process orientation, 83–84
  teaching speech to nonverbal
    children, 81–82
Language acquisition device (LAD), 82–
  83
Language Behavior Therapy, 36
Language conditioning, 35
  and conditioned anxiety, 188–189
Language disorders and intervention,
  91–95
  hearing-impaired children, 94–95
  language-delayed children, 91
  mentally retarded children, 91–94
  stuttering, 91
Language repertoires, 155
  abnormal behavior and verbal–
    cognitive repertoires, 163–164
  correspondence and self-instructional
    training, 157
  dysfunctional behavior and, 155–164
  emotional behavior, control of, 158–
    161
  labeling and reasoning repertoires,
    regulatory functions of, 161–162
  overt behavior, control of, 156
  self-regulatory systems and plans,
    157–158
  verbal-motor repertoires, 158
Language-cognitive personality system,
  108–111,118–119
Language-cognitive repertoire and
  depression, 233–238
Learned helplessness, 233
Learned resourcefulness:
  defined, 144
  and epilepsy, 147
  and self-regulation, 144–148
Learning:
  and adaptive behavior, 207
  cumulative-hierarchical theory of, 96–
    97,105,257–258
  multilevel theory, 130
  theories of: *see* Learning theories

Learning, Language, and Cognition, 36
Learning theories, 84
  competing, 27–29
  of language, 34
Locus of control, 142
Logical positivism, 16–17
Low self-administration of positively
    valenced emotional stimuli (LF-
    SARD), 239

Maturational theories of child develop-
    ment, 257–258
Measurement level of theory, 112–
    121,125
  BBRs, original learning of, 113–114
  personality repertoires, 114–121
Mentally retarded children, 266
  language acquisition by, 91–94
  parental speech, 93–94
Minnesota Multiphasic Personality
    Inventory (MMPI), 116,232
Models: *see* Conditioning models
Motor skills, 111
Multilevel-theory-construction method,
    52
Multilevels of paradigmatic behavior-
    ism, 23–26,27–43,130
  abnormal psychology level of the
    theory, 42–43
  basic learning theory level, 27–33
  child development level of the theory,
    37–38
  human learning theory level, 33–37
  personality level of the theory, 38–42
  research establishing, 71–74

New York State Commission on Quality
    of Care for the Mentally Disabled
    (1987), 284–285

Opengate, 284–285

Paradigm; defining characteristics of, 60
Paradigmatic behaviorism, 14–54
  and abnormal behavior, 271–276
  applied, 7–8
  and behavior therapy, 3–13,293–317
  Boulder model, 7
  and child clinical psychology: *see*
    Child clinical psychology
  contribution to new knowledge, 309–
    314
  defined, 16
  depression, theory of, 227–238
  as framework: *see* Paradigmatic
    behaviorism as framework theory
  measurement level of theory: *see*

Measurement level of theory
  multilevels: *see* Multilevels of
    paradigmatic behaviorism
  new insights and treatments, 309–
    310
  origin of, 5
  "personality" defined within, 103–104
  personality level of theory, 8
  physical attributes, influence of, 106
  research foundations: *see* Research
    foundations of paradigmatic
    behavior
  three-function learning theory, 30–32
  unification of, 302–309
  validity of, research establishing, 78–
    80
  viewed as applied science or dogma,
    315–317
Paradigmatic behaviorism as a frame-
    work theory, 43–52, 190–193
  connective-meaning function, 44–45
  curriculum planning function, 50–52
  heuristic function, 45–49
  world view function, 49–50
Parent–child verbal interaction, 86
  dynamic interaction perspective, 89–
    90
  effect, question of, 87–91
  home environment, importance of,
    95–96
  language control of overt behavior,
    156–157
  language-delayed children, 91
  mentally retarded children, 93–94
  parental language-teaching hypothe-
    sis, arguments for, 88–89
  parental speech characteristics, 86–87
  professional guidance for parents, 96
  stuttering, 91
Part-to-whole method, 19–22
Peak shift phenomenon, 73
Pedolinguistics, 85
Personal efficacy, 146
Personality:
  and behavioral assessment: *see*
    Personality and behavioral assess-
    ment
  bridging theory of, 41
  concept of, 260–262
  defined, 100,103–104
  and depression, 229,231
  level of theory: *see* Personality level
    of theory
  and self-regulation, 128–129,140–144
Personality and behavioral assessment,
    98–125
  assumed causes of behavior, 100

Personality and behavioral assessment
(*cont.*)
behavioral sample, inference from,
101–102
dividing issues, 98–102
indirect interaction of, 105
interactional viewpoint, 102–103,105
Personality level of theory, 8,38–42,47–
48,102–112,125
and basic behavioral repertoires,
103–106
emotional-motivational system, 107–
108
language-cognitive system, 108–111
sensory-motor system, 111–112
tripartite conception, 106–112
Personality repertoires, assessment of,
47
see also Basic behavioral repertoires
behavior, 113,119
emotional-motivational system, 114–
116
environment-behavior interactions,
113,120–121
language-cognitive system, 118–119
present stimulus situation, 113,119
sensory-motor system, 117–118
Personality-environment interaction,
105
Personality-environment–personality
interaction, 105–106
Personalized system of instruction (PSI),
79
Phobic anxiety, 9–10,173–200
affective responses, role of, 194–195
agoraphobia, 177,185
AIDS, 205
cancer, 205
conceptual and critical issues, 193–
198
dogs, 185–186,260
imagery, role of, 184–186
interface between affect, behavior,
and cognition, 193–194
language conditioning and, 183–184
preparedness theory, 175
rabbits, 188–189
rats, 204
selectivity of phobias, 175
self-verbalizations, effect of, 186–187
semantic conditioning interventions,
189–190
simple conditioning models, inadequacies of, 174–177
snakes, 175–176,188–189,204
of speeches, 216
spiders, 175,204

Physical attributes, influence of, 106
Pleasant Events Schedule, 239,311
Positive counterconditioning, 196
Preparedness theory of phobic anxiety,
175
Primary appraisal, 141,194
Primary depression, 221–222
Problem solving, 75–78
Process-regulating cognitive (PRC)
repertoires, 127,133–134
and self-regulation, 134–140
PSI, 79
Psychoanalysis and part-to-whole
method, 19–20
Psychology:
disunification of, 17–19
separatism of, 13
Psychopathology, 24,42–43
Psychotherapies, integration of, 47
Psychotic–neurotic distinction, 222–
224,225

Rabbits, 188–189
Radical behaviorism, 17,21,46,154
personalized system of instruction, 79
Rathus Assertiveness Inventory, 117
Rats, 204
Reasoning repertoires, 161–162
Reciprocal determinism, 182
Reinforcement:
emotional response, 67–68
reinforcing stimulus, 31
token, 60
Reinforcement Survey Schedule, 116
Relaxation, 208–210
cue-controlled techniques, 214–215
role of imagery in, 169
Representation, 141
Research Diagnostic Criteria, 242
Research foundations of paradigmatic
behavior, 57–79
aggression, basis of, 62–63
contributions to the behavioral
engineer, 58–61
demonstrating the validity of
principles, 69–71
dyslexia as a learning phenomenon,
63–65
functional behavioral repertoires,
62,74
implicit events, indirect observation
of, 65–68
multilevel nature, establishing, 71–74
research base, 60–61
social behavioral approach, 61–78
stuttering, speech fluency in, 74–75
Reward, role of imagery in, 170–171

Robert Giffard Hospital Center:
Behavioral Module, 277
controversy, 277–278
evaluating the new program, 282–284
organizational aspects of new
program, 278–279
original program, 276–277
program objectives and components,
279–282
Rule-governed behavior, 39
Rules of sequence, 207

Schema, 185
Schizophrenia, 272,283
Schizophrenic speech, 81
Secondary depression, 221–222
Self control: *see* Self-regulation
Self-Control Schedule (SCS), 145
Self-efficacy theory, 41,138–139,179–
182
Self-regulation, 126–149
consciousness versus unconsciousness,
130–131
and depression, 143,148
and epilepsy, 147
expectancies' effect on process of,
139–140
illusion of control phenomenon, 146
and information processing, 129–130
and learned resourcefulness, 144–148
model of; flowchart description, 137
and personality, 128–129,140–144
and process-regulating cognitions,
134–140
self-efficacy judgments, 138–139
situations, role of, 140–144
systems and plans, 157–158
unified model of, 132–134,137,139–
140
Self-reinforcement and depression, 235
Self-Reinforcement Questionnaire, 242
Self-verbalizations, 196
and emotional arousal, 187
and phobic anxiety, 186–187
Semantic behavior therapy of anxiety
disorders, 201–219
cue-controlled techniques, 214–215
desensitization, 208
hierarchies, role of, 218
instructional desensitization,
215–216
interventions, 208–217
language, 205
relaxation, 208–210
sensitization, 212–214
therapist–client relationship, 216–217
Semantic Hierarchy of Anxiety

Mediating-Stimuli (SHAMS), 210–
211
Semantically Aversive Disturbing
Events (SADE), 212
Sensitization, 212–214
Sensory-motor personality system, 111–
112
assessment of, 117–118
Sensory-motor repertoire and depression, 231–233
Situations and self-regulation, 140–144
Snakes, 175–176,188–189,204,205
Social Behaviorism, 11
Social behaviorism, 4–5,154–155
applications with severely handicapped people: *see* Handicapped
people
defined, 5
fundamental characteristics, 5
individualizing programs, 286–287
methodology, 60
misuse of principles, 284–285
organizational behavior change; case
study, 276–284
policy and practice issues, 284–287
problem solving, analysis of, 75–78
research demonstrating the validity
of principles, 69–71
social integration, 285–286
types of research important in
development of, 61–78
Social learning theories, 22,23,29,47
integration of antecedent, consequent,
and mediational systems, 178
Social skills, dysfunctional, 232
Speech, schizophrenic, 81
Speech anxiety, 163
Speeches, 216
Spiders, 175,204,205
Staats–Heiby theory of depression,
220–246
Stanford–Binet intelligence test, 118
Strong Vocational Interest Blank, 107–
108,116
Study of Values, 116
Stuttering, 91
research foundations of speech
fluency in, 74–75
Subjective anxiety scale (SUDS), 210

*The Best of Both Worlds? A Critique of
Cognitive Social Learning Theory*,
22
Theories:
construction of: *see* Theory construction
framework: *see* Framework theories

Theories (*cont.*)
  heuristic function of, 45–49
Theory construction:
  generalization by exclusion, 99
  multilevel, hierarchical approach, 98–
    99
  natural sciences versus psychology
    and behavioral science, 17–19
Three-function learnng theory: *see* A-R-
    D theory
Triple-response-mode concept of fear,
    121–122
  social competence, example of, 122–
    125

UCR, 174
UCS, 174
Unconsciousness: *see* Consciousness
  versus unconsciousness

Unemployed patients, treatment of, 50
Unified theory, 46
Unipolar depression, 221,224–225
  implications for classification, 238–
    240
Unpleasant Events Schedule, 242

Verbal Behavior, 84
Verbal labels, 159
Verbal–cognitive repertoires, 163–164
Verbal-image repertoire, 166–167
Verbal-motor repertoires, 39,40
  elements of, 158
Vicarious learning, 33–34

Wechsler intelligence test, 118
Words: *see* Language